THE WORLD OF
JESUS AND THE
EARLY CHURCH

THE WORLD OF JESUS AND THE EARLY CHURCH

Identity and Interpretation in
Early Communities of Faith

CRAIG A. EVANS

EDITOR

HENDRICKSON
PUBLISHERS

The World of Jesus and the Early Church
© 2011 by Hendrickson Publishers Marketing, LLC
P. O. Box 3473
Peabody, Massachusetts 01961-3473

ISBN 978-1-59856-825-7

Printed in the United States of America

First Printing — December 2011

Library of Congress Cataloging-in-Publication Data

The world of Jesus and the early church : identity and interpretation in
  early communities of faith / edited by Craig A. Evans.
    p. cm.
  Proceedings from a series of conferences and symposia.
  Includes bibliographical references (p.   ) and indexes.
  ISBN 978-1-59856-825-7 (alk. paper)
    1. Church history—Primitive and early church, ca. 30–600—
  Congresses. 2. Bible—Criticism, interpretation, etc.—Congresses.
  3. Abels, Janet Jiryu.v Congresses. I. Evans, Craig A.
  BR165.W77 2011
  270.1´0901—dc23
                          2011029660

CONTENTS

Part One: Identity in Jewish and Christian Communities of Faith

PREFACE

The World of Jesus and the Early Church gradually emerged from a series of scholarly conferences and symposia. One was held at Acadia Divinity College of Acadia University, in Wolfville, Nova Scotia, Canada. Two others were held at Midwestern Baptist Theological Seminary in Kansas City, Missouri. The editor is grateful to the Hayward Lectures endowment that supported the conference at Acadia and to Mr. G. Richard Hastings, whose generosity made possible the founding of The Hastings Institute for the Study of the Dead Sea Scrolls and Christian Origins, which in turn supported the conferences on the campus of Midwestern. Thanks are also due President Harry Gardner of Acadia Divinity College and President R. Philip Roberts of Midwestern Baptist Theological Seminary, whose vision and commitment to scholarship make scholarly conferences possible, productive, and very enjoyable. The editor is also grateful to Mr. Jeremy Johnston, who is currently pursuing his doctorate in biblical studies, for compiling the indexes. And finally, on behalf of the contributors, the editor dedicates our studies to the memory of Douglas Edwards, who died in November 2008. At the conference held at Acadia, Doug presented two stimulating papers on village life in Galilee. He is missed.

Craig A. Evans
Acadia Divinity College

Contributors

Stephen J. Andrews
Midwestern Baptist Theological Seminary

Keith Bodner
Crandall University

George J. Brooke
University of Manchester

Mark A. Chancey
Southern Methodist University

John J. Collins
Yale University

Torleif Elgvin
Evangelical Lutheran University College

Craig A. Evans
Acadia Divinity College

Paul Foster
University of Edinburgh

Shimon Gibson
University of the Holy Land

Larry Hurtado
Universitiy of Edinburgh

Margaret Y. MacDonald
St. Francis Xavier University

Dorothy M. Peters
Trinity Western University

James A. Sanders
Claremont School of Theology

Abbreviations

General

AD	*anno Domini*
b.	*Bavli,* Babylonian Talmud
BCE	before the Common Era
c./ca.	*circa,* about
CD	Cairo Damascus
CE	Common Era
ch(s).	chapter(s)
d.	died
D	Damascus (rule)
DSS	Dead Sea Scrolls
esp.	especially
ESV	English Standard Version
frag(s).	fragment(s)
HB	Hebrew Bible
l(l).	line(s)
LDAB	Leuven Database of Ancient Books
LXX	Septuagint
m.	*Mishnah*
mm	Masorah magna
mp	Masorah parva
MT	Masoretic Text
NRSV	New Revised Standard Version
NT	New Testament
n(n).	note(s)
OT	Old Testament
PBI	Pontifical Biblical Institute
rev.	revised
t.	Tosefta
viz.	*videlicet,* namely
v(v).	verse(s)
y.	*Yerushalmi,* Jerusalem Talmud

Journals and Series

AB	Anchor Bible
ABD	*Anchor Bible Dictionary*
ABRL	Anchor Bible Reference Library
ANRW	*Aufstieg und Niedergang der römischen Welt: Geschichte und Kultur Roms im Spiegel der neueren Forschung*
ARWAW	Abhandlungen der Rheinische-Westfälischen Akademie der Wissenschaften
AUSS	*Andrews University Seminary Series*
BA	*Biblical Archaeologist*
BAR	*Biblical Archaeology Review*
BASOR	*Bulletin of the American Schools of Oriental Research*
BETL	Bibliotheca Ephemeridum Theologicarum Lovaniensum
BHS	*Biblia Hebraica Stuttgardensia*
BibOr	Biblica et orientalia
BICS.SP	Bulletin of the Institute of Classical Studies of the University of London—Supplementary Papers
BIS	Biblical Interpretation Series
BJS	Brown Judaic Studies
BR	*Biblical Research*
BRev	*Bible Review*
BSac	*Bibliotheca sacra*
BTB	*Biblical Theology Bulletin*
CBNTS	Coniectanea Biblia: New Testament Series
CBQ	*Catholic Biblical Quarterly*
CBQMS	Catholic Biblical Quarterly Monograph Series
CIL	*Corpus inscriptionum latinarum*
CIS	Copenhagen International Seminar
CP	*Classical Philology*
CRINT	Compendia rerum iudiacarum ad Novum Testamentum
DJD	Discoveries in the Judaean Desert
DSD	*Dead Sea Discoveries*
EDB	*Eerdmans Dictionary of the Bible* (ed. David Noel Freedman; Grand Rapids, MI: Eerdmans, 2000)
FOTL	Forms of the Old Testament Literature
FRLANT	Forschungen zur Religion und Literatur des alten und Neuen Testaments
HS	*Hebrew Studies*
HThKAT	Herders theologischer Kommentar zum alten Testament
HTR	*Harvard Theological Review*
HUB	Hebrew University Bible
IAA	Israel Antiquities Authority
ICC	International Critical Commentary

IEJ	*Israel Exploration Journal*
JAOS	*Journal of the American Oriental Society*
JBL	*Journal of Biblical Literature*
JHS	*Journal of Hellenic Studies*
JQR	*Jewish Quarterly Review*
JRS	*Journal of Roman Studies*
JSJSup	Journal for the Study of Judaism in the Persian, Hellenistic, and Roman Periods Supplement Series
JSNT	*Journal for the Study of the New Testament*
JSNTSup	Journal for the Study of the New Testament: Supplement Series
JSOT	*Journal for the Study of the Old Testament*
JSOTSup	Journal for the Study of the Old Testament: Supplement Series
JSPSup	Journal for the Study of the Pseudepigrapha: Supplement Series
JSS	*Journal of Semitic Studies*
JSSSup	Journal of Semitic Studies Supplement
LCL	Loeb Classical Library
LNTS (JSNTS)	Library of New Testament Studies
NEA	*Near Eastern Archaeology*
NovT	*Novum Testamentum*
NTOA.SA	Novum Testamentum et Orbis Antiquus: Series archaeologica
NTS	*New Testament Studies*
NTTS	New Testament Tools, Studies, and Documents
OBO	Orbis biblicus et orientalis
OECGT	Oxford Early Christian Gospel Texts
PEQ	*Palestine Exploration Quarterly*
RB	*Revue biblique*
RBL	*Review of Biblical Literature*
RelSRev	*Religious Studies Review*
RevQ	*Revue de Qumran*
SBL	Society of Biblical Literature
SBLABib	Society of Biblical Literature Academia Biblica
SBLEJL	Society of Biblical Literature Early Judaism and Its Literature
SBLMS	Society of Biblical Literature Monograph Series
SNTSMS	Society for New Testament Studies Monograph Series
SBLSP	Society of Biblical Literature Seminar Papers
SBLSymS	SBL Symposium Series
STDJ	Studies on the Texts of the Desert of Judah
SVTP	Studies in Veteris Testamenti pseudepigrapha
TSAJ	Texte und Studien zum antiken Judentum
TynBul	*Tyndale Bulletin*
VT	*Vetus Testamentum*
VTSup	Supplements to Vetus Testamentum
WBC	Word Biblical Commentary
WUNT	Wissenschaftliche Untersuchungen zum Neuen Testament

Hebrew Bible (Old Testament)

Gen	Genesis
Exod	Exodus
Lev	Leviticus
Num	Numbers
Deut	Deuteronomy
Josh	Joshua
Judg	Judges
1–2 Sam	1–2 Samuel
1–2 Kgs	1–2 Kings
1–2 Chr	1–2 Chronicles
Neh	Nehemiah
Job	Job
Ps(s)	Psalm(s)
Prov	Proverbs
Isa	Isaiah
Jer	Jeremiah
Ezek	Ezekiel
Dan	Daniel
Joel	Joel
Nah	Nahum
Hab	Habakkuk
Zech	Zechariah

New Testament

Matt	Matthew
Mark	Mark
Luke	Luke
John	John
Acts	Acts
Rom	Romans
1–2 Cor	1–2 Corinthians
Eph	Ephesians
Phil	Philippians
Col	Colossians
1–2 Thess	1–2 Thessalonians
1–2 Tim	1–2 Timothy
Titus	Titus
Heb	Hebrews
Jas	James
1–2 Pet	1–2 Peter
Jude	Jude
Rev	Revelation

Apocrypha

4 Ezra	2 Esdras 3–14
Jud	Judith
1 Macc	1 Maccabees
Sir	Sirach/Ecclesiasticus
Tob	Tobit

Pseudepigrapha

1–3 En.	*1–3 Enoch*
Jub.	*Jubilees*
Ps. Sol.	*Psalms of Solomon*

Ancient Sources

Aristides
    Apol.   *Apology for the Christian Faith*
Dionysius of Halicarnassus
    Ant. rom.   *Antiquitates romanae*
Josephus
    Ag. Ap.   *Against Apion*
    Ant.   *Jewish Antiquities*
    J.W.   *Jewish War*
Philo
    Prob.   *Quod omnis probus liber sit (That Every Good Person Is Free)*
    Spec. Laws   *On the Special Laws*
Plautus
    Ps.   *Pseudolus*
Pliny the Elder
    Nat.   *Naturalis historia (Natural History)*

Apostolic Fathers

Barn.	*Barnabas*
1-2 Clem.	*1-2 Clement*
Did.	*Didache*
Herm. Man.	*Shepherd of Hermas, Mandate(s)*
Herm. Vis.	*Shepherd of Hermas, Vision(s)*
Ign. *Pol.*	Ignatius, *To Polycarp*
Pol. *Phil.*	Polycarp, *To the Philippians*

Dead Sea Scrolls

1QH^a	(=1Q35) *Hodayot* or *Thanksgiving Hymns*
1QpHab	(=1Q14) *Pesher Habakkuk*
1QS	*Serek Hayakhad* or *Rule of the Community*
1QS^b	(=1Q28b) *Rule of Benedictions*
4Q88	*Apostrophe of Judah*
4Q174	(=4QFlor) *Florilegium*
4Q203	(=4QEnGiants^{a,c} ar) *Book of the Giants*
4Q213, 4Q214	(=4QTLevi^{a–f} ar) *Aramaic Levi*
4Q228	(=4QJub, but 4Q288 just cites *Jubilees*)
4Q282	Unidentified Fragments B
4Q285	(=*Sefer Hamilhamah, Rule of War*)
4Q370	(=*Exhortation Based on Flood*)
4Q387b	(=*Apocryphon of Jeremiah C*)
4Q401	(=4QSirSabb) *Songs of the Sabbath Sacrifice*
4Q403	(=4QSirSabb) *Songs of the Sabbath Sacrifice*
4Q418	(=4QInstruction)
4Q491	(see *War Scroll*)
4Q504	(=4QDibHam) *Words of the Luminaries*
4Q524	(=4QTemple) *Temple Scroll*
4Q541	(=4QapocLevi) *Apocryphon of Levi*
4QAmram	(=4Q543–548) *Visions of Amram*
4QExod^b	(=4Q13)
4QGen^g	(=4Q7)
4QMMT	(=4Q394–399) *Miqsat Ma'ase ha-Torah*
4QpNah	(=4Q169) *Pesher Nahum*
4QpPs^a	(=4Q171) *Commentary on Psalms*
4QS	(=4Q255–264) *Rule of the Community*
4QSD	(=4Q265) *Serek Damascus*
4QS^e	(=4Q259) *Serek Damascus*
4QSam^{a–c}	(=4Q51–53)
11Q13	(=11QMelch) *Melchizedek*
11QPs^a	(=11Q5) *Psalms Scroll*
11QT	(=11QTemple^{a,b}=11Q19–20) *Temple Scroll*
War Scroll	(=1QM + 1Q33 *Milkhamah*)
CD	(Cairo Damascus, Damascus Document)

INTRODUCTION

Archaeology concerns itself with the study of the remains of material culture. These remains include the durable items uncovered by excavations, items such as pottery, stoneware, building materials, inscriptions, coins and other valuables, glass, ostraca, tools, various other metal utensils, and the like. The remains of material culture also include writings of one sort or another, writings that may or may not have survived into modern times through scribal transmission, such as the biblical writings, or writings of which we knew nothing until modern discovery. The papyri of Egypt and the leather scrolls of the Dead Sea region represent the bulk of such writings.

All of these materials shed light on how people lived in antiquity. How they lived, how they worked, how they associated with one another, how they communicated, and what they believed are the questions that drive modern research and archaeological excavation. Constructing answers to these questions in turn sheds light on the texts that we regard as authoritative or normative, such as biblical texts. And, of course, the biblical texts shed light on what we uncover through archaeology and discovery. It is through this interpretive reciprocity—the archaeological discovery clarifying the text and the text clarifying the archaeological discovery—that we are able to make significant progress in understanding what went before us and why we are what we are today.

The chapters that make up the present collection are focused on the early Jewish and Christian communities of faith—how these communities lived, how they developed, what they believed, what they regarded as authoritative Scripture, and how they understood it. The papers fall into two parts. The first part is concerned with community identity, how communities understood and defined themselves, and how these identities in some cases changed over time. The second part is concerned with how the early Jewish and Christian communities interpreted Scripture and how Scripture—whether text or the scriptural artifact itself—informed the community as to how it should understand and define itself and, in light of this understanding and definition, to know how it should live as a community.

The first part begins with John Collins's study of the development of community (or communities as the case seems to be) as seen in the literature of Qumran, in early references and descriptions of the Essenes, and in the archaeology of Qumran. Collins believes that the evidence indicates that the *yahad*, or community, was an "association dispersed in multiple settlements." Understood this way, the discrepancies, recensions, and (in places) lack of coherence in the Qumran rule books make sense. Not all rule books (such as various recensions of the Serek Scrolls) were composed at Qumran or in one period of time. Collins also takes a new look at the origin of the *yahad*. He suspects the community did not begin with a quarrel between the Teacher of Righteousness and the Wicked Priest, as has been supposed. Collins thinks this quarrel was a later development. With respect to the ruins at Qumran, he wonders if the site was originally a Hasmonean outpost and only later became an Essene compound. In any case, Collins wisely recommends that interpretation of the scrolls not be tied too closely to Qumran, for at most Qumran was but one settlement of the community; it was never the community in its entirety.

Part One continues with Torleif Elgvin's study of the conception of the heavenly temple, in what ways it was compared with the temple in Jerusalem, and in what ways it was understood in various early Jewish and Christian settings. Elgvin begins with depictions of God as king of heaven, as seen in the OT and in later intertestamental writings, including the DSS. He shows how early Christian writings build upon these older traditions in conceiving of a heavenly temple and a reigning Messiah Jesus. Elgvin concludes his study with an analysis of the book of Revelation and ponders in what ways the crises of the Neronian persecutions and the Jewish revolt might have shaped the Christian community's understanding of God's rule in heaven and the image and function of the heavenly temple.

Dorothy Peters looks at the boundaries of canon and the various communities of faith that treasured the contents of canon, even if these contents were not always identical. She probes the factors that determined what kept certain books within the emerging canon of Scripture and other books on the margins or just outside the boundaries of canon. Peters's study sheds important light on how it is that some books, such as *Jubilees* and *1 Enoch*, were regarded as authoritative in some circles and not in others and, in turn, on what implications there might be for understanding the respective communities that variously included or excluded the writings on the margins.

The next three studies focus on village and family life in Galilee and in the larger Roman world. Mark Chancey reviews several important but disputed areas in the study of villages, cities, and the economy of Galilee in the time of Jesus and his earliest followers. For example, Chancey calls our attention to the sharply divergent assessment of the economy in Galilee, how some scholars envision pressures brought on by commercial farming, geared to the needs of the urbanization of Galilee under the tetrarch Herod Antipas, while others speak of the benefits urbanization brought to the economy. The first model assumes tensions between rural inhabitants and urban inhabitants. The second model assumes close, collaborative economic ties. Chancey warns that at present the data are insufficient to form models as definitive as these. He brings his study to a close with a review of what was known of taxation, Roman or otherwise, and of large estates and commercial farms in Galilee before the Jewish revolt. Chancey concludes by admitting that "economics and urban-rural relations still pose the most difficult questions to answer."

Margaret MacDonald explores what is known about Christian families in the Roman world, with special attention to the presence and role of children in early Christian house churches and how the houses became church buildings. Her aim is to bring the level of precision seen in recent studies of the family to the study of children, a much neglected area of study. MacDonald begins her discussion with a review of what has been learned of the design and function of the early Christian house church. Among other things, there is evidence of segregated seating for men and women, even though there is evidence of female leadership and patronage in early churches. MacDonald also explores the complications and dangers faced by children and mothers who were slaves, as well as Christian women who were married to non-Christian men, women who could lose custody of their children should the new faith lead to an end of the marriage. Children's various activities, living space, and acquaintances are reviewed. MacDonald concludes with a new look at Eph 6:1–4, an often overlooked reference to the education of children in the Ephesians household code.

Part One concludes with two studies concerned with a rather grim topic: execution and burial. These studies touch on the dark side of community life, that of conflict and death. The first study by Craig Evans calls attention to the importance of family burial tombs, with reference to the Jewish custom of ossilegium, or reburial of the bones. Of special interest is the literary and archaeological evidence that indicates that even executed criminals were eventually buried in their family tombs. One case is especially interesting, in that we might have a situation in which the bones of a man who had murdered a member of his family were interred in the family tomb, in a chamber adjacent to the chamber in which the bones of the murder victim had been placed. That the bones of the murderer would be reburied in the family tomb (as Jewish law and custom permitted but did not require) is remarkable and may attest to the strength of family bonds, even in a postmortem setting.

The chapter by Shimon Gibson, a well-known archaeologist working in Israel, brings to light new evidence relating to Jesus' appearance before Pontius Pilate, the Roman governor of Judea and Samaria. One of the difficult facts of life and community for the Jewish people in their homeland was submission to foreign authority, whether to a puppet Herodian prince in Galilee or Gaulanitis or to the Roman prefect in Judea. More than any other story in the Gospels, there is certainty among scholars and commentators that Jesus was tried in front of the Roman prefect Pontius Pilate at the Praetorium in Jerusalem, and that this led to his being sentenced to death and subsequently crucified. Gibson examines the oft-cited testimony of Roman historian Tacitus, who in the early second century wrote, "Christus, the founder of the name, had undergone the death penalty in the reign of Tiberias, by sentence of the procurator (*sic*) Pontius Pilate, and the pernicious superstition (*exitiabilis superstitio*) was checked for a moment." Gibson reviews a number of scholarly problems relating to the details of Jesus' hearing before Pilate, suggesting that on the basis of recent work and a new appreciation of the evidence for the western gateway of the Roman Praetorium (identified with the old palace of Herod the Great) in Jerusalem the diverse accounts of the Gospels may now be better understood. Gibson argues that the gateway was accessible to the inhabitants of the city, was situated outside the private zone of the Praetorium palace buildings, and was in proximity to the military barracks where Jesus would have been temporarily incarcerated prior to the trial.

The chapters in Part Two focus on how authoritative Scripture was interpreted in diverse community settings. George Brooke considers how Scripture is interpreted in the DSS. His interest is not merely how Scripture was interpreted in the past, but how these insights may help people today who regard Scripture as authoritative for faith and practice. Brooke rightly notes that the interpretation of Scripture in the scrolls should not be limited to examples of explicit interpretation, such as we see in the *pesharim*, or eschatological commentaries on the prophets and Psalms, but should include the many examples of implicit interpretation that we see in the *Temple Scroll* or the various *Reworked Pentateuch* scrolls. But Brooke also takes into consideration a variety of other texts, such as hymns, poetry, and prayers, that incorporate words and themes from Scripture. The chapter concludes with a brief consideration of the various settings in which Scripture was studied.

Keith Bodner's study of the Samuel scrolls at Qumran shows how a community can read, reread, and recite old, familiar stories in rich new ways. He finds that the Qumran material makes a quantifiable literary contribution for biblical exegetes in the often-neglected realms of plot, character, irony, motif, theme, temporal and spatial settings, point of view, intertextuality, structural design, and keywords. In this way the Qumran texts of Samuel provide modern interpreters with an idea of the reception history of these compelling narratives. Bodner finds that while the major details in the MT and the Samuel scrolls of Qumran are often uniform, unique variations in the scrolls frequently come in the form of gap-filling or matters of characterization with a sense of vibrancy and creativity, with what could be called an attuned sensitivity to storytelling flow and intent. Finally, Bodner suggests that the Samuel scrolls provide insight into the history of interpretation, since some of the variants indisputably testify to a dynamic understanding and application of the story; that is, an active engagement with the text, as though it is being read with a sense of imaginative vitality. One may wonder if these modifications originated in settings of story telling and oral performance. If they did, they may give us an important glimpse into the role authoritative narrative played in community life.

Stephen Andrews treats readers to a study that focuses on the oldest attested Hebrew Scriptures. As almost everyone knows, the Bible scrolls found in the vicinity of the Dead Sea reach back in time some one thousand years closer to the biblical period itself. But what many readers may not know is that there are quotations of OT Scripture that reach back into time much further than even the scrolls. Recently, however, the Khirbet Qeiyafa inscription has grabbed a lot of attention, with claims that we may have evidence of scribal literacy in the tenth century BCE, perhaps in the very court of Israel's famous King David. One scholar finds in the ostracon laws pertaining to social justice and to the protection of widows and orphans, perhaps alluding to Mosaic law. But Andrews believes the parallels and claims are much overdrawn. He concludes his chapter with a review of the famous

Nash Papyrus, which contains the Ten Commandments, and the silver amulets from Ketef Hinnom, one of which contains an abridged form of the priestly blessing found in Num 6:24–26. The accumulated evidence, Andrews tells us, suggests that these amulets were worn not for magical purposes but as a confessional statement.

James Sanders, founder and long-serving president of the Ancient Biblical Manuscript Center in Claremont, California, reviews the progress of *Biblia Hebraica Quinta* in the context of other major editions of the Hebrew Bible, especially in the light of the contribution made by the Dead Sea scripture scrolls. Sanders points out that one of the major results of a half century of study of the scrolls has been clearer understanding of the history of transmission of the Hebrew text and hence a gradual growth in appreciation of the MT's being made up of five integral elements: consonants, vowels, accents, intervals, and *masorot*. Along with the recent, fuller recovery of the actual Masoretic phenomenon in critical study of the text, largely boosted by close study of the scrolls, has been a gradual shedding of bias against the MT's being a Jewish propaganda device in the perennial Jewish-Christian, and then later critical, debates about the meanings of biblical texts. The Biblia Hebraica (BH) series stands as an ongoing witness to that recovery. The respective faith-community perspectives of various versions of the text—whether Hebrew, Greek, or other languages—are now recognized and appreciated for what they are and what they contribute. Each has its place in the history of the transmission and interpretation of Scripture.

Our collection of studies concludes with chapters by two NT scholars, both on the theology faculty of the University of Edinburgh. Larry Hurtado asks what the earliest Christian manuscripts tell us about their readers in the first few centuries of the Christian movement. He focuses on the physical and visual features of earliest Christian manuscripts, in order to consider what we can learn from them about those who prepared and read them. The manuscripts that Hurtado considers are among the earliest artifacts of Christianity. The oldest of these manuscripts are probably the earliest Christian artifacts extant, with some of them dating to the late second century CE, a few perhaps a bit earlier. Hurtado finds that these early manuscripts show that Christians of this early period had already developed a sense of particularity, a distinctive corporate identity as Christians, and were developing and deploying expressions of this identity in their production of copies of their texts, particularly their most cherished ones, those that they read in churches as Scripture.

Paul Foster speaks directly to the question of the antiquity of these earliest manuscripts. He agrees with Hurtado that these manuscripts can and do tell us much about the communities that copied, read, and studied them. He also agrees that they are very old. But with regard to other scholars he finds it necessary to caution against the temptation of dating these manuscripts to times earlier than the evidence itself allows. As a test case Foster examines the well-known Papyrus Egerton 2, which some have claimed reaches back to the first century, possibly predating the Gospel of Mark. He shows how some paleographers were quite inaccurate in their dating of this papyrus and suggests that the lessons learned here be

applied to some of the Greek NT papyri that some scholars, perhaps out of apologetic interests, are tempted to date too early. Foster rightly concludes that there is
no need to engage in special pleading in attempts to make the evidence "better"
than it really is. The NT manuscript evidence is remarkably strong, especially in
comparison with other literature from late antiquity. Acccordingly, NT scholars
are encouraged by Foster to celebrate the number and diversity of third-century
manuscript witnesses to the text that forms the focus of their scholarly attention.

Part One

Identity in Jewish and Christian Communities of Faith

1

The Site of Qumran and the Sectarian Communities in the Dead Sea Scrolls

John J. Collins

The first batch of scrolls discovered in 1947 near Qumran, by the Dead Sea, famously included the Rule of the Community, or *Serek Hayakhad*, also known as 1QS.[1] The press release issued by Millar Burrows on behalf of the American Schools of Oriental Research on April 11, 1948, said that this text "seemed to be a manual of discipline of some comparatively little-known sect or monastic order, possibly the Essenes."[2] The idea that this "monastic" sect lived at Qumran did not arise immediately. Initially the ruins at Qumran were thought to be the remains of a Roman fort. But when Roland de Vaux and Lankaster Harding began to excavate the site in November–December 1951, they found a jar, identical to the ones in which the first scrolls had been found, embedded in the floor of one of the rooms. They inferred that the scrolls were related to the site after all. In his account of the excavation, Harding wrote:

> it would appear, then, that the people who lived at Khirbet Qumran deposited the scrolls in the cave, probably about A.D. 70. The situation fits in well with Pliny the Elder's account of the Essenes, who had a settlement "above Engeddi," and the ruin itself, with its peculiar cemetery which is without parallel in other sites in Jordan, is clearly not an ordinary defensive or agricultural post.[3]

The association of the scrolls with the site was cemented in 1952, when the Bedouin discovered Cave 4, with a trove of more than five hundred manuscripts, at the edge of the marl plateau, literally a stone's throw from the ruins. Several other caves containing scrolls were discovered in the immediate vicinity.

---

[1] This chapter reflects John J. Collins, *Beyond the Qumran Community: The Sectarian Movement of the Dead Sea Scrolls* (Grand Rapids: Eerdmans, 2010). See also Collins, "Sectarian Communities in the Dead Sea Scrolls," in *The Oxford Handbook of the Dead Sea Scrolls* (Timothy H. Lim and John J. Collins, eds.; Oxford: Oxford University Press, 2010), 151–72.

[2] J. C. VanderKam, *The Dead Sea Scrolls Today* (2nd ed.; Grand Rapids: Eerdmans, 2010), 10.

[3] G. Lankaster Harding, "Khirbet Qumrân and Wady Murabbaʿat: Fresh Light on the Dead Sea Scrolls and New Manuscript Discoveries in Jordan," *PEQ* 84 (1952): 109.

Once the connection between the scrolls and the site of Qumran had been established, it became customary to refer to the community described in 1QS as "the Qumran community," and to suppose that Qumran was the sectarian settlement *par excellence*. According to J. T. Milik, this rule was the work of the Teacher and "gave its special character to Qumrân monastic life in the first strict phase of Essenism."[4] Frank Moore Cross argued that "the term *yahad*, 'community,' seems to apply to the community *par excellence*, i.e., the principal settlement in the desert. The Qumrân settlement is probably unique, not only in being the original 'exile in the desert,' the home of the founder of the sect, but also in following a celibate rule."[5] Cross allowed that it was "possible, but not probable . . . that more than one community could be termed the *yahad*."[6] Thus the tendency developed to regard Qumran as the setting for all the scrolls, or at least for the community described in 1QS.

Another Rule Book

Almost from the beginning, however, it was realized that the situation was more complicated than that. It was immediately apparent that there was some relationship between the newly discovered Community Rule and a text that had been discovered in the Cairo Geniza in 1896, which had come to be known as the Damascus Document (or CD, Cairo Damascus) because of references to a new covenant in the land of Damascus. This document also described a sectarian movement. Not only were there similarities in the organization of the communities described in the two rule books, but also CD contained several code names that now reappeared for the first time in the scrolls. These included "Teacher of Righteousness," "sons of Zadok," and "man of the lie." The relationship was subsequently confirmed when fragments of the Damascus Rule were found in Qumran Cave 4.[7] In 1955, Burrows wrote:

> The form of the organization and its rules are found in the Damascus Document and the Manual of Discipline. We have seen that these two documents have a great deal in common, though there are sufficient differences to show that they do not come from exactly the same group. They may represent different branches of the same movement or different stages in its history, if not both.[8]

Milik supposed that the Damascus Rule was a secondary development, drawn up by "a fairly important group" who "left the community at Qumrân and settled in the region of Damascus, without, however, abandoning the priestly charac-

---

[4] J. T. Milik, *Ten Years of Discovery in the Wilderness of Judea* (trans. John Strugnell; Studies in Biblical Theology 26; London: SCM, 1959), 87.

[5] Frank Moore Cross, *The Ancient Library of Qumran* (New York: Doubleday, 1958; repr., Sheffield: Sheffield Academic Press, 1995), 71.

[6] Ibid.

[7] J. M. Baumgarten, ed., on the basis of transcriptions by J. T. Milik, with contributions by S. Pfann and A. Yardeni, *Qumran Cave 4. XIII: The Damascus Document (4Q266–273)* (DJD 18; Oxford: Clarendon Press, 1996).

[8] Millar Burrows, *The Dead Sea Scrolls* (New York: Viking, 1955), 230.

ter of the movement's theology, and remaining in communion with the 'mother house.'"[9] Cross also supposed that 1QS was the older rule and that CD was a secondary development.[10]

More recent scholarship, however, has generally favored the priority of CD.[11] The Damascus Rule preserves the older, simpler form of community structure, while the Community Rule, or Serek, is more developed. In CD, the admission process requires only a simple oath. This simple process is also found in 1QS 5:7c–9a, but it is followed by a much more elaborate, multiyear process in 1QS 6. The Damascus (D) community required the contribution of two days' salary per month. The Serek requires full community property. The D rule places restrictions on sexual activity. The Serek does not speak of women or children at all. The Damascus Rule is critical of the Jerusalem temple. The Serek imagines the community as an alternative temple. Each of these cases suggests that the line of development was from the more primitive kind of organization found in the D rule to the more elaborate provisions of the Serek. It is not the case that one rule simply superseded the other. Both were copied throughout the first century BCE. Equally, there is no evidence that the differences between the two rules were due to a schism. Rather, it appears that within one broad movement some people opted for a stricter, more demanding form of community life.

Multiple Settlements

The *yahad*, however, cannot be identified simply with one settlement in the wilderness, "the Qumran community." We read in 1QS 6:

> In this way shall they behave in all their places of residence. Whenever one fellow meets another, the junior shall obey the senior in work and in money. They shall eat together, together they shall bless and together they shall take counsel. *In every place where there are ten men of the council of the community*, there should not be missing amongst them a priest . . . And in the place in which the ten assemble there should not be missing a man to interpret the law day and night, always, one relieving another. (1QS 6:1c–8a)[12]

"The council of the community" cannot be distinguished from "the community" or *yahad*. The plain meaning of this passage is that the *yahad* consists of multiple communities, with a minimum of ten members.[13] Some scholars have tried to deny this by arguing that the passage refers to members traveling outside of

---

[9] Milik, *Ten Years of Discovery*, 90.

[10] Cross, *The Ancient Library of Qumran*, 71 n.2.

[11] P. R. Davies's *The Damascus Covenant: An Interpretation of the Damascus Document* (JSOTSup 25; Sheffield: JSOT, 1982) was a pivotal book in this regard. The priority of the Community Rule is still defended by Eyal Regev, *Sectarianism in Qumran: A Cross-Cultural Perspective* (Berlin: de Gruyter, 2007), 163–96.

[12] The passage is attested in 4QS[d], although the text is fragmentary.

[13] See John J. Collins, "The Yahad and 'The Qumran Community,'" in *Biblical Traditions in Transmission: Essays in Honour of Michael A. Knibb* (ed. Charlotte Hempel and Judith Lieu; JSJSup 111; Leiden: Brill, 2005), 81–96.

community[14] or that the "places of residence" are temporary structures. But multiple settlements are just what we should expect if the movement in question is identical with the Essene sect, as most scholars suppose. Josephus writes of the Essenes: "They have no one city, but many settle in each city; and when any of the sectarians come from elsewhere, all things they have lie available to them."[15] Josephus clearly assumes that Essenes, apparently of the same order, live in many cities. Similarly, Philo says that the Essenes "live in a number of towns in Judaea, and also in many villages and large groups."[16] Scholarship seems to have lost sight of these statements about the Essenes when it focuses exclusively on the site of Qumran.

The view that that the *yahad* was an association dispersed in multiple settlements may also shed light on one of the more puzzling aspects of the Qumran rule books. The fragments of Cave 4 show that both the D rule and the Serek existed in different recensions and that both were copied repeatedly during the first century BCE. Sarianna Metso has made a convincing argument that some later copies of the Serek preserve earlier redactional stages, while the most developed edition, in 1QS, is found in the earliest manuscript.[17] Philip Davies has questioned whether the rules reflect actual community practice: "If the 'rule' is a rule, there can be only one version in effect at any one time. The paradox obliges us to reconsider our premises: is 1QS a 'community rule' at all?"[18] But as Metso has argued, "it was not academic interest which motivated the Qumranic scribes in their editorial work but rather the changes which had taken place in the life and practices of the community."[19] If we bear in mind that there were many settlements of the *yahad*, however, a new explanation becomes possible. Not all the scrolls found at Qumran were copied on site. Some may have been brought there from different settlements, which may have been operating with different editions of the Community Rule.[20] In short, the different forms of the Serek may not have been copied side by side in the same community but may have been in effect in different communities at the same time. (This possibility also undercuts the question raised by Davies as to

---

[14]Sarianna Metso, "Whom Does the Term Yahad Identify?" in *Biblical Traditions in Transmission: Essays in Honour of Michael A. Knibb* (ed. Charlotte Hempel and Judith Lieu; JSJSup 111; Leiden: Brill, 2006), 213–35.

[15]Josephus, *J.W.* 2.124.

[16]Philo, *Apologia pro Iudaeis* 1; G. Vermes and M. D. Goodman, *The Essenes According to the Classical Sources* (Sheffield: JSOT Press, 1989).

[17]Sarianna Metso, *The Textual Development of the Qumran Community Rule* (STDJ 21; Leiden: Brill, 1997), 105. This view is disputed by Philip Alexander, "The Redaction History of Serek ha Yahad: A Proposal," *RevQ* 17 (Milik Festschrift, 1996), 437–53.

[18]Philip Davies, "Redaction and Sectarianism in the Qumran Scrolls," in *Sects and Scrolls: Essays on Qumran and Related Topics* (South Florida Studies in the History of Judaism 134; Atlanta: Scholars Press, 1996), 151–61, here 157.

[19]Sarianna Metso, "In Search of the Sitz im Leben of the Community Rule," in *The Provo International Conference on the Dead Sea Scrolls* (ed. D. W. Parry and E. Ulrich; STDJ 30; Leiden: Brill, 1999), 310.

[20]As suggested by Alison Schofield, "Rereading S: A New Model of Textual Development in Light of the Cave 4 *Serekh* Copies," *DSD* 15 (2008), 96–120; eadem, *From Qumran to the Yahad: A New Paradigm of Textual Development for the Community Rule* (STDJ 77; Leiden: Brill, 2009).

whether the Serek was a community rule at all.) Scrolls from various communities would have been brought to Qumran for hiding in time of crisis.

Reference to Qumran?

Do the DSS, or the Serek in particular, ever refer to a settlement at Qumran?

Needless to say, the text never indicates a specific location. It does, however, speak of a group that is to go to the wilderness to prepare there the way of the Lord. From the early days of scholarship on the scrolls, scholars have seen here a specific reference to the settlement by the Dead Sea.

The passage is found in 1QS 8. The opening section (8:1–4a) announces that there shall be "in the council of the community twelve men and three priests, perfect in everything that has been revealed from all the law" (8:1). This section is followed by three paragraphs, each of which begins with the phrase "when these are in Israel." The first of these, beginning in 8:4b, claims for the sectarian group the function of atonement, which was traditionally proper to the temple cult. The second paragraph begins in 8:12b: "when these are a community in Israel[21] . . . they shall be separated from the midst of the dwelling of the men of iniquity, to go to the wilderness to prepare there the way of Him, as it is written, 'in the wilderness prepare the way of **** . . .' This is the study of the law, which he commanded by the hand of Moses." The third paragraph, beginning in 9:3, reads, "when these are in Israel in accordance with these rules in order to establish the spirit of holiness in truth eternal." This passage is not found in 4QSᵉ, which lacks 8:15–9:11. The paragraph beginning in 9:3 seems to duplicate 8:4b–10 and may be a secondary insertion.[22]

In the early days of scrolls scholarship, the twelve men and three priests were understood as an inner council.[23] It is not apparent, however, that they have any administrative role. In an influential article published in 1959, E. F. Sutcliffe dubbed them "The First Fifteen Members of the Qumran Community."[24] In this he was followed by Jerome Murphy-O'Connor, who labeled the passage "an Essene manifesto."[25] This view has been widely, though not universally, accepted. Michael Knibb spoke for many when he wrote:

> This material thus appears to be the oldest in the Rule and to go back to the period shortly before the Qumran community came into existence; it may be regarded as

---

[21] The word ליחד ("a community") is inserted above the line and appears to be missing in 4QSᵈ.

[22] So Sarianna Metso, *The Textual Development of the Qumran Community Rule* (STDJ 21; Leiden: Brill, 1997), 72.

[23] So Milik, *Ten Years of Discovery*, 100.

[24] E. F. Sutcliffe, "The First Fifteen Members of the Qumran Community," *JSS* 4 (1959): 134–38.

[25] Jerome Murphy-O'Connor, "La Genèse Littéraire de la Règle de la Communauté," *RB* 66 (1969): 528–49. See also Michael Knibb, *The Qumran Community* (Cambridge Commentaries on Jewish Writings of the Jewish and Christian World 200 BC to AD 200 2; Cambridge: Cambridge University Press, 1988), 129.

reflecting the aims and ideals of conservative Jews who were disturbed by the way in which the Maccabean leaders were conducting affairs, and whose decision to withdraw into the wilderness was motivated by the desire to be able to observe strictly God's laws in the way that they believed to be right. It probably dates from the middle of the second century BC.[26]

This view does not withstand a close analysis of the text.

The text of 1QS 8:1, "In the council of the community (there shall be) twelve men and three priests," can be read in either of two ways. The twelve men and three priests can be taken to constitute the council of the community or to be a special group within it. It is possible to take the verse to mean that the twelve men and three priests are a special subgroup within the council of the *yahad*. (The council of the *yahad* is simply the *yahad* itself). This is in fact how they are understood in 1QS 8:10–11: "When these have been established in the fundamental principles of the community for two years in perfection of way, they shall be set apart as holy within the council of the men of the community." They are not, then, a council in the sense of an administrative or executive body. Rather, they are an elite group set aside for special training. The establishment of such a group is necessary for the completion of the *yahad*: "when these exist in Israel the council of the community is established in truth" (8:5). The group in question cannot be taken to constitute the whole *yahad*, at any stage of its existence.[27] Rather, as Leaney already saw, "the community or movement out of which it arose must have been represented by groups dispersed throughout the land."[28] The elite group does not break away from the *yahad*, nor does it found a separate organization. It may be said to found a new community, but it is a community that is an integral part of the broader *yahad*. The text (1QS 8:10–11) says quite clearly that certain people who have been established in the community for two years will be set apart as holy in its midst. In the extant text, the antecedent is the group of twelve men and three priests.

Unfortunately, we do not know what part this group played in the history of the movement. The numbers have symbolic significance, referring to the twelve tribes and three priestly families,[29] and we cannot be sure that this group ever came to be. Moreover, the command to prepare in the wilderness the way of the Lord is taken from Scripture and is interpreted allegorically in the text:

> As it is written: In the desert prepare the way of ****, in the wilderness make level a highway for our God. This is the study of the law which he commanded through the hand of Moses, in order to act in compliance with all that has been revealed from age to age, and according to what the prophets have revealed through his holy spirit.[30]

---

[26] Knibb, *Qumran Community*, 129.

[27] See further Collins, "The Yahad and 'The Qumran Community,'" 88–90; also Shane A. Berg, "An Elite Group within the Yahad: Revisiting 1QS 8–9," in *Qumran Studies: New Approaches, New Questions* (ed. Michael T. Davis and Brent A. Strawn; Grand Rapids: Eerdmans, 2007), 161–77.

[28] A. R. C. Leaney, *The Rule of Qumran and Its Meaning* (London: SCM, 1966), 210–11.

[29] Milik, *Ten Years of Discovery*, 100.

[30] G. J. Brooke, "Isaiah 40:3 and the Wilderness Community," in *New Qumran Texts and Studies* (ed. G. J. Brooke and F. García Martínez; STDJ 15; Leiden: Brill, 1994), 117–32.

Symbolism does not preclude literal enactment, and the fact that this text was found beside an inhabited site in the wilderness is hard to dismiss as mere coincidence. Accordingly, the suspicion persists that the retreat of this pioneering group to the wilderness marked the beginning of "the Qumran community." If so, it should be noted that it did not arise from a schism in a parent group and did not by itself constitute the *yahad* but was part of a larger whole. It would also, of course, have to have grown in size. But while the identification of this group with the founding of the Qumran community is attractive, it is by no means certain.

If the passage in 1QS 8 does indeed refer to the beginnings of the settlement at Qumran, then that settlement would appear to be an offshoot of the main association, or perhaps a kind of retreat center where people could devote themselves to the pursuit of holiness to an exceptional degree. There is nothing to suggest that this settlement would become the headquarters or motherhouse of the sect. Neither, it should be noted, is there any mention of a motherhouse in the Greek and Latin accounts of the Essenes. Pliny writes about an Essene settlement near the Dead Sea because he happens to be giving an account of that geographical region. He does not indicate any awareness of other Essene settlements. Philo and Josephus, however, emphasize that the Essenes live in multiple locations, with no indication that any one took precedence.[31] The passage in 1QS 8, in any case, is too enigmatic to allow us to deduce much about a settlement in the wilderness, and its historical and geographical value remains uncertain.

The Date of the Movement

In light of what we have seen, the attempt to correlate the ruins of Qumran with the life of the sect known from the scrolls appears hazardous. The common assumption in older scholarship that the Teacher "led his flock to the desert" is unsubstantiated. If 1QS 8 is indeed a reference to "the move to the desert," then presumably the *yahad* had been in existence for some time before that happened. The only clue to the date of this passage is provided by the paleographic date of the manuscript of 1QS, which has been estimated at 75 BCE, plus or minus twenty-five years, and falls within the same range as Jodi Magness's date for the founding of the settlement at Qumran.[32] This coincidence, however, only keeps open the possibility of a reference in 1QS 8. It does not establish its probability.

For more than fifty years there has been a consensus that the sectarian movement described in the scrolls developed in the middle of the second century BCE.[33] This consensus has rested on two main considerations. One is a brief and elliptic

[31] Philo, *Apologia pro Iudaeis* 1; Josephus, *J.W.* 2.124.
[32] Jodi Magness, *The Archaeology of Qumran and the Dead Sea Scrolls* (Grand Rapids: Eerdmans, 2002), 68.
[33] For an overview see J. C. VanderKam, "Identity and History of the Community," in *The Dead Sea Scrolls after Fifty Years: A Comprehensive Assessment* (ed. Peter W. Flint and J. C. VanderKam; 2 vols.; Leiden: Brill, 1999), 2:507–23; Philip R. Callaway, *The History of the Qumran Community: An Investigation* (JSPSup 3; Sheffield: Sheffield Academic Press,

narrative of sectarian origins in CD 1, and the other concerns the conflict between the Teacher of Righteousness and the Wicked Priest, described in the biblical commentaries or *pesharim*.

The passage in CD 1 reads as follows:

> He left a remnant to Israel and did not deliver it up to be destroyed. And in the age of wrath, three hundred and ninety years after He had given them into the hand of King Nebuchadnezzar of Babylon, He visited them, and caused a plant root to spring from Israel and Aaron to inherit His Land and to prosper on the good things of His earth. And they perceived their iniquity and recognized that they were guilty men, yet for twenty years they were like blind men groping for the way. And God observed their deeds, that they sought Him with a whole heart, and He raised for them a Teacher of Righteousness to guide them in the way of his heart.

It is universally acknowledged that the figure of 390 years is symbolic. (It is derived from Ezek 4:5, where the prophet is told to lie on his left side and bear the punishment of the house of Israel for 390 days, representing the years of the punishment of the house of Israel.) Nonetheless, most scholars have accepted the number as approximately correct. This would point to a date in the early second century BCE. Some twenty years then elapsed before the coming of the Teacher. The decisive break is usually thought to have been a reaction to the usurpation of the high priesthood by Jonathan Maccabee in 152 BCE. Jonathan is then identified as the "Wicked Priest" mentioned in the *pesharim*, or commentaries, on the prophets. The archeology of the site of Qumran, as explained by de Vaux, was thought to lend support to this reconstruction of the history. This consensus was formulated with minor variations by Milik, Cross, and Geza Vermes.[34]

But in fact there is no reason to think that the 390 years of CD is any more reliable than Dan 9, which calculates the period from the destruction of Jerusalem to the persecution under Antiochus Epiphanes as 490 years (70 weeks of years; in fact the period in question was only about 418 years). As Vermes has pointed out, "all the extant evidence proves that Jews of the early post-biblical age possessed no correct knowledge of the length of the duration of Persian rule."[35] The 390 years of CD 1 is a symbolic number for the period of time between the destruction of Jerusalem and the beginning of the last times. It is probably safe to say that a considerable time had elapsed since the destruction, but the number cannot be pressed to yield even an approximate date.

1988), 11–27. The consensus view has been defended recently by Hanan Eshel, *The Dead Sea Scrolls and the Hasmonean State* (Grand Rapids: Eerdmans, 2008), 1–27.

[34] Milik, *Ten Years of Discovery*, 44–98; Cross, *The Ancient Library of Qumran*, 88–120; Geza Vermes, *Les manuscrits du désert de Juda* (1953; 2nd ed.; Paris: Desclée, 1954), 70–104. Compare Geza Vermes, *The Complete Dead Sea Scrolls in English* (rev. ed.; London: Penguin, 2004), 49–66. Cross identified Simon Maccabeus, rather than Jonathan, as the Wicked Priest.

[35] Geza Vermes, "Eschatological Worldview in the Dead Sea Scrolls and in the New Testament," in *Emanuel: Studies in the Hebrew Bible, Septuagint, and Dead Sea Scrolls in Honor of Emanuel Tov* (ed. S. M. Paul et al.; VTSup 94; Leiden: Brill, 2003), 482 n. 4. Compare Eshel, *The Dead Sea Scrolls and the Hasmonean State*, 31.

It has been widely assumed that the usurpation of the high priesthood by the Maccabees was a decisive factor in the formation of the sect.[36] The high-priestly succession, traditionally within the Zadokite line, had been disrupted during the so-called Hellenistic Reform by Jason (who was from the high-priestly family) and Menelaus (who was not), as reported in 2 Macc 4. After the death of Menelaus, Alcimus held the office for some three years (162–160 or 159 BCE).[37] After this, there was a period known as the *intersacerdotium*, when the office of high priest was vacant, until Jonathan Maccabee was appointed high priest by the Syrian king Alexander Balas.[38] The members of the *yahad* are often called "sons of Zadok" in the scrolls, and the Teacher of Righteousness is sometimes called "the priest." Many scholars have assumed that the Teacher and his followers, as Zadokite priests, objected to the usurpation of the office by the Maccabees. This is thought to be the basis for the enmity between the Teacher and the "Wicked Priest" in the *pesharim*. But in fact the scrolls never claim that the ruling high priests were illegitimate. The reasons for separation given in the Damascus Document and 4QMMT concern the cultic calendar and matters of legal observance. At no point is any mention made of the legitimacy of the high priest. Neither can the use of the sobriquet "the Wicked Priest" in the *pesharim* be taken to imply that the high priest was illegitimate. The *pesharim* often qualify the wickedness of the priest in question, but at no point do they accuse him of usurping the high priesthood.[39] It seems highly unlikely that this issue would go unmentioned, if it were a major reason for the formation of the sect.

If the usurpation of the high priesthood was not a causative factor in the formation of the sect, this removes one of the major reasons for dating the origin of the sect to the middle of the second century BCE. It also opens up the possibility that the conflict between the Teacher and the Wicked Priest was not the original rift that caused the separation of the sect, but may have occurred some time later.

New light was shed on the question of the origins of the sect by the text called "Some of the Works of the Torah," 4QMMT, a fragmentary text found in six manuscripts in Qumran Cave 4 (4Q394–399). The first public presentation of this text, at a conference in Jerusalem in 1984, led to a revolution in the study of the scrolls, as it states explicitly that the group represented by the author "have separated ourselves from the majority of the people" because of halakic disagreements.[40] The issues in question are primarily ones of holiness and purity (the holiness of Jerusalem and the "camp," the purity of liquid streams, sacrifice and tithing, forbidden

---

[36] This hypothesis was first proposed by Vermes, *Les manuscrits du désert de Juda*, 79. See J. C. VanderKam, "Identity and History of the Community," in *The Dead Sea Scrolls after Fifty Years: A Comprehensive Assessment* (ed. Peter W. Flint and J. C. VanderKam; 2 vols.; Leiden: Brill, 1999), 2:509–10.

[37] See J. C. VanderKam, *From Joshua to Caiaphas: High Priests after the Exile* (Minneapolis: Fortress, 2004), 226–44.

[38] Josephus, *Ant.* 13.146. See VanderKam, *From Joshua to Caiaphas*, 244–50.

[39] Compare Alison Schofield and J. C. VanderKam, "Were the Hasmoneans Zadokites?" *JBL* 124 (2005): 73–87: "while the community opposed Hasmonean ruler-priests, there is no surviving indication that they considered them *genealogically* unfit for the high priesthood" (83).

[40] Elisha Qimron and John Strugnell, eds., *Qumran Cave 4: V. Miqsat Maʿase Ha-Torah* (DJD 10; Oxford: Clarendon Press, 1994), 59 (Composite text, C 7).

sexual unions, etc.).[41] Some twenty issues are cited. A whole section of the text is devoted to laying out the solar calendar, although this may be a separate document annexed to 4QMMT secondarily.[42] While the scriptural basis of the disputed issues is not made explicit, it is evidently assumed throughout. The issues raised are "precepts of the Torah." They are presented by juxtaposing opposing arguments; "we say" as opposed to "they do." In all cases the views of the "we" group are stricter than those of their opponents. The views of the opponents generally correspond to those attributed to the rabbis in the Mishnah and are consequently thought to be those of the Pharisees.[43] The text concludes:

> We have written to you some of the precepts of the Torah according to our decision, for your welfare and the welfare of your people. For we have seen (that) you have wisdom and knowledge of the Torah . . . so that you may rejoice at the end of time, finding that some of our practices are correct.[44]

Most scholars have accepted the editors' suggestion that this text, which may be viewed as a halakic treatise,[45] was addressed to an individual leader of Israel, most probably a Hasmonean high priest.[46] The conclusion reads:

> and also we have written to you some of the works of the Torah which we think are good for you and for your people, for we have seen that that you have wisdom and knowledge of the Torah. Reflect on all these matters and seek from him that he may support your counsel and keep far from you the evil scheming and the counsel of Belial, so that at the end of time, you may rejoice in finding that some of our words are true. And it shall be reckoned to you as justice when you do what is upright and good before him, for your good and that of Israel.[47]

Most scholars believe that the addressee in this passage must have been a ruler of Israel.[48] In any case, the text provides the author's understanding of the reasons for separation from the rest of Israel.

There is evidence that the Teacher at least once reached out to his opponents in an attempt to persuade them. According to 4QpPs[a] fragments 1–10, col. 4:8–9, the Wicked Priest sought to murder the Teacher "and the Torah which he sent to him." Most probably, this was the same "Torah" that was rejected by the Man of the Lie. Elisha Qimron and John Strugnell made the attractive proposal that the document

---

[41] See Elisha Qimron, "The Halakha," in *Qumran Cave 4: V. Miqsat Maʿase Ha-Torah* (ed. Elisha Qimron and John Strugnell; DJD 10; Oxford: Clarendon Press, 1994), 123–77.

[42] See John Strugnell, "MMT: Second Thoughts on a Forthcoming Edition," in *The Community of the Renewed Covenant* (ed. Eugene Ulrich and J. C. VanderKam; Notre Dame, IN: University of Notre Dame, 1994), 61–62; Hanne von Weissenberg, *4QMMT: Reevaluating the Text, the Function, and the Meaning of the Epilogue* (STDJ 82; Leiden: Brill, 2009), 141.

[43] Regev, *Sectarianism in Qumran*, 98.

[44] Composite text C 26–30; cf. Elisha Qimron and John Strugnell, eds., *Qumran Cave 4: V. Miqsat Maʿase Ha-Torah* (DJD 10; Oxford: Clarendon Press, 1994), 63.

[45] The initial suggestion of the editors that this text was a letter is widely rejected. See already Qimron and Strugnell, *Qumran Cave 4*, 113–14.

[46] Qimron and Strugnell, *Qumran Cave 4*, 121.

[47] 4QMMT C 26–32.

[48] See, e.g., Regev, *Sectarianism in Qumran*, 104.

in question is none other than the text we know as 4QMMT,[49] and the proposal has been taken up by such diverse scholars as Michael Wise and Hanan Eshel.[50]

It is generally agreed that the interpretation of the Torah found in 4QMMT is opposed to that of the Pharisees.[51] In the words of Lawrence Schiffman, "When mishnaic texts preserve Pharisee-Sadducee conflicts over the same matters discussed in the Halakhic Letter, the views of the letter's authors match those of the Sadducees."[52] We need not conclude that the authors were Sadducees,[53] but at least they were anti-Pharisaic. The Pharisees were embroiled in conflicts especially in the early first century BCE. They clashed especially with Alexander Jannaeus, the Hasmonean king who ruled from 103 to 76 BCE. At one point the Pharisees led a revolt against him, on the grounds that he was not fit to be high priest, and he responded by having some six thousand people killed. He later crucified around eight hundred of his opponents. On his deathbed, however, he advised his queen Salome Alexandra to make peace with the Pharisees. She did so, and entrusted them with the government. According to Josephus "she permitted the Pharisees to do as they liked in all matters, and also commanded the people to obey them; and whatever regulations, introduced by the Pharisees in accordance with the tradition of their fathers, had been abolished by her father-in-law Hyrcanus, these she again restored. And so, while she had the title of sovereign, the Pharisees had the power" (*Ant.* 13.408–409). She appointed Hyrcanus II high priest, and he served in that capacity until 67 BCE. He later had a second term (63–40). We should not be surprised if the reversal of royal attitude toward the Pharisees and their rulings provoked a protest from the other sects. This is perhaps the time in Hasmonean history when a high priest was most likely to take action against people who were contesting the Pharisaic halakah. Josephus says that the Pharisees tried to persuade the queen to kill those who had urged Alexander to put the eight hundred to death, and that they themselves assassinated some of them. This struggle for sectarian hegemony provides a plausible context for the conflict between the Teacher and both the Wicked Priest and the Man of the Lie.[54] In contrast, we have no evidence

---

[49] Qimron and Strugnell, *Qumran Cave 4*, 175.

[50] Michael Owen Wise, *The First Messiah* (San Francisco: HarperSanFrancisco, 1999), 65–68; Hanan Eshel, "4QMMT and the History of the Hasmonean Period," in *Reading 4QMMT: New Perspectives on Qumran Law and History* (ed. J. Kampen and M. J. Bernstein; SBLSymS 2; Atlanta: Society of Biblical Literature, 1996), 53–65; Eshel, *The Dead Sea Scrolls and the Hasmonean State*, 46–47.

[51] See Qimron and Strugnell, *Qumran Cave 4*, 123–77; Y. Sussmann, "Appendix 1. The History of the Halakha and the Dead Sea Scrolls," in Qimron and Strugnell, *Qumran Cave 4*, 179–200.

[52] L. H. Schiffman, *Reclaiming the Dead Sea Scrolls* (Philadelphia: Jewish Publication Society, 1994), 86–87.

[53] Other factors besides halakah would have to be taken into account. See the comments of J. C. VanderKam and Peter W. Flint, *The Meaning of the Dead Sea Scrolls* (San Francisco: HarperSanFrancisco, 2002), 250–52.

[54] See now Michael O. Wise, "The Origins and History of the Teacher's Movement," in *The Oxford Handbook of the Dead Sea Scrolls* (Timothy H. Lim and John J. Collins, eds.; Oxford: Oxford University Press, 2010), 92–122.

for sectarian conflict in the time of Jonathan Maccabeus. Even though Josephus introduces the three schools of thought in the time of Jonathan (*Ant.* 13.171), it is only at the end of the long reign of John Hyrcanus (135/4–104 BCE) that sectarian affiliation becomes an important issue for the high priest (*Ant.* 13.288–298).

Qumran

Roland de Vaux had proposed that the settlement at Qumran had been established in the mid-second century BCE, but he admitted that the earliest phase was poorly attested. The small amount of pottery from period 1a is indistinguishable from that of 1b, and there are no coins associated with it.[55] Magness points out that neither the pottery nor the coins provide evidence for any settlement before 100 BCE and concludes that "it is reasonable to date the initial establishment of the sectarian settlement to the first half of the first century BCE (that is, some time between 100–50 BCE)."[56] It should be noted that the *yahad* was not a single settlement, at Qumran or elsewhere, and there is no hard evidence linking the Teacher to the site of Qumran. The beginnings of the *yahad*, and the activity of the Teacher at least in part, should be dated to a time before the settlement of the site (assuming that Qumran was a settlement of the sect).[57] But in any case, the archeological evidence does not provide any solid support for the second-century dating of the Teacher or the community.

There has been raging controversy as to whether Qumran should be considered a sectarian site at all.[58] The sheer proximity of the caves, especially Cave 4, to the site, weighs heavily in favor of the view that the scrolls were related to the site, as does the fact that a jar identical to the ones in which the first scrolls were found was embedded in the floor of one of the rooms. It seems overwhelmingly likely that Qumran was a sectarian settlement at the time when the scrolls were hidden. This does not necessarily require that it was always a sectarian settlement. Several archeologists have tried to reconstruct the development of the site from its architecture. They regard the roughly square structure in the center of the complex, with the tower at its northwest corner, as the original nucleus. Jean-Baptiste Humbert regards this structure as a residence;[59] Yitzar Hirschfeld and Magen and

---

[55] Roland de Vaux, *Archaeology and the Dead Sea Scrolls* (Oxford: Oxford University Press, 1973), 4–5. See the summary by VanderKam, "Identity and History," 501–4.

[56] Magness, *Archaeology of Qumran*, 65.

[57] Torleif Elgvin, "The Yahad Is More Than Qumran," in *Enoch and Qumran Origins: New Light on a Forgotten Connection* (ed. G. Boccaccini; Grand Rapids: Eerdmans, 2005), 273–79.

[58] Yitzhar Hirschfeld, *Qumran in Context* (Peabody, MA: Hendrickson, 2004); Katharina Galor et al., eds., *Qumran: The Site of the Dead Sea Scrolls: Archaeological Interpretations and Debates, Proceedings of a Conference Held at Brown University, November 17–19, 2002* (STDJ 57; Leiden: Brill, 2006).

[59] Jean-Baptiste Humbert, "Reconsideration of the Archaeological Interpretation," in *Khirbet Qumrân et 'Aïn Feshkha: II Études d'anthropologie, de physique et de chimie, Stud-*

Peleg regard it as a fortress.[60] All these scholars assume that the nature of the site changed after the Roman conquest, when the Hasmoneans were no longer in a position to fortify the area. Humbert allows that it became a sectarian settlement in the later phase of its occupation. Whether the square structure was the original nucleus of the site, however, remains hypothetical.

While some of the suggestions about the original nature of the site (rustic villa, pottery factory) border on the ridiculous, the idea that it might have been a fortress is not inherently implausible. It is agreed that there was a fort there in the pre-exilic period. The site was evidently destroyed by military assault in 68 CE. De Vaux believed that the Romans maintained a small garrison there after the site was destroyed in 68 CE. He noted that "from the plateau of Qumran the view extends over the whole of the western shore from the mouth of the Jordan to Ras Feshka and over the whole southern half of the sea."[61] In the Hasmonean era there was a chain of fortresses in the general area of the Dead Sea. Most of these were built in the wake of the expansion of the Hasmonean state under John Hyrcanus, Aristobulus, and Alexander Jannaeus. The northern end of this chain was Alexandrion-Sartaba and Dok, near Jericho.[62] The fortress of Kypros protected the main road to Jerusalem. There were fortified docks at Rujm al-Bahr and Khirbet Mazin, south of Qumran. Inland from Qumran was Hyrcania. Far to the south stood Masada. On the Jordanian side of the Dead Sea was the fortress of Machaerus, built by Alexander Jannaeus as a bulwark against the Nabateans. It would be surprising if the Hasmoneans had allowed a group that was bitterly critical of them to build an establishment in the middle of this area. The cemetery with predominantly male burials could conceivably be explained on the hypothesis that the site was a military fort. It would be more difficult to explain the great number of stepped pools, assuming that these are correctly identified as *miqvaoth*. The viability of the fortress hypothesis depends on the date at which the pools were dug. At least some of them were evidently in existence before the earthquake, which is still most plausibly identified as the one in 31 BCE. But the earthquake was fully three decades after the Roman conquest. The problem is that clear stratigraphic evidence of the date of construction of the pools is lacking.

The idea that Qumran was originally a fortress or early warning station, as part of the Hasmonean chain of defenses, and that it became a sectarian settlement only after the Roman conquest, is attractive in some respects. But it is an *a priori*

---

ies of Anthropology, Physics, and Chemistry (ed. Jean-Baptiste Humbert and Jan Gunneweg NTOA.SA 3; Fribourg: Academic Press, 2003), 419–25, here 422.

[60] Hirschfeld, *Qumran in Context*, 60; Y. Magen and Yuval Peleg, "Back to Qumran: Ten Years of Excavation and Research, 1993–2004," in *Qumran: The Site of the Dead Sea Scrolls: Archaeological Interpretations and Debates, Proceedings of a Conference Held at Brown University, November 17–19, 2002* (ed. Katharina Galor et al.; STDJ 57; Leiden: Brill, 2006), 55–113.

[61] De Vaux, *Archaeology and the Dead Sea Scrolls*, 42.

[62] The fortress of Dok was in existence before the Hasmoneans rose to power. See 1 Macc 9:50; 16:11–17; Josephus, *Ant.* 13.6, 230–234. This is where Simon Maccabeus was murdered by Ptolemy, son of Abubus.

hypothesis that lacks empirical archeological data to support it. No evidence has yet been adduced to show that the stepped pools were constructed late, or indeed that the square building was the original core of the settlement.[63] Moreover, we do not know what the Hasmoneans thought of the *yahad*. The conflict between the Teacher and the Wicked Priest surely loomed larger from a sectarian than from a Hasmonean perspective. The rulers may not have perceived the sect as a threat at all. In short, there is enough uncertainty about the history and nature of the site to cast doubt on the long-established view that the site was constructed by the Teacher and his followers, but there is not enough evidence to establish the view that it was a Hasmonean fortress that underwent a major change after the Roman conquest. If the site was a military outpost or served some other non-religious function in the Hasmonean era, then the famous passage in 1QS 8:13–14, about going to the wilderness to prepare the way of the Lord, could not be a reference to the settlement at Qumran.

Conclusion

Much remains uncertain about the archeology of the site, although de Vaux's interpretation, as modified by Magness, has not by any means been discredited. The site was surely a sectarian settlement in the first century CE, and it is probably still easiest to suppose that it was already such in the Hasmonean period. But in any case the interpretation of the scrolls should not be tied too closely to that of the site. At most, Qumran was one settlement of the *yahad*. It was never the *yahad* in its entirety. There is no good evidence that it was the headquarters or motherhouse of the sect. The fact that the scrolls were hidden there is due to the remote location, not necessarily to the primacy of the settlement. Even the Community Rule (*Serek Hayakhad*) was not written specifically for a community at Qumran, although it may have applied to that community among others. The *yahad*, and still more the new covenant of the Damascus Rule, was not an isolated monastic community, as has sometimes been imagined, but was part of a religious association spread widely throughout the land. Despite the lure of convenience, it is time we stopped referring to it as "the Qumran community."

---

[63] Hanan Eshel, "Qumran Archaeology," *JAOS* 125 (2005): 389–94, says that "since the pottery found in the foundation trenches of the building has not yet been published, we have no data on which to base a precise date for the construction."

2

From the Earthly to the Heavenly Temple: Lines from the Bible and Qumran to Hebrews and Revelation

Torleif Elgvin

Among the NT writings, Hebrews and Revelation have a particular interest in God's heavenly temple. We hear about sacrifice at the heavenly altar, a high priest in the image of the angelic Melchizedek, incense rising before the heavenly throne, and angels singing and acting in God's presence. Texts from the OT and the scrolls provide an important background for central concepts in these two writings.[1]

Old Testament Foundations

Some OT texts describe God marching forward from his holy mountain surrounded by angelic forces. According to Deut 33:2, "YHWH came from Sinai, and dawned over them from (Mount) Seir, he shone forth from Mount Paran, He came with myriads of holy ones" (i.e., angels). Similar descriptions are found in Judg 5:4–5, Ps 68:8–9, and Hab 3:3.

The rule of thumb in the OT is that God is invisible to mortals. But he can make exceptions and allow people to see his throne and to gaze at his presence. Exodus 24:9–11 preserves the memory of Moses and the elders of Israel, dining with and receiving a vision of God enthroned above a sapphire floor. In 1 Kgs 22:19–23 we encounter the prophet Mika son of Yimla who sees into God's presence and listens to God's dialogue with his angels about Israel's fate below.

Other OT texts describe God's change of address. He moved from Sinai and into his new dwelling at the temple in Zion. At the holy mountain his glory was

[1] This chapter draws on two more technical articles that have been recently published: Torleif Elgvin, "Priests on Earth as in Heaven: Jewish Light on the Book of Revelation," in *Echoes from the Caves: Qumran and the New Testament* (ed. F. Garcia Martinez; STDJ 60; Leiden: Brill, 2009), 257–78; idem, "Temple Mysticism and the Temple of Men," in *The Dead Sea Scrolls: Text and Context* (ed. Charlotte Hempel; STDJ 90; Leiden: Brill, 2010), 227–42.

revealed in thunder, smoke, and blowing of the horn. In the desert his presence was seen as a pillar of smoke and light. After his move, priestly tradition remembers that God at central moments let his glory be visibly revealed in the sanctuary, probably as a shining cloud (Exod 40:34; 1 Kgs 8:10–11, cf. Exod 24:16; Isa 6:4).

In the ancient Near East the temple could be perceived as a symbolic mountain and God's abode. Thus, biblical authors would transfer traditions connected to the Sinai revelation to Zion and the temple, God's elect place of dwelling. Descriptions of God at march, not from Sinai but from Zion in Ps 50:1–4 and Ps 68 (vv. 17, 25–30, 36), are examples of this theological transfer. The hymns proclaiming "the Lord is king" (Pss 93; 96–99) describe the enthroned Lord marching forth to judge his enemies and redeem his people, similar to the early descriptions of God revealing himself from Sinai. At this stage of tradition the place of God's appearance would be Zion and the temple.

Isaiah 6 portrays the sanctuary as the place in which Isaiah was called to be a prophet. Isaiah was probably standing in the courts of the temple when God opened his eyes. In this vision earthly and heavenly sanctuaries converge, as do priestly and prophetic tradition. The Jerusalemite Isaiah, his vision, and his subsequent legitimating report presuppose basic elements of the priestly tradition at home in this temple: God's abode in the temple, the enthroned Lord surrounded by angelic beings, angelic praise, smoke filling the temple, incense altar, human impurity and need for cleansing and atonement, and divine communication with humankind. According to Isa 6, priestly procedures go on in the heavenly temple.

In Isa 40:1–9, the prologue to the Isaianic Book of Consolation, we hear angelic voices commissioned by the God of Israel. This chapter has usually been understood as the calling of the exilic prophet Second Isaiah. Scholars such as Ulrich Berges see the speaker of Isa 40–55 not as an individual but as a group of Levitic singers, a group that stands forth with prophetic identity and treasures both hymnic traditions from the temple and the heritage from the prophet Isaiah.[2] Such an understanding of these texts would make Isa 40–55 another example of the converging of priestly and prophetic tradition. In this context it should be remembered that biblical and postbiblical sources assign the Levites a central role in temple liturgies.

According to the Priestly source of the Pentateuch (Exod 25:9, 40), the tabernacle is built according to the model that was shown to Moses on the mountain. For later tradition (1 Chr 28:19; Ps 11:4; Heb 8:5; Acts 7:44) this model is not an architectural blueprint but refers to a vision given to Moses of the heavenly temple that serves as model for the earthly sanctuary: For Heb 8:2–5 this is "the true tabernacle, which the Lord pitched, not man," and the earthly temple is only "a copy and shadow of the heavenly things."

The idea of the earthly temple as a counterpart to the heavenly one would enable temple singers below to see themselves in unison with angelic singers above. Since the time of Isaiah God's people here below have been singing "Holy, holy,

---

[2] U. Berges, *Jesaja 40–48. Übersetzt und ausgelegt von Ulrich Berges* (HThKAT, Freiburg: Herder, 2008), 38–43.

holy is the Lord of Hosts," tuning themselves into the heavenly song. Psalm 22:4 knows that the Lord, enthroned over the cherubim in the Holy of Holies (cf. Exod 25:22), rules over the praises of Israel. This verse demonstrates that earthly temple singers envisioned themselves in communion with angels singing before God's throne. When the Levites were singing, their praises were elevating God's throne, as we sing in some modern choruses.

Some Second Temple psalms (Pss 11:4–7; 25:14; 73:23–26, cf. Job 19:25–27; Prov 3:32, "his council is with the upright ones" [author's translation]) demonstrate a charismatic piety in which the singer may gaze upon the face of the Lord and be taken into his intimate council. The "council of God" was previously the prerogative of elect prophets (1 Kgs 22:19–22; Jer 23:18, 22). These psalms suggest that Levites singing these psalms entertained a hope of visionary experience. Jon Levenson describes the expectations of pilgrims and those seeking asylum in the temple who could be forced to stay there for years: "The apogee of the spiritual experience of the visitor to the Temple was a vision of God . . . Psalm 11 asserts a reciprocity of vision: YHWH, enthroned in His Temple, conducts a visual inspection of humanity, and those found worthy are granted a vision of his 'face.'"[3] The hymn concludes with the promise, "the upright shall gaze his face." These singers would easily take the promise of Isa 33:17, "Your eyes will see the king in his beauty," to their hearts. Psalm 11:4 indeed understands the temple below as an earthly antitype to a heavenly archetype. Within this concept a vision of the above for the pious one below is easily understood.

Intertestamental and New Testament Texts

Priestly and Levitic tradition continued to treasure the hope of divine revelation to individuals in the temple. The historian Josephus reports revelations to the high priest Jaddus at the time of Alexander the Great (*Ant.* 11.326–328) and to the Hasmonean high priest Yohanan Hyrcanus (ruled 135–105 BCE; *Ant.* 13.282–283). According to rabbinic tradition, an angel could appear to the high priest in the sanctuary during the Yom Kippur liturgy.[4] And according to Luke, NT figures continue this tradition: the priest Zechariah encounters the angel in the temple, Simon and Anna receive revelation of the Messiah in the temple, and Stephen had a vision of the enthroned Son of Man (Luke 1:5–23; 2:25–38; Acts 7:55–56). Stephen's vision probably took place in the meeting room of the high council, located in the temple precincts or its immediate surroundings. The book of Revelation reflects visionary access to the heavenly sanctuary, although in this case the seer is distanced from the (fallen) earthly temple.

---

[3] Jon Levenson, "The Jerusalem Temple in Devotional and Visionary Experience," in *Jewish Spirituality: From the Bible through the Middle Ages* (ed. Arthur Green; 2 vols.; London: SCM, 1989), 1:32–61, here 43.

[4] A tradition connected with Shimon the Righteous in *t. Sotah* 13.8; *y. Yoma* 5.2; *Lev R* 21.12; *b. Yoma* 39b; *b. Menahot* 109b.

The priestly writings of *Aramaic Levi* and *Jubilees* (from the third and second centuries, also preserved outside of Qumran) conceive of a priestly ministry in unison with the angels. In the *Aramaic Levi Document* 6:5, Levi, the forefather of priests and Levites, is told by Isaac, "You are near to God and near to all his holy ones."[5] Similarly, *Jub* 31:14 foresees Levi "serving in his temple like the angels of the presence and like the holy ones."

Some hymns from the pre-Maccabean temple specifically reflect the concept of a union between earthly and heavenly worshipers. In the *Hymn to the Creator* in 11QPs[a], God marches forth accompanied by the tumult of mighty waters (cf. Ezek 1:24), and angelic powers surround God's throne in praise.

> Great and holy are you, Lord, holy among the holy ones from generation to generation. At his fore marches majesty, at his rear, the tumult of many waters. Loving kindness and truth surround his face; truth, justice and righteousness uphold his throne. He divided darkness from light, preparing the dawn with the knowledge of his heart. When all his angels saw it, they rejoiced in song—for he had shown them what they knew not: decking out the mountains with food, fine sustenance for all who live. Blessed be he who made the earth by his power, and established the world by his wisdom. By his understanding He stretched forth the heavens and brought out [the wind] from [his] trea[sure stores.]

The threefold use of "holy" recalls Isa 6:3. The benediction "Blessed be he" shows a liturgical setting in which earthly singers praise their God. The angels are described singing when they witnessed God's act of creation. Our temple singers would not imagine the angels turning mute in the continuation.

Similar tunes are heard in 4Q88, *Apostrophe of Judah*, where the singer instructs stars and angels to join the jubilation of Judah at the festivals in the temple: "Let heaven and earth give praise in unison, let all the twilight stars give praise! Rejoice, Judah, rejoice and be glad! Make your pilgrimages, fulfill your vows . . . For you, O Lord, are etern[al,] your glory endures forever."

The Sabbath liturgy contained in the presectarian *Words of the Luminaries* echoes Ezekiel and the threefold "holy" from Isa 6 in its vision of heaven and earth praising the Creator (4Q504 frags. 1–2, col. 7). In the preserved text the word "holy" occurs twice; a third can be emended:

> Give thanks . . . to his holy name forever . . . all the angels of the holy firmament, [from down below up] to the heavens, the earth and all its schemers, [praise his holy name, yea, even the]great [abyss], Abaddon, the waters and all that is [in them, praise him] always[, the earth with]all its creatures, forever.

Among those participating in the choir are angels of the holy firmament, a term echoing Ezekiel's throne vision (Ezek 1:22–26) and perhaps alluding to Exod 24:9–11. *Words of the Luminaries*' links with later synagogue liturgy suggest a common Israelite setting for these daily prayers; the most logical one would be Levitic liturgy in the temple.[6]

---

[5] The reference to *Aramaic Levi* follows J. C. Greenfield, M. E. Stone, and E. Eshel, *The Aramaic Levi Document: Edition, Translation, Commentary* (SVTP 19; Leiden: Brill, 2004).

[6] Cf. T. Elgvin, "Qumran and the Roots of the Rosh Hashanah Liturgy," in *Liturgical Perspectives: Prayer and Poetry in Light of the Dead Sea Scrolls* (ed. Esther G. Chazon; STDJ

In the *Songs of the Sabbath Sacrifice*, found in eight copies in Qumran and Masada, the earthly conductor directs the praises of the angels. At times he asks the earthly singers to join (4Q403 1 i 36–37): "Rejoice, you who exult in [knowing him, with] a song of rejoicing among the wondrous godlike angels. Exalt his glory with the tongue of all who exalt His wondrous knowledge, with the mouth of all who chant [to Him]." These songs may have their origin in the Levitic choir of the pre-Maccabean temple, and they demonstrate how the singing Levites saw themselves in line with the angelic choir above. God is indeed "enthroned over the praises of Israel."

I now turn to a non-hymnic composition, a presectarian "testament of Levi" in Aramaic from the early second century BCE. The text of 4Q541 frag. 9 portrays an end-time priest whose teaching and words are like the words of heaven. Tested through trials, his teaching and sacrificial ministry will lead to a renewal of the world:

> He will transmit [to the]m his [w]isdom. And he shall make atonement for all those of his generation, and he shall be sent to all the children of his people. His words are like the words of heaven, and his teaching is like the will of God. Then the sun everlasting will shine and its fire will give warmth unto the ends of the earth. It will shine on darkness; then darkness will vanish from the earth, and mist from the dry land.

Although this priest is earthly, his ministry gives resonance in the heavenly realms. Such a description suggests a relation to priestly circles that conceived of the officiating temple priest as being linked to and in line with the heavenly temple and the angels serving above.

A connected tradition, evidenced in the Greek *Testament of Levi* 3:4–6; 5:1–2; 8:18–19 and *Aramaic Levi* 4:4–13 refers to the ascent of Levi to the heavenly realms. A central blessing from the Qumran community refers to the officiating high priest standing in the midst of angels in the heavenly sanctuary (1QSb 3–4).

> May the Lord bless you and set you, perfected in honor, in the midst of the holy angels; [may he re]new for you the [eternal] covenant of the priesthood. May he make a place for you in the holy [habitation.] May he ju[dge a]ll princes by the measure of your works, all [leaders] of the nations by what you say. He has justified you from all [defilement,] chosen you and placed you at the head of the holy angels. . . . May you [abide forever] as an angel of the presence in the holy habitation, to the glory of the God of host[s. May you] serve in the temple of the kingdom of God, ordering destiny with the angels of the presence, a Council of the Community [with the holy angels] forever, for all the ages of eternity! . . . May he establish you as holy among his people, as the "greater [light" (Gen 1:16) to illumine] the world with knowledge, and to shine upon the face of many [with wisdom leading to life.

A related rabbinic tradition judges the officiating high priest as more important than the angels (*y. Yoma* 5.2). Neither angels nor the son of man are present in the tent of meeting on Yom Kippur, but only the high priest and God. The two last texts quoted above provided the matrix that enabled a sectarian author to coin

---

48; Leiden: Brill, 2003), 49–67.

the "Self-Glorification Hymn" on the messianic high priest, modeled upon the Teacher of Righteousness, the priest who founded the community. This hymn, here quoted from 4Q491, exists in two versions and was included in the *Thanksgiving Hymns* of the community.

> God has given me] a mighty throne in the congregation of the angels. None of the ancient kings shall sit on it, and their nobles [shall] not[be there.] There are no]ne comparable [to me in] my glory, no one shall be exalted besides me; none shall come against me. For I have dwelt on[high, and resided] in the heavens . . . I am reckoned with the angels and my abode is in the holy assembly. . . . Wh]o has experienced contempt like me? Who is comparable to me in my glory? . . . Who has borne troubles like me? And who like me [has refrain]ed from evil? I have never been taught, but no teaching compares [with mine.] Who then shall assault me when [I] ope[n my mouth?] Who can endure the utterance of my lips? Who shall challenge me and compare with my judgment? Fo]r I am reck[oned] with the angels, [and] my glory with that of the sons of the King.

Heavenly Temple and Christology in Hebrews

These priestly texts provide a living background for the Christology of Hebrews. This Jewish Christian author knows other NT writings that testify to Jesus as messianic prophet and royal messiah, as the Wisdom of God who speaks with the Lord's own authority, and as the Suffering Servant. In the choir of early Christian voices that give expression to the meaning and importance of Jesus' ministry he wants to add one central element from his treasured tradition: that the high priest has a dual ministry, earthly and at the same time officiating in the heavenly sanctuary. He wants to supplement the words about the "Son of Man as a ransom for many" (Mark 10:45), the blood of Jesus "poured out for many for the forgiveness of sins" (Matt 26:28), and Paul's words of Christ as a "sacrifice of atonement" (Rom 3:25). Drawing on his priestly and Levitic heritage the author of Hebrews describes Jesus as the ultimate high priest, who sacrificed himself on Golgotha, which takes the place of the earthly temple. But at the same time Jesus is officiating in the real and heavenly sanctuary, before the throne of God.

According to Heb 4:10 and Heb 6:20, Jesus has "become a high priest forever, in the order of Melchizedek," fulfilling the messianic promise of Ps 110:4. Three texts from Qumran cast new light on the figure of Melchizedek and the argument and exegesis of Hebrews. 4Q *Visions of Amram,* a priestly writing in Aramaic from the early second century BCE, describe the prince of light and the prince of darkness, the two angelic powers who rule over humankind. The prince of darkness is named Melki-resh'a ("My king is evil"). The name of his counterpart is not preserved in the six fragmentary copies of this work, but he was no doubt called Melchi-zedeq ("My king is righteousness"). This angelic ruler of the sons of light is divine (perhaps not in the Nicean sense of the word); he brings healing and saves people from the power of death. As leader of God's heavenly army he takes on the role that other texts ascribe to the archangel Michael.

In a fragmentary context in the *Songs of the Sabbath Sacrifice* one of the angels is referred to as ". . .]zedeq, priest in the assemb[ly of God" (4Q401 11 3). We may with confidence restore the name of the angel as Melchi]zedek. These liturgical songs thus conceive of Melchizedek as an angel with a priestly ministry in the heavenly sanctuary, perhaps as a counterpart to the service of priests in the earthly temple.

From Cave 11 comes the "Melchizedek text," a biblical commentary on the Year of Jubilee and God's forthcoming redemption of his people. In this text Melchizedek is an angelic redeemer who leads the battle against the evil powers. "He shall atone for all the sons of [light] . . . and release th[em from the debt of a]ll their sins . . . he will deliver all the captives from the power of B]elial." It is he who is spoken of in Isa 52:7, "Your God reigns," he is the God who "holds judgment among the godlike ones" (Ps 82:1). "The year of God's favor" (Isa 61:2, cf. Luke 4:19) is here rendered as "the year of Melchiz[edek]'s favor" (11Q13 2 i 8–16).

The first two writings come from a wider priestly tradition in Judea;[7] the third was probably authored in the priestly-led Qumran community early in the first century BCE. Together they testify to the concept of an angelic Melchizedek, priest and prince in God's assembly. A similar picture of Melchizedek emerges in *2 Enoch*, a Jewish apocalypse from the first century CE, preserved in Slavonic. The idea of a heavenly Melchizedek probably crystallized in priestly exegesis of Gen 14 and Ps 110:4. The names of Abraham's antagonists were read symbolically: The king of Gomorra is Birsha ("son of wickedness"), while the king of Sodom is Bera ("son of evil"). We may speculate if these priests read Gen 14 as referring to an earthly visit of the angelic Melchizedek, who helped Abraham in his fight against the evil powers.

How is Melchizedek described in Hebrews? He is "without father or mother . . . without beginning of days and end of life; like the Son of God he remains priest forever." In contrast to earthly priests who die he is "declared to be living" (Heb 7:3, 8). Jesus appears as priest like Melchizedek not because of his ancestry (he was not of the tribe of Levi) but "on the power of an indestructable life" (Heb 7:15–16).

When we recognize the thoroughly priestly character of Hebrews it is hard to escape the conclusion that this author shares a similar image of Melchizedek as that evolving from *2 Enoch* and the Qumran writings discussed above.[8] Our author is a priest or Levite who reinterpreted the Melchizedek tradition in light of the Jesus event: Melchizedek prefigures the priestly ministry of Jesus, who brought himself forth as a sacrifice on the cross, and at the same time in the heavenly sanctuary, "he entered heaven itself to appear for us in God's presence" (Heb 9:24). In contrast to Pharisaic theology this author subscribed to a priestly, perhaps Sadducean, axiom, based on Leviticus and temple tradition: "without the shedding of

---

[7]On the provenance of the *Songs of the Sabbath Sacrifice*, see P. Alexander, *Mystical Texts* (London: T&T Clark, 2006), 97, 129.

[8]Thus H. W. Attridge, *The Epistle to the Hebrews: A Commentary on the Epistle to the Hebrews* (Philadelphia: Fortress, 1989, 186–215); A. Aschim, "Melchizedek and Jesus: 11QMelchizedek and the Epistle to the Hebrews," *The Jewish Roots of Christological Monotheism: Papers from the St. Andrews Conference on the Historical Origins of the Worship of Jesus* (SupJSJ 63; C. C. Newman, J. R. Davila, and G. S. Lewis, eds.; Leiden: Brill, 1999), 129–47.

blood there is no forgiveness" (Heb 9:22). As Hebrews probably read Gen 14 as referring to an earthly visit of the heavenly Melchizedek, he also would appear as a biblical foreshadow of the incarnation of Christ, who "for a little while was made lower than the angels" (Heb 2:7–9).

We have surveyed Qumran texts that prefigure NT motifs and that easily could be interpreted as prophecies of Jesus. In my understanding these texts and their authors could have been used by God to prepare his people for the "fullness of time."

Not only priests and Levites are connected with the angelic assembly. This is true also for the whole congregation: "You have come to the heavenly Jerusalem . . . to thousands of angels in joyful assembly, to the church of the firstborn whose names are written in heaven" (Heb 12:22–23). Through Christ's sacrifice every believer now has access through the veil (of the Holy of Holies) and into God's presence (Heb 6:19; 10:20), a privilege previously accessible only to the high priest on the Day of Atonement.

Such a democratization of priestly privileges had a precursor in the community that produced the Qumran writings. The Qumran community regarded the physical temple as polluted. Therefore angelic liturgies had to be sung outside the Jerusalem temple to secure pure liturgical partners for the angels. This community conceived of itself as a spiritual temple with its members in liturgical communion with the heavenly sanctuary and the officiating angels. The singers therefore saw themselves as successors of purified priests and Levites in sacrificial and liturgical temple service. In the liturgical celebration of the community lay Israelites had access to a mystical experience previously cherished by temple priests and Levites. A member's identification with the praying "I" in the *Thanksgiving Hymns* would give the faithful access to the source of mystical revelation and communion with God. According to these hymns, the purified one "can take his stand in your presence with the perpetual host and the spirits . . . in a jubilating union" (*Thanksgiving Hymns* 19:16–17). As part of the community where praise and supplication rose like incense before the heavenly throne as a "sacrifice of thanksgiving" (4Q174 1:7), the non-priestly member was transformed to some kind of priestly status. This spiritual renewal would be seen as a sign of the community of the end times (Joel 3:1–5, cf. Num 11:25; Acts 2:14–36).

The mystical prayer and praise of this community may be seen as a precursor of the Pharisees' and early Jewish Christians' realization of the idea of a "kingdom of priests" (cf. Exod 19:6; Isa 61:6; 1 Pet 2:5; Eph 2:21–22; Rev 1:6; 5:8, 12; *Avot de Rabbi Nathan* 4, where Johanan ben Zakkai is attributed with the dictum that acts of loving-kindness provide an atonement as effective as the temple sacrifices).

Temple and Priesthood in Revelation

In contrast to the priestly-led Qumran community, for Revelation the new community of the Messiah realizes the priesthood of all believers; leadership by priests or Levites is not needed to establish the new priestly ministry. The introductory greeting states that Christ by his blood "has made us a kingdom, priests for God his father" (Rev 1:6). Revelation 5:10 recalls this proclamation; Christ has "made them a kingdom, priests to God," and adds that the priestly believers shall "rule on the earth," a promise that will be realized in the millennium: "They shall be priests with him and rule with him for a thousand years" (Rev 20:6).

The acknowledgement of the presentic eschatology of John the seer suggests that the vision of the multitude in Rev 7:9–17 may be interpreted as a description of the full community of believers partaking in the heavenly worship.[9] This multitude serves God night and day in his temple, similar to the ministry of Levitic singers who served God in praise day and night in the temple (Pss 134; 135:1–2).

Revelation 5:8 and 8:3–4 describe the prayers of the holy ones (viz., the believers on earth) as incense rising before God's heavenly throne, conveyed through the censers of heavenly beings. The priests' offering of incense before the veil to the Holy of Holies is a colorful image of Second Temple Judaism. The silence in heaven (Rev 8:1) signifies the time during which the angel burns the incense on the altar to accompany the prayers of the saints. The same thought is found in rabbinic tradition: when Israel comes to pray, the angels are silent. The temple is the starting point both for John and the rabbis: during the morning and evening service of the temple incense was burned while the community (as well as Jews elsewhere in the land) was praying outside the temple (Exod 30:1–10; Judg 9:1; Luke 1:10; Acts 3:1).[10] The ascending smoke of incense was seen as symbolizing and assisting the ascent of prayers to God in heaven. The association of prayer with incense goes back to OT times (cf. Ps 141:2, "Let my prayer be counted as incense before you") and continues in Revelation and Hebrews (cf. Heb 13:15, "Let us offer up a sacrifice of praise to God").

Revelation 5 and 8 show an intimate relation between the believers' praise and prayers and the burning of incense in the heavenly temple. The believers' priestly ministry is connected with the heavenly realms both in John's apocalypse and in Hebrews (Heb 4:14–16; 9:11–12; 10:19–22). The angelic hymns in Rev 4–5 were likely used in earthly liturgies in Asia Minor, perhaps before John's experience and certainly thereafter. Therefore, there is already now a union between the heavenly and earthly singers. If John came from a Levitic background and was at home in the temple watches where God's servants praised him night and day, it is easy to understand that he conceives of an unending priestly ministry with the prayers of the church steadily rising in the heavenly sanctuary.

John's description of angelic priestly ministry is indebted to Jewish tradition treasured by Levites and priests. The angels' priestly ministry is elaborated in the visions of the sanctuary (Rev 4–5; 8:1–4). Further, angels come out from the altar before they are sent to minister on earth (Rev 8:5; 14:18; 16:7; cf. 9:13). The image of angels being sent out from the altar can owe their inspiration to the Levitic temple guard, which under the command of the high priest's deputy was

---

[9] H. Ulfgard. *Feast and Future: Revelation 7:9–17 and the Feast of Tabernacles* (CBNTS 22; Stockholm: Almquist & Wiksell, 1989), 61–68, 100–104.

[10] R. Bauckham, *The Climax of Prophecy: Studies in Revelation* (Edinburgh: T&T Clark, 1993), 70, 83; D. E. Aune, *Revelation 6–16* (WBC 52B; Nashville: Nelson, 1997), 511–15.

responsible for checking the inventory of the temple and guarding the temple precincts (cf. Luke 22:4; John 18:3; Acts 4:1; 5:24–26). The line of deduction would thus be "as on earth so also in heaven."

In Rev 7:3 and 9:4 God's servants on earth are sealed with the name of the Lamb on their foreheads (cf. Rev 14:1; Ezek 9:4). This feature may be connected to their priestly ministry. In the ancient Near East, priests could be marked with the name of their god on their foreheads (cf. the inscription over Aaron's forehead, "sanctified to the Lord" [Exod 28:36–37]). Houses or sanctuaries could be dedicated through an inscription on the doorpost to the king or the godhead. The believers, who before the eyes of the world are sanctified to the Lamb, are thus fulfilling Deut 6:8, where the words of God on the foreheads realize the priestly prerogative of every Israelite male in the time of the Babylonian exile, a time without a temple.[11] Revelation 22:3–4 describes the ultimate service before God's throne where the elect serve God with his name on their foreheads, not any more the name of the Lamb, as there is no more need for the open witness to the Lamb before the world.

As is the case in Paul's writings, the believers on earth are designated "the saints" or "the holy ones" (Rev 5:8; 8:3; 11:8, etc.). In the OT and intertestamental literature "holy ones" regularly refers to angels. But in some texts this usage is extended to those elect and sanctified. Some Qumran texts use "the holy ones" or similar expressions about the end-time community or the priests. As all priestly service was sanctified to God, the particular use of "holy ones" within the early Christian community may be explained through an eschatological democratization of priestly prerogatives to all believers.

In Rev 15:2–4 the victorious ones are portrayed standing on the sea of glass and fire, singing with harps. The sea of glass and fire is reminiscent of the firmament below God's throne in Exod 24:9–11 and Ezek 1:24. But the designation "sea" also recalls the "sea" for purification purposes in the Jerusalem temple (1 Kgs 7:23–25, 39, 44). The victorious ones of Rev 15:1–4 are those who have purified themselves by the blood of the Lamb. So this passage merges traditions of visions of the divine throne with the concept of purification, both central elements of the temple tradition.

More than any other first-century Jewish writing, Revelation is permeated by temple symbolism. The promise that the faithful will become a pillar in God's temple (Rev 3:12; cf. 1 Kgs 7:21; Isa 22:15) can be compared with the thresholds of the temple that partake in the praise of the king in the *Songs of the Sabbath Sacrifice* (4Q403 1 i 41). The believer portrayed as a temple pillar may be a derivation of the community seen as a spiritual temple, a concept well known from the Qumran Community that recurs in NT epistles (1QS 7:5–10; 4Q174 1–3 i 6–7; 1 Pet 2:5–10; Eph 2:20–22).

In Rev 4:1 and Rev 11:19 God's temple in heaven is opened (cf. the opened door before the believer in Rev 3:20). The opening of the door to the sanctuary

---

[11]T. Elgvin, *Hør, Israel! Ved disse ord skal du leve! Tekster og tider i 5 Mosebok* (Oslo, Norsk Luthersk Forlag, 2000), 45–8, O. Keel, "Zeichen der Verbundenheit: Zur Vorgeschichte und Bedeutung der Forderungen von Deuteronomium 6, 8f. und Par." in *Mélanges Dominique Barthelemy: études bibliques offertes à l'occacion de son 60e anniversaire* (ed. P. Casetti et al.; Göttingen: Vandenhoeck & Ruprecht, 1981), 159–240, pp. 193–217.

was a well-known image in the ancient world. Of particular importance is the rabbinic tradition that the doors of the temple were opened forty years before its destruction, so that rabbi Yohanan ben Zakkai had to reproach them (*b. Yoma* 39b, cf. a similar incident reported by Josephus, *J.W.* 6.293–294). In all three texts the opening of the doors is related to end-time judgment. Hebrews uses related but different terminology—the way through the curtain to the inner sanctum has been opened by Christ (Rev 6:19; 4:14–16; cf. the tearing of the veil in Matt 27:51).

The seer notes that there is still a covenantal ark in the heavenly sanctuary (Rev 11:19). As long as the holy ones on earth lift up their prayers as incense rising before God's throne, there must be a sanctuary above with an altar (Rev 6:9; 8:3, 5; 9:13; 11:1; 14:18; 16:7). But in the end there is no temple, only God's throne (Rev 20:11), a temple source (Rev 22:1–2), and God's city, the new Jerusalem. God the Almighty and the Lamb are their temple (Rev 21:22–23). Jeremiah 3:16–17 may lay behind Rev 21–22 as a proof text; this passage on the restoration of Israel describes Jerusalem, Gentiles coming to Zion, and the Lord's throne, but no ark of the covenant. In its description of the end-time Zion without a temple Revelation differs from other Jewish groups who expected a restored temple in the end times.[12]

In Rev 15:5–8 the heavenly temple is opened and the temple filled with the smoke of God's glory and power. Here again we encounter priestly terminology, albeit belonging to the all-Israelite Scriptures. There are a number of parallels between Rev 1–8 and the daily temple sacrifices described in *Mishna Tamid.*[13] Knowledge of such procedures was the prerogative of priests and Levites.

In other texts (Rev 7:17; 21:6; 22:1–2) we encounter the temple source with living water, running water. The image of the temple source with paradisiac connotations goes all through the HB (cf. Gen 2:10–14; Ps 46:5; Ezek 47:1–12; Joel 4:18; Zech 13:1; 14:6) and is often connected to end-time scenarios. In Qumran this tradition often recurs in the *Thanksgiving Hymns* and 4Q*Instruction*. Both writings testify that the "opened fountain" of Zech 13:1 is a reality in the community of the end time (4Q418 81 1, 12; 1QH^a 9:4; 10:18; 13:10, 12, 13; 14:17–18; 16:8; 18:31, cf. Sir 24:23–33).

In Rev 7:15 God will raise his dwelling over the martyrs. The biblical background of this image may be found in Isa 4:5–6, a promise that God will spread over Zion a cover. But we also recall Ps 84 of the Levitic sons of Korah, who long to dwell in the temple and gaze upon God in its precincts (cf. Ps 11:4–7).

Revelation's War Ideology

Revelation recasts Jewish eschatological tradition on the militant Messiah and his army. In the lion-like Lamb and his followers these hopes are transformed and fulfilled through the sacrificial death of the Lamb. The 144,000 (Rev 7:3–8; 14:1–5)

---

[12] The only exception is the contemporary apocalypse *4 Ezra,* which does not mention any temple in the messianic millennium (7:26–28). Only the Torah will abide forever (9:31–37).

[13] J. Paulien, "The Role of the Hebrew Cultus, Sanctuary, and Temple in the Plot and Structure of the Book of Revelation," *AUSS* 33 (1995): 245–64, pp. 252–57, 263.

represent the end-time army of this Messiah, those who are following him faithfully, even unto death. Revelation uses holy war language while transferring it to non-military means of triumph over evil.

The concept of war in heaven with repercussions on earth has parallels in the early 4Q*Visions of Amram* (ca. 200–150 BCE) and the later 11Q*Melkizedek*, both preserving priestly traditions with dualistic features. Here we encounter Melchizedek as the end-time judge of Belial and his army. And he will redeem those belonging to him in the great Year of Jubilee and freedom. The parallels to the ruling Lamb as well the rider on the white horse (Rev 19:11–21) are many. Both Hebrews and John the seer are indebted to priestly traditions on Melchizedek as God's vigilant viceroy.

These two texts and the *Songs of the Sabbath Sacrifice* illuminate Revelation's royal terminology, where both God and Christ are designated with royal titles. In Rev 11:14–19 God has taken on kingship (cf. the recurring image of God as king in the *Songs of the Sabbath Sacrifice*). In Rev 1:5 Jesus is Lord over the kings of the earth, and in Rev 19:16 he is proclaimed "King of kings and Lord of lords." Those who belong to him have themselves been made royal priests.

Another feature of the book's war ideology is the conviction that the priestly believers shall "rule the earth" or "rule the land." The declaration of the believers as royal priests in the introduction (Rev 1:6) probably refers to believers who shall rule the land, as is explicitly stated in Rev 5:10. In the letter to Laodicea the victorious believer shall sit with the Lord on his throne (Rev 3:21), and in the letter to Thyatira the victorious one will rule the Gentiles with an iron rod (Rev 2:26–27), similar to the description of the end-time Messiah in the main part of the book (Rev 12:5; 19:15–16). As the enthroned Messiah shall rule by an iron rod, so shall his church. These verses should be interpreted in connection with the millennium of Rev 20, a limited time during which the Messiah rules on earth together with the faithful: "They shall be priests with him and rule with him for a thousand years" (Rev 20:6).

The concepts of royal believers ruling the land may be indebted to the painful loss of the land of Judea in 67–70 CE, a close memory of John the seer.[14] Further, "priests ruling the land" would for a Jewish reader recall the rule of the Hasmonean (Maccabean) high priests (164–38 BCE). 4Q*Apocryphon of Jeremiah C* describes three bad priests who did not walk in God's ways (4Q387 frg. 2 col. III, lines 5–7; frg. 3 lines 4–8), probably Jason, Menelaus, and Alcimus (174–169 BCE). These three priests, as well as the Hasmoneans, could be antitypes for the end-time priests who shall rule in the name of the Lamb-like Messiah. The loss of

---

[14]I am indebted to David Aune's introduction and commentary to Revelation: D. E. Aune, *Revelation 1–5* (WBC 52A; Nashville: Nelson, 1997). For him, Revelation is the product of an apocalyptically oriented Judean who migrated to the province of Asia in Asia Minor during or after the great Jewish revolt (66–70 CE). At some stage in his career he joined the Jesus movement and was recognized as a Christian prophet by congregations in Asia. His book may have developed through a lengthy process of literary growth. It reflects the traumatic experience of the crushing of the great Jewish revolt as well as local persecution of Christians in Asia Minor in the 90s.

the land in the great revolt, as well as the OT background, suggest that we should first read these passages as "ruling the land" and only secondarily as "ruling the earth." The wider universal dimension could indicate that John the seer's eschatology developed during the decades following the great revolt.

Jerusalem still occupies a central role for the author. Toward the end of the millennium Satan and his earthly allies will encircle the "beloved city" of Jerusalem (Rev 20:9). This city is also called "the camp of the holy ones," recalling the Qumran designations "the congregation of Jerusalem" and "Jerusalem, who is the holy camp" and "capital of the camps of Israel" (*War Scroll* 3:11; 4QMMT B 60–62). Revelation 21–22 perceives the eschatological fulfillment as Jerusalem created anew. A similar hope is articulated in the contemporary Jewish apocalypse *4 Ezra*: the preexistent, hidden Jerusalem will appear and be rebuilt for the world to come (*4 Ezra* 7:26; 8:52; 10:39, 44). But in the messianic kingdom, which precedes the world to come, God's Messiah will rebuild the city of Zion (*4 Ezra* 13:29–50).

The Messiah ruling the Gentiles with an iron rod is an image from the messianic Ps 2, which recurs in the early Pharisaic *Pss. Sol.* 17:23–24 where the royal Messiah is called "to smash the arrogance of sinners like a potter's jar; to shatter all their substance with an iron rod; to destroy the unlawful nations with the word of his mouth."[15]

In the generation following another war lost, that of Bar Kokhba, Jewish Christians would again raise the hope of an earthly millennium around Zion, as evidenced in *Testament of the Twelve Patriarchs* and *Lives of the Prophets*. Jewish-Christian theology permeates these Jewish writings, which were edited by Jewish-Christian hands in the second century.[16] Also here we find the hope that redeemed Israel will return to the land.

Revelation, the *Testament of the Twelve Patriarchs*, and *Lives of the Prophets* reflect the outcome of two different Jewish revolts with messianic flavor (66–70 CE and 132–136 CE). After both of them, Jewish Christians looked forward to a true messiah who would rule the land in a millennial kingdom.

Conclusion

I have suggested that the author of Revelation was a priest or Levite who had resided in Judea. Temple theology and priestly traditions belong to the heritage

[15] Another text illuminating the background of Revelation is the *Gabriel Inscription*. This text, written in ink on stone in the late first century BCE, is formed as a prophetic revelation from the angel Gabriel about Jerusalem threatened by enemy armies (cf. Rev 20). Then God commissions angelic hosts to fight the evil forces under the leadership of Michael (cf. Rev 11). He sends three angelic shepherds to visit his people and prophecy for them, and then calls these shepherds back to their place (cf. Rev 11, two witnesses prophecy on earth before they are killed by the Beast). See M. Henze, ed., *Hazon Gabriel: New Readings of the Gabriel Revelation* (Atlanta: Society of Biblical Literature, 2011).

[16] T. Elgvin, "Jewish Christian Editing of the Old Testament Pseudepigrapha," in *Jewish Believers in Jesus: The Early Centuries* (ed. O. Skarsaune and R. Hvalvik; Peabody, MA: Hendrickson, 2007), 278–304.

of all Israel; they are not the property of priestly circles alone. But the cumulative evidence of priestly traditions that have set their stamp on John the seer forces the question: Is John a priest or Levite who transforms the traditions that framed him in light of the Christ event (cf. Acts 4:36; 6:7, which refer to the Levite Barnabas and "many priests" who joined the Jesus camp)? John the seer represents a priestly or Levitic milieu with much in common with the frustrated theologians of Qumran. In the 50s and 60s they are, as members of the Jesus camp, at odds with the Sadducean leaders of the temple.

The visions of Rev 4 onwards show John's struggle with understanding God's hidden plans during and after the great revolt, in the aftermath of Nero's persecutions. The visions of the enthroned Lamb give meaning through the destruction of the temple and the end of sacrifices. The same is true for the interpretation of the prayers of the believers as incense rising before the divine throne. The visions in the main part of the book and the (perhaps later) vision of the ruling Christ in Rev 1:9–18 assure John and his circles that the Jesus movement *is* the legitimate successor of the temple with its divine presence on earth. Opposition from Jewish leaders in Smyrna and Philadelphia in the 90s confirm for John that Israel is now divided on the issue of the lion-like Lamb and Messiah.

Can there be a connection between the milieus that framed Hebrews and the book of Revelation? Hebrews knows of the heavenly temple, but the proceedings of this sanctuary are treated in the form of a treatise with scriptural exegesis, not in the form of a visionary writing or apocalypse. But Hebrews also proclaims the believers' union with the angels officiating above: "you have come to the city of the living God, the heavenly Jerusalem, to thousands of angels, to a holy convocation" (Heb 13:22–23). This author shares a realized eschatology like that of John of Patmos: The end times have broken in and the believer partakes in this new reality. While Revelation has access to heavenly liturgies and revelations on how God's plan for history and his people is unveiled in the present and the future, Hebrews has its interest in the central liturgical event in the heavenly temple, the ultimate high-priestly sacrifice of Christ prefigured by the Yom Kippur sacrifices. Revelation conveys more than Hebrews about the consequences of Christ's sacrifice for the church in the world. For John, the primary image for Christ is the Lamb, not the ultimate high priest, although Rev 1:12–18 depicts Christ as the royal high priest. Also Hebrews knows the priestly ministry of all believers, since Christ has opened for them a road through the curtain into the heavenly sanctuary (Heb 4:14–16; 10:19–22). Hebrews and Revelation may derive from priestly milieus that were able to produce both theological treatises and apocalyptic visions.

3

The Scrolls and the Scriptures on the Margins: Remembered in Canons or Forgotten in Caves

Dorothy M. Peters

Scriptures Bound and Unbound: Authority without Bible and Canon

The story of "The Scrolls and Scriptures on the Margins" could be told in many ways by the many different voices within Judaism and Christianity through-out the millennia.[1] In our day, Ethiopian Orthodox Christians speaking of *1 Enoch* or *Jubilees* as scripture to their Jewish, Catholic, or Protestant friends, whose Bibles do not include these books, might see puzzlement in their faces. Likewise, even otherwise biblically literate Jews and Protestants may be unfamiliar with Maccabees, Baruch, Tobit, Sirach, Judith, and Wisdom of Solomon, books collected within the canons of the Catholic and Orthodox traditions but not within their own. The complex diversity of the story only increases when the voices of people living during the Second Temple or intertestamental period begin to be heard.

Given the many and diverse voices around the conversational table through-out the millennia, the terms of this chapter's title need to be understood lest they muddy the discussion and handicap its conclusions. "Margins" demands a mutually agreed upon boundary between what was and was not perceived to be scripture, while "scriptures" begs the question, "Whose scripture?" and "During which period?"

The table of contents in any modern Bible helpfully lists the individual writings bound within its covers, while its very construction excludes all others. In contrast, a cave is more open-ended than a book and its scrolls not bound together. In his contribution to this volume, George Brooke writes about the "journey from author-ity to canon" taken by the Jewish scriptures in the Second Temple period including

---

[1] I am grateful to my graduate student, Jeffrey Spence, for his many helpful suggestions at the editing stage of this chapter.

those "literary works that never completed the journey."[2] With that in mind, it is important to unbind postcanon-formation understandings of "Bible" and "canon" from Second Temple conceptions of "authority" and "authoritative scripture."

Let us imagine for a moment the Qumran library from the perspective of a first-century CE scribe composing a new commentary on Genesis. Paying a visit to Cave 4, he finds numerous copies of Genesis, copies of the *Reworked Pentateuch* alongside earlier commentaries of Genesis, an exposition on the flood, and figures from Genesis incorporated into new historical retellings. Close at hand are the Aramaic books of Enoch, the *Book of Giants*, and other Aramaic writings purporting to contain the words of Noah, Levi, Jacob, Judah, and Joseph. Our scribe is pleased to find multiple copies of *Jubilees*, an innovative Hebrew reworking of Genesis composed two centuries earlier that explicitly linked Genesis to Moses. The various editions of Deuteronomy remind him of the fresh intertextual connections between Genesis and Deuteronomy that he and some of his friends in the community have discovered, insights he is hoping to include in the new commentary.

What the scribe would *not* find in the cave, however, would be a notice posted reminding him to replace the scrolls in their proper categories: biblical scrolls to the right, non-biblical scrolls on the left, and the marginally biblical scrolls in between. Because the canon of the Hebrew Bible was not closed until later that century, the concept of an exclusive scripture list shared by all Jews was not yet known.[3] In fact, some books eventually canonized by mainstream Judaism may never have attained authoritative scriptural status at Qumran. For example, the biblical book of Esther was not preserved at Qumran, and Chronicles, while preserved, may have had limited authority.[4]

Because of its flexibility, "authoritative scripture" may be a term more suitable for use in this period than either "Bible" or "canon." A text could gain or lose authority over time. Its authoritative status could be transient and time-bound or prove to be persistent and timeless. That said, the familiar categories of "biblical" and "non-biblical" are almost inescapable as descriptors because of their long established use. The best we can do is put them to work within carefully defined boundaries. Therefore, "biblical" will be used adjectivally in this chapter as shorthand for identifying texts and figures from the HB or Protestant OT while guarding against assumptions about a particular writing's authoritative status at Qumran based on its final resting place, either in various canons or caves.

---

[2] See in the present volume G. J. Brooke, "The Dead Sea Scrolls and the Interpretation of Scripture," 139.

[3] For a helpful historical chronology and background for many Second Temple writings, see Craig A. Evans, *Ancient Texts for New Testament Studies: A Guide to the Background Literature* (Peabody, MA: Hendrickson, 2005).

[4] On the status of Esther and Chronicles, see George J. Brooke, "Between Authority and Canon: The Significance of Reworking the Bible for Understanding the Canonical Process," in *Reworking the Bible: Apocryphal and Related Texts at Qumran. Proceedings of a Joint Symposium by the Orion Center for the Study of the Dead Sea Scroll and Associated Literature and the Hebrew University Institute for Advanced Studies Research on Qumran, 15–17 January, 2002* (ed. E. G. Chazon, D. Dimant, and R. A. Clements; Leiden: Brill, 2005), 85–104, here 87–91.

We continue with some strategies that scribe-interpreters used for acknowledging authority and for claiming authoritative scriptural status for their own writings. Then, in the third section, we survey selected scriptures on the margins and discuss the correlations of authoritative status to the language in which the texts were composed, the texts and figures to which they were anchored, and the stance toward the relationship between Jews and Gentiles.

Scribes and Scriptures: Acknowledging and Claiming Authority

Acknowledging Authority: Affirming Previously Written Scriptures

How a scribal community acknowledged the authoritative status of a particular writing is sometimes difficult to distinguish from the ways that they claimed authoritative status, but there are several helpful indicators. The first is found in the material evidence of the scrolls, and the second is found within the writings themselves.

The material evidence, as fragmentary as it is, can still hint at the strength and the duration of a text's authority. For example, the act of collecting the books of the Torah onto a single scroll served to acknowledge heightened authoritative scriptural status. By extension, the collection of separate books of Enoch onto a single scroll suggests either an attempt to claim a heightened authority for the books or an acknowledgment of authority already recognized.

The number of copies preserved is another indicator. That nineteen copies of Genesis and fifteen or sixteen copies of *Jubilees* were preserved in comparison with a single copy of Chronicles and only one copy of the *Genesis Apocryphon* may indicate their comparative authoritative strength. Furthermore, whether or not a text continued to be copied throughout the history of the movement, whether an older text was scraped off from the leather and written over with a different composition, or whether scribes bothered to repair a torn scroll may be indicators for the durability or marginality of authoritative status.

How scribes cited and used earlier writings within new compositions also served to acknowledge authority.[5] For example, excerpts of writings could be combined within a single text[6] or explicit citations from scripture followed by contemporizing interpretation.

> [16] [But You] [17] [are eternal, O Lᴏʀᴅ, my holy God, we will not die.] [5:1] *You have marked them for judgment; . . .* [3] This passage means that God will not exterminate his people

---

[5] In an effort to assess perceptions of what were perceived to be inspired writings by the early church fathers, Craig Allert compares citations from both canonical and non-canonical books. Craig D. Allert, *A High View of Scripture? The Authority of the Bible and the Formation of the New Testament Canon* (Grand Rapids: Baker Academic, 2007), 60–65. This method is also useful for assessing the authoritative status of individual writings among the DSS.

[6] 4QTestimonia (4Q175) contains excerpts from Numbers, Deuteronomy, and Joshua.

through the Gentiles;[4] on the contrary, He will give the power to pass judgment on the Gentiles to his chosen. (1QpHab 4:16–5:4, citing and interpreting Hab 1:12–13a)[7]

What was perceived to be authoritative scripture (italicized above) is clearly differentiated from its *pesher* or interpretation.

Citations were sometimes prefaced with formulas, following patterns in already recognized scripture. The formula "as it is written in the book of the Torah of Moses" (Josh 8:30)[8] is echoed in the *Community Rule* citation of Isaiah:

> . . . as it is written, "In the wilderness prepare the way of the Lord, make straight in the desert a highway for our God the Lord, make stra]ight in the desert a highway for our God" (1QS 8:13–14, citing Isa 40:3).

Most citations in the DSS are from biblical books, but the book of *Jubilees*—known by its full title as "The Book of the Divisions of the Times according to their Jubilees and Their Weeks" (CD 16:3–4)—is also cited using the familiar formula: "For thus is it written in the Divisions of [the Times . . ." (4Q228 frag. 1, col. i, line 9).

Claiming Authority: Anchoring Writing to Scriptural Texts and Figures

When closely linked to already recognized scripture, interpretations may come to attain authoritative status themselves. Even today, Christians most consciously adhering to the persistent and timeless authority of *sola scriptura* ("scripture alone") may, in practice, submit themselves to the authority of teachers perceived to be inspired interpreters of their scriptures. Holding fast to the interpretative words of a teacher is sometimes viewed as holding fast to the words of God. Yet, even those teachers who claim to be authoritative interpreters of their scriptures are likely aware of the transient nature of their authority, and few, if any, would dare claim that they were speaking or writing the Bible.

During the Second Temple period, by contrast, it is not inconceivable that some teachers and scribes believed that their words could one day be received as authoritative scripture. Again, it is worth remembering the distinction made earlier between a closed canonical Bible and a developing collection of authoritative scriptures. One of the most important ways that scribes routinely claimed authority was to anchor their work to scriptural figures and texts by attaching superscriptions, placing first person speeches into the mouths of biblical characters, updating already accepted scriptures, and bookending new writing between sections of the more ancient narrative.

While not included in the psalter of the HB, Ps 151 is nevertheless included in the psalters of the Greek LXX and the Orthodox and Slavonic Bibles and among the biblical psalms in the great Psalms scroll (11QPs^a). In the latter, it appears in

---

[7] All translations of the DSS, unless otherwise noted, are taken from Martin G. Abegg Jr., James E. Bowley, and Edward M. Cook, "Qumran Sectarian Manuscripts," *Accordance Bible Software* 8.05 (Altamonte Springs, FL: Oaktree Software Specialists, 2008) and Michael Wise, Martin Abegg Jr., and Edward Cook, *The Dead Sea Scrolls: A New Translation* (1996; rev. ed., New York: HarperCollins, 2005).

[8] All Bible references are adapted from the NRSV.

two separate Hebrew versions, each with its own superscription attributing the psalm to David.

> A Hallelujah of David, Son of Jesse . . . He sent his prophet, Samuel, to anoint me, to make me great. My brothers went out to meet him, handsome of figure and appearance . . . But he sent and fetched me from behind the flock and anointed me with holy oil, and he made me leader of his people and ruler over the children of his covenant. (excerpts from 11QPsᵃ: 151A:1–7).[9]

The explicitly autobiographical voice of the psalm sets it apart as different from the biblical psalms associated with David but, even so, it was treasured within more than one tradition and included in the canonical psalter.

From a postcanon-formation perspective, it may seem obvious that all Jews during the Second Temple period viewed Moses as the primary authoritative figure to whom and through whom God revealed his words and that they viewed the Mosaic Torah as the fundamental record of divine revelation. However, there were other texts later deemed marginal that claimed authority by anchoring to other figures viewed as revealers. For example, Enoch, a virtual extra in the Genesis cast of characters, played a leading role in the Aramaic Enoch books. Enoch, along with other figures from Genesis, including Noah and Levi, received and transmitted divine revelation most commonly through angels, dreams, and visions in their various literary incarnations especially in the Aramaic texts among the DSS.

First person speeches placed into the mouth of a biblical character—a practice called pseudepigraphy—strengthened a text's claim to authority, especially when the interpretative writing imitated already recognized scripture. Second Temple authors would have observed that Moses had spoken to the Israelites in the first person, recounting God's words as spoken from the mountain (Deut 5). Centuries later, an author gives Enoch speech:

> Enoch, a righteous man whose eyes were opened by God, who had the vision of the Holy One and of heaven, which he showed me. From the words of the watchers and holy ones I heard everything; and I heard everything from them, I also understood what I saw. (*1 En.* 1:2)[10]

During the prehistory of the Qumran sectarians, it appears that the authority of biblical texts and figures was less centralized than it became later when it shifted more decisively to Moses. Bookending was a scribal strategy signaling this shift whereby a reinterpreted version of a previously known text was adapted within a fresh retelling of the narrative and anchored to another text or figure.

For example, in Genesis a previously known story about the "sons of gods" who married "daughters of men" (Gen 6:1–4) was tersely summarized and recontextualized within the Noah narrative. Subsequently, in the oldest layer of the

---

[9] Martin Abegg Jr., Peter W. Flint, and Eugene Ulrich, trans., *The Dead Sea Scrolls Bible: The Oldest Known Bible Translated for the First Time into English* (San Francisco: HarperSanFrancisco, 1999).

[10] All translations from *1 Enoch* are taken from George W. E. Nickelsburg and J. C. VanderKam, *1 Enoch: A New Translation* (Minneapolis: Fortress, 2004).

Enochic *Book of Watchers,* it is Noah who hears from God within a greatly expanded story about the angelic "sons of gods" and human women in which Enoch is not even mentioned (*1 En.* 6–11). However, once these chapters were bookended by Enoch's speeches in *1 En.* 1–5 and *1 En.* 12–36, the primary authoritative figure in *Watchers* is no longer Noah, but Enoch.[11]

Subsequently, in *Jubilees,* the tradition crossed over from Aramaic into Hebrew and the Enoch and Noah narratives were recontextualized within a divine revelation given to Moses by an angel on Mount Sinai (*Jub.* 1:1). While *Jubilees* honored the historical grandfathered authority of Noah and especially of Enoch— and, presumably, the writings anchored to them—it was now Moses who was presented as the primary revealer, the one who received and transmitted the most complete and reliable revelation from God.

Using these interpretive strategies, scribes were able to update their scriptures for new generations facing different challenges within their social contexts. If the authority of their contemporizing interpretations was recognized, they could even be received as scripture. This practice may have been legitimized by examples found by the community within the Hebrew scriptures, where original and updated versions co-existed as authoritative scripture. For example, scribes well-acquainted with their scriptures could not have failed to notice that Deut 5:1–22 was a reformulation of the Ten Words originally spoken by God and then written by the finger of God (Exod 20:1–17; 34:1). By linking their own interpretations to Moses, they were justified in believing that they, too, were authentically expressing "the law already accepted as authoritatively Mosaic."[12]

The Jews of the Qumran community were not the only Jews who were reading Moses in new ways. In Matthew's Gospel, Jesus states, "Do not think that I have come to abolish the law or the prophets; I have come not to abolish but to fulfill" (Matt 5:17), adding:

> You have heard that it was said to those of ancient times, "You shall not murder"; and "whoever murders shall be liable to judgment." But I say to you that if you are angry with a brother or sister, you will be liable to judgment. (Matt 5:21–22a)

Jesus offers a contemporizing interpretation of Mosaic Torah but, unlike the interpretations found in the DSS, he speaks explicitly on his own authority ("But I say to you . . ."). His widespread popularity would suggest that Jesus was accepted, at least initially, as an authoritative voice by many who gathered to listen. Later, as his words and the accounts of his life, death, and resurrection were collected and written down in various forms, some could not take the next step of receiving them as authoritative scripture. However, others could and did. Ultimately, Jesus'

---

[11] For a comprehensive study on a history of traditions of Noah in the DSS, including the practice of bookending and recontextualizing traditions, see Dorothy M. Peters, *Noah Traditions in the Dead Sea Scrolls: Conversations and Conversations in Antiquity* (SBLEJL 26; Atlanta: Society of Biblical Literature, 2008), 173–89.

[12] For a discussion on discourses linked to their founders, see Hindy Najman, *Seconding Sinai: The Development of Mosaic Discourse in Second Temple Judaism* (JSJSup 77; Leiden: Brill, 2003), 12–13.

innovative reworking of the Ten Words in Exodus and Deuteronomy completed the journey from authority into canon, into the Bible of those communities of faith for whom the primary authoritative revealer, fulfilling and superseding Moses, was now Jesus.

Candidates for Scriptures on the Margins among the Dead Sea Scrolls

We now come to a survey of selected scriptures on the margins, divided into three categories. The first includes writings connected to the books of the Greek LXX and/or writings later canonized within the Roman Catholic and Orthodox traditions. The second surveys some of the Aramaic reworkings of Genesis, and the third category surveys some of the Hebrew reworkings of scripture anchored to Moses and his Torah.

Scriptures on the Margins: The Apocrypha/Deuterocanonicals

The Greek LXX[13] followed by the Roman Catholic and Orthodox canons included books and parts of books not canonized within the HB: Maccabees, Baruch, Tobit, Sirach, Judith, Wisdom of Solomon, as well as additional psalms and Daniel and Esther material. The DSS preserved some of these: additional Hebrew psalms, a Hebrew version of Sirach (Ben Sira), Aramaic court tales with similarities to the books of Esther and Daniel, and both Aramaic and Hebrew copies of Tobit.

Psalms and Ben Sira

As mentioned earlier, Ps 151 was canonized within the Greek LXX, Orthodox, and Slavonic Bibles and preserved in the great Psalms Scroll (11QPsalms[a]), a scroll that also contained Pss 154 and 155 known from some manuscripts of the ancient Syriac Psalter of Eastern Orthodox Christianity and that contained, for example, these verses: "Form a community to make known his salvation, and do not hesitate in making known his might and his majesty to all the simple one" (Ps 154:4); "My trust, O Lord, is befo[re] you. I cried 'O Lord,' and he answered me, [and he healed] my broken heart" (Ps 154:17). All in all, fifteen compositions not found in any modern Bible appear among the forty Psalms scrolls at Qumran, attesting to a Psalter that was still open and still fluid with respect both to the number of psalms and their ordering.[14]

Known variously from the Greek version as Sirach or Ecclesiaticus, portions of The Wisdom of Ben Sira were found in two scrolls at Qumran.[15] However, the Cave 11 copy of Ben Sira is an independent canticle placed after Ps 138 and appearing in a form substantially different from the Greek version (Sir

---

[13] Copies of the Greek Septuagint found in Cave 7 include 7QSeptuagint Exodus (7Q1) and 7QEpistle of Jeremiah (7Q2), possibly a copy of the Epistle of Jeremiah.

[14] Abegg, Flint, and Ulrich, *The Dead Sea Scrolls Bible*, 506–7, 572–73, and 579–80.

[15] 2QSir (2Q18); 11QPs[a] (11Q5). A third copy was found at Masada (Mas 1h).

51:13–30).[16] While this canticle may have been sung as scripture at Qumran, its presence in the psalter cannot be proof that the entire book of Ben Sira was authorized as scripture. Only a few words are extant on the copy deposited in the less important Cave 2. It is possible that this scroll, like others, came to Qumran among the personal possessions of new initiates into the Community. Ben Sira would be a strange theological bedfellow with the sectarian scrolls, in any case. For example, its argument for free will (Sir 15:11–17) is somewhat at odds with sectarian predeterminism (1QS 2:1–10) and, while the sectarian scrolls promoted additional wisdom gained from esoteric knowledge made known to select individuals (1QS 5:11–12; 9:18–19; CD 3:13–15), Ben Sira advocated a wisdom derived largely from Torah and, therefore, accessible to all.[17]

Daniel Stories of the Exile

Stories about Daniel were composed during the Second Temple period in Aramaic, Hebrew, and Greek. They were copied and translated, and some eventually were collected within the various canons of scripture. Other stories, however, failed to be transmitted and were lost until the discovery of the DSS.

Preserved among the scrolls are eight copies of the intriguingly composed biblical book[18] in which Aramaic court stories (Dan 2:4b–7:28) were selected and bookended by Hebrew portions (Dan 1:1–2:4a; 8:1–12:13). In the Aramaic stories, Daniel and friends are portrayed as living successfully albeit sometimes precariously in the Diaspora whereas Dan 9, Hebrew, expresses a longing for the restoration of Jerusalem and the sanctuary. Daniel 9 also introduces deuteronomic language of confession and repentance, of curse and oath, and the transgression of Torah, effectively shifting the focus from Daniel as the primary revealer and interpreter of dreams and vision to Moses and the written Torah.

The LXX collected Susanna, the Prayer of Azariah and the Song of the Three Young Jews, and Bel and the Dragon among the Daniel stories. Of these, 4QDaniel-Suzanna (4Q551) has parallels to the Susanna story in the LXX. In addition, there are as many as nine previously unknown Aramaic scrolls connected to Daniel. For example, in 4QPseudo-Daniel[a–c] (4Q243–245), Daniel explains the history of Israel to an apparently interested King Belshazzar. 4QPrayer of Nabonidus (4Q242) evokes the biblical story of King Nebuchadnezzar's loss of sanity and his return of reason once the king prays to the "Most High."[19]

[1]The words of the pra[y]er of Nabonidus, king of [Ba]bylon, [the great] kin[g, when he was smitten] [2]with a severe inflammation . . . Beca[use] I was thus changed, [becoming

---

[16]So Peter W. Flint, "Noncanonical Writings in the Dead Sea Scrolls; Apocrypha, Other Previously Known Writings, Pseudepigrapha," in *The Bible at Qumran: Text, Shape, and Interpretation* (ed. P. W. Flint; Studies in the Dead Sea Scrolls and Related Literature; Grand Rapids: Eerdmans, 2001), 80–123, here 92. This essay provides an easily accessible and compact assessment of the scriptural status of many of the scriptures on the margins discussed in this chapter.
[17]See the Prologue to Sirach and Sir 34:1–8.
[18]1QDan[a–b] (1Q71–72), 4QDan[a–e] (4Q112–116), and 6QpapDan (6Q7).
[19]See also 4QAramaic Apocalypse (4Q246); 4QApocalypse? (4Q489); 4QFourKingdoms[a–b] (4Q552–553).

like a beast, I prayed to the Most High,] [4]and He forgave my sins. An exorcist—a Jew, in fact, a mem[ber of the community of exiles—came to me and said,] [5]"Declare and write down this story, and so ascribe glory and gre[at]ness to the name of G[od Most High."] (4Q242 frags. 1–3, ll. 1–5; cf. Dan 4:28–37)

Like those stories in biblical Daniel, the focus of these newly rediscovered texts portray Daniel's influence in the court before a succession of kings who come to acknowledge the Most High and his revelation transmitted to and through Daniel. While these non-canonized Daniel stories, at some point, may have been perceived as authoritative scripture, they were not recontextualized and reinterpreted within Hebrew and Mosaic bookends, and ultimately were marginalized. On the other hand, the authoritative life of those Daniel stories aligned with Moses was extended and eventually canonized.

Esther-Like Tales of the Court

While no copies of the book of Esther known from the HB or the Greek LXX were found at Qumran, the Aramaic Tales of the Persian Court (4Q550[a–e]) have some similarities. Conflict and intrigue in the palace court swirl around the cast of characters that include a Persian king who demands that the court archives be read to him, a Jewish servant, and, of course, a princess.

The writings focus on the living of a peaceful Jewish life among the Gentiles in the Diaspora and, more specifically, on gaining status within court. The wider genre (including Tobit and the Daniel cycle) is set in Persian or neo-Babylonian courts and, with the exception of some of the stories in Dan 1–6, demonstrates a positive attitude toward the reigning monarch.[20] Perhaps the stance toward Gentiles was too positive for some tastes when reread later in different contexts when relationships were more adversarial between Jews and Gentiles. If so, any scriptural authority these texts enjoyed may have been diminished, increasingly bound to the specific times and places in which and where they were written.

Tobit

Likely composed in Aramaic, the book of Tobit is a novella preserved at Qumran in four Aramaic copies and one Hebrew copy.[21] Alone among his countrymen, Tobit faithfully went to Jerusalem to observe the festivals (Tob 1:6) until exiled to Nineveh, where he lived under the rule of a succession of foreign kings. He served Shalmaneser under whom he had "favor and good standing" (Tob 1:13), and when he died, he was buried with great honor in Nineveh (Tob 14:2). Even while it is important to the narrator that Tobit was honored and respected in a

---

[20]So Sidnie White Crawford, "4QTales of the Persian Court (4Q550a–e) and Its Relation to Biblical Royal Courtier Tales, Especially Esther, Daniel, and Joseph," in *The Bible as Book: The Hebrew Bible and the Judaean Desert Discoveries* (ed. Emanuel Tov; London: The British Library and Oak Knoll Press in association with The Scriptorium: Center for Christian Antiquities, 2002), 121–37, here 132.

[21]4Q papTobit[a] ar (4Q196), 4Q Tobit[b–e] (4Q197–4Q200) dated mostly to the first century BCE. See Michael D. Coogan, ed., *The New Oxford Annotated Apocrypha* (3rd ed.; Oxford: Oxford University Press, 2001), 12.

foreign land, Tobit's faithful obedience to the law of Moses even while in exile is emphasized (Tob 1:8), as is his loyalty to Jerusalem (Tob 14:5–7). The fact that Tobit was translated into Hebrew suggests an effort to extend the authority of this book. Eventually Tobit was preserved in the Catholic and Orthodox canons while other Aramaic courtier tales were marginalized.

Scriptures on the Margins: Aramaic Reworkings of Genesis

At Qumran, the language of scriptural authority was more obviously Hebrew. Yet the prevalence of Aramaic books suggests that authoritative status may not always have been attributed solely to Hebrew texts. The Aramaic retellings of Genesis acknowledge divine revelation as most commonly transmitted through dreams, visions, and angels. The characters routinely speak in the first person and reliably transmit knowledge and wisdom orally to their children and grandchildren by means of exhortation and last testaments and by means of written form through sacred books handed down from father to son.

Enoch, Noah, and Abram: The Enoch Books and Genesis Apocryphon

Composed in Aramaic between the third century BCE and into the first century CE, the Enochic books making up *1 Enoch* were known previously, in their entirety, only in Ethiopic. Four of the five Enochic books—*Book of Watchers* (*BW*), the *Astronomical Book* (*AB*),[22] the *Dream Visions* (*DV*), and the *Epistle of Enoch* (*EE*) appended by a *Birth of Noah* story, were preserved on eleven or twelve fragmentary scrolls, in four separate caves, either singly or in collections.[23] This indication of high interest in the writing should be kept in tension with the observation that most copies date to the earlier periods of Community history; therefore, it is possible that the earlier scriptural status of the books gradually transitioned into a grandfathered historical authoritative status.

The laconic description of Enoch in Genesis, "Enoch walked with God; then he was no more, because God took him" (Gen 5:21–24), left spacious exegetical gaps within which Enoch could flourish. The cosmos recreated for Enoch by later exegetes was peopled with angels, good and bad. The angelic Watchers transgressed their boundaries, intermarrying with women and bringing dangerous knowledge (e.g., weapons and cosmetics) into the world (*1 En.* 6). The right kind of angels, by contrast, revealed the right kind of trustworthy knowledge to Enoch who, in turn, became a reliable transmitter of divine revelation to the rest of humanity (*1 En.* 1–2).

First Enoch was cited in the pre-Nicene church fathers[24] and was eventually canonized in the Ethiopian Orthodox Bible, but there is evidence of a shared

---

[22] The Ethiopic form, the *Book of Luminaries*, abbreviates what was likely a much longer work.

[23] 4QEn^{a-f} ar (4Q201–207); 4QEnastr ar^{a-d} (4Q208–211). For translation and commentary, see George W. E. Nickelsburg, *1 Enoch 1* (Minneapolis: Fortress, 2001).

[24] *Epistle of Barnabas* cites *1 En.* 89:61–64 and *1 En.* 90:17 with the introduction formula, "concerning which it is written as Enoch says" and cites *1 En.* 89:56–57 with the introductory formula, "For Scripture says." Allert, *A High View of Scripture?* 46.

thought world from even earlier. For example, in *Watchers*, the Watchers who were responsible for bringing evil, violence, and bloodshed to the world were to be bound "until the day of their judgment" and then "led away to the fiery abyss" where they would be confined forever (*1 En.* 10:11–15). In Matthew, Jesus speaks of the "eternal fire prepared for the devil and his angels" (Matt 25:41; cf. 2 Pet 2:4, Jude 6), and the book of Jude recognizes Enoch as a prophet, citing from *Watchers*:

> . . . Enoch, in the seventh generation from Adam, prophesied, saying, "See, the Lord is coming with ten thousands of his holy ones, to execute judgment on all, and to convict everyone of all the deeds of ungodliness that they have committed in such an ungodly way, and of all the harsh things that ungodly sinners have spoken against him." (Jude 14–15, citing *1 En.* 1:9)

While the *Book of Parables* included in the Ethiopic collection was not found at Qumran, nine copies of a *Book of Giants* preserved in four caves retell an alternative version of the Watchers story. Four giants are named (Ohya, Hahya, Mahway, and Gilgamesh) who have disturbing dreams of water, uprooting, and fire. They send Mahway as their representative to Enoch for an interpretation of these nightmares.[25] In response, a tablet "in the very handwriting of Enoch the noted scribe" addressed to the Watcher Shemihaza, announces divine judgment by flood because of the "harm" done to the earth by the Watchers and their progeny. It calls on them to loosen the bonds binding them to evil and to pray (4Q203 frag. 8 lines 1–15). These points have no parallel in other Enochic books and, while the *Book of Giants* was linked to Enoch, it was not included among the five that eventually comprised *1 Enoch*. Perhaps the tradition collectors shied away from stories portraying their authoritative revealer, Enoch, speaking with the giants, speaking to God (or his angels) about the giants, transmitting God's words—even of judgment—back to the giants, and calling the giants to prayer!

There are no direct citations from the books of Enoch in the DSS, yet Enochic traditions permeate many of the scrolls. For example, the sole copy of *Genesis Apocryphon* claims to recount the "Book of the Words of Noah" (1Q20 5:29) and presents Noah as an authoritative revealer and transmitter of divine revelation: "an emissary of the Great Holy One proclaimed to me . . ." (1Q20 6:15). In its own version of the birth of Noah, Lamech is worried that Noah was fathered by the Watchers and not by him. Yet, while Lamech does not accept the passionate assertions of his wife, Batenosh, he does accept the reassurances of his grandfather, Enoch, as authoritative (1Q20 2).

In the Abram narrative, three advisors come from the Egyptian court asking Abram for the "knowledge of goodness, wisdom, and righteousness," and it is the

---

[25] Copies include 1QGiants[a–b] (1Q23–24), 2QGiants (2Q26), 4QGiants[a] (4Q203), 4QGiants[b–d] (4Q530–532), 4QGiants[e] (4Q556), 4QGiants[f] (4Q206 2–3) originally published as part of 4Q556, and 6QGiants (6Q8). For an extended treatment, see Loren Stuckenbruck, *The Book of Giants from Qumran: Texts, Translation, and Commentary* (Tübingen: Mohr Siebeck, 1997). J. T. Milik believes that 4QGiants[a] originally was part of 4QEn[c] and has argued, not without controversy, that an earlier "Enochic Pentateuch" originally included the *Book of Giants* and was replaced later by the *Parables*. J. T. Milik, *The Books of Enoch: Aramaic Fragments of Qumran Cave 4* (Oxford: Clarendon Press, 1976), 58.

"Book of the Words of Enoch" from which he reads (1Q20 19:24–26). Overall, the relationship between Abram's family and the Egyptians is presented as being risky but also with potential of mutual benefit. Abram lays his hands on his head of the Egyptian king and prays for him, exorcising an evil spirit and healing him from the plague of impotency. In appreciation, the king gives many gifts not only to Sarai but also to Hagar (1Q20 20:16–33). While this narrator may have attempted to claim authority for the *Genesis Apocryphon* by anchoring it to favorite authoritative revealers, it is difficult to know whether an authoritative status was ever recognized.

Levi: The Aramaic Levi Document

An archetypical Levi is portrayed in the *Aramaic Levi Document* (*ALD*) as a wise and priestly figure given to heavenly visions and anchoring a hereditary line of priests that reached back to Noah (*ALD* 10:10) and forward to Levi's priestly descendents (*ALD* 13).[26] This new Levi is no longer violent (cf. Gen 34; 49:5); instead, violence is attributed to the Shechemites: "I was eighteen when I killed Shechem and destroyed the workers of violence. I was nineteen when I became a priest" (*ALD* 2:1; 12:6–7). In fact, Levi is subtly distanced from the sword. In the text, the "kingdom of the sword" is described as "fighting and battle and chase and toil and conflict and killing and hunger" (*ALD* 4:9).

Levi encourages his descendents to be like Joseph and so not all Gentiles were to be viewed as enemies. Those who learned wisdom would not a foreigner in every land and nation to which he would go but would, instead, be like a "brother" honored and sought after for wisdom (*ALD* 13:4–10).

Levi traditions continue in other writings. Other Aramaic texts claim to contain the first person speech of Jacob (4Q537), Levi's son, Qahat, (4Q542), and the words of Amram, Moses' father (4Q543–548). In Hebrew, Levi is re-formed in *Jubilees* and, outside of the DSS, in the Greek *Testament of Levi*. In both texts, Aramaic Levi traditions become aligned more closely to Moses. The prevalence of *ALD* among the scrolls and the effort made to extend its authority in its afterlife is suggestive of its status as authoritative scripture particularly in the early history of the sect.

Scriptures on the Margins: Hebrew Reworkings of Moses and Torah

The authority of Aramaic texts unmediated by Moses and Torah may have faded through the margins with the arrival of the back-to-Moses and back-to-Hebrew movements connected to Hasmonean rule in the second and first centuries BCE. In their place, Hebrew increasingly became the language in which authoritative texts were written.

---

[26]Composed as early as the third century BCE, *ALD* was previously known from Cairo Genizah; the seven fragmentary copies among the DSS include 1QTLevi (1Q21), 4QLevi[a] ar (4Q213), 4QLevi[b] ar (4Q213a), 4QLevi[c] ar (4Q213b), 4QLevi[d] ar (4Q214), 4QLevi[e] ar (4Q214a), and 4QLevi[f] ar (4Q214b). For full treatment of the text, see Jonas C. Greenfield, Michael E. Stone, and Esther Eshel, *The Aramaic Levi Document: Edition, Translation, and Commentary* (SVTP; Leiden: Brill, 2004).

The Temple Scroll

The *Temple Scroll*, a reworking of Exod 34–Deut 23 that records changes of first person speech in the mouth of Moses to first person speech in the mouth of God,[27] has provoked the tongue-in-cheek title "pseudo-God."[28] For example, where Moses says, "if you obey the voice of the LORD your God by keeping all his commandments that I [Moses] am commanding you today" in Deut 13:18, the *Temple Scroll* substitutes "provided you obey *Me* by keeping all *My* commandments that I [the LORD] hereby command you this day" (11Q19 55:13–14).

This is clearly a claim for authoritative scriptural status. The practice of pseudepigraphy or falsely ascribing words, while sounding vaguely dishonest to modern ears, was nevertheless a respected genre in antiquity that acknowledged and honored the authoritative voice it was interpreting. Deuteronomy itself had provided patterns for Second Temple scribes to follow as they updated, interpreted, and developed earlier authoritative texts linked to Moses. Perhaps these scribes felt that these changes and even the creation of new laws, such as the "Feast of New Oil," the "days of Wood Offering," and the "Feast of Wine" (11Q19 11:11–13; 43:8), were authentic expressions of "the law already accepted as authoritatively Mosaic."[29] It is unlikely that the *Temple Scroll* was written to replace Torah. Rather, it appears to have acknowledged and extended the Mosaic authority of Torah as scripture at the same time as it claimed authority for itself.[30]

4Q Reworked Pentateuch

4Q Reworked Pentateuch (4QRP)[31] has similarities to the Samaritan Pentateuch, but the number and nature of the variants and expansions make it difficult to classify unambiguously as a version of the Pentateuch. Even so, a strong case could be made for its status as authoritative scripture. The number of texts outnumber some other biblical books, and 4QRP itself claims authority as an extension of Mosaic Torah. For example, the "wood festival" noted in the *Temple Scroll* is introduced on good authority: "the Lord spoke to Moses, saying . . ."

---

[27] See 4QTemple (4Q524), 11QTemple[a] (11Q19), 11QTemple[b] (11Q20), 11QTemple[c] (11Q21).

[28] Moshe J. Bernstein, "Pseudepigraphy in the Qumran Scrolls: Categories and Functions," in *Pseudepigraphic Perspectives: The Apocrypha and Pseudepigrapha in Light of the Dead Sea Scrolls. Proceedings of the [Second] International Symposium of the Orion Center for the Study of the Dead Sea Scrolls and Associated Literature, 12–14 January 1997* (ed. E. G. Chazon and M. E. Stone; STDJ 31; Leiden: Brill, 1999), 1–26, here 19.

[29] Najman, *Seconding Sinai*, 12–13.

[30] Daniel Falk's language of "extending the scriptures" is helpful since it does not force the distinction between texts as either "supplementary or complementary to Scripture." Daniel K. Falk, *The Parabiblical Texts: Strategies for Extending the Scriptures among the Dead Sea Scrolls* (Companion to the Qumran Scrolls/Library of Second Temple Studies 8/63; New York: T&T Clark, 2007), 2.

[31] Cf. 4Q365 frag. 6a col. ii + frag. 6c lines 1–8 with Exod 15:25 and 4Q364 frag.4b–e col. ii lines 19–26 with Gen 31:10–13.

Expansions include Jacob's dream of the mating of the goats[32] and seven additional lines of Miriam's song:[33]

> [5] [Miriam the prophetess, the sister] [6] [of Aaron,] took [a timbrel in her hand and a] ll the women went out after her with [timbrels and with dances. She answered.] . . . (4Q364 6b 5-6) . . . [1] *with an olive branch [. . .]* [2] *for the pridefulness [. . .* [3] *You are great, O deliverer [. . .* [4] *the enemy's hope has perished [. . .]* [5] *they have perished in the mighty waters, the enemy [. . .]* [6] *Praise him in the heights, you have given salvation [. . .]* [7] *[who has] done glorious things [. . .]* [8] Moses led [Isra]el onward from the sea. (4Q365 frag. 6a col. ii + frag. 6c lines 1-8)

Whether or not 4QRP was an edition of the biblical text or whether it was intended as an interpretation or extension may have had little bearing on its practical authority or its status as scripture. If authority is disconnected from the degree to which a text adheres to a particular version of the biblical text, then even a book like *Jubilees* containing significant interpretative changes may have been treasured as authoritative and contemporized scripture.

Jubilees

Composed between 160 and 150 BCE, *Jubilees*, preserved in fifteen or sixteen copies, the latest dating to the mid-first century CE,[34] was cited like scripture (see above), and its oldest extant copy repaired instead of discarded. The complete book of *Jubilees* was previously known only in Ethiopic within the canon of the Ethiopian Orthodox Church.

Jubilees functioned as a rebuttal of those Jews living in the Hellenistic world who "sought to do away with the commands of the Torah that separated Jew and non-Jew, arguing that such laws were not original" and who believed that "[t]here was an ancient, better time, a golden age, when such separatist legislation was not in force."[35] By bookending biblical Genesis and pre-Sinai Exodus (Gen 1–Exod 16:1) within a divine revelation to Moses, *Jubilees* confirmed for its readers that the Torah was already recorded on heavenly tablets prior to Sinai and that their ancestors were subject to it.

Thus, in *Jubilees*, Noah offers his sacrifice with the proper animals after the flood (*Jub.* 7:3–5) and both Isaac and Ishmael observe the Feast of Firstfruits with their father, Abraham (*Jub.* 22:1–2). Abram is portrayed as a prototypical faithful Israelite living in the midst of a people that worshipped other gods.

---

[32] Cf. 4Q365 6a ii + 6c 1–7 with Exod 15:25 and 4Q364 4b–e col. ii, 19–26 with Gen 31:10–13.

[33] The expansion between Exod 15:21–22 is italicized.

[34] 1QJub[a–b] (1Q17–18), 2QJub[a–b] (2Q19–20), 3QJub (3Q5), 4QJubilees? (4Q176a–b), 4QJub[a] (4Q216), 4QpapJub[b]? (4Q217), 4QJub[c–g] (4Q218–222), 4QpapJub[h] (4Q223–224), 11QJub (11Q12).

[35] So J. C. VanderKam, "The Origins and Purposes of the *Book of Jubilees*," in *Studies in the Book of Jubilees* (ed. M. Albani, J. Frey, and A. Lange; TSAJ 65; Tübingen: Mohr Siebeck, 1997), 3–24, here 21–22.

Yet, a curious tension exists between the nearness and distance in Abram's relationship with his Chaldean family and neighbors in Ur. Abram prays to the Creator and learns writing from his father, Terah, but then temporarily separates himself from his idol-worshipping father. He burns down the house of idols in his community but solves the problems of the crows that were eating up the seed and helpfully teaches the carpenters how to make his new plow invention (*Jub.* 11–12). Thus, while the archetypical Abram is permitted to be helpful to the foreigner who would regard his words, he separated himself from foreign idols and from the people who worshipped them.

Conclusion

In conclusion, the DSS reveal a broader range of scripture authoritative for Jews of antiquity than is found in any Bible today. Some of the writings possessed a persistent and timeless authority while the authority of others was transient, bound more closely to the times and places in which they were composed. While it may not be possible to identify with any certainty the characteristics of those writings that either persisted as scriptures or were marginalized by the community of the DSS, there are several observable trends.

First, there is a trend toward the centralization of authority in Moses. In the earlier history of the movement, the primary authoritative revealer might be Enoch, Noah, Levi, Daniel, or Moses, alone or in combination with one of the others. Over time, however, some of the texts were bookended by and subordinated to newly authoritative texts anchored to Moses while the authority of Aramaic texts not reworked into Hebrew compositions seems to have diminished.

Second, the corollary of the first point is that the language of authority increasingly became Hebrew and decreasingly Aramaic. In broad strokes, then, the DSS written in Hebrew and anchored securely to Moses persisted as authoritative scripture even in the later history of the sect at the same time that the scrolls written in Aramaic and anchored to Enoch, Noah, Levi, and Daniel as primary authoritative revealers tended to drift toward the margins.

There is still much exciting study to do toward identifying the elements contributing either to the persistence or marginality of a text's authoritative status for the Qumran community. Therefore, this next point is just a preliminary observation. The Aramaic texts tend to hold a generally more optimistic view of a potentially positive relationship between Israel and the Gentiles than do the Hebrew texts. While this chapter surveyed only several Hebrew texts, the larger DSS corpus of authoritative Hebrew texts do trend increasingly toward a more cautious and even hostile view of the outsider as the margins between those inside and outside the Qumran sectarian group were increasingly more sharply defined.[36] It may be that one of the elements contributing to the persistence of authoritative scripture for this particular sectarian group was the fortification of boundaries rather than bridges between those within the group and those outside.

---

[36] Peters, *Noah Traditions*, 187–88.

Finally, the sheer number and variation of interpretations of scriptures found among the DSS attest to the deep love that the people of Qumran had for the writings they so carefully copied, interpreted, and preserved. For them, the revelation of God through their various ancestors still lived and breathed in their day, and by interpreting this revelation for a new generation, the authority of these texts was extended and enlarged. The writings that we might disparagingly think of as marginal may have been honored as grandfathers by those who preserved them, books possessing wisdom and authority still heard down through the generations.

4

DISPUTED ISSUES IN THE STUDY OF CITIES, VILLAGES, AND THE ECONOMY IN JESUS' GALILEE

Mark A. Chancey

It has often been observed that the current phase of the quest for the historical Jesus is inseparable from the quest for the historical Galilee. Jesus' home region has taken pride of place, so to speak, in much of the research of the past thirty years. Although this heightened attention has resulted in genuine advances in our understanding of the Galilean social setting, questions about the economic situation and urban-rural relations are still a matter of considerable debate.[1] For some scholars, Herod Antipas's rebuilding of Sepphoris and construction of the wholly new city of Tiberias elevated the quality of life, at least in socio-economic terms, for much of the region's population, while for others the rise of those cities facilitated the exploitation and oppression of rural Galileans.

In scholarly quarters where the view that most rural Galileans suffered severe economic turmoil under Antipas is near orthodoxy, the parables function as a key set of evidence. Thus, a landowner can readily hire day laborers to work in his vineyard because economic pressures have driven so many family farmers off their own land (Matt 20:1–16). The absentee owner of a large estate can easily find tenant farmers for the same reason (Mark 12:1–12; Luke 20:9–19; Matt 21:33–46). A manager tries to curry favor by slashing the debts of his associates, illustrating the widespread and growing debt faced by Galileans (Luke 16:1–9).

In this view, the economic pressures assumed by the parables are explained as consequences of the actions and policies of Herod Antipas, especially his efforts at

---

[1]Morten Hørning Jensen thoroughly canvasses the literature in *Herod Antipas in Galilee* (WUNT 2/215; Tübingen: Mohr Siebeck, 2006). See also Phillip A. Harland, "The Economy of First-Century Palestine: State of the Scholarly Discussion," in *Handbook of Early Christianity: Social Science Approaches* (ed. Anthony J. Blasi, Jean Duhaime, and Paul-André Turcotte; Walnut Creek, CA: Altamira, 2002), 511–28; Mark Rapinchuk, "The Galilee and Jesus in Recent Research," *Currents in Biblical Research* 2 (2004): 197–222; and Halvor Moxnes, "The Construction of Galilee as a Place for the Historical Jesus—Part II," *BTB* 31 (2001): 64–77.

urbanization. The cities required a reorientation of the distribution of agricultural products; whereas farmers had once focused on growing crops primarily for their own subsistence, they now had to produce surplus crops to feed the cities. Taxes and rents imposed by the parasitic cities and their elites combined to facilitate this transfer of foodstuffs. But taxes served not only to feed the cities; tax increases would have been necessary just to build them. The cities themselves served as centers for the collection of taxes for Antipas and perhaps also for Rome. Antipas minted his own bronze coins to facilitate payment of taxes. These intertwining policies of taxation and monetization pushed family farmers beyond what they were able to produce, causing them to seek loans from city-based lenders and to sell their lands to city-dwelling estate owners. Some farmers became tenants on what had been their own lands, others were forced to become day laborers, others became artisans and craftsmen, others resorted to begging, and still others turned to social banditry. It is within this context of a debilitating economic crisis that we must place the historical Jesus, with his call for a type of kingdom that differed from the tetrarchy of Antipas and the empire of Rome.[2]

Other scholars, however, see Galilee in an entirely different light. The late Douglas R. Edwards, for example, was an eloquent and influential proponent of the view that the reign of Antipas and his city-building activities had positive effects on the region as a whole. Increases in the number and size of villages indicate a flourishing rural population and ample agricultural production. Urban-rural relations were generally positive, and cities and villages had close economic ties. Markets played an important part in the regional economy, in addition to both reciprocity and redistribution exchange systems. The political stability of Antipas's reign allowed for economic stability, as well. "The Galilee envisioned as teeming with people and villages able to provide strangers sustenance, a Jewish Galilee cultivated extensively, rich in produce and diverse occupations, seems right on target."[3]

---

[2] This amalgamation of arguments is drawn from a variety of sources, the following of which are representative: William R. Herzog II, *Parables as Subversive Speech: Jesus as Pedagogue of the Oppressed* (Louisville: Westminster/John Knox, 1994); idem, *Jesus, Justice, and the Reign of God* (Louisville: Westminster/John Knox, 2000); Douglas E. Oakman, *Jesus and the Peasants* (Eugene, OR: Cascade Books, 2008); idem, *Jesus and the Economic Questions of His Day* (Lewiston, NY: Edwin Mellen Press, 1986); K. C. Hanson and Douglas E. Oakman, *Palestine in the Time of Jesus: Social Structures and Social Conflicts* (2nd ed.; Minneapolis: Fortress, 2008); Richard A. Horsley, *Jesus and Empire: The Kingdom of God and the New World Disorder* (Minneapolis: Fortress, 2003); idem, *Covenant Economics: A Biblical Vision of Justice for All* (Louisville: Westminster/John Knox, 2009); idem, *Archaeology, History, and Society in Galilee: The Social Context of Jesus and the Rabbis* (Valley Forge, PA: Trinity Press International, 1996); idem, *Galilee: History, Politics, People* (Valley Forge, PA: Trinity Press International, 1995); and numerous other works; John Dominic Crossan, *The Historical Jesus: The Life of a Mediterranean Peasant* (San Francisco: HarperSanFrancisco, 1991); idem, *The Birth of Christianity* (San Francisco: HarperSanFrancisco, 1998); and idem, *God and Empire: Jesus against Rome, Then and Now* (San Francisco: HarperSanFrancisco, 2007).

[3] Douglas R. Edwards, "Identity and Social Location in Roman Galilean Villages," in *Religion, Ethnicity, and Identity in Ancient Galilee* (ed. Jürgen Zangenberg, Harold W. Attridge, and Dale B. Martin; WUNT 210; Tübingen: Mohr Siebeck, 2007), 357–74, quote

A growing number of scholars, however, express uncertainty about the whole issue of social and economic conditions. The most notable is perhaps Morten Hørning Jensen, who searched in vain for archeological evidence of decline at rural sites. He found instead growing villages that that included "public buildings, industrial activities, and local upper-class quarters." He concluded his book-length study with a carefully nuanced assertion: "it is not concluded that the urban-rural relationship was symbiotic or reciprocal rather than parasitic. Instead, it is asserted that it is unwarranted to place Antipas in the middle of a deterioration process which 'must have' taken place under him. There are no indications of such a process either in the archaeological record or in the literary sources."[4] More recently, David A. Fiensy has offered words of caution for scholars at both ends of the spectrum.[5] In particular, Fiensy questions the extent to which large estates were absorbing farms and urban elites were driving rural Galilean villagers into debt and poverty. His reservations on this subject are especially notable because his earlier work on land tenure was influential in shaping the notion that such processes were endemic throughout first-century Palestine.[6] Other scholars known for their expertise in Galilean studies have raised similar questions.[7]

---

from 373; see also idem, "The Socio-Economic and Cultural Ethos of the Lower Galilee in the First Century: Implications for the Nascent Jesus Movement," in *The Galilee in Late Antiquity* (ed. Lee I. Levine; New York: Jewish Theological Seminary of America, 1992), 53–73; idem, "First Century Urban-Rural Relations in Lower Galilee: Exploring the Archaeological and Literary Evidence," in *Society of Biblical Literature 1988 Seminar Papers* (Atlanta: Scholars Press, 1988), 169–82; and Edwards and Peter Richardson, "Jesus and Palestinian Social Protest: Archaeological and Literary Perspectives," in *Jesus and Palestinian Social Protest: Archaeological and Literary Perspectives* (ed. Anthony J. Blasi, Jean Duhaime, and Paul-André Turcotte; Walnut Creek, CA: Altamira, 2002), 247–66. See also Eric M. Meyers, "Jesus and His Galilean Context," in *Archaeology and the Galilee: Texts and Contexts in the Graeco-Roman and Byzantine Periods* (ed. Douglas R. Edwards and C. Thomas McCollough; South Florida Studies in the History of Judaism 143; Atlanta: Scholars Press, 1997), 57–66. The work of Sean Freyne has also been influential on this subject, although his position has shifted over the years. Some of his most important essays are included in his *Galilee and Gospel* (Boston: Brill Academic Publishers, 2002).

[4] Jensen, *Herod Antipas*, 258.

[5] David A. Fiensy, "Assessing the Economy of Galilee in the Late Second Temple Period: Five Considerations," in Ralph Hawkins and David A. Fiensey, eds., *The Galilean Economic Life in the Time of Jesus* (in preparation); "Ancient Economy and the New Testament," in *Understanding the Social World of the New Testament* (ed. Dietmar Neufeld and Richard E. DeMaris; London: Routledge, 2010), 194–206; and *Jesus the Galilean: Soundings in a First Century Life* (Piscataway, NJ: Gorgias Press, 2007), 43–59.

[6] David A. Fiensy, *The Social History of Palestine in the Herodian Period: The Land Is Mine* (Lewiston, NY: Edwin Mellen Press, 1991).

[7] See, for example, Milton Moreland, "The Jesus Movement in the Villages of Roman Galilee: Archaeology, Q, and Modern Anthropological Theory," in *Oral Performance, Popular Tradition, and Hidden Transcript in Q* (ed. Richard A. Horsley; Semeia Studies 60; Atlanta: Society of Biblical Literature, 2006); and J. Andrew Overman, "Jesus of Galilee and the Historical Peasant," in *Archaeology and the Galilee: Texts and Contexts in the Graeco-Roman and Byzantine Periods* (ed. Douglas R. Edwards and C. Thomas McCollough; South Florida Studies in the History of Judaism 143; Atlanta: Scholars Press, 1997), 67–73. Jonathan L. Reed tries to move the discussion in a new direction in his provocative study, "Instability in Jesus'

As has also often been noted, what makes the range of positions found in contemporary scholarship so remarkable is that all draw from the same set of evidence: archeological finds and literary texts such as the NT, Josephus, and rabbinic materials. What leads scholars to such different conclusions is more often than not their choice of interpretive models.[8] Some, like Edwards, look at the evidence through the lens of a model that assumes that the ancient economy included at least some of the aspects of a market economy. In contrast, those who perceive Roman, Herodian, and civic elites as driving a thoroughgoing redistribution of income from the masses to themselves utilize very different economic models. The latter scholarly camp deserves considerable credit for generally being more intentional and explicit about their selection and application of models. All scholars, after all, bring their assumptions to the data, and the use of models only makes those assumptions clearer and more subject to challenge and review.

Scholars who argue that urban exploitation of rural Galileans was driving peasants to the point of destitution generally subscribe to lines of reasoning that go back to classical historian Moses Finley[9] and macrosociologists Gerhard Lenski and John Kautsky.[10] All three scholars regarded cities as centers of elite power that facilitate the transfer of resources from the masses. Of the three, Finley has by far been the most influential and received the most attention in classical studies, and for this reason I will focus for a moment primarily on his model of the ancient economy. As it turns out, historians are increasingly questioning Finley's model, and many of their critiques seem quite pertinent for the debate over Galilee.[11]

Galilee: A Demographic Perspective," *JBL* 129 (2010): 343–65. Reed also explored these issues in "Reappraising the Galilean Economy: The Limits of Models, Archaeology, and Analogy," an unpublished conference paper delivered at the 2008 meeting of the Westar Institute.

[8] On this point, see especially Fiensy's thought-provoking discussion in "Assessing the Economy of Galilee." For a broader look at the use of models in historical Jesus research, see F. Gerald Downing, "In Quest of First-Century CE Galilee," *CBQ* 66 (2004): 81–82. Oakman provides a helpful overview of several influential theorists in "The Ancient Economy," in *Jesus and the Peasants*, 53–69.

[9] M. I. Finley, "The Ancient City," *Comparative Studies in Society and History* 19 (1977): 305–27, and *The Ancient Economy* (Berkeley: University of California Press, 1973).

[10] Gerhard E. Lenski, *Power and Privilege: A Theory of Social Stratification* (Chapel Hill: University of North Carolina Press, 1966); Gerhard Lenski and Jean Lenski, *Human Societies: An Introduction to Macrosociology* (4th ed.; Chapel Hill: University of North Carolina Press, 1982); John H. Kautsky, *The Politics of Aristocratic Empires* (Chapel Hill: University of North Carolina Press, 1982). For reviews of their influence, see Douglas E. Oakman, "Models and Archaeology in the Social Interpretation of Jesus," in *Social Scientific Models for Interpreting the Bible: Essays by the Context Group in Honor of Bruce J. Malina* (ed. John J. Pilch; BIS 53; Leiden: Brill, 2001), 102–31; and Dennis C. Duling, "Empire: Theories, Methods, Models," in *The Gospel of Matthew in its Roman Imperial Context* (ed. John Riches and David C. Sim; JSNTSup 276; London: T&T Clark International, 2005), 49–74. On Finley and his influences (especially Karl Polanyi), see Sharon Lea Mattila, "Jesus and the 'Middle Peasants': Challenging a Model of His Socioeconomic Context" (unpublished PhD dissertation, University of Chicago, 2006), 99–141.

[11] Many of the critiques leveled by classicists against Finley (or at least some of the applications of his ideas) seem equally applicable to aspects of the Lenski and Kautsky models, at least as they are applied within NT studies.

Finley argued that ancient cities were parasitical centers of consumption that drained resources from surrounding rural areas. Economic interactions between ancient cities and villages were typically not reciprocal, mutually beneficial, and market driven, with cities selling manufactured goods to villages and villages selling produce to cities. To the contrary, the level of manufacturing in cities was minimal. Rural-urban economic relations were largely redistributive, with the resources of poor rural villagers shifting to rich urban elites through rents and taxation. Although peasants had previously raised just enough food for subsistence, they were now compelled to generate a surplus to feed the cities. In many cases, they were unable to increase agricultural production sufficiently. The result was debt, eventually land loss, and increased poverty. Keith Hopkins later modified Finley's model to emphasize the importance of monetization, market relations, and trade, but he still envisioned the economy as largely redistributive, rather than reciprocal. Hopkins argued that peasants had to sell produce to obtain coins to pay rents and taxes, and provinces had to generate income through exports to pay taxes to Rome.[12] The points of contact between Finley's model, whether in its original or modified form, and the depiction above of exploitative urban-rural relations in Galilee are obvious.

Finley's model has increasingly been challenged because of its inability to encompass the variegated data from the Roman world,[13] so much so that Fiensy rightly summarizes, "In the discipline of classical history, they are now in the post-Finley era."[14] Sharon Lea Mattila comments, "Indeed ancient socioeconomics is perhaps the subject about which there has been the *least* consensus since the appearance of Finley's book in 1973."[15] In his review of the attacks on Finley's model

---

[12] Keith Hopkins, "Rome, Taxes, Rent, and Trade," *Kodai* 6/7 (1995–1996): 41–75; idem, "Taxes and Trade in the Roman Empire," *JRS* 70 (1980): 101–25.

[13] For examples of the onslaught of challenges to the hegemony of Finley's model, see the following: J. G. Manning and Ian Morris, eds., *The Ancient Economy: Evidence and Models* (Palo Alto, CA: Stanford University Press, 2005), especially J. G. Manning, "The Relationship of Evidence to Models in the Ptolemaic Economy (332 BC–30 BC)," 163–85; and Richard Saller, "Framing the Debate over Growth in the Ancient Economy," 223–38; Lukas de Blois and John Rich, eds., *The Transformation of Economic Life under the Roman Empire* (Amsterdam: J. C. Gieben, 2002), especially Lukas de Blois, H. W. Pleket, and John Rich, "Introduction," ix–xx, Peter Fibiger Bang, "Romans and Mughals: Economic Integration in a Tributary Empire," 1–27, and Willem M. Jongman, "The Roman Economy: From Cities to Empire," 28–47; David J. Mattingly and John Salmon, eds., *Economies Beyond Agriculture in the Classical World* (London: Routledge, 2001); Walter Scheidel and Sitta von Reden, eds., *The Ancient Economy* (New York: Routledge, 2002); Walter Scheidel, Ian Morris, and Richard P. Saller, eds., *The Cambridge Economic History of the Greco-Roman World* (Cambridge: Cambridge University Press, 2008); W. V. Harris, "Between Archaic and Modern: Some Current Problems in the History of the Roman Economy," in *The Inscribed Economy: Production and Distribution in the Roman Empire in the Light of* Instrumentum Domesticum (ed. W. V. Harris; Ann Arbor: Journal of Roman Archaeology, 1993), 12–29.

[14] Fiensy, "Assessing the Economy of Galilee."

[15] Mattila, "Jesus and the 'Middle Peasants,'" 111. Mattila questions whether Finley's views ever reigned among classicists, suggesting that scholarship that regards Finley's position as dominant ignores the "'Hundred Year's War' specifically over the subject of ancient socioeconomic relations" (110).

in the 1990s, Ian Morris, who is himself quite sympathetic to Finley's position, dubs one set of objections as the "empiricist critique." Morris writes, "Empiricist studies tend to foreground details at the expense of formal argument and methodological exposition, drawing attention to the richness, variety and irreducible uniqueness of individuals, institutions, and states in the ancient world."[16] Susan E. Alcock echoes this type of critique, arguing that "far more thought needs to be given to the manner in which cultural, ethnic, or religious difference skewed economic choice and behavior in different parts of the Eastern Empire."[17]

Roger S. Bagnall's regional study of Roman Egypt illustrates the complexity of local variations. Thanks to the preservation of so many papyri by its dry climate, Egypt is the Roman province for which we have the most evidence of economic relations. Bagnall's findings differ sharply from what Finley's model would suggest. In his analysis, leasing, credit, and marketing created close ties between city and village, but not all villagers were bad off, and cities were not wholly parasitic. He notes the difficulty of applying an overarching model to this mass of data and to the larger Roman economy.[18]

Similarly, Walter Scheidel emphasizes that Roman cities evolved in different ways and had varying impacts on the surrounding areas.[19] Critiquing the notion that all cities were merely centers of consumption, he writes, "Because of . . . differences in context, it would not make much sense to treat the Greco-Roman or 'ancient' city as a stable and uniform institution or attribute to it a single function or location within a particular system of production as a whole."[20] Scheidel does not completely abandon the Finley model but notes that realities on the ground were more varied and complicated. Suggesting a greater role for markets, reciprocal relations, and artisans, he proposes that cities could simultaneously be both parasites and economic stimuli.

In defense of Finley, he himself recognized the validity of these sorts of critiques. He emphasized that the complexity and variety of ancient economic relations hampered the development of a universally applicable model. "The model must . . . be complicated," he reasoned, "because the isolated city-country unit exists only in very primitive societies or in the imagination of Utopian writers." Commenting further, he noted, "Hypothetically, the economic relationship of a city to its countryside . . . can range over a whole spectrum, from complete para-

---

[16] Ian Morris, "Foreword," in Moses I. Finley, *The Ancient Economy* (updated ed.; Berkeley: University of California Press, 1999), ix–xxxvi, quote from xxvi.

[17] Susan E. Alcock, "The Eastern Mediterranean," in *The Cambridge Economic History of the Greco-Roman World* (ed. Walter Scheidel, Ian Morris, and Richard P. Saller; Cambridge: Cambridge University Press, 2008), 671–97, quote from 696.

[18] Roger S. Bagnall, "Evidence and Models for the Economy of Roman Egypt," in *The Ancient Economy: Evidence and Models* (ed. J. G. Manning and Ian Morris; Palo Alto, CA: Stanford University Press, 2005), 187–204.

[19] Walter Scheidel, "Demography," in *The Cambridge Economic History of the Greco-Roman World* (ed. Walter Scheidel, Ian Morris, and Richard P. Saller; Cambridge: Cambridge University Press, 2008), 38–86.

[20] Ibid., 81.

sitism at one end to full symbiosis at the other."[21] His caveats, however, have not always been given the weight they deserve in recent biblical scholarship.

The following discussion briefly explores the scholarly position that in Jesus' Galilee, exploitation by Roman, Herodian, and civic elites led to large-scale poverty and landlessness among the peasant majority. It does so by focusing on three issues: taxation, monetization, and the role of large agricultural estates. It raises what Ian Harris would call "empiricist critiques," noting that the available data do not unambiguously support conclusions reached primarily through the application of social-scientific models, and it underscores the importance of Galilee's particular historical and political development. Rather than offering definitive answers, it is intended to suggest areas that merit further investigation.

We can begin with a certainty: Galileans paid taxes. But there the certainty ends. Despite attempts to estimate what proportion of Galilean production various types of taxes and tolls consumed, we are largely in the dark about the combined taxation rate.[22] Were there three layers of taxation, one imposed by the Romans, another by Antipas, and a third consisting of the half-shekel tax due annually to the Jerusalem temple?[23] If Rome taxed Galileans, did it do so directly or indirectly, in the latter case by demanding tribute from Antipas, which he paid from the taxes that his own officials collected?

Most scholars who have studied ancient taxation in depth have ruled out rather quickly the possibility that Rome collected some sort of per capita tax (a poll tax or *tributum capitis*) or property tax (*tributum soli*) directly from Galileans in the early first century. Galilee's status as part of a client kingdom would have made such a policy highly unlikely; direct taxation by the Romans presumably would not have occurred until the region passed into the hands of Roman governors mid-century.[24] The more pertinent question is whether or not Rome taxed Galileans indirectly by demanding tribute from Antipas, and if so how often it expected such tribute. Any such demand imposed upon Antipas would have been at least partially passed on to his subjects through his own tax collection system.

The question is difficult to answer because although Josephus includes detailed discussions of occasional tribute paid to Rome—for example, first-century BCE payments from Jerusalem to Julius Caesar—he nowhere indicates that such payments were a regular, recurring phenomenon, a notable silence in light of the remarkable amount of information he provides us about the Herodian dynasty and other client rulers.[25] The second-century CE historian Appian also discusses tribute from client kingdoms, even mentioning Herod the Great, but only in a

---

[21] Finley, *The Ancient Economy*, 125.

[22] Harland compares various views in "The Economy of First-Century Palestine," 521–22.

[23] Horsley, *Archaeology, History, and Society in Galilee*, 78, and *Galilee*, 139.

[24] On the administrative history of Galilee, see Mark A. Chancey, *The Myth of a Gentile Galilee* (Cambridge: Cambridge University Press, 2002), 52.

[25] Fabian E. Udoh discusses the pertinent passages in *To Caesar What Is Caesar's: Tribute, Taxes, and Imperial Administration in Early Roman Palestine (63 BCE–70 CE)* (BJS 343; Providence: Brown Judaic Studies, 2005).

passing reference.[26] Thus, while it is indisputable that client rulers occasionally sent money to Rome, how often they did so is unknown.

It is noteworthy that the two most detailed studies of client kings—by P. C. Sands a century ago and David Braund in 1984—concluded that evidence for regular, annual payment of taxes or tribute by client kings to Rome was lacking.[27] Braund, however, allowed for the possibility that client rulers were expected to send some sort of indemnity payment, if not outright tribute, an argument that K. C. Hanson has rightly characterized as a distinction without a difference.[28] Fabian E. Udoh's recent study of taxation in early Roman Palestine, by far the most thorough treatment of the subject available, came to a similar conclusion as Sands and Braund, arguing that evidence for regular client king payments to Rome was mostly lacking.[29] When wrestling with this issue, interpreters are thus faced with an interesting dilemma: to what extent should they be swayed by particular social-scientific models or cross-cultural comparisons that regard tribute as a fundamental component of imperial rule, and to what extent should they be guided (even limited) by the available evidence—evidence that is itself subject to multiple interpretations? The bottom line is that the impact of Rome's financial expectations of Antipas upon his subjects is extraordinarily difficult to calculate.

Regardless of whether or how often he needed tribute for the Romans, Antipas clearly gathered tax revenue for his own needs. It is his tax collectors that the Gospels depict as so unpopular. Many scholars have sensibly pointed out that Sepphoris and Tiberias would have been the central nodes of Galilee's tax collection system and as such would have generated at least some resentment among the region's many villagers. In addition to per capita taxes and property taxes, Galileans would have had to pay various other taxes, tolls, and duties. But was their combined weight crushing, or at least heavy enough to generate the impression that they were oppressive?

Udoh's comprehensive study is again instructive. When discussing the taxes of Antipas's father, Herod the Great, Udoh cites the long lists of different taxes that one encounters in the scholarly literature: the poll tax, property tax, income tax, salt tax, crown tax, sales tax, fishing tolls, customs duties, occupational taxes. Udoh demonstrates that such lists are often constructed by pulling together references from different regions and historical periods. He writes, "This procedure, which allows each scholar the convenience of [citing] . . . any number of taxes that the scholar might choose from Ptolemaic, Seleucid, and Roman systems of taxation, is obviously arbitrary. It cannot establish within any certainty what taxes

[26] Appian, *Bella Civilia* 5.75.318–319, discussed in Udoh, *To Caesar What Is Caesar's*, 137–43 and Jack Pastor, *Land and Economy in Ancient Palestine* (London: Routledge, 1997), 109–10.

[27] P. C. Sands, *The Client Princes of the Roman Empire* (Cambridge: Cambridge University Press, 1908), 127–39; David Braund, *Rome and the Friendly King: The Character of the Client Kingship* (London: Croom Helm; New York: St. Martin's Press, 1984), 63–66, 184.

[28] K. C. Hanson, "The Galilean Fishing Economy and the Jesus Tradition," *BTB* 27 (1997): 99–111.

[29] Udoh, *To Caesar What Is Caesar's*.

were actually paid" in the time of Herod.[30] The same point is true when discussing the taxes of Antipas. Some of the types of taxes identified above were collected, but which ones, how many, and what was their combined weight? Because the evidence itself does not tell us, any proposed tabulations of the overall tax burden are dictated to a considerable degree by the choice of interpretive models.

The economic impact of Antipas's building projects is likewise difficult to assess. The rebuilt Sepphoris and the young Tiberias were indeed the largest cities that Galilee had ever seen, and they introduced Greco-Roman architecture into the region on a new scale. Archeological evidence for their growth is abundant, especially for Sepphoris. But that evidence demonstrates that the growth of their populations and cityscapes occurred gradually and that their architectural heyday was in the second century, not the first.[31] Their costs of construction must have been substantial, but we need not imagine that building expenses were covered solely by tax revenues and tolls. As Jonathan L. Reed has pointed out, Antipas may well have had royal land that grew dates and balsam, and we know practically nothing about his possessions in Perea. He might also have relied upon the euergetism of local elites to defray his costs.[32]

Although the topic of the temple tax leads us away from our focus on Galilean urban-rural relations, a brief comment is merited because of the frequency with which it appears in discussions of Galilee's tax burden and economic conditions. It is sometimes claimed that the annual half-shekel tax paid to the Jerusalem temple was an alien burden forced upon Galileans a century earlier by their Hasmonean conquerors and thus a relatively recent introduction that would have generated popular resentment.[33] We need not enter into the full thicket of issues regarding perceptions of the tax, the proportion of the population that paid it, and the extent to which it exacerbated economic difficulties; stories such as that of Peter and the coin-dispensing fish clearly indicate that the question of whether to pay it was a matter of discussion (Matt 17:24–27). But the archaeological evidence does shed light on one aspect of the debate. It is increasingly clear that the majority of first-century CE Galileans were not descendents of ancient Israelites whose roots went back to the Northern Kingdom or descendents of pagans who dwelled in the region in the Ptolemaic and Seleucid periods.[34] Galilee had been largely depopulated after the Assyrian conquest in the eighth century BCE, severing any significant linkage between the ancient Israelite population and the later population. The

---

[30] Ibid., 160.

[31] Chancey, *Greco-Roman Culture*; Reed, "Instability in Jesus' Galilee," 343. As Alcock notes, such growth was the norm throughout the Roman East in the second century ("Eastern Mediterranean," 686).

[32] Reed, "Reappraising the Galilean Economy." Euergetistic inscriptions from this period are notably lacking, however.

[33] Horsley in numerous publications (for example, *Jesus and Empire*, 60).

[34] Chancey, *Myth of a Gentile Galilee*, and "Archaeology, Ethnicity, and First-Century CE Galilee: The Limits of Evidence," in *A Wandering Galilean: Essays in Honour of Sean Freyne* (ed. Zuleika Rodgers with Margaret Daly-Denton and Anne Fitzpatrick McKinley; JSJSup 132; Leiden: Brill, 2009), 205–18; Jonathan L. Reed, *Archaeology and the Galilean Jesus: A Re-examination of the Evidence* (Harrisburg, PA: Trinity Press International, 2000).

Hasmonean conquest in the late second or (more likely) early first century BCE had also resulted in significant populations shifts. Many of the region's Gentile inhabitants appear to have left, and new settlers from Judea arrived, thrived, and multiplied. Surveys and excavations show that many Roman-period settlements had their origins in the Hasmonean period. Galilean Jews in the time of Jesus thus had a southern orientation that dated back to the arrival of Judean colonists under the Hasmoneans. Those colonists brought the temple tax with them from Judea when they moved northwards. The temple tax was a natural part of the Jewish Galilean orientation, not something new imposed upon a forcibly converted pagan population or an older northern Israelite population.

Questions regarding taxation are closely tied to questions about monetization. Some scholars have argued that Antipas facilitated the region's monetization in order to expedite tax collection and the creation of debt.[35] Antipas was indeed the first ruler to strike coins in Galilee.[36] Because his coins were bronze rather than silver, they functioned economically as small change, not as the basis for large monetized payments. Their primary purpose, in fact, must have been political. First and foremost, they advertised Antipas's stature as a significant client ruler. Some bore inscriptions referring to Tiberias, epigraphically proclaiming his creation of a new city and underscoring his loyalty to the emperor for whom that city was named. These coins were important as propaganda, but archeology suggests that there were not very many of them—too few, in fact, to have been any sort of common currency for first-century Galilee. Older Hasmonean coins continued to be the primary source of bronze, and Tyre (and to a lesser extent, Sidon) provided the region's silver. Therefore, Antipas's minting activities did not significantly hasten the process of monetization. The introduction of Hasmonean coinage a century earlier had already had a much greater effect, though even in the Common Era bartering and payments in kind still played significant roles in the economy. Increases in coinage in the second and third centuries CE moved the region further along the scale toward monetization.[37] The timing of increased monetization corresponds to the significant increase in the number of Roman troops stationed in Palestine, with one legion remaining in Jerusalem after the first revolt and a second headquartered in the Jezreel Valley in the early second century. Because Roman troops were paid with silver, an influx of troops resulted in a corresponding influx in silver and, in turn, a need for more bronze to use as small change.[38] In

---

[35] William E. Arnal, *Jesus and the Village Scribes* (Minneapolis: Fortress, 2001); John Dominic Crossan and Jonathan L. Reed, *Excavating Jesus: Beneath the Stones, Behind the Texts* (San Francisco: HarperSanFrancisco, 2001), 69–70; Herzog, *Parables as Subversive Speech*, 72, 206; Herzog, *Jesus, Justice, and the Reign of God*, 106.

[36] Chancey, *Greco-Roman Culture and the Galilee of Jesus*, 166–92; Jensen, *Herod Antipas*, 187–217.

[37] Jensen, *Herod Antipas*, 203–17, making good use of Danny Syon, "Tyre and Gamla: A Study in the Monetary Influence of Southern Phoenicia on Galilee and the Golan in the Hellenistic and Roman Periods" (unpublished PhD dissertation, Hebrew University [Jerusalem] 2004); Chancey, *Greco-Roman Culture and the Galilee of Jesus*, 166–92.

[38] Jonathan Roth, "The Army and the Economy in Judaea and Palestine," in *The Roman Army and the Economy* (ed. Paul Erdkamp; Amsterdam: J. C. Gieben, 2002), 375–97; cf. Con-

light of this larger set of evidence about monetary patterns in Galilee, the suggestion that Antipas's minting activities radically shifted the methods and amount of tax collection or the processes of debt creation appears inaccurate.[39]

The issue of monetization is closely tied to that of land ownership.[40] Key questions include: the role of city-based land owners and creditors; the relative number of small landowners who lost their farms because of inability to pay taxes, tolls, and other debts; the rate at which such small property owners became tenant farmers, seasonal workers, day laborers, desperation-driven artisans, slaves, and social bandits; and the extent to which Galilee was commercialized, with fields that had once been devoted to polycropping for the purposes of feeding families and villages now converted to monocropping to assure adequate food for the cities and maximum profits for large estate owners.[41] On all of these points, as it turns out, the Galilean evidence is more ambiguous than is often acknowledged, as a consideration of the overarching topic of large agricultural estates demonstrates.

The Zenon papyri, a collection of documents from the third century BCE, attest to large agricultural estates in Ptolemaic Galilee. Scholars have sometimes proposed that the pattern of landholdings from that period would have remained steady as Galilee shifted hands to the Seleucids, then to the Hasmoneans, and then to the Herodian dynasty, with the result that large estates stayed mostly intact over the centuries. In light of what we now know about settlement patterns in Galilee, however, this seems unlikely. The Hasmonean conquest would have significantly disrupted patterns of property ownership. After the Hasmoneans' arrival, some older communities were abandoned, others were taken over by Jewish colonists, and numerous new communities sprang up. Such changes pose insurmountable difficulties for those who would rely on early Hellenistic papyri to understand the early Roman period.

As for the first century CE itself, literary sources offer ample evidence for large estates at various places throughout Palestine, particularly at the time of the revolt.[42] Josephus, for example, held land near Jerusalem (*Vita* 422, 429), and

---

stantina Katsari, "The Monetization of the Roman Frontier Provinces," in *The Monetary Systems of the Greeks and Romans* (ed. W. V. Harris; Oxford: Oxford University Press, 2008), 242–67.

[39] The chronological pattern is similar to that of Commagene, where client rulers produced a modest amount of bronze coins, but the number of coins multiplied dramatically after full Roman annexation. See Margherita Facella, "The Economy and Coinage of Commagene (First Century BC–First Century AD)," in *Patterns in the Economy of Roman Asia Minor* (ed. Stephen Mitchell and Constantina Katsari; Swansea: The Classical Press of Wales, 2005), 225–50.

[40] For example, Crossan and Reed, *Excavating Jesus*, 69; Hanson and Oakman, *Palestine in the Time of Jesus*, 95–99; John S. Kloppenborg, *The Tenants in the Vineyard: Ideology, Economics, and Agrarian Conflict in Jewish Palestine* (WUNT 195; Tübingen: Mohr Siebeck, 2006), 284–313; Sean Freyne, *A Jewish Galilean* (London: T&T Clark, 2004), 44–45.

[41] The claim of "commercializion" and the resultant reorientation of Galilee's agriculture from polycropping to monocropping reflects Kautsky's influence; see Crossan, *Birth of Christianity*, 157–59, 229–30; Crossan and Reed, *Excavating Jesus*, 54, 61, 69–70, 114–15; and Herzog, *Parables as Subversive Speech*, 72 and 206.

[42] Fiensy, *Social History of Palestine*, 21–73; Kloppenborg, *Tenants in the Vineyard*, 284–313; Pastor, *Land and Economy*.

Crispus, a Herodian official from Tiberias, had estates beyond the Jordan (*Vita* 33). For Galilee itself and the adjacent areas, however, the evidence is more limited. Antipas would have had royal possessions in Galilee, though their size and location is unknown. The fact that Queen Berenice had grain stored at Beth She'arim (*Vita* 119–120) in southwestern Galilee may indicate the proximity of a royal estate, and Fiensy suggests that much of the Jezreel Valley, just south of Galilee, would have been royal land and large estates.[43] A reference to imperial granaries at Gischala may signify that an imperial estate was located in that part of Upper Galilee (*Vita* 71–73). If so, its presence would not be entirely surprising, since the Romans had by that time assumed direct control of the area; alternatively, rather than the harvest of imperial land, Josephus could have had in-kind taxes produced by villagers in mind. Rabbinic materials from subsequent centuries refer to large estates, although they suggest a predominance of small landholdings.[44] And, of course, there are Jesus' parables, which presuppose that listeners would have been familiar with large agricultural estates.

Archeological finds also indicate the presence of large land holdings in the larger region of Palestine.[45] The most famous example is provided by the numerous field towers built at regular intervals in Samaria in the third century BCE. Their systematic distribution over a large area strongly suggests that they were overseen by governing authorities. Many were still in use centuries later in the early Common Era, but their ownership by then is unclear.[46] Other evidence comes in the form of spacious rural villas, most of which would have been associated with sizable landholdings. The nearest first-century example is a fortified residence at Ramat Ha-Nadiv, northeast of Caesarea Maritima, that was abandoned around the time of the Jewish revolt.[47] Such villas were more the exception than the rule for much of the Roman East; as Alcock notes, they were far less common there than in western parts of the empire like Italy.[48]

---

[43] Fiensy, *Jesus the Galilean*, 43–45.

[44] Zéev Safrai, *The Economy of Roman Palestine* (London: Routledge, 1994), 322–28.

[45] In addition to Fiensy, Kloppenborg, and Pastor, see Safrai, *The Economy of Roman Palestine*, 85–99, and Yizhar Hirschfeld, "Jewish Rural Settlement in Judaea in the Early Roman Period," in *The Early Roman Empire in the East* (ed. Susan E. Alcock; Oxford: Oxbow, 1997), 72–88.

[46] Shimon Dar, *Landscape and Pattern: An Archaeological Survey of Samaria 800 BCE– 636 CE* (BAR International Series 308; Oxford: BAR, 1986), 88–125.

[47] Yizhar Hirschfeld, "Ramat Ha-Nadiv," in *The New Encyclopedia of Archaeological Excavations* (ed. Ephraim Stern et al.; Jerusalem: Israel Exploration Society, Washington, DC: Biblical Archaeology Society, 2008), 5:2004–6. Hirschfeld also identifies several settlements in the Dead Sea region (including Qumran) as agricultural estates in *Qumran in Context: Reassessing the Archaeological Evidence* (Peabody, MA: Hendrickson, 2004), 211–30. On later evidence, see Yizhar Hirschfeld, "Farms and Villages in Byzantine Palestine," *Dumbarton Oaks Papers* 51 (1997): 33–71.

[48] Alcock, "The Eastern Mediterranean," 686; cf. Alexandra Chavarrîa and Tamara Lewit, "Archaeological Research on the Late Antique Countryside," in *Recent Research on the Late Antique Countryside* (ed. William Bowden, Luke Lavan, and Carlos Machado; Late Antique Archaeology 2; Leiden: Brill, 2004), 3–51, esp. 19–20.

Despite the extensive archaeological work undertaken in Galilee in recent decades, however, no first-century CE large estates or rural villas have been discovered there. Reviews of published excavation reports simply turn up short in this regard. Perhaps the most significant data for this point is the recently published survey of Uzi Leibner. Leibner's team surveyed an area of approximately 285 square kilometers in eastern Lower Galilee, identifying fifty settlement sites north and west of Tiberias. "It should . . . be noted," he observed, "that none of the small sites seem like an estate or a villa."[49] It is precisely this lack of specifically Galilean data that has caused Fiensy to reconsider his earlier arguments about the pervasiveness of such estates.[50]

Nor are dramatic shifts in ownership patterns, with debt causing small farms with diverse crops to be absorbed into large estates devoted primarily to mono-cropping, the only way to explain how the modest-sized cities of Sepphoris and Tiberias were fed. As the population of Galilee grew, so did the areas settled and the areas cultivated. Here again, Leibner's survey is instructive, tracing in vivid detail both the explosion in the number of rural sites and their growth in size.[51] Part of the explanation for how sufficient food was produced for the new cities is simply that agricultural productivity increased as more land was farmed. This general pattern—growing population, new settlements, new cultivation, higher productivity—is paralleled elsewhere in the empire at this time as well.[52] If large estates were less numerous in Galilee than is often speculated, the proposal that profit-motivated monocropping by large landholders was to a large degree replacing the polycropping of smallholders is seriously undermined. It is worth empha-sizing that the primary source for the theory of extensive monocropping is neither archeological data nor ancient literary references but anthropological theory.[53] Furthermore, while it is true that literary sources attest to large estates, sources at-test to the continuation of smaller farms as well.[54] My point is not to argue for the absence of large estates in Galilee, which would be an untenable position in light of the parables, but to point out the how little we know about the precise role they played in land ownership and economic patterns.[55]

---

[49] Uzi Leibner, *Settlement and History in Hellenistic, Roman, and Byzantine Galilee* (TSAJ 127; Tübingen: Mohr Siebeck, 2009), 348; cf. Safrai, *The Economy of Roman Pales-tine*, 95–96.

[50] Fiensy, "Assessing the Economy of Galilee."

[51] Leibner, *Settlement and History*; see also Rafael Frankel, Nimrod Getzov, Mordechai Aviam, and Avi Degani, *Settlement Dynamics and Regional Diversity in Ancient Upper Gali-lee: Archaeological Survey of Upper Galilee* (IAA Reports 14; Jerusalem: Antiquities Author-ity, 2001), 110–14.

[52] Alcock, "Eastern Mediterranean," 678–82; cf. Elio Lo Cascio, "The Early Roman Em-pire: The State and the Economy," in *The Cambridge Economic History of the Greco-Roman World* (ed. Walter Scheidel, Ian Morris, and Richard P. Saller; Cambridge: Cambridge Uni-versity Press, 2007), 619–47, esp. 619.

[53] On the lack of evidence for monocropping, cf. Jensen, *Herod Antipas*, 249 n. 208, and especially the important discussion in Gary Gilbert's review of Crossan and Reed, *Excavat-ing Jesus*, posted in June 2003 at *RBL* (www.bookreviews.org).

[54] See especially Safrai's examination of rabbinic sources in *The Economy of Roman Palestine*.

[55] The cautious approach to this issue modeled by Pastor and Fiensy, who emphasize the gaps in our evidence, seems well warranted. See Pastor, *Land and Economy*, and Fiensy,

This review of taxation, monetization, and large estates has been painted in admittedly broad strokes, with complicated issues addressed with only brief treatments. Nonetheless, even a brief investigation like this one suggests that many of the claims that we so often take for granted—claims of economic oppression, heavy taxation, land consolidation, and so forth—have less concrete support in the evidence than is often supposed. The problem is not that these claims are inherently unreasonable; they are plausible and may well be correct. The problem, in my opinion, is that they are sometimes held too confidently, when other interpretive options are also possible and might even make better sense of the empirical data. The fact that claims of thoroughgoing deprivation are far from proven does not necessarily mean that claims of widespread economic prosperity are accurate, either. At this point, we simply do not know. Given the messy and incomplete state of our evidence, it is perhaps understandable that such different understandings of the Galilean economy should stand side by side in the literature. As Finley insightfully noted on another issue, "These are all arguments from silence, it will be objected, to which I reply that, given the nature of the sources, the issue comes down to how we interpret the silence."[56]

Returning to the parables and the extent to which they illuminate economic conditions in Galilee: The question is not whether or not there were *any* city-dwelling absentee landlords, *any* large estates, *any* day laborers, *any* tenant farmers—clearly there were; the Bible tells us so. The question, to reiterate, is one of scale. How widespread were these phenomena? How typical were they? How did the emergence of cities contribute to their development? How was the activity of Jesus related to them?

The critiques above should not be interpreted as a broad indictment of the use of models. As noted earlier, every scholar brings some sort of interpretive lens to the data, and the deliberate use of models serves an important function by making the nature of that lens clearer for all, as well as by often facilitating a more rigorous assessment of the data. Problems arise, however, when the choice of model predetermines the interpretive outcome. As Jensen has admirably demonstrated, when a scholar examines Galilee through the lens of a model built upon the foundational assumption that urban elites redistributed wealth from peasants to themselves through rent and taxes, it is no surprise that she or he finds exactly that. With many such models, Jensen observes, "Too much is explained with too little."[57] Similarly, Fiensy stresses the importance and usefulness of models but also comments, "The model should not become 'proxy data.'" He explains, "Proxy data, as I understand them, are constructing hypothetical scenarios not supplied by the ancient evidence but by 'likelihood, analogy, or comparison.'"[58] What is needed

---

"Assessing the Economy of Galilee," "Ancient Economy and the New Testament," and *Jesus the Galilean.*

[56] Finley, *The Ancient Economy*, 136.

[57] Jensen, *Herod Antipas*, 259.

[58] Fiensy, "Assessing the Economy of Galilee," quoting Jean Andreau, "Twenty Years after Moses I. Finley's *Ancient Economy*," in *The Ancient Economy* (ed. Walter Scheidel and Sitta von Reden; New York: Routledge, 2002), 33–49. See also David A. Fiensy, review of

is not only a full-scale sifting of the literary and archaeological data but also a rigorous comparison of the strengths, weaknesses, and applicability of competing economic models.

The investigation of ancient economics is in flux. There is a general recognition that a universalizing model is problematic, and it is not clear what is going to replace the old orthodoxy of the parasitic city. As one scholar has observed, "At present the study of the ancient economy might be compared to a minefield, full of perils for the unsuspecting scholar."[59] The perils are no less great even for the suspecting scholar who ventures into the contested terrain of economic conditions in Galilee. For all we have learned about Galilee in the third quest, economics and urban-rural relations still pose the most difficult questions to answer.

Palestine in the Time of Jesus: Social Structure and Social Conflicts, by K. C. Hanson and Douglas E. Oakman, eds., *CBQ* 70 (2008): 842–44.

[59] Morris Silver, review of Scheidel and von Reden, *The Ancient Economy*, in EHNet, posted January 2003 at http://eh.net/book_reviews/ancient-economy.

5

CHILDREN IN HOUSE CHURCHES IN LIGHT OF NEW RESEARCH ON FAMILIES IN THE ROMAN WORLD

Margaret Y. MacDonald

Over the past decade, there have been several important studies on early Christian families.[1] Given that the primary meeting place for early Christian groups was the "house" until at least 150 CE (by the end of the second century houses began to be remodeled into buildings specifically for worship), scholars have sought to understand how various forms of domestic architecture may have influenced church spaces and community life in the regions where early Christianity arose.[2] With no extant archeological evidence from this early period that allows confident identification of particular house churches (early evidence is disputed), scholars have relied on wide-ranging evidence concerning domestic space and investigations by experts on the interaction between domestic space and social identity. There have been studies on family relations generally, as well as works on slaves and women. Children, however, have received comparatively little attention.

Existing monographs on children and childhood in early Christianity—and they are not very numerous—contain important insights but mainly take the form of surveys and reflect diffuse interests (understandable, given the preliminary stage

---

[1] See especially Carolyn Osiek and David L. Balch, *Families in the New Testament World: Households and House Churches* (Louisville: Westminster John Knox, 1997); Halvor Moxnes, ed., *Constructing Early Christian Families: Family as Social Reality and Metaphor* (London: Routledge, 1997); Geoffrey S. Nathan, *The Family in Late Antiquity* (London: Routledge, 2000); Jan Willem Van Henten and Athalya Brenner, eds., *Family and Family Relations as Represented in Early Judaisms and Early Christianities: Texts and Fictions* (Leiden: Deo, 2000); David L. Balch and Carolyn Osiek, eds., *Early Christian Families in Context: An Interdisciplinary Dialogue* (Grand Rapids: Eerdmans, 2003); Carolyn Osiek and Margaret Y. MacDonald, with Janet Tulloch, *A Woman's Place: House Churches in Earliest Christianity* (Minneapolis: Fortress, 2006).

[2] On the evolution of the house church, see especially Michael L. White, *The Social Origins of Christian Architecture,* vol. 1: *Building God's House in the Roman World: Architectural Adaption Among Pagans, Jews, and Christians;* vol. 2: *Texts and Monuments for the Christian Domus Ecclesiae and Its Environment* (Valley Forge, PA: Trinity Press International, 1996–1997).

of scholarship).[3] Detailed, textually specific treatments are just now beginning to appear.[4] But in general, works on children and childhood in the New Testament era lack the sophisticated attention to context that has been a trademark of scholarship on early Christian families—scholarship that has frequently benefited from interdisciplinary exchanges, especially with historians of the Roman family. My main goal in this chapter is to explore some promising lines of enquiry with respect to how this rich interdisciplinary perspective and focus on families in context can shed light on children in house churches. It will be important to consider not only how children in house churches contributed to the development of early Christianity but also how, in turn, childhood was influenced by participation in early church communities.[5] In the final section of the chapter, I will concentrate on one specific body of early Christian evidence from the early period (50–150 CE) found in several NT and apostolic father works, the familial ethical discourse, commonly known as the household codes (Col 3:18–4:1; Eph 5:21–6:9; 1 Pet 2:18–3:7; 1 Tim 2:8–15; 5:1–2; 6:1–2; Titus 2:1–10; *Did.* 4:9–11; *Barn.* 19:5–7; *1 Clem.* 21:6–9; Ign. *Pol.* 4:1–5:2; Pol. *Phil.* 4:2–3). I will argue that a focus on children and childhood can lead to new insight with respect to the significance of the inclusion of these codes in early Christian texts and the impact of the codes in community life.[6]

Families and Household Space

Thorough investigation of children and childhood in early Christianity calls for a focus on context—the life of house churches—to be at the center of investigation, in much the same way as the 1997 study by Carolyn Osiek and David L. Balch on families in the NT world placed this concern with context at the center.[7] Part of the challenge with respect to understanding families in the NT era involves the need to investigate Jewish and Greek families of the Hellenistic era as well as

---

[3] See, for example, Peter Müller, *In der Mitte der Gemeinde: Kinder im Neuen Testament* (Neukirchen-Vluyn: Neukirchener, 1992); W. A. Strange, *Children in the Early Church: Children in the Ancient World, the New Testament, and the Early Church* (Carlisle: Paternoster, 1996); Peter Balla, *The Child-Parent Relationship in the New Testament and Its Environment* (WUNT 155; Tübingen: Mohr Siebeck, 2003); O. M. Bakke, *When Children Became People: The Birth of Childhood in Early Christianity* (trans. Brian McNeil; Minneapolis: Fortress, 2005); Cornelia B. Horn and John W. Martens, *"let the little children come to me": Childhood and Children in Early Christianity* (Washington, DC: The Catholic University Press of America, 2009).

[4] See, for example, Reidar Aasgaard, "Paul as a Child: Children and Childhood in the Letters of the Apostle," *JBL* 126 (2007): 129–69; Reidar Aasgaard, *The Childhood of Jesus: Decoding the Apocryphal Infancy Gospel of Thomas* (Eugene, OR: Cascade Books, 2009); Marcia J. Bunge, ed., *The Child in the Bible* (Grand Rapids: Eerdmans, 2008).

[5] For preliminary work on this topic see chapters on infancy and childhood in Osiek and MacDonald, *A Woman's Place.*

[6] For a more detailed treatment of children in the household codes of Colossians and Ephesians, see Margaret Y. MacDonald, "A Place of Belonging," in *The Child in the Bible* (ed. Marcia J. Bunge; Grand Rapids: Eerdmans, 2008), 278–304.

[7] See Osiek and Balch, *Families in the New Testament World.*

Roman families, including families of the eastern Mediterranean world in regions that were more or less Romanized. Scholars of early Christianity need to take account of recent scholarship about housing in the Roman era,[8] informed by the growing understanding of the interaction between Greek and Roman influences, the varying degrees of Romanization in the provinces, and the sometimes uneasy relationship between public space and private space, with implications for gender constructions and the lives of women.[9] The archeological evidence for house churches later than our era gives us a sense of the difficulty of drawing implications for the important participation of women; artistic and inscriptional evidence suggests female leadership and patronage, but the existence of separate rooms, courtyard benches, and the placement of inscriptions may indicate some separation of men and women during worship—also implied by some early Christian texts, though all later than the NT era (e.g., third-century *Didascalia Apostolorum* XII).[10] By the first century CE it is was common for Roman women to join their husbands at dinner parties in contrast to earlier Greek times; but we must also allow for local variation and perhaps more traditional practices in some eastern regions when seeking to understand the options for women and children participating in the meetings of the house church, which involved a common meal.

Of particular importance when we think about house churches is that the usual modern western division between private domestic space associated with private homes, and outside public, work space associated with the workplace is not applicable to this ancient context. Workshops and businesses were often closely linked to domestic quarters, and even the grandest of houses made room for the regular and formal visits of clients to their patrons, as institutionalized elements of the daily routine. It is very misleading to think of the modern nuclear family when trying to envision ancient households, which perhaps more closely resemble nineteenth-century southern plantations or modern urban family businesses.[11] Kinship (relations between husbands and wives, children and parents, brothers and sisters) was important in ancient households, but the inclusion of slaves in family life and the ongoing involvement of former slaves, clients, and dependent workers mean that we must think of the house church infrastructure as one that was set up for a broad

---

[8]See Michele George, "*Servus* and *domus*: The Slave in the Roman Household," in *Domestic Space in the Roman World: Pompeii and Beyond* (ed. A. Wallace-Hadrill and R. Laurence; Portsmouth, RI: Journal of Roman Archaeology Supplementary Series 22, 1997), 15–24; idem, "Domestic Architecture and Household Relations: Pompeii and Romans Ephesos," *JSNT* 27 (2004): 7–25; Andrew Wallace-Hadrill, *Houses and Society in Pompeii and Herculaneum* (Princeton: Princeton University Press, 1994); idem, "Domus and Insulae in Rome: Families and Housefuls," in *Early Christian Families in Context* (ed. David L. Balch and Carolyn Osiek; Grand Rapids: Eerdmans, 2003), 3–18.

[9]See L. Nevett, *House and Society in the Ancient Greek World* (Cambridge: Cambridge University Press, 1999); Shelley Hales, *The Roman House and Social Identity* (Cambridge: Cambridge University Press, 2009).

[10]See discussion in Rainer Riesner in "What Does Archaeology Teach Us about House Churches?" *Tidsskrift for Teologi og Kirche* 78 (2007): 159–85, here 168.

[11]Charles H. Talbert, *Ephesians and Colossians* (Paideia Commentaries on the New Testament; Grand Rapids: Baker Academic, 2007), 151.

enterprise. This has important implications for the involvement of children, who would have been present at every activity. As will be discussed further below, even the ideological divide between slave and free often had little bearing on the lives of children, as free and slave children were frequently raised together by the slave caregivers and found in the spaces where slaves lived and worked.

Economic, civic, and religious interests cannot be clearly distinguished in the ancient household. In addition to the close association of shops and rooms for entertaining clients, homes of Gentiles typically included small shrines known as *lorariums*, where offerings were made to the *Lares* (household spirits), to Vesta (goddess of the hearth), and to the *genius* (the guardian spirit of the family), and wall paintings depicting mythological stories.[12] This merging of religious, familial, and what we would think of as broadly political interests can also be seen in Jewish evidence from the period. To offer one example from textual evidence, when Flavius Josephus wrote his apologetic work to illustrate the respectability and civility of the Jewish population, he argued that marriage between Jews under the law was a central feature of identity, closely tied to the Jewish conception of God and the temple (*Ag. Ap.* 2.190–203).

The earliest house church that we can identify with certainty is usually understood to be the third-century house church at Dura Europos (the House of St. Peter at Capernaum is very difficult to evaluate though its identity as the earliest house church continues to be defended by some scholars).[13] Because of the lack of definite archeological evidence for early house churches, it must be admitted that scholars of early Christianity differ in how they envision the nature of household space. In light of the lack of definitive evidence for the early period, it is probably best to remain open to a variety of possibilities. Moreover, textual evidence as a whole (Christian, Jewish, and Greco-Roman) often makes it difficult to determine what type of housing is envisioned because the "house" terminology of Greek *oikos, oikia,* and Latin *domus* are terms that could refers to house buildings (physical dwellings) of various kinds but also to households, including material goods and slaves, as well as immediate family or even to family lineage.

---

[12] On how these various features of ancient households can help us to understand the lives of NT characters see Richard A. Ascough, *Lydia: Paul's Cosmopolitan Hostess* (Collegeville, MN: Liturgical Press, 2009), 34–35.

[13] See the valuable survey of the archeological evidence by Riesner in "What Does Archaeology Teach Us about House Churches?" He identifies one example as certain (Dura Europos), one recent discovery (Kefar Othnay near Megiddo), and three other cases as disputed (House of Leontis, Beth Shean; House of Peter, Capernaum, Cenacle Building, Jerusalem). Riesner favors the position of some scholars that the House of Peter has indeed been uncovered at Capernaum and represents the earliest house church (174–78). But this remains disputed by White (see n. 2 above) and Peter Richardson, "Architectural Transitions from Synagogues and House Churches to Purpose-Built Churches," in *Common Life in the Early Church: Essays Honoring Graydon F. Snyder* (ed. J. V. Hills; Harrisburg, PA: Trinity Press International, 1998), 373–89, here 387, among others. For a survey that deals with regions associated with Pauline Christianity, such as Corinth, see Bradley Blue, "Acts and the House Church," in *The Book of Acts in Its Greco-Roman Setting* (ed. W. J. Gill and Conrad Gempf; vol. 2 of *The Book of Acts in Its First-Century Setting* (ed. Bruce Winter; Grand Rapids: Eerdmans, 1994), 119–221.

In Roman law a *domus* was any place where a property owner (a *paterfamilias*) resided. Often the term *familia* is employed to refer to all the persons and objects under the legal power (*patria postestas*) of the *paterfamilias* rather than the nuclear group implied by the English term "family." One of the most remarkable features of this hierarchal, property-based system is that sometimes the male term for property owner (*paterfamilias*) was retained even in cases where the property owner was a woman—such as in the case of some wealthy, independent widows.[14] Emphasis on control of property, including ownership of individual persons, is central to the concept of *oikonomia* ("household management"). The NT household codes (e.g., Col 3:18–4:1) are a form of household management ethics (see below) that have much in common with ancient notions of the organization of the household and its civic and religious significance for the good of society as a whole.

In thinking about the specific types of houses involved in NT communities, there is some evidence that some of the first believers met in very modest apartment houses, in rooms above shops of various kinds. This is implied by the scene in Troas (Acts 20:7–12) discussed further below, but also perhaps by the placement of Tabitha on a bier in an upper room (Acts 9:37, 39 cf. Acts 1:13).[15] Acts points to other housing possibilities, however, suggesting reasonable-size houses. The mother of John Mark seems both to manage her own household and to host a house church; she has a house large enough to host a good number (*hikanoi*) of the believing community.[16] In my work with Carolyn Osiek on women in house churches, we argued in favor of a variety of possibilities, writing the following:

> We need first to talk about what kinds of houses are envisioned. . . . Some Christian groups must certainly have met in more modest accommodations, even in some grimier apartment houses (*insulae*) or "tenement churches," as Robert Jewett has called them. But there is no reason, given the ample evidence of the ownership of some rather spacious houses of Pompeii by persons of modest social status but less modest wealth, why groups of worshipping Christians, like their Jewish and Mithraist neighbors, could not have met is a peristlyled *domus* (a building featuring a colonnade). It seems best to leave open the possibility of a variety of different configurations for house-church meetings in the early years at least. The households of Stephanas and of Prisca and Aquila in Corinth (1 Cor 16:15, 19) are likely to have been *domus*, even if ever so modest. "Those from Chloe" (1 Cor 1:11) may have been messengers to Paul in Ephesus, therefore away from home in Corinth, but they may also be members of a gathering in more modest circumstances, since no household (*oikos*) of Chloe is mentioned. In the case of this group, however, it is also possible that Chloe herself is not a Christian but a large number of her household are.[17]

---

[14] Osiek and MacDonald, *A Woman's Place*, 154–55. See Richard P. Saller, "*Pater Familias, Mater Familias*, and the Gendered Semantics of the Roman Household," *CP* 94:182–97.

[15] On upper rooms as assembly halls in Acts, see Riesner, "What Does Archaeology Teach Us about House Churches?" 181.

[16] Ascough has argued that Lydia probably lived in "at least a medium-sized house." See *Lydia*, 33–35, esp. 34.

[17] Osiek and MacDonald, *A Woman's Place*, 10–11. See also Osiek and Balch, *Families in the New Testament World*, 5–6.

Ideally, when the material evidence permits, one should try to link texts to the particular housing possibilities found in particular geographic centers. Recent debate concerning Corinth, for example, is instructive both for illustrating the variety of possibilities and for demonstrating how scholars may have been too quick to neglect very modest arrangements in considering the house-church setting.

The extent to which members of the Corinthian congregation participated in the life of the Roman villa with triclinium and atrium or peristyle, even given the reference to the seemingly well-to-do Gaius who is a "host to the whole church" (1 Cor 14:23; Rom 16:23), is a subject of debate. In part, this is because the dating and significance of archeological evidence at Corinth remains uncertain.[18] But it is also because significant scholarly discussion continues, especially since Justin Meggit's challenge to the "new consensus" rooted in the work of Gerd Theissen and others, about the social status of the Corinthians.[19] This "new consensus," which is still upheld by many scholars, posits a social diversity with some members coming from the more well-to-do and the majority from the lower social status. While many are not prepared to accept Meggitt's description of the social location of the Corinthians as that of absolute poverty,[20] at the very least, as David Horrell notes, "Meggitt has forcefully highlighted how little firm evidence there is to identify any of the Corinthian Christians known to us as elite, wealthy, aristocratic or upper class."[21]

For our purposes, the question of what type of space might have functioned as a house church is perhaps less important than the diversity of experiences of domestic space shared by the socially diverse members of house-church communities. For example, the slaves associated with a villa like that at Anaploga (one of the few houses excavated at Corinth with some parts at least going back to Paul's era) might well have found themselves at church meetings in other very different quarters, such as the buildings east of the theater, which seem to have been comprised of butchery kitchens with families residing in second- or possibly third-story, one- or two-room dwellings.[22]

---

[18] See especially David G. Horrell, "Domestic Space and Christian Meetings at Corinth: Imagining New Contexts and the Buildings East of the Theatre," *NTS* 50 (2004): 349–69. Horrell critiques the influential work of Jerome Murphy-O'Connor that associates house church life with the Roman villa. See Jerome Murphy-O'Connor, *St. Paul's Corinth: Texts and Archaeology* (3rd rev. and expanded ed.; Collegeville, MN: Liturgical Press, 2002).

[19] Justin J. Meggitt, *Paul, Poverty, and Survival* (Edinburgh: T&T Clark, 1998).

[20] See, for example, D. B. Martin, "Review Essay: Justin J. Meggitt, *Paul, Poverty, and Survival,*" *JSNT* 84 (2001): 51–64.

[21] Horrell, "Domestic Space and Christian Meetings at Corinth," 358. According to Horrell, Meggitt's critique of the identification of Erastus (Rom 16:23) as an elite individual is especially significant. He has highlighted the problems with the identification of Erastus with the Erastus mentioned in the inscription as having laid the theater pavement in return for being elected aedile. Among other issues, the dating of this inscription is problematic. See Justin J. Meggitt, "The Social Status of Erastus [Rom 16:23]," *NovT* (1996): 218–23.

[22] Horrell, "Domestic Space," 387. Horrell indicates the size of such quarters as 10x5 meters. Exercising "disciplined imagination," he notes that "this is the kind of space that might well have been occupied by small traders and business folk, not too different in social level from artisans like Prisca and Aquila, and Paul himself. Such people were not

Slaves are explicitly mentioned in 1 Cor 7:21, and while their relationships with masters is of concern in this text, the identity of the masters as believers (or not) is left unstated. Given the direct reference to the slaves of unbelievers as part of Pauline communities elsewhere (cf. 1 Tim 6:1–2; 1 Pet 2:18–19), however, it would be best not to rule out their presence in Corinth. The multifaceted experience of slaves is increasingly being taken into account by scholars of early Christianity as they seek to understand the complex relationship between textual evidence and material evidence of various kinds. Studies of inscriptional evidence and funerary monuments are drawing attention to the circumstances of slave children, who are often forgotten when the issue of slaves in early Christianity is discussed.

Awareness of the overlapping categories of "slave" and "child" is leading scholars to ask new questions about texts dealing with slaves and familial relations more broadly. First Corinthians 7:12–16 is, arguably, the only passage in the undisputed letters of Paul where he refers to the concrete presence of children in the community, but awareness of overlapping categories of identity can help us understand the complex experience of early church family life and demands of allegiance. In one of the most obscure verses in all of the NT (1 Cor 7:14), Paul uses a reference to the children of marriages between believers and non-believers as one of his main arguments as to why such marriages should be preserved and presents this in a way that conveys the impression that this argument will be convincing, even obvious, to the Corinthians; he states that otherwise the children would be unclean, but now they are "holy." We catch only a glimpse here of the concrete challenges of life in house-church communities. The presence and identity of children serves a point of focus in the precarious relations between believers and non-believers. But the children in question are not necessarily freeborn. Inscriptional evidence includes the use of marital terminology to refer to slave families even if such marriages and family relations among slaves had no legal standing in the Roman world.[23] Members of Paul's audience may have been living a wide variety of scenarios. For example, the audience may have included slave women who brought their children to meetings and whose non-believing "husbands" were the domestic slaves of non-believers of high social status. Slave or free, mothers involved in mixed marriage were especially vulnerable. In the case of free women, divorce would almost inevitably lead to loss of access to children, who remained under the control of the authority of the father in such circumstances. Slave women who

---

from the lowest strata; they may have owned one or two slaves and been able to afford some 'luxuries', as the wall painting in building three indicate—so this alternative scenario does not by any means presume that such a domestic setting implies a host that was poor in the sense of living at or around the subsistence level." On modest housing as the basis for the Pauline mission see also R. Jewett, "Tenement Churches and Communal Meals in the Early Church: The Implications of a Form-Critical Analysis of 2 Thessalonians 3:10," *BR* 38 (1993): 23–43.

[23] Here the work of Dale Martin has been especially influential. See especially *Slavery as Salvation: The Metaphor of Slavery in Early Christianity* (New Haven: Yale University Press 1990), 2–7; idem, "Slave Families and Slaves in Families," in *Early Christian Families in Context: An Interdisciplinary Dialogue* (ed. David L. Balch and Carolyn Osiek; Grand Rapids: Eerdmans, 2003), 207–30.

brought their children to meetings without the knowledge of the *paterfamilias* could face brutal consequences.

Children in the House-Church Setting

This mixing of slave and free and overlapping of categories of identity is especially important when we consider the life of children in house churches. In investigating the life of these communities, it is crucial to keep in mind that children were constantly present in every type of domestic setting—there was no escaping them in either a *domus* with a large retinue of slaves and clients or in much simpler spaces. In comparison with modern architectural structures, ancient houses were more open and generally lacking in our concerns for privacy. Even what we would understand as the most private of activities—lovemaking—would frequently not escape the gaze of children.[24] Moreover, there is very little evidence for separate slave quarters, and slaves and slave children may well often have slept in such places as kitchens, storerooms, or on the floor of the master's bedroom.[25]

As part of the complexity of family relations that would have a bearing on church communities, it is important to recognize that children crossed barriers between slave and freeborn existence. In essence, childhood for many freeborn persons involved automatic—though temporary—membership in the slave *familia*.[26] Free and slave children were also present at banquets and celebrations such as weddings, with slave children sometimes working as servers, readers, and entertainers.[27] Slaves and freeborn children were frequently cared for by the same slave caregivers and lived in the same spaces on a daily basis. Sometimes slave children were adopted as pseudo-siblings of freeborn children. In her study of childhood in the Roman world, Beryl Rawson draws attention, for example, to an altar dedicated by Publicia Glypte for her infant son and *uerna* (a term that usually refers to house-born slaves). From Rome and dating from the early second century, the inscription reads as follows, with the dedication for each child in columns side by side: "To the departed spirits of Nico, her sweet son, who lived 11 months and 8 days and Eutyches, her home-born slave, who lived for 1 year, 5 months and 10 days; dedicated by Publicia Glypte." Rawson offers the following description:

> Above the inscription are sculpted two figures of the little boys in togas, each holding a scroll, with a scroll-box between them at their feet. The togas and the appurtenances

---

[24] See Beryl Rawson, *Children and Childhood in Roman Italy* (Oxford: Oxford University Press, 2003), 214. See also Osiek and MacDonald, *A Woman's Place*, 93. On children witnessing sexual activity, it is interesting to consider Quintillian's arguments (*The Orator's Education* 1.2.8) in favor of sending children out to school rather than being tutored at home, where they will inevitably witness corruption: "They see our mistresses, our boy lovers; every dinner party echoes with obscene songs; things are to be seen which it is shameful to name" (LCL).

[25] See especially Michele George, "Domestic Architecture and Household Relations: Pompeii and Roman Ephesos," *JSNT* 21 (2004): 7–25.

[26] Rawson, *Children and Childhood*, 216.

[27] See Nepos, *Atticus* 13; Rawson, *Children and Childhood*, 154–56, 187–91.

of schooling are clearly prospective, foreshadowing the boys' futures (now cut off) as well-educated citizens. The representation of Eutyches is especially optimistic, as a slave would not normally look forward to a liberal education or wear a toga; but Glypte advertises what had been her intention—to give Eutyches his freedom and to raise him as a citizen and as a foster brother to Nico. The sculpture and the pediment of stone appear to be of Telephus, suckled by a hind, thus alluding to a fostering relationship. Glypte has raised the two boys almost as twins. Eutyches may have already been a surrogate son during Glypte's pregnancy, and she could have looked forward to having him as playmate and companion for her natural son, perhaps also to be suckled by the same nurse.[28]

There is plenty of counterevidence to suggest that playmates who crossed the slave-free divide would grow up to be worlds apart as adults,[29] but Rawson's example reminds us that the lines of status and identity could overlap significantly even with respect to a parent's aspirations for the children of the household.

Education offered another opportunity for the exchange between slave and free. Slaves (usually male slaves) accompanied freeborn children to school (*paidagogos*), and sometimes such schooling was arranged in terms of a type of home schooling whereby a tutor was hired to teach a few children of neighboring households.[30] It does not take a great leap of the imagination to see how such trips might be blended with visits to a house where church groups met. In short, the mixing of slaves and free children must have created many opportunities for contact with early church groups. One wonders if such adventures lie behind the polemical critique of Celsus in the second century in which the early Christians are accused of encouraging the recruitment of unruly, rebellious, and inadequately supervised children. He refers to children in house and workshop settings being encouraged "to leave father and their schoolmasters, and go along with the women and little children who are their playfellows to the wooldresser's shop, or to the cobbler's or the washerwoman's shop, that they may learn perfection" (Origen, *Against Celsus* 3.55).[31]

Especially when we consider non-elite housing in a neighborhood of the type identified by Horrell, with two-room dwellings as a possible locus for Corinthian church meetings, it is easy to understand how children could easily spill into house church meetings; the neighborhood for non-elite children was essentially the playground of non-elite children. For poorer families living in urban tenement houses in particular, the neighborhood (a world of crowded living conditions, shops, and outdoor life) offered a social network and perhaps one of the few real sources of protection and identity.[32] Here we might consider the case of the youth (*neanias, pais*) Eutychus who was present at the church gathering in an upper room dwelling in Troas (more than likely the type of housing buildings uncovered east of

---

[28] Rawson, *Children and Childhood*, 260–61.

[29] See Margaret Y. MacDonald, "Slavery, Sexuality, and House Churches: A Reassessment of Col 3.18–4.1 in Light of New Research on the Roman Family," *NTS* 53 (2007): 94–113.

[30] See full discussion in Osiek and MacDonald, *A Woman's Place*, 86–87.

[31] Origen, *Contra Celsum* (trans. Henry Chadwick; Cambridge: Cambridge: University Press, 1953).

[32] Rawson, *Children and Childhood*, 211.

the theater in Corinth)[33] described in Acts 20:7–12. But the account in Acts gives us a brief glimpse into the kind of atmosphere in which the presence of children was taken for granted. He had been listening to Paul but had fallen asleep "as [the apostle] talked still longer." Having been seated in the window, he fell to his death three floors to the ground—a reminder of the vulnerability of children in crowded urban dwellings. In the end the youth was miraculously cured by Paul.

The world of children must be included in any scholarly reconstruction of the house church. From the experiences of childhood of most of the population of the Roman world as described by historians, we must also be ready to accept that children would have come into church groups largely by chance. The second-century apologist Aristides refers to Christians rescuing orphans from those who treat them harshly (*Apol.* 15), and orphans are often mentioned in conjunction with widows in early Christian texts (e.g., Jas 1:27; *Herm. Man.* 8:10; *Herm. Vis.* 2:4:3; *Barn.* 20:2). We do not know how such children came into contact with early church groups, but the neighborhood atmosphere may offer an important clue. Maybe children living in particularly harsh circumstances found solace among these communities; essentially abandoned or left unsupervised for large portions of the day, these children perhaps were adopted by communities by default.

Children and Household Management Discourse

With insight into the presence of children in household and neighborhood space, it is valuable to turn our attention to the ethical instructions concerning the child-parent relationship in the household codes. Colossians and Ephesians offer the first indisputable evidence for children being singled out for exhortation in group assemblies where Pauline letters were read aloud and of the valuing of the child-parent relationship (Col 3:20–25; Eph 6:1–4). When these texts are read with an understanding of the complex circumstances of children, new questions and perspectives arise.

Much of what was said about family life in the NT period was rooted in the ethics of the classical era. It is now generally accepted that the early Christian household code, for example, had its origins in discussions of household management, often including the same three pairs of relationships (husband-wife, master-slave, parent-child), among philosophers and moralists from Aristotle (see *Politics* 1.1253b–1260b26) onward.[34] Important studies on children and childhood in the classical Greek period are potentially useful in tracing the evolution of children's roles in the ancient *topos* of household management and for determining

---

[33]Horrell has seen a connection between the kind of domestic space described in Acts and the buildings east of the theater in Corinth but has not drawn attention to the fact that this is an episode involving a child. See "Domestic Space and Christian Meetings in Corinth," 368–69.

[34]David L. Balch, *Let Wives Be Submissive: The Domestic Code in 1 Peter* (SBLMS 26; Chico, CA: Scholars Press, 1981); idem, "Neopythagorean Moralists and the New Testament Household Codes," *ANRW* II.26.1 (1992): 380–411.

the function of stereotype in the representation of children.[35] In some cases there were notable transformations with the passage of time. While Aristotle resisted the equation of slave and son when it came to the authority of the *paterfamilias*,[36] scholars have noted that the Roman concept of the authority of fathers and heads of households—*patria potestas*—often placed greater emphasis on the obedience of children in household management ethics than did earlier Greek models.[37] Like Colossians, the encomium of Rome given by Dionysius of Halicarnassus (30–7 BCE) speaks of children honoring and obeying parents in all things and includes the three pairs of relationships in the same order as Colossians (*Ant. rom.* 2.26.1–4). But at some distance from Colossians, which instructs fathers not to provoke their children (Col 4:1), Dionysius stresses the severe punishment of children who disobey and notes that Roman law gives greater power to the father over his son than to the master over his slaves (*Ant. rom.* 2.27.1). Jewish and pagan authors both tended to express divine sanction for parental authority in the strongest possible terms with God or the gods as models for parents or fathers. For Philo of Alexandria "parents . . . are to their children what God is to the world" (*Spec. Laws* 2.225–227, trans. Colson, LCL; cf. 2.231; 4.184; cf. Josephus, *Ag. Ap.* 2.206). For Hierocles in "How to Conduct Oneself towards Parents," parents are images of the gods (see Stobaeus, *Anthology* 4.25.53; cf. Iamblichus, *Life of Pythagoras* 22.18–19).[38]

Although it is not explicit in the case of children, a similar analogical principle may be at work in Ephesians' use of the marriage metaphor to speak of the relationship between Christ and the church, but there are also several indications in the household codes, including the call for mutual submission in Eph 5:21, that church groups viewed human authority in familial relations as qualified and only secondary to the authority of the Lord. Judith M. Gundry-Volf has drawn attention to the fact that we do not find the parallels between parents and God or the gods in the household codes that are widely attested elsewhere. Such parallels were not used to motivate behavior in the household codes, and ultimately parents stand alongside their children under the Lord. This introduces the possibility of a type of critical tension between the authority of children and the authority of parents.[39]

Recent work on ancient society calls for a reassessment of the hierarchical codes on the basis of the complexities of family life and overlap between categories, such as "child" and "slave" or "slave" and "parent." To date, interpreters have tended to take the household codes involving clear-cut categories and idealized relationships at face value, but, as noted above, recent work on families encourages

---

[35] See M. Golden, *Children and Childhood in Classical Athens* (Baltimore: John Hopkins University Press, 1990); J. Neils and J. H. Oakley, *Coming of Age in Classical Greece: Images of Childhood from the Classical Past* (New Haven: Yale University Press, 2003).

[36] See Aristotle, *The Nicomachean Ethics* 8.1160b23–1161a10.

[37] Balch, *Let Wives Be Submissive*, 54. For full discussion of this shift see MacDonald, "A Place of Belonging," 283–84.

[38] On this issue and for further reference, see Müller, *In der Mitte der Gemeinde*, 320.

[39] Judith M. Gundry-Volf, "The Least and the Greatest: Children in the New Testament," in *The Child in Christian Thought* (ed. Marcia J. Bunge; Grand Rapids: Eerdmans, 2001), 56.

us to consider the impact of these codes in light of complex family circumstances involving overlapping and multiple identities, including attachment of some members to non-believing households (1 Tim 6:1–2; 1 Pet 3:1–6). If one takes the household codes at face value, they do address the community in a manner that presumes that all members will find their place within the categories, even though some members may be living in circumstances that substantially differ from the ideal (e.g., the Christian ideal of permanency in marriage has never eradicated divorce). In the case of children, several possible situations come to mind: Should the child whose father is a non-believer obey him in all things? What of the slave whose parents are slave believers, but whose master is a non-believer? How would such a child "hear" the household code instructions?[40] Particularly in the case of Colossians, it is important to recognize that the codes do not state that members belonging to the various pairs of relationships are all Christians.[41] In light of the great likelihood that the audiences addressed in household codes lived in complex circumstances, it is best not to view them as "hardened rules"; it is important to acknowledge that household regulations may have been applied in flexible and perhaps even inconsistent ways.[42]

Treatment of the categories in the codes also raises the question of how one should define children and childhood as they are reflected in the household codes. Although the suggestion that the household codes of Colossians and Ephesians primarily refer to relations between adult children and parents has remained a minority position,[43] the exhortations almost certainly had a bearing on such relations. Especially in the case of girls, who were frequently married when they were adolescents to much older men, it is important to consider their ongoing education by older females throughout the process of a first marriage and the birth of a first child, as seems to be presumed by the author of the Pastoral Epistles who admonished older women to teach younger women (2 Tim 1:5; 3:15; Titus 2:3–5). For girls, marriage was the most visible marker of adulthood, but the difference between child and wife was a matter of small degree. The household ceremony involving the bride's offering of her dolls and toys to the household gods or to Venus on the eve of her wedding celebration reminds us that by our standards

---

[40] On these questions, see further MacDonald, "A Place of Belonging," 293.

[41] With respect to Colossians, Jean-Noël Aletti has argued that the author of Colossians does not make the Christian allegiance of both partners explicit. See *Saint Paul Épitre aux Colossiens: Introduction, Traduction et Commentaire* (Paris: Galbalda, 1993), 250. Specifically referring to Ephesians, but equally applicable to other texts that contain household codes, Turid Karlsen Seim has argued that the code may well have spoken (even primarily) to women and slaves who were subject to non-believing heads of households ("A Superior Minority: The Problem of Men's Headship in Ephesians 5," in *Mighty Minorities? Minorities in Early Christianity—Positions and Strategies* [ed. D. Hellholm, H. Moxnes, and T. K. Seim; Oslo: Scandinavian University Press, 1995], 167–81). For the alternate view, see Andrew T. Lincoln, *Ephesians* (Word 42; Dallas: Word Books, 1990), 403; and E. Best, *A Critical and Exegetical Commentary on Ephesians* (ICC; Edinburgh: T&T Clark, 1998), 524.

[42] See MacDonald, "Slavery, Sexuality, and House Churches."

[43] See M. Gärtner, *Die Familienenerziehung in der alten Kirche* (Cologne: Bohlau, 1985), 36–37.

these young brides were adolescent girls, probably between the ages of twelve and sixteen.[44] But in some ways the Romans seem wiser than we moderns with our associations of particular rights and privileges with specific biological ages (from voting to driving). Romans tended instead to focus on flexible stages of development rather than rigid age demarcation signaling the end of childhood. There was little age demarcation in Roman society until late antiquity.[45]

New research on children in the Roman world is also raising questions about the intersection between the addresses to children in the codes and NT ethics more generally. For example, a recent Dutch-language work by Christian Laes examines the whole of the empire (including the Greek East) and treats the sensitive issues of child labor and the sexual use of children, especially child slaves who were sometimes adopted as "pet" children.[46] The latter raises interesting questions about the intersection between early Christian teaching on sexual morality, slavery, and children. The use of slaves as sexual outlets was such a widespread expectation that the NT silence on the matter is curious.[47] But there are some indirect indications that the treatment of slaves in early church communities may have included respect for their families and resistance to sexual violation. The promise of inheritance to slaves in Col 3:24, for example, is especially striking, perhaps revealing that slaves and free ultimately are worthy of honor as brothers and sisters in the Lord.[48] Moreover, the household codes of Colossians and Ephesians are both preceded with ethical discourse that exhibits considerable interest in sexual ethics more broadly. This, combined with the fact that concern with holiness and purity shapes the metaphorical treatment of marriage in Eph 5:22–33, suggests that an interest in sexual ethics runs just under the surface of the treatment of household relations in the codes. Such overlapping interests are very much in keeping with comparative Jewish teaching. In addition to displaying a concern for familial

---

[44] Among Roman girls there was no true coming-of-age ceremony as in the case of the boys with the *toga uirilis*. Rawson notes the flexibility concerning the age of the boy undergoing the ceremony: "a boy might go through the ritual of attaining manhood by changing his boyhood garb (*the toga praetexta*) for the *toga uirilis*. Ages known for this ceremony range from 13–18. Parents' freedom in deciding when the boy was ready and when there was an appropriate occasion is another example of the flexibility of concepts of stages of development in Roman society" (142). With respect to the encouragement of asceticism in early Christianity, and Paul's advice in 1 Cor 7, it is interesting to note the link between adulthood and intercourse in boys: "Celsus (2. I. 17–21) claimed that most childhood illnesses disappeared by the time of a boy's puberty or first intercourse. This suggests that the two events, puberty and first intercourse, were thought to be not far apart. What sexual partners were available to well-born boys, given that girls of their own class were not generally available? Slaves and prostitutes are the obvious answers. If Cicero's picture of Clodia is more widely applicable, liberated society ladies might also have provided this service" (142).
[45] See Rawson, *Children and Childhood*, 134–45.
[46] See Christian Laes, *Kinderen bij de Romeinen: Zes Eeuwen Dagelijks Leven* [Children among the Romans: Six Centuries of Daily Life] (Leuven: Uitgeverij Davidsfonds NV, 2006).
[47] See especially Jennifer A. Glancy, *Slavery in Early Christianity* (Oxford: Oxford University Press, 2002).
[48] See full discussion in MacDonald, "Slavery, Sexuality, and House Churches."

relations more generally, Philo of Alexandria, for example, treats exposure, infanticide, abortion, and abandonment—topics that appear in the ethical discourse of the apostolic fathers (e.g., *Barn.* 19:5; *Did.* 2:2), which overlaps or comes immediately after the NT teaching.[49]

By way of a final theme, I would like to draw attention to the interesting and often overlooked reference in the Ephesians household code to the education of children. The first explicit encouragement of the education of children in Eph 6:1–4 is followed by various indicators in the Pastoral Epistles that education (including that of girls and adolescents by older women) was an important feature of house-church life (e.g., 2 Tim 1:5; 3:15; Titus 2:3–5), and the sustained interest in Christian socialization of children in household ethics of the apostolic fathers (e.g., *1 Clem.* 21:6, 8; *Did.* 4:9; Pol. *Phil.* 4:2; cf. *Herm. Vis.* 2:4:3). Here there is also important comparative material from Jewish sources to consider. The DSS, which are cited increasingly frequently in an attempt to understand the thought world of Ephesians, contain intriguing material concerning the education of children. As highlighted recently by Cecilia Wassen, the Damascus Document and the Rule of the Congregation (1QSa), in particular, reflect married communities and include several prescriptions concerning children.[50] For example, while the Damascus Document bars children from participating in communal meetings (4Q266 8 i 6–9 [cf. 1QM 7:3–6]), it also outlines the process by which children make the transition from childhood to adulthood (CD 15:5–10).[51] The Rule of the Congregation (1QSa 1:6–8) lists several stages in the life of a member, including childhood, which is devoted to studies in the Torah while the child is gradually introduced to deeper insights.[52] This document also recounts a special meeting—probably the renewal of covenant ceremony—in which children's presence is highlighted (1QSa 1:4–5; cf. Col 3:20–21; Eph 6:1–2).[53] These communal priorities are in keeping with the little-recognized emphasis on the education and treatment of children as a key aspect of Jewish identity in Josephus's apologetic work (*Ag. Ap.* 1.60; 2.202–204; 2.173–174, 178). Within this broad comparative framework, several key questions arise: Will using the lens of the child and childhood reveal new aspects of the household management material found in both Jewish and early Christian sources of this period? Was the education of children central to the identity of certain Jewish and early Christian groups? How does consideration of the education of children and place of children in household morality affect our vision of the social location of church groups in comparison with Greco-Roman associations and schools?

---

[49] See Adele Reinhartz, "Parents and Children: A Philonic Perspective," in *The Jewish Family in Antiquity* (ed. Shaye Cohen; BJS 289; Atlanta: Scholars Press, 1993), 61–88; idem, "Philo on Infanticide," *Studia Philonica Annual* 4 (1992): 42–58.

[50] See Cecilia Wassen, *Women in the Damascus Document* (SBLABib 21; Atlanta: Society of Biblical Literature; Leiden: Brill, 2005), 164–68.

[51] Ibid., 133–36.

[52] See Lawrence Schiffman, *The Eschatological Community of the Dead Sea Scrolls* (SBLMS 38; Atlanta: Scholars Press, 1989), 14–16.

[53] Wassen, *Women in the Damascus Document*, 136–38.

Comparison of early Christian ethical texts to Josephus's works suggests that children were a more important factor in the apologetic intent of these texts than is often realized. In *Against Apion*, a work roughly contemporary with Colossians and Ephesians, Josephus responds to anti-Jewish propaganda after the destruction of the temple in 70 CE.[54] In an effort to convince his audience that Judaism is compatible with imperial values, Josephus gives a rarely recognized prominent place to the treatment of children by Jews. As the head of the family enjoys the honor of a harmonious and ordered household, Jews are united in belief under the Law as under a father and master (*Ag. Ap.* 2.174); consequently, even women and dependents (*tōn oikētōn*, literally the ones belonging to the household—children and probably also slaves) will state that piety (*eusebeia*—a concept closely associated with matters of family and reflecting state loyalty and Roman imperial values) is their primary motivation (*Ag. Ap.* 2.181).[55] In fact, in Josephus's thought, the Law is the primary education tool and children are literally reared under its tutelage—it is indeed something that is observed and absorbed from infancy (*Ag. Ap.* 2.173, 178). Although Josephus reinforces the authority of fathers over their children in the strongest possible terms—where rebellious sons might even be stoned (*Ag. Ap.* 2.206; Deut 21:18–21; Lev 20:9; cf. Philo, *Spec. Laws* 2.232; cf. 2.217; Deut 21:18–21; Lev 24:13)—he also states that Jews treasure their children, rejecting practices associated with other nations: they raise all of their children, and women are not to cause abortions, lest they be charged with infanticide (*Ag. Ap.* 2.202–203; cf. Philo, *Spec.Laws*, 3.108–19). Josephus also contrasts the conventions associated with the birth of a child among Jews with that of the nations in a striking manner. While the birth of Roman child provides a pretext for a "wild party," the birth of a Jewish child is an occasion for sobriety, followed by commitment to educate the child, including the teaching of reading and training in the laws and the traditions of the ancestors (*Ag. Ap.* 2.204; cf. Philo, *Hypothetica* 7.14). In Josephus's discourse, the education of children can even emerge as the highest priority of Jews: "Above all we pride ourselves on the education of our children, and regard as the most essential task in the life the observance of our laws and pious practices, based thereupon, which we have inherited" (*Ag. Ap.*1.60, trans. Thackeray, LCL).[56]

This text can help us to appreciate the significance of the instruction to fathers to bring up children "in the discipline and instruction of the Lord" (Eph 6:4). Yet, the Greek term *paideia* ("discipline") employed in Eph 6:4 can refer not only to

---

[54] See Martin Goodman, "Josephus' Treatise *Against Apion*," in *Apologetics in the Roman Empire: Pagans, Jews, and Christians* (ed. Mark Edwards, Martin Goodman and Simon Price, in association with Christopher Rowland; Oxford: Oxford University Press, 1999), 50–51. *Against Apion* was composed sometime after the *Antiquities* in 90 CE. I accept the position of those who view Colossians and Ephesians as pseudonymous: Colossians is frequently dated between 60 and 80 CE and Ephesians between 80 and 90 CE.

[55] The Romans prized the virtue of *pietas*, which they associated with loyalty to gods, state, parents, and family. It was a virtue frequently linked to the obedience of children. See Rawson, *Children and Childhood*, 223.

[56] Here I am following closely my earlier discussion in "A Place of Belonging," 286–88. See a fuller discussion of this text there.

the upbringing of a child but also to the formation of an adult—the instruction delivered by fathers, like training in the Law, thus comes under the category of lifelong learning (to use a modern phrase) and calls to mind the flexible approach to the end of childhood among Roman families described previously. Here it is interesting to note that 2 Tim 3:16 presents "training in righteousness" as one of the purposes of Scripture. That learning extends indefinitely from the time of early childhood is suggested by a call for Timothy to continue in what he has already learned, including the sacred writings that he has known from childhood (*brephos*; literally "infancy"; cf. 2 Tim 1:5).[57]

Conclusion

By way of brief concluding remarks, I would like to suggest that a focus on children and house churches and the use of families as a major category of analysis for early Christian texts can cause us to rethink much about early Christian communities. Even highly conventional instructions like the household codes can emerge in a new light—at least they do not appear quite as straightforward. The impact of household codes needs to be envisioned within the context of urban neighborhoods and domestic spaces where free and slave children played together. The increasing interest among archeologists in the lives of ordinary people and domestic life is of enormous importance in understanding the life of house churches and what was at stake in Christian commitment. The overlap between the categories of slave, parent, and child is a key feature of this complex picture and needs to be kept in mind when one considers the familial audiences of house churches who heard the household codes. Although not emphasized by scholars who have tended to view the codes as interbelieving directives, it is also important to keep in mind that such audiences most likely included some slave, child, and female members who were under the authority of a non-believing household head.

The NT includes metaphorical language of liberation that is difficult to assess in terms of social relations (e.g., Col 2:13–15; 3:24). But such language does invite us that to view slaves and slave children as honored members of the community even though the hierarchical structures of the household are not abolished. The Roman world offered many opportunities for the adoption of slaves and slave families who had been kidnapped or captured in war as well as slaves born in households or adopted as foundlings.[58] Moreover, in an urban neighborhood, the

---

[57] On the process of lifelong learning (but specifically with respect to female members of the community), see Osiek and MacDonald, *A Woman's Place*, 90–92.

[58] Glancy, *Slavery in Early Christianity*, notes that after the Jewish war, the slave markets of the empire were flooded with captives. Many have dated Colossians to approximately this time period, about the year 70. Glancy notes that Rome's great wars of expansion had slowed down by the first century, "but occasional wars throughout the provinces and at the edges of the Empire meant a continuing, if episodic, supply of captives as slaves" (77). She speculates that at least a small number of these slaves would have been members of the emerging Christian group (78).

house church may have offered a place of belonging to abandoned and orphaned children who found their way into church meetings. Chance encounters may well have turned into opportunities for the evangelization and education of children, which are so derided by second-century pagan interests. Such assertions do involve a certain degree of imaginative reconstruction because definitive evidence is so scarce. But comparison of the household codes with Josephus's apologetic discourse in particular highlights the very real importance of the treatment and education of children in assertions of group identity. As we envision of the life of early church communities, there is much emerging from the study of families in the Roman world to suggest that we should attribute to children a greater place of importance and more space to play, learn, and grow in house churches.

6

The Family Buried Together Stays Together: On the Burial of the Executed in Family Tombs

Craig A. Evans

The Jewish people buried their dead, then later gathered the bones and placed them in containers called ossuaries or in a vault or pit set aside for this purpose. The practice of gathering the bones of the deceased is called ossilegium, or secondary burial (cf. *y. Mo'ed Qatan* 1.5, 80c: "At first they would bury them in ditches, and when the flesh had decayed, they would gather the bones and bury them in ossuaries").[1] How far back this practice may be traced and where the practice originated are major questions that lie at the heart of the debate surrounding the significance of the numerous ossuaries found in and around Jerusalem, dating to the Herodian period (c. 35 BCE–70 CE).[2]

The question before us concerns the fate of the remains of those executed. In the Roman world the executed, especially the crucified, were often left unburied. In the Jewish world the executed were buried, but not in the family tomb, at least not initially. Jewish literature suggests that after one year the skeletal remains of the executed, that is, of those who had died dishonorably, could be relocated and reburied in the family tomb. But is the literature supported by archeological finds? And what of the remains of the executed who may have committed murder against members of their own families? As it so happens, archeology may shed light on this intriguing question.

Jewish Burial Customs in Late Antique Palestine

In the Jewish world burial took place the day of death, or, if death occurred at the end of the day or during the night, burial took place the following day.

---

[1] On ossilegium in the time of Jesus and the early church, see C. A. Evans, *Jesus and the Ossuaries: What Jewish Burial Practices Reveal about the Beginning of Christianity* (Waco, TX: Baylor University Press, 2003).

[2] On the origins of ossilegium, see E. M. Meyers, *Jewish Ossuaries: Reburial and Rebirth* (BibOr 24; Rome: Pontifical Biblical Institute Press, 1971).

Knowing this lends a great deal of pathos to some otherwise familiar Gospel stories. We think of the story of the widow from the city of Nain: "As he approached the gate of the town, a man who had died was being carried out. He was his mother's only son, and she was a widow; and with her was a large crowd from the town" (Luke 7:12). Her only son had died that day or the evening before. Her sorrow is at its rawest when Jesus encounters her. We also think of the desperate father who hurries Jesus to his home, hoping he will arrive in time to heal his dying daughter: "When Jesus came to the leader's house [he] saw the flute players and the crowd making a commotion" (Matt 9:23). As it turns out, before they arrived, the girl had died and the funeral process, complete with music and weeping, was already under way.[3]

Following death, the body is washed and wrapped. We can find this custom mentioned in several episodes in the Gospels and elsewhere. We see it in the story of Lazarus, who was bound and wrapped with cloths (John 11:44). The body of Jesus is wrapped in a clean linen shroud (Matt 27:59; Luke 23:53; John 19:40). The body of Ananias is wrapped and buried (Acts 5:6); so also Dorcas, who "became ill and died. When they had washed her, they laid her in a room upstairs" (Acts 9:37). Moreover, the corpse was usually perfumed (Josephus, *Ant.* 15.61; for spices, see *Ant.* 17.196–99; John 19:39–40).

The day of burial was the first of seven days of mourning (*Semahot* 12.1). This is clearly stated by first-century Jewish historian Josephus, in reference to the death, burial, and funeral of Herod the Great (d. 4 BCE): "Now Archelaus [Herod's oldest surviving son] continued to mourn for seven days out of respect for his father—the custom of the country prescribes this number of days—and then, after feasting the crowds and making an end of the mourning, he went up to the temple" (Josephus, *Ant.* 17.200). The custom of seven days of mourning arose from Scripture itself: Joseph "observed a time of mourning for his father seven days" (Gen 50:10); and, in reference to the remains of king Saul and his sons, Israelite men "took their bones and buried them under the tamarisk tree in Jabesh, and fasted seven days" (1 Sam 31:13).

Mourning normally took place at the tomb's entrance or within the tomb itself. This is why archeologists sometimes find a portion of the floor carved out more deeply, allowing mourners to pray standing upright, according to the Jewish custom.[4] Of course, standing inside the tomb was why the corpse was perfumed. Many perfume bottles and jars have been found in tombs and burial caves. One can only imagine how unpleasant the tomb would have become by the sixth and seventh days. Lamps and lamp niches have also been found in tombs, because of the need for light.

---

[3] Life expectancy was short at this time. More than half of the population died before age thirty. For a recent survey, see Y. Nagar and H. Torgeë, "Biological Characteristics of Jewish Burial in the Hellenistic and Early Roman Periods," *IEJ* 53 (2003): 164–71.

[4] An example of a section of floor that has been more deeply carved can be seen in the partially opened tomb on the Mount of Olives at Dominus Flevit.

One year after death it was customary to gather the bones and place them in a bone niche or in an ossuary. This is sometimes called secondary burial. This is readily observed in the archeological excavations of Jewish tombs in the time of Jesus. Thousands of ossuaries have been recovered (whether properly or looted) from tombs in the vicinity of Jerusalem.[5] The practice of ossilegium is also attested in later rabbinic literature: "When the flesh had wasted away they gathered together the bones and buried them in their own place" (*m. Sanhedrin* 6:6); "My son, bury me at first in a niche. In the course of time, collect my bones and put them in an ossuary but do not gather them with your own hands" (*Semahot* 12.9; cf. *Semahot* 3.2). The custom of the interval of twelve months from primary burial to secondary burial is also attested in rabbinic literature (cf. *b. Qiddushin* 31b).

For executed criminals, however, the rules were different. Criminals were to be buried properly, but not in places of honor, such as the family tomb. This is clearly taught in the earliest writings of the rabbis: "They did not bury (the executed criminal) in the burying-place of his fathers. But two burying-places were kept in readiness by the Sanhedrin, one for them that were beheaded or strangled, and one for them that were stoned or burnt" (*m. Sanhedrin* 6:5); "Neither a corpse nor the bones of a corpse may be transferred from a wretched place to an honored place, nor, needless to say, from an honored placed to a wretched place; but if to the family tomb, even from an honored place to a wretched place, it is permitted" (*Semahot* 13.7). Not only was the body of a criminal not to be buried in a place of honor, but also no public mourning for executed criminals was permitted: "they used not to make [open] lamentation . . . for mourning has place in the heart alone" (*m. Sanhedrin* 6:6).

These are the burial customs of the Jewish people. But did the Jewish people always bury the dead? Was burial important to them? Were they willing to leave people unburied, such as executed criminals? These questions must be asked, because in Roman-controlled Palestine execution normally was at the discretion of Roman authority. Sometimes the executed were crucified, and often the crucified were left unburied. Was this the peacetime practice in first-century Palestine?[6]

---

[5] See L. Y. Rahmani, *A Catalogue of Jewish Ossuaries in the Collections of the State of Israel* (Jerusalem: Israel Antiquities Authority, 1994). Rahmani catalogues some 895 ossuaries. About 30 percent of them are inscribed, usually with the names or nicknames of the deceased.

[6] The archeological examples that will be considered are all from Jerusalem and its immediate vicinity. The Galilean examples mentioned in the Gospels are relevant nevertheless, for the burial customs of Jews in Galilee and Jews in Judea were not significantly different. The differences in sepulture in and around Jerusalem mostly concern urbanization, higher density of population, and greater affluence. The customs and practices themselves are essentially identical. For more on this topic, see M. Aviam, "Regionalism of Tombs and Burial Customs in the Galilee During the Hellenistic, Roman, and Byzantine Periods," in *Jews, Pagans, and Christians in the Galilee: Twenty-five Years of Archaeological Excavations and Surveys: Hellenistic to Byzantine Periods* (Rochester, NY: University of Rochester Press, 2004), 257–313; E. Regev, "Family Burial, Family Structure, and the Urbanization of Herodian Jerusalem," *PEQ* 136 (2004): 109–31.

Jewish Beliefs and the Necessity of Burial

In the Mediterranean world of late antiquity proper burial of the dead was regarded as sacred duty, especially so in the culture and religion of the Jewish people. The first reason for providing proper burial was for the sake of the dead themselves. The importance of care for the dead and their proper burial is well attested in Scripture, from the amount of attention given to the story of Abraham's purchase of a cave for the burial of Sarah (Gen 23:4–19), to the burial accounts of the patriarchs and monarchs of Israel. Of special interest is the story of Jacob's body taken to the land of Canaan, to be buried in a tomb that he had hewn (Gen 50:4–14). So also Joseph; though buried in Egypt, his bones were exhumed and taken with the Israelites at the time of the exodus, to be buried eventually in Canaan (Gen 50:22–26; Josh 24:32). The bones of the slain Saul and his sons were buried in Jabesh (1 Sam 31:12–13). David later commended the men who did this (2 Sam 2:5: "May you be blessed by the Lord, because you showed this loyalty to Saul your lord, and buried him!"). Saul's bones were later taken to the land of Benjamin (2 Sam 21:12–14).

The wicked and divinely judged were buried, too, such as those in the wilderness who were greedy for meat (Num 11:33–34), or individual criminals who were executed (Deut 21:22–23). Israel's enemies, slain in battle, were buried (1 Kgs 11:15). Even the eschatological enemy hosts of Gog were to be buried (Ezek 39:11–16). To leave the dead, even enemy dead, lying about unburied was to bring a curse on the land (Deut 21:22–23). Explaining Jewish ethical obligations, Josephus states: "We must furnish fire, water, food to all who ask for them, point out the road, not leave a corpse unburied [*ataphon*], show consideration even to declared enemies" (*Ag. Ap.* 2.211; cf. 2.205). In an imaginative retelling of Jacob's grief upon hearing (falsely) that his son Joseph had been killed by wild animals and that nothing of him remained for burial, Philo has the patriarch affirm that had his son died in some other manner and had his corpse been found lying beside the road, even the "cruelest of men" would have taken pity and "deemed the custom of burial to be its due" (*De Iosepho* 22–27).

A second reason for burying the dead is to avoid defilement of the land of Israel. This requirement is grounded in the Mosaic law: "When someone is convicted of a crime punishable by death and is executed, and you hang him on a tree, his corpse must not remain all night upon the tree; you shall bury him that same day, for anyone hung on a tree is under God's curse. You must not defile the land that the Lord your God is giving you for possession" (Deut 21:22–23). It is also expressed in Ezekiel: "They will set apart men to pass through the land regularly and bury any invaders who remain on the face of the land, so as to cleanse it. . . . Thus they shall cleanse the land" (Ezek 39:14, 16). The requirement for burial of the criminal is emphasized because of the temptation to neglect the burial of a murderer or traitor. A law would hardly be necessary for the burial of others, whose family members would have needed no encouragement to see to proper and honorable burial of the deceased.

Deuteronomy's law of burial for the condemned and executed remained current at the turn of the era, though not without some important modification, as seen in its elaboration in the Temple Scroll, one of the DSS, where we read: "If a man is a traitor against his people and gives them up to a foreign nation, so doing evil to his people, *you are to hang him on a tree until dead.* On the testimony of two or three witnesses he will be put to death, and they themselves shall hang him on the tree. If a man is convicted of a capital crime and flees to the nations, cursing his people and the children of Israel, *you are to hang him, also, upon a tree until dead.* But you must not let their bodies remain on the tree overnight; you shall most certainly bury them that very day. Indeed, anyone hung on a tree is accursed of God and men, but you are not to defile the land that I am about to give you as an inheritance [Deut 21:22–23]" (11QT 64:7–13a = 4Q524 frag. 14, ll. 2–4; with emphasis added). Whereas Deut 21:22–23 speaks of one put to death and then hanged, 11QTemple speaks of one hanged "until dead." That is, death is understood to follow hanging on the tree, not preceding it. Most think crucifixion is in view in this latter instance (as also in 4QpNah frags. 3–4, col. i, ll. 6–8, and perhaps also in 4Q282i, which refers to the hanging up [probably crucifixion] of those who lead the people astray).[7] It is also important to note that this form of execution is linked to treason.

It should also be observed that the requirement to bury the executed person the day of his death is emphasized. The reason given for taking the bodies down and burying them the day or evening of death is to avoid defiling the land, for the executed person is "cursed of God." This is probably the rationale that lies behind the concern regarding the burial of slain enemy soldiers, as in 1 Kgs 11:15 and Ezek 39:11–16, but also as envisioned in 4Q285, where Israel and the Messiah (the "Branch of David and "Prince of the Congregation") have slain the Roman legions and their emperor, where the priests give oversight to the burial of the enemy.

What is important here is that even in the case of the executed criminal, proper burial was anticipated. Various restrictions may have applied, such as being forbidden burial in one's family tomb—at least until the flesh had decomposed—or not being allowed to mourn publicly, but burial was to take place, in keeping with the scriptural command of Deut 21:22–23 and the Jewish customs that had grown up alongside it.

Archeological Evidence of Burial in the Roman Era

The important discovery in 1968 of an ossuary (ossuary no. 4 in Tomb I, at Giv'at ha-Mivtar) of a Jewish man named Yehohanan, who had obviously been crucified, provides archeological evidence and insight into how Jesus himself may have been crucified. The ossuary and its contents date to the late 20s CE, that is, during the administration of Pilate, the very Roman governor who condemned

---

[7] For detailed discussion of these texts from Qumran, see G. L. Doudna, *4Q Pesher Nahum: A Critical Edition* (JSPSup 35; CIS 8; London: Sheffield Academic Press, 2001), 389–433; Y. Yadin, *The Temple Scroll* (3 vols.; Jerusalem: Israel Exploration Society, 1977–1983), 2:288–91.

Jesus to the cross.[8] The remains of an iron spike (11.5 cm in length) are plainly seen still encrusted in the right heel bone (or calcaneum). Those who took down the body of Yehohanan apparently were unable to remove the spike, with the result that a piece of wood (from an olive tree) remained affixed to the spike. Later, the skeletal remains of the body—spike, fragment of wood, and all—were placed in the ossuary. Forensic examination of the rest of the skeletal remains supports the view that Yehohanan was crucified with arms apart, hung from a horizontal beam or tree branch. However, there is no evidence that his arms, or wrists, were nailed to this cross beam.

The lack of nails or spikes in the hands or wrists of Yehohanan is consistent with a reference in Pliny the Elder (23–79 CE), who refers to rope being used in crucifixion (cf. *Nat.* 28.4).[9] Nevertheless, it is recorded by others that many victims of crucifixion did have their hands or wrists nailed to the beam. Writing in the second century BCE Plautus refers to a crucifixion victim whose "arms and legs are double-nailed" (*Mostellaria* 359–61). At the beginning of the second century CE Plutarch asks, "Will you nail him to a cross or impale him on a stake?" (*Moralia* 499D). A third-century author described it this way: "Punished with limbs outstretched . . . they are fastened (and) nailed to the stake in the most bitter torment, evil food for birds of prey and grim picking for dogs" (*Apotelesmatica* 4.198–200). One Latin inscription found in Pompeii reads: "May you be nailed to the cross!" (*CIL* IV.2082: *in cruce figarus*). Another reads: "Samius (says) to Cornelius, Get hung!" (*CIL* IV.1864: *Samius Cornelio suspendre*). According to Plautus (*Pseud.* 335), a pimp said to a slave, "Go to an evil cross!" (*i in malam crucem*). All of these curses are the equivalent to the modern imprecation: "Go to hell!"

Yehohanan's leg bones were broken, but there is disagreement over how and when they were broken (i.e., while still on the cross, or after being taken down). Some think that the breaks in the lower leg bones of Yehohanan, including the cut to the talus bone of the foot, are due to *crurifragium*, the breaking of a victim's bones to hasten his death. Others do not think the talus suffered such an injury. Indeed, the talus under question may belong to one of the other two individuals whose skeletal remains had been placed in the ossuary. Accordingly, the conclusion that Yehohanan's leg bones were broken before death and decarnation is disputed. Because of the age and degraded condition of the skeletal materials, a measure of uncertainty remains.[10]

---

[8] For a selection of studies concerned with this find, see Y. Yadin, "Epigraphy and Crucifixion," *IEJ* 23 (1973): 18–22 + plate; J. Zias and E. Sekeles, "The Crucified Man from Giv'at ha-Mivtar: A Reappraisal," *IEJ* 35 (1985): 22–27; J. Zias and J. H. Charlesworth, "Crucifixion: Archaeology, Jesus, and the Dead Sea Scrolls," in *Jesus and the Dead Sea Scrolls* (ed. J. H. Charlesworth; ABRL; New York: Doubleday, 1992), 273–89 + plates.

[9] J. W. Hewitt, "The Use of Nails in the Crucifixion," *HTR* 25 (1932): 29–45. Hewitt rightly recognized that the arms of some crucifixion victims were tied with rope and that only the feet or ankles were nailed.

[10] On the problem of determining bone damage before or after death, see N. J. Sauer, "The Timing of Injuries and Manner of Death: Distinguishing among Antemortem, Perimortem, and Postmortem Trauma," in *Forensic Osteology: Advances in the Identification of Human Remains* (ed. K. R. Richards; 2nd ed.; Springfield, IL: Charles C. Thomas, 1998), 321–32.

If Yehohanan's legs were broken before death, we then know not only that he was taken down and buried (as indicated by the discovery of his remains in an ossuary) but also that his death was intentionally hastened. The most likely and most compelling reason for hastening death in this manner was so that his corpse could be taken down from the cross and placed in a tomb before nightfall, as Scripture commands (Deut 21:22–23) and as Jewish custom required. The Romans had no reason to expedite death by crucifixion; they would prefer just the opposite.

Also found in the tombs discovered at Giv'at Ha-Mivtar were the remains of a woman who had been decapitated. Whether she was murdered or executed is not clear.[11] (Below I shall give reasons why I think she probably was executed.) However, we may have the skeletal remains of another person who, like Yehohanan, was executed and whose remains eventually were placed in a family tomb. These remains were found in a cluster of tombs on Mount Scopus, north of Jerusalem.[12] In Tomb C the skeletal remains of a woman (aged fifty to sixty) give clear evidence of having been attacked. Her right elbow suffered a deep cut that severed the end of the humerus (elbow). Because there is no sign of regrowth or infection, it is surmised that she died from the attack.

In Tomb D, which contains the remains of persons related to those interred in Tomb C, were the remains of a man (aged fifty), who had been decapitated. It is plausible to speculate that this man had been executed, quite possibly for having murdered the female relative in Tomb C. However, physical anthropologist Joe Zias doubts that the man had been executed, because his neck had been struck twice. Being struck twice, he reasons, suggests an act of violence rather than a judicial execution.[13] Zias could be correct, of course, but we should not assume that judicial beheadings were always neatly done and did not require more than one stroke of the sword or axe. One only needs to be reminded of the several badly aimed strokes that finally took off the head of James, Duke of Monmouth, in 1685.[14] Apparently the executioner was intoxicated. His first stroke buried the axe in the duke's shoulder! Mary Queen of Scots fared no better a century earlier, when in 1586 her cousin, Elizabeth I, had her executed for treason. It took the executioner three strokes to take off her head.

---

[11] The gender of these remains is not certain. This decapitated person may have been a man. For study, see N. Haas, "Anthropological Observations on the Skeletal Remains from Giv'at ha-Mivtar," *IEJ* 20 (1970): 38–59; J. Zias, "Anthropological Evidence of Interpersonal Violence in First-Century A.D. Jerusalem," *Current Anthropology* 24 (1983): 233–34; P. Smith, "The Human Skeletal Remains from the Abba Cave," *IEJ* 27 (1977): 121–24. According to Haas, the "atlas, the axis vertebrae and the slope of the occipital bone (were) broken into sharp slivers . . . produced by a heavy blow of a blunt weapon, such as a mace" (44). But Smith and Zias do not agree. Zias speaks of "decapitation" (234), while Smith speaks of a "severed head," stating that "the cuts were made with a sword rather than an axe" (123).

[12] The Mount Scopus tomb was excavated in 1979 by Gershon Edelstein of Israel's Department of Antiquities (now the Israel Antiquities Authority).

[13] Zias, "Anthropological Evidence of Interpersonal Violence," 223–34.

[14] The official number is five, but other versions place the number of strokes as high as seven or eight.

Multiple cuts, as others might contend, do not in fact argue against interpreting beheadings as judicial executions. I have reviewed the evidence of hundreds of Roman-era skeletons that have been excavated (mostly in Britain, though some in North Africa and elsewhere in the Roman Empire) and have been found to have suffered decapitation. In about one half of the cases two or more strokes of the sword or axe were required before the head was separated from the body.[15]

Of special interest for this topic was the discovery of the mass grave left behind in the aftermath of the bloody battle of Towton, in fifteenth-century Britain.[16] Although dating from a much later period, the skeletal remains are nevertheless quite instructive because the weapons employed and the manner of fighting were essentially the same as those from the earlier Roman period. Approximately one half of the several hundred slain had suffered fatal head wounds, and the other half had suffered fatal sword or spear thrusts through the body. Only one victim suffered decapitation, and it may have been a postmortem insult, not the actual cause of death.[17] The point is this: If no one—or at most only one—was decapitated in pitched battle, where combatants were armed with axes and swords, what is the probability that someone suffered decapitation in a domestic altercation? I think it is rather slim.

Accordingly, the man in Giv'at Ha-Mivtar tomb D is probably another individual who suffered the death penalty—even if it took two strokes to finish the job—and whose skeletal remains, in due course, were placed in the family tomb. With all due respect to Joe Zias, I believe this means that we apparently have found three executed persons—one by crucifixion and two by beheading—who were buried according to Jewish customs in the time of Jesus. This means that they were given primary burial (most likely in a place of dishonor, that is, in one of the tombs reserved for executed criminals) and subsequently their skeletal remains were gathered and placed in ossuaries, which in turn were placed in their family

---

[15] I recommend J. L. McKinley, "A Decapitation from the Romano-British Cemetery at Baldock, Hertfordshire," *International Journal of Osteoarchaeology* 3 (1993): 41–44; A. Boylston, "Evidence for Weapon-Related Trauma in British Archaeological Samples," in *Human Osteology: In Archaeology and Forensic Science* (ed. M. Cox and S. Mays; London: Greenwich Medical Media, 2000), 357–80, esp. 367–68. McKinley and Boylston review a number of cases involving decapitation, observing that multiple strokes were the norm. See also M. Harmon, T. I. Molleson, and J. L. Price, "Burials, Bodies and Beheadings in Romano-British and Anglo-Saxon Cemeteries," *Bulletin of the British Museum of Natural History: Geology* 35 (1981): 145–88; R. J. Watt, "Evidence for Decapitation," in *The Roman Cemetery at Lankhills* (ed. G. Clarke; Winchester Studies 3: Pre-Roman and Roman Winchester; Oxford: Clarendon Press, 1980), 342–44 + plate XVII. I should also mention the ongoing excavation at Ridgeway in Dorset, United Kingdom, where a mass burial was discovered in 2009. Oxford Archaeology staff members are conducting the excavation. The remains of some fifty beheaded men, probably viking raiders (c. 910–1030 CE), have been unearthed. Angela Boyle, senior osteologist, reports that most of the skeletons "exhibit evidence of multiple blows to the vertebrae," caused by "a large, very sharp weapon such as a sword" (as reported on the Oxford Archaeology web page). I also thank Dr. Jane Evans, British Geological Survey, for the information that she provided.

[16] The battle took place in 1461 and confirmed the crown for Edward IV (d. 1483).

[17] V. Fiorato, A. Boylston, and C. Knüsel, eds., *Blood Red Roses: The Archaeology of a Mass Grave from the Battle of Towton AD 1461* (Oxford: Oxbow, 2000).

burial vaults, all according to the laws and customs related in ancient Jewish literature. Archaeology, so far as it goes, corroborates what is claimed in the literary remains from this period. The Gospel accounts of the women going to Jesus' tomb early Sunday morning, to perfume his body and mourn privately, are completely in step with the literature and archaeology of death and burial.

What I find especially intriguing about the Mount Scopus tomb is not that an executed man was buried in his family tomb (for we have seen this in at least two other cases), but that this man may have been executed for the murder of a family member (i.e., the woman with the injured elbow). It seems that the Jewish custom of permitting criminals proper burial in the family tomb even extended to those who committed murder against one's own family. The lapse of one year, the wasting away of the flesh, and the theological belief that in this passage of time and physical decomposition the "sins of the flesh" had in some sense been atoned for made possible a family reunion of sorts. Apparently, once family always family, and so even the blackest of sheep were to slumber amid the remains of kith and kin.[18] This observation lends further support to studies that have shown just how cohesive the Jewish family was in late antiquity.

But why have we found the buried remains of only three or four executed Jews in pre-AD 70 Israel? Surely many more than these were executed. And if other executed persons were buried properly, as I have argued they would have been, then why have we not found many more skeletons of executed persons? Accordingly, it has been argued by some that, in light of the thousands of Jews crucified in the first century in the vicinity of Jerusalem, the discovery of only one properly buried crucifixion victim is proof that the normal Roman practice of not permitting burial must have obtained, even in Jewish Palestine. On the basis of this logic perhaps one should conclude that Jesus was not buried either.[19]

At least four objections must be raised against this inference. First, almost all of the bones recovered from the time of Jesus are poorly preserved, especially the smaller bones of the feet and hands, which will normally provide evidence, if any, of crucifixion. It was the presence of the nail in the right heel of Yehohanan that made it clear that he had been crucified. The presence of the nail was a fluke. It was

---

[18] The strong familial bond, along with the practice of ossilegium, is probably what lies behind Jesus' surprising exhortation to the would-be disciple who requests time to "bury (his) father": "Follow me," Jesus tells the man, "and let the dead bury their own dead" (Matt 8:22). Viewed in the light of ossilegium and how the dead were understood, Jesus has told this man to allow the family members already interred in the family tomb to see to the reburial of his father's bones. For support of this interpretation, see B. R. McCane, "'Let the Dead Bury Their Own Dead': Secondary Burial and Matt 8:21–22," *HTR* 83 (1990): 31–43. On the idea of life (even if greatly diminished) still present in the bones, see Meyers, *Jewish Ossuaries*, 12–16. This idea provided a major part of the motivation to have one's bones buried in Israel, in one's family tomb. A number of those interred in tombs at Beth Shearim, Galilee, had at first been buried outside the land of Israel. The bones of some had been transported from as far away as Rome.

[19] This argument has been advanced by John Dominic Crossan, *Who Killed Jesus? Exposing the Roots of Anti-Semitism in the Gospel Story of the Death of Jesus* (San Francisco: HarperCollins, 1995).

due to the sharp end being bent back (like a fishhook), perhaps because the nail struck a knot in the upright beam. When Yehohanan was taken down from the cross, the nail could not be extracted. Accordingly, no statistics should be inferred from this unusual find.

Second, many crucifixion victims were scourged, beaten, and then tied to the cross, not nailed. Thus, skeletal remains would leave no trace of the trauma of crucifixion. Accordingly, we do not know that Yehohanan is the only crucifixion victim discovered in a tomb. Several other crucifixion victims may have been found without our knowing it.

Third, the best-preserved skeletons are found in the better-constructed tombs, within bone pits or in ossuaries. These tombs were mostly those of the rich or middle class, not the poor. The poor were usually buried in the ground, or in smaller natural caves. Not many of their skeletons have been found and when found the small bones are poorly preserved, if preserved at all. The significance of this point is that it is the poor who are most likely to be crucified, not the wealthy and powerful. Accordingly, those skeletons most likely to provide evidence of crucifixion are the skeletons least likely to survive, whereas the best-preserved skeletons are the ones least likely to have belonged to those who had been crucified.

Fourth, the vast majority of the thousands of Jews crucified and left unburied in the first century, in the vicinity of Jerusalem, died during the rebellion of 66–70 CE. They were not buried because Rome was at war with the Jewish people and had no wish to accommodate Jewish sensitivities, as Rome normally did during peacetime. It was during peacetime—indeed, during the administration of Pontius Pilate—that both Yehohanan and Jesus of Nazareth were crucified. That both were buried, according to Jewish customs, should hardly occasion surprise. Jewish priestly authorities were expected to defend the purity of Jerusalem (or at least give the appearance of doing so), while Roman authorities acquiesced to Jewish customs and sensitivities, as Philo and Josephus relate.[20]

The archeological evidence suggests that Jesus and other Jews executed in peacetime Israel were buried, not in honor but properly, in accordance with Jewish laws and customs. In the case of Jesus of Nazareth the expectation would have been to collect his skeletal remains approximately one year after death and transfer them from the place of dishonor to a place of honor, such as his family tomb or some other burial place. Burial customs and laws permitted this, and the strong social and family ties of the Jewish people of late antiquity expected it. However Jesus of Nazareth may have been viewed by family and acquaintances in the immediate aftermath of his execution, the anticipation of the gathering and reburying of his bones in the family tomb would have been more than probable.

---

[20] Philo, *De Legatione ad Gaium* 300: Romans normally do "not to disturb the customs which throughout all the preceding ages had been safeguarded without disturbance by kings and by emperors"; Josephus, *Ag Ap.* 2.73: Romans do not require "their subjects to violate their national laws."

7

THE TRIAL OF JESUS AT THE JERUSALEM PRAETORIUM: NEW ARCHAEOLOGICAL EVIDENCE

Shimon Gibson

More than any other story given in the Gospels concerning events in the life of Jesus, there is general agreement among NT historians and commentators that he was tried (c. 30 CE) in front of the Roman prefect Pontius Pilate at the praetorium in Jerusalem (Mark 15:2–20; Matt 27:11–31; Luke 23:2–25; John 18:28–19:16) and that this event ultimately resulted in his being sentenced to death and subsequently crucified.[1]

While none would disagree with the basic elements of this story, the historical credibility of the details of the trial proceedings, as given in the Gospels, has been seriously questioned, especially in view of contradictions and discrepancies that crop up in these accounts.[2] What some critics find particularly doubtful are

---

[1] All quotations from the Gospels are taken from the NRSV. I am grateful to Craig Evans for inviting me to contribute this chapter, and to Mareike Grosser for going over the manuscript and correcting the bibliography. It is dedicated to the memory of Doug Edwards.

[2] Joseph Klausner, *Jesus of Nazareth: His Life, Times, and Teaching* (New York: Macmillan, 1945); Joel Carmichael, *The Death of Jesus* (London: Gollancz, 1963); Paul Winter, "The Trial of Jesus," *Commentary*, September (1964): 35–41; idem, *On the Trial of Jesus.* (Berlin: de Gruyter, 1974); S. G. F. Brandon, *The Trial of Jesus of Nazareth* (London: Batsford, 1968); David Flusser, *Jesus* (New York: Herder & Herder, 1969), 116–32; idem, *Judaism and the Origins of Christianity* (Jerusalem: Magnes Press, 1988), 588–92; Tibor Horvath, "Why Was Jesus Brought to Pilate?" *NovT* 11/3 (1969): 174–84; T. A. Burkill, "The Trial of Jesus,'" *Vigiliae Christianae* 12/1 (1958): 1–18; idem, "The Condemnation of Jesus: A Critique of Sherwin-White's Thesis," *NovT* 12/4 (1970): 321–42; William Riley Wilson, *The Execution of Jesus: A Judicial, Literary, and Historical Investigation* (New York: Scribners, 1970); Michael Grant, *Jesus* (London: Rigel, 1977), 156–66; Fergus Millar, "Reflections on the Trial of Jesus," in *A Tribute to Geza Vermes* (ed. P. R. Davies and R. T. White; Sheffield: JSOT Press, 1990), 356–81; E. P. Sanders, *The Historical Figure of Jesus* (London: Allen Lane, 1993), 265–74; John Dominic Crossan, *Who Killed Jesus? Exposing the Roots of Anti-Semitism in the Gospel Story of the Death of Jesus* (New York: HarperCollins, 1996), 82–117; John Dominic Crossan and Jonathan L. Reed, *Excavating Jesus: Beneath the Stones, Behind the Texts* (New York: HarperCollins, 2001), 264–71; Simon Légasse, *The Trial of Jesus* (London: SCM,

the spoken words that were purportedly made by the key participants at the trial, namely, by Jesus and Pilate. Furthermore, some researchers have expressed doubts as to whether the proceedings described in the Gospels were even legal in terms of the Roman judicial system as practiced in the provinces at that time.[3] There are even those who would discount the historical accuracy of the basic storyline of the trial narrative, particularly the version given in the Fourth Gospel, on the grounds that the trial must have taken place behind closed doors and therefore could not have been witnessed by supporters of Jesus but only by a handful of Roman officials.[4] This has led some researchers to take the extreme stance of dismissing the entire trial narrative—except for some of the very basic elements of the story—as a literary creation devoid of historical content.[5]

The chapter cautiously argues against taking such a negative approach to the subject of the trial of Jesus as portrayed in the Gospels. The basis for this conclusion is a new study I have made on the overall layout of the palace of Herod the Great, which later became the seat of the Roman governor when in residence in Jerusalem, the praetorium. My work also highlights previously unpublished archeological discoveries pertaining to the appearance of the western gateway of the palace/praetorium, which I think is the Gate of the Essenes referred to by Josephus.[6] This monumental gateway had inner and outer gates flanked by large towers, and these gates were separated one from the other by a large, open, and paved court at its center, with a rocky area on its north. In the first century CE, the gateway undoubtedly provided direct access to the palace grounds, which incorporated palace residences, an ornamental pleasure garden, and military barracks. Remarkably, these archeological remains fit very well with John's description of the place of Jesus' temporary incarceration and the trial in front of Pilate, and with the two topographical features that are mentioned by him, the *lithostrotos* and *gabbatha*.

The purpose of this chapter, therefore, is to provide the reader with a reassessment of the historical, topographical, and archeological evidence available regard-

1997); Darrell L. Bock, *Jesus According to Scripture: Restoring the Portrait from the Gospels* (Grand Rapids: Baker Academic, 2002); Marcus J. Borg and John Dominic Crossan, *The Last Week: A Day-by-Day Account of Jesus's Final Week in Jerusalem* (New York: HarperCollins, 2006); Craig A. Evans and N. T. Wright, *Jesus, the Final Days: What Really Happened* (Louisville: Westminster John Knox, 2009).

[3] A. N. Sherwin-White, *Roman Society and Roman Law in the New Testament: The Sarum Lectures, 1960–61* (Oxford: Clarendon Press, 1965); Haim Cohen, *The Trial and Death of Jesus* (Old Saybrook, CT: Konecky & Konecky, 1968); R. Larry Overstreet, "Roman Law and the Trial of Christ," *BSac* (October–December 1978): 323–32; Earl Schwartz, "The Trials of Jesus and Paul," *Journal of Law and Religion* 9/2 (1992): 501–13.

[4] G. A. Wells wrote emphatically: "There were thus no Jewish witnesses to report the trial," in *The Jesus of the Early Christians: A Study in Christian Origins* (London: Pemberton, 1971), 99.

[5] Crossan, *Who Killed Jesus?* 117; see also Crossan and Reed, *Excavating Jesus*, 264–71.

[6] Shimon Gibson, "Suggested Identifications for 'Bethso' and the 'Gate of the Essenes' in the Light of Magen Broshi's Excavations on Mount Zion," in *New Studies in the Archaeology of Jerusalem and Its Region* (ed. Joseph Patrich et al.; 4 vols.; Jerusalem: IAA, 2007), 1:29*–33*.

ing the situation of the palace/praetorium and its various parts. It was here the trial of Jesus took place, and on this matter there is almost unanimous agreement among scholars.[7] But there is less agreement on whether the trial took place inside or adjacent to the praetorium. What I will suggest is that the monumental gateway uncovered in excavations on the western side of the palace/praetorium should now be considered a reasonable candidate for the place where the trial of Jesus took place.

The Arrest of Jesus and the Proceedings at the House of Caiaphas

Following his arrest by soldiers and the temple police at the garden of Gethsemane, Jesus was subsequently taken to the house of Joseph Caiaphas for questioning (Mark 14:54, 66–68; Matt 26:58, 69, 71; Luke 22:55; John 18:15–19; see Fig. 1).

At the time of Jesus' arrest, Caiaphas (18–36 CE) was the officiating high priest.[8] Mark for some reason does not mention the name of the high priest, but Matthew states quite clearly that Jesus was brought "to the house of Caiaphas the high priest" (Matt 26:57). In the Gospel of John, however, Jesus was first taken to Annas (or Ananus I), the father-in-law of Caiaphas. The exact location of the Annas/Caiaphas household (if this was a combined building complex) is unknown, though later Byzantine tradition situated it in the area of Mount Zion on the western side of the city, not far from the supposed Roman governor's palace.[9] It may conceivably have been situated close to the first-century palaces of Agrippa and Berenice, which are said by Josephus (*J.W.* 2.427) to be in the general area of the Upper City. Appointed by Valerius Gratus, Caiaphas had a complicated career and was ultimately deposed by Vitellius, governor of Syria, in the same year that Pilate was removed from office. Caiaphas belonged to a powerful and influential family, and it seems he had a son named Elioeneiai ben ha-Kayyaf.[10] Archeological work has brought to light a rock-hewn cave to the south of the city that may have served as the Caiaphas family tomb.[11]

---

[7] See Charles W. Wilson, *Golgotha and the Holy Sepulchre* (London: PEF, 1906), 41–44; R. Eckardt, "Das Praetorium des Pilatus," *Zeitschrift des Deutschen Palästina-Vereins* 34 (1911): 39–48; Pierre Benoit, "Prétoire, Lithostroton et Gabbatha," *RB* 59 (1952): 531–50; Jean-Pierre Lémonon, *Pilate et le Gouvernement de la Judée: Textes et Monuments* (Paris: Gabalda, 1981), 117–24. Bargil Pixner disagreed with this location; see Bargil Pixner, "Noch einmal das Prätorium. Versuch einer neuen Lösung," *Zeitschrift des Deutschen Palästina-Vereins* 95 (1979): 56–86.

[8] Klausner, *Jesus of Nazareth*, 339–40; Helen K. Bond, *Caiaphas: Friend of Rome and Judge of Jesus?* (London: Westminister John Knox, 2004).

[9] Gustaf Dalman, *Sacred Sites and Ways: Studies in the Topography of the Gospels* (London: SPCK, 1935), 328–30; Pierre Benoit, "Le Prétoire de Pilate à L'Époque Byzantine," *RB* 91/2 (1984): 161–77.

[10] See references to this family in rabbinical sources: *m. Parah* 3:5; *t. Yebamoth* 1.10.

[11] In 1990 a rock-hewn tomb was accidentally unearthed on the north side of the modern neighborhood of Talpiot, a couple of kilometers to the south of ancient Jerusalem.

Jesus was interrogated by Caiaphas at his house in front of an impromptu assembly of Sanhedrin council members. The Sanhedrin was the principal Jewish authoritative body in Jerusalem at that time. On the following morning, additional members of the council came to Caiaphas's house and following a consultation a decision was made to turn Jesus over to Pilate for trial. Luke presents things a bit differently: Jesus' being interrogated in the morning and without witnesses. Considerable scholarly debate has taken place in regard to the extent and limits of the Sanhedrin's powers during the first century CE, with the current consensus of opinion leaning toward the view that it was able to exercise quite a few of its judicial powers on social and religious matters.[12] While the Sanhedrin was a form of high court or senate, it is unclear whether the full forum of this body would have convened specifically to deal with the matter of Jesus, especially since it was just before the Passover festivities. The Sanhedrin would normally convene at the Chamber of Hewn Stone near the temple, but never apparently at night.[13] If this meeting did take place, which was highly unusual, it was more likely to have been an *ad hoc* assembly of select members of the Sanhedrin (the Council, *bouleutes*, in Mark 15:43) that convened in order to determine whether or not Jesus should be

---

Excavations were immediately undertaken by archaeologist Zvi Greenhut. The tomb was a typical one of the first century, nothing lavish, with a roughly rectangular central chamber with a standing pit, and with four *kokhim* in its walls. There were twelve ossuaries, five of them inscribed, and two of them were particularly exciting. One had a scratched inscription reading "Yehosef bar Qayafa" (Joseph son of Caiaphas) and "Yehosef bar Qafa" on the other side. Another ossuary was simply inscribed "Qafa," or Caiaphas: Zvi Greenhut, "The 'Caiaphas' Tomb in North Talpiyot, Jerusalem,'" 'Atiqot 21 (1992): 63–72; David Flusser, "Caiaphas in the New Testament," 'Atiqot 21 (1992): 81–87. For a critical view of the significance of these finds, see W. Horbury, "The 'Caiaphas' Ossuaries and Joseph Caiaphas," *PEQ* 126 (1994): 32–48; Craig A. Evans, *Jesus and the Ossuaries: What Jewish Burial Practices Reveal about the Beginning of Christianity* (Waco, TX: Baylor University Press, 2003), 107–8; idem, "Excavating Caiaphas, Pilate, and Simon of Cyrene: Assessing the Literary and Archaeological Evidence," *Jesus and Archaeology* (ed. J. H. Charlesworth; Grand Rapids: Eerdmans, 2006), 323–40. Undoubtedly, this tomb belonged to the priestly family of Caiaphas. It may even have had a prominent monument outside that could be seen from a distance. None has been found, but it might have been dismantled in antiquity or may even have been accidentally bulldozed before excavations began. Similarly, the tomb monuments in the Kidron Valley are very impressive, whereas the actual hewn burial chambers attached to them are quite simple. So I am not too bothered by the simplicity of the tomb as an argument for it not being the Caiaphas family tomb.

[12] Geza Vermes, *The Passion* (London: Penguin, 2005).

[13] It is unclear whether there was a single Sanhedrin, or, alternatively, two supreme bodies by that name in Jerusalem, a political and a religious one; if so, then the latter was also known as the *bet din ha-gadol*; see Hugo Mantel, "Sanhedrin," *Encyclopedia Judaica* (2nd ed.; 2007), 18:22–23. The Council Chamber, or the Xystus, should be identified with a substantial and well-preserved building situated due west of Wilson's Arch along the western wall of the Temple Mount. It was first investigated by Charles Warren in 1868, who named it the "Masonic Hall". Additional chambers with pilasters in its walls with well-preserved Corinthian capitals, have recently been uncovered by the Israel Antiquities Authority immediately west of the so-called Masonic Hall, and the whole complex dates to the Herodian period. My thanks to Alexander Onne and his team for allowing me to visit these on-going excavations.

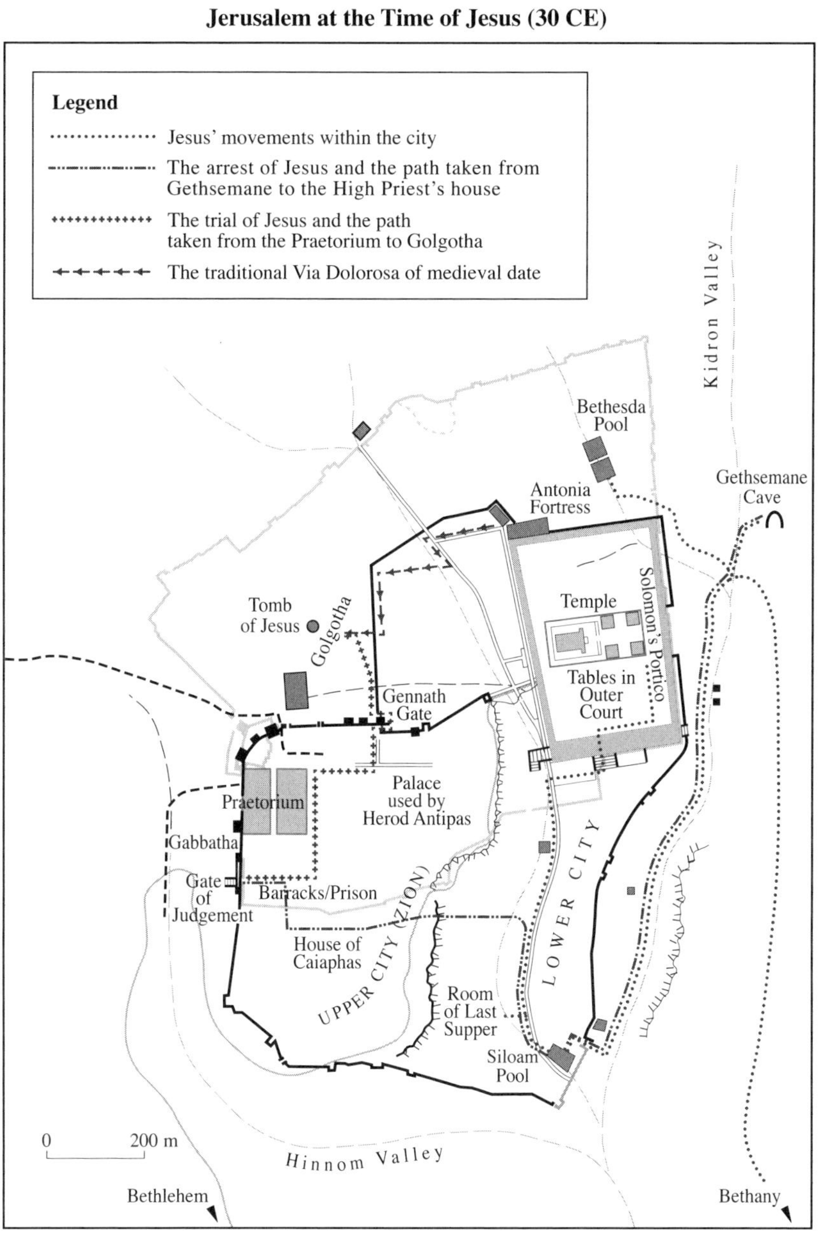

Jerusalem at the Time of Jesus (30 CE)

Legend

················ Jesus' movements within the city

─·─··─··─··─ The arrest of Jesus and the path taken from
Gethsemane to the High Priest's house

✦✦✦✦✦✦✦✦✦✦ The trial of Jesus and the path
taken from the Praetorium to Golgotha

←←←←← The traditional Via Dolorosa of medieval date

Kidron Valley

Bethesda Pool

Gethsemane Cave

Antonia Fortress

Solomon's Portico

Temple

Tomb of Jesus

Golgotha

Tables in Outer Court

Gennath Gate

Palace used by Herod Antipas

Praetorium

Gabbatha

LOWER CITY

Gate of Judgement

Barracks/Prison

House of Caiaphas

UPPER CITY (ZION)

Room of Last Supper

Siloam Pool

0   200 m

Hinnom Valley

Bethlehem

Bethany

Fig. 1: Map of Jerusalem at the time of Jesus (c. 30 CE).
Drawing: Vered Shatil. Copyright: S. Gibson

charged with blasphemy based on the reports provided by witnesses. Alternatively, this last-minute meeting may have been arranged by concerned members of the council, perhaps even instigated by Joseph of Arimathea, to see if Jesus might be willing to admit to a lesser charge so that he need not stand trial with the Romans on the more serious charge of sedition or claims to kingship.[14] This might explain why when following his arrest at Gethsemane Jesus was not led directly to the Roman barracks for imprisonment and to await trial but was first brought to the home of the high priest. Ordinarily, the Sanhedrin should have been concerned with the preservation of human life (see *m. Makkot* 1:10), but Jesus may have had enemies on the council who were not sympathetic to his message. What is absolutely certain is that the Sanhedrin had no jurisdiction on matters of sedition or insurrection, and such accusations could have been dealt with only by the Romans. For this reason John says "the Jews replied [to Pilate], 'We are not permitted to put anyone to death'" (John 18:31).

Pontius Pilate

Pontius Pilate was the supreme Roman authority at that time in Judea (26–36 CE) and was of equestrian rank within the lower ranks of Roman nobility.[15] In the Gospels he was called "governor," but Josephus, as well as Tacitus (*Annales* XV.44:3), refers to him as "procurator." A stone fragment of a monumental Latin inscription found at Caesarea in 1961, reading "[Po]ntius Pilatus / [Praef]ectus Iuda[ea]e," indicates that Pilate's correct title was *praefectus* over the province of Judea.[16] This dedicatory inscription was apparently for an edifice at Caesarea called Tiberieum, which was built by Pilate in honor of the emperor Tiberias (14–37 CE).[17] This edifice may have been a lighthouse on the edge of the harbor, or perhaps a building associated with the Roman imperial cult.[18] It is not surprising that Pilate would have wanted to embellish Caesarea with additional buildings since his own official resi-

---

[14]Horvath, "Why Was Jesus Brought to Pilate?" 180.

[15]See the excellent study by Helen K. Bond, *Pontius Pilate in History and Interpretation* (SNTSMS 100; Cambridge: Cambridge University Press, 1998). For the suggestion that Pilate took up office earlier in 19 CE, see Daniel R. Schwartz, "Pontius Pilate," in *The Anchor Bible Dictionary* (ed. David Noel Freedman et al.; 6 vols.; New York: Doubleday, 1992), 5:395–401.

[16]For the circumstances of the discovery of the inscription with a map and photographs showing where it was found, see Antonio Frova, "L'Inscrizione di Ponzio Pilato a Cesarea," *Rendiconti, Classe di Lettere, Instituto Lombardo* 95 (1961): 419–34. The supposition that Pilate was procurator still sometimes persists in the literature; see Laurna L. Berg, "The Illegalities of Jesus' Religious and Civil Trials," *BSac* 161 (July–September 2004): 330–42, here 335.

[17]Menahem Stern, ed., *Greek and Latin Authors on Jews and Judaism* (3 vols.; Jerusalem: Israel Institute of Science and Humanities, 1980), 2:89, 92; Evans, *Jesus and the Ossuaries,* 45–47.

[18]For the suggestion that the Tiberieum was a lighthouse, see G. Alföldy, "Pontius Pilatus und das Tiberieum von Caesarea Maritima," *Scripta Classica Israelitica* 18 (1999): 85–108; a building for the Roman imperial cult, see Joan E. Taylor, "Pontius Pilate and the Imperial Cult in Roman Judaea," *NTS* 52 (2006): 555–82.

dence was situated there at the praetorium, in the area of the old palace of Herod the Great, remains of which have been uncovered in recent excavations.[19]

Josephus depicts Pilate as a cruel, ruthless, and brutal person. Philo also describes him as guilty of "venality, violence, robbery, assault, abusive behavior, frequent executions without trial, and endless savage ferocity" (*Legatio ad Gaium* 301–302).[20] Early on in Pilate's rule he brought military standards bearing the imperial image into Jerusalem, thereby provoking substantial rioting. But the picture of Pilate provided in the Gospels is quite different. He is portrayed there as an indecisive and compassionate man, and surprisingly also a believer in Jesus' innocence, which is not at all credible in my opinion.[21] He was undoubtedly a hard and manipulative man, and this comes across in the devious way in which he conducted the suppression of a protest made by the inhabitants of Jerusalem who accused him of misusing the *korban* temple funds for the construction or restoration of a water aqueduct to Jerusalem: "Large numbers of the Jews perished, some from the blows they received, others trodden to death by their companions in the ensuing flight. Cowed by the fate of the victims, the multitude was reduced to silence" (*J.W.* 2.177).[22] There is also the reference to Pilate being involved at some point in the spilling of Galilean blood in Jerusalem (Luke 13:1). Six years after the death of Jesus, Pilate used inordinate violence by massacring Samaritans and killing several of their leaders (36 CE); this brutality eventually led to him being recalled to Rome (Josephus, *Ant.* 18.85–87).

In view of his propensity for violence as a means of achieving his ends, would Pilate have even bothered giving a low-ranking individual such as Jesus a trial, when this matter might conceivably have been dealt with by a Roman subordinate? Perhaps at any other time of the year this might have been the case, but, I

---

[19] Acts 23:35. For the praetorium at Caesarea, see Kathryn L. Gleason, "The Promontory Palace at Caesarea Maritima: Preliminary Evidence for Herod's *Praetorium*," *Journal of Roman Archaeology* 11 (1998): 41–52; Joseph Patrich, "A Chapel of St. Paul at Caesarea Maritima," *Liber Annuus* 50 (2000): 363–82. See also Hannah M. Cotton and Werner Eck, "Governors and Their Personnel on Latin Inscriptions from Caesarea Maritima," *The Israel Academy of Sciences and Humanitis Proceedings* 7/7 (2001): 215–40. Cotton and Eck (216) use the term *praetorium* to refer not just to the official residence of the Roman governor in the promontory palace, but to the entire complex of buildings extending between the circus to the north and the city wall to the south. The circus is probably the same as the "great stadium" where Pilate set up his tribunal (Josephus, *J.W.* 2.172).

[20] For the possibility that the hostility expressed in Josephus and Philo may not be entirely accurate, see Raymond E. Brown, *The Death of the Messiah: From Gethsemane to the Grave: A Commentary on the Passion Narratives in the Four Gospels* (2 vols.; New York: Doubleday, 1998), 1:695–97.

[21] See the opposing views of Stephen J. Patterson, "Pilate in the Dock: For the Prosecution," *BRev* 20/3 (2004): 30–32; and Paul L. Maier, "Pilate in the Dock: For the Defense," *BRev* 20/3 (2004): 27–30, 32.

[22] I think the reason for the riots was that the funds were diverted for the construction or restoration of the high-level aqueduct, which would have benefitted the Upper City, particularly the area of the praetorium and especially its gardens, whereas the low-level aqueduct extended all the way to the temple and the rest of the city; funds used for that purpose would have made more sense to the populace.

think, because of the sensitivities of the Passover week, it is more than likely Pilate would have wanted to deal with the matter himself so as to ensure a firm outcome. The assembly of the Sanhedrin had seemingly not been able to resolve the matter, and Pilate was probably afraid that if he was not seen to be dealing with the matter decisively, unrest on the street might quickly turn into a full-blown insurrection. Pilate would not have wanted a long, drawn-out trial and would have insisted that Jesus be dispatched to his death without delay.

The fact that Pilate was wary of the inhabitants of Jerusalem and at times did try to take heed of the mood of the crowd is made clear from the episode of the iconic standards, which probably occurred not long after he had taken up office (26 CE). Pilate's soldiers arrived in Jerusalem—probably entering through the Gate of the Essenes (see below)—for winter encampment, and they brought with them their standards bearing the imperial image and entered the city at night.[23] The soldiers would have gone directly to the barracks within the praetorium on its south side, which might even have had provision for a special shrine (*sacellum*) to contain the standards. The soldiers did not intend to transfer them to the Antonia fortress, which might reasonably have caused severe offense to Jews owing to its proximity to the temple.[24] The inhabitants of Jerusalem, we are told by Josephus, were in an uproar because they felt their "laws [that] permit no image to be erected in the city" had been broken, even though the praetorium was an independent compound cut off from the rest of the city (*J.W.* 2.169–174). Hence, the protestors made their way to Caesarea, where they demonstrated *en masse* against the standards. Pilate finally capitulated, and the standards were removed from Jerusalem.

The Place of the Trial Based on the Gospels

While Pilate's official residence was at Caesarea on the Mediterranean coast, there can be no doubt that on the occasions when he stayed in Jerusalem, particularly during the Jewish festivities, he took up residence at Herod's old palace situated on the west side of the city, also known as the praetorium (Fig. 2). The word *praetorium* might refer to a palace or a judicial or military seat, but it is likely that in Jerusalem it referred to the entire palace compound, which on the north included palatial buildings used for residential purposes and on the south, military barracks. This general use of the term *praetorium* creates difficulties when trying to establish the exact location of the trial of Jesus.

Mark, Matthew, and Luke tell us what happened at the trial, but without providing much information about the place where it was conducted and the actual program of the proceedings. Mark has the following:

---

[23]Josephus, *Ant.* 18.55, described these as "busts of the emperor that were attached to the military standards." For a detailed study of the episode of the standards, see Carl H. Kraeling, "The Episode of the Roman Standards at Jerusalem," *HTR* 35/4 (1942): 263–89.

[24]Contrary to Kraeling, "The Episode of the Roman Standards," 280, who assumes that the standards were taken to the Antonia.

Fig. 2: Aerial view of the upper Hinnom Valley showing the place of the palace/praetorium in the present-day Armenian Garden behind the city wall. Photograph: Richard Cleave. Copyright: RØHR Productions

As soon as it was morning, the chief priests held a consultation with the elders and scribes and the whole council. They bound Jesus, led him away, and handed him over to Pilate. Pilate asked him, "Are you the King of the Jews?" He answered him, "You say so." Then the chief priests accused him of many things. Pilate asked him again, "Have you no answer? See how many charges they bring against you." But Jesus made no further reply, so that Pilate was amazed (Mark 15:1–5).[25]

---

[25] William Sanger Campbell, "Engagement, Disengagement and Obstruction: Jesus' Defense Strategies in Mark's Trial and Execution Scenes (14:53–64; 15:1–39)," *JSNT* 26/3 (2004): 283–300.

Mark then goes on to relate how Pilate offered clemency for a prisoner in view of the upcoming Passover holiday, hoping that the crowd of Jews would choose Jesus. Many scholars do not regard this story as historical.[26] In fact, there is nothing tangible in the sources of the period to suggest that such a Roman clemency existed at times of Jewish festivities in Judea or elsewhere.

Setting aside the complications and contradictions about the trial as set forth in the Gospels, what is certain is that Jesus was ultimately condemned to death by Pilate, who was the supreme Roman authority in Jerusalem at that time, and then summarily executed by crucifixion, which was a Roman and not a Jewish method of execution. In this regard, Josephus, writing in the years following the fall of Jerusalem in 70 CE, provides a clear, albeit concise, reference to these events which is in my opinion entirely believable: "Pilate, upon hearing him [Jesus] accused by men of the highest standing among us, had condemned him to be crucified" (*Ant.* 18.64). Tacitus, writing about eighty or so years after the death of Jesus, also says the sentence was carried out by Pilate: "Christus, the founder of the name, had undergone the death penalty in the reign of Tiberius, by sentence of the procurator [*sic*] Pontius Pilate, and the pernicious superstition (*exitiabilis superstitio*) was checked for a moment" (*Annales* 15.44.3).[27]

Mark 15:8 does not tell us very much about the location of the trial of Jesus, except that at one point the crowd "went up" to Pilate, perhaps indicating that he was seated at an elevated spot at the place of the trial.[28] Matthew adds that Pilate "was sitting on his judgment-seat" (*bema*) and that a crowd was "gathered together" at the tribunal (Matt 27:17–19). Pilate's judgment seat (a throne or bench) may have been of the same kind used by Herod the Great's son, the tetrarch Philip. Josephus wrote that during Philip's travels "the throne on which he sat when he gave judgment accompanied him wherever he went. And so, whenever anyone appealed to him for redress along the route, at once without a moment's delay the throne was set up wherever it might be. He took his seat and gave the case a hearing" (*Ant.* 18.107). Governors in Roman-controlled territories ordinarily dispensed justice in a public arena such as in a court or open square adjacent to the praetorium, with a judgment seat set up on a raised platform with access steps along one side (Latin *tribunal*; Greek *bema*). In Mark the impression is that the trial of Jesus was outdoors, especially since Jesus was later led away into the inner grounds of the palace (*aule*) at the praetorium (Mark 15:16). This is also the impression in Matt 27:27: "Then the soldiers of the governor took Jesus into the governor's headquarters, and they gathered the whole cohort around him." This has led some scholars, notably Raymond E. Brown, to infer that Jesus was taken from the first outdoor location for a private interrogation *inside* the praetorium building.[29] However, the fact

---

[26] Burkill, "The Condemnation of Jesus," 327; Crossan, *Who Killed Jesus?* 111.

[27] Menaham Stern, ed., *Greek and Latin Authors*, 89; *Annales* xv. 44 (trans. J. Jackson; LCL; London: Heinemann, 1951), 4:283.

[28] On the role of the crowd at the trial, see Brown, *Death of the Messiah*, 720–22; Brian E. Messner, "Pontius Pilate and the Trial of Jesus: The Crowd," *Stone-Campbell Journal* 3 (2000): 195–207.

[29] Brown, *Death of the Messiah*, 705.

that Jesus was subsequently taunted by a large number of soldiers at the second location goes against such an interpretation. Moreover, as we shall see, the layout of the gateway and the adjacent palace, garden, and barracks suggests a different reconstruction of events, with Jesus being led from the public court of the gateway into a court in front of the barracks or to the actual barracks, to which there would have been no access for the public. Unlike Mark and Matthew, Luke does not say anything about the place of the trial or its setting.[30]

The Gospel of John provides additional information about the location of the trial that does not appear in the synoptic narratives.[31] Jesus was led from the house of Caiaphas "into the praetorium and it was early, and they [the priests] themselves entered not into the praetorium, that they might not be defiled, but might eat the Passover" (John 18:28–29).[32] Pilate "therefore went out to them" to find out what the accusation was. This description makes it clear that the place was situated outside the praetorium proper and near a gate, and that Jesus was eventually incarcerated or held in a prison nearby. The priests might have ventured within the gate but no further for fear of becoming ritually impure, a common fear among Jews at that time.[33] We are then told that Pilate went in and out of the praetorium, with Jesus being scourged, and then he "went out again," all of which suggests that the actual trial took place in an open space (John 18:33, 38; 19:4, 13). Jesus was eventually brought out to the place of the tribunal wearing a crown of thorns and purple robes, a sight that inflamed the crowd, and then was taken back into the praetorium grounds with Pilate following (John 19:5, 9). John 19:13 tells us that Pilate subsequently brought Jesus outside again and that he then sat on his judgment seat (*bema*) at an elevated rocky place (*gabbatha*) next to the place called the stone pavement (*lithostrotos*). The information provided by John fits well with what one gathers from Josephus regarding the Roman tribunal being situated at

---

[30] Joseph B. Tyson, "The Lukan Version of the Trial of Jesus," *NovT* 3/4 (1959): 249–58; Paul W. Walaskay, "The Trial and Death of Jesus in the Gospel of Luke," *JBL* 94/1 (1975): 81–93.

[31] David Rensberger, "The Politics of John: The Trial of Jesus in the Fourth Gospel," *JBL* 103/3 (1984): 395–411; Bart D. Ehrman, "Jesus' Trial Before Pilate: John 18:28–19:16," *BTB* 13 (1983): 124–31; Peter-Ben Smit, "The Final Verdict: A Note on the Structure of Jesus' Trial in the Gospel of John," *RB* 115/3 (2008): 383–95.

[32] Brown takes John 18:28–29, 33, 38; 19:4, 9 to mean that Jesus was led into the praetorium building, but as we shall see it can also be understood that Jesus was taken into the praetorium compound, to which the city inhabitants would not have been given access; see Brown, *Death of the Messiah*, 705.

[33] Shimon Gibson, "Stone Vessels of the Early Roman Period from Jerusalem and Palestine: A Reassessment," in *One Land—Many Cultures: Archaeological Studies in Honour of S. Loffreda* (ed. G. Claudio Bottini, Leah Di Segni, and L. Daniel Chrupcala; Jerusalem: Franciscan Printing Press, 2003), 287–308; idem, "Jewish Purification Practices and the Bethesda Pools in Jerusalem," *Proche-Orient Chrétien* 55 (2005): 270–93; idem, "New Excavations on Mount Zion in Jerusalem and an Inscribed Stone Cup/Mug from the Second Temple Period," in *New Studies in the Archaeology of Jerusalem and Its Region* (ed. David Amit et al.; 4 vols.; Jerusalem: IAA, 2010), 4:32*–43*; idem, "The Archaeology of Jesus in Jerusalem," in *Loy H. Witherspoon Lecture Booklet in Religious Studies* (Charlotte: University of North Carolina at Charlotte, 2009).

an elevated location on the west side of the praetorium (see below). The reference to a stone pavement would indicate that this place had a large open court with flagstones. Dalman's estimation was that this place "was a paved terrace erected for the purpose of public transactions."[34] The Aramaic (not Hebrew, as in John) word *gabbatha* does not refer to the pavement but to another feature at the place of the trial, and the word may have been derived from *gabbeta*, meaning "height"; the Hebrew equivalent would have been *gibath* or *gabath*.[35]

The Palace of Herod/Praetorium

Over the past century, scholars have debated the location of the praetorium mentioned in the Gospels, with suggestions that it was at the Antonia fortress, which was situated on a high, rocky outcrop at the northwest corner of the Temple Mount; or that it was at Herod's palace on the west side of the city on the summit of the Upper City.[36] Nowadays, a consensus of opinion exists among scholars that the trial of Jesus took place at Herod's palace.[37]

It is highly unlikely that Jesus was tried at the Antonia, since it served primarily as a military observation tower (*pyrgos*) with a specific function: to keep an eye on the activities of the Jewish worshipers on the Temple Mount and to prevent rioting or demonstrations there. It was to this spot, one will remember, that Paul was later brought after having been saved from the temple mob (Acts 21:30–36). The tower was also too cramped for it to serve as the residence and headquarters of the governing official. As a controlling maneuver this was the place where the Romans kept the Jewish high priest's vestments. Archeological work shows that hardly anything has survived of the actual structure of the Antonia fortress except for the rock-cut base itself on the northwest of the Temple Mount. Judging by the very limited size of the rock base which I have measured (90 m x 40 m), it would appear that this fortress was no more than a very large and high tower with turrets at its corners, and with a flight of broad steps leading down into the temple area.[38]

Herod's palace lay at the northwest angle of the Upper City, in the area spanning the distance between the present-day citadel, *Kishle*, and Armenian Garden. It was built in the fifteenth year of Herod's reign (i.e., in 25 BCE). Following the deposing of Herod's son Archelaus in 6 CE, the palace was used thereafter as the

---

[34]Dalman, *Sacred Sites and Ways*, 337.

[35]Ibid., 335. See the use of the word to denote a prominent height in the toponym Gabath Saul (i.e., Gibeah of Saul/Tell el Ful) mentioned in Josephus, *J.W.* 5.51; see Eyal Regev, "Josephus on Gibeah: Versions of a Toponym," *The Jewish Quarterly Review* 89/3–4 (1999), 351–59. For additional place names, see Yoel Elitzur, *Ancient Place Names in the Holy Land: Preservation and History* (Winona Lake, IN: Eisenbrauns, 2004), 177, 297, 300.

[36]Dalman, *Sacred Sites and Ways*, 335–36; Brown, *Death of the Messiah*, 706–10.

[37]Benoit, "Prétoire," 531–50; Lémonon, *Pilate et le Gouvernement de la Judée*, 117–24.

[38]For a new assessment of the date of the construction of the Antonia and surrounding buildings, see Shimon Gibson, "The Excavations at the Bethesda Pool in Jerusalem: Preliminary Report on a Project of Stratigraphic and Structural Analysis," *Proche-Orient Chrétien* (forthcoming).

military and civic headquarters of the Roman governors in Jerusalem. The fact that Herod's palace was used by Pontius Pilate as his residence becomes clear from the episode of the votive round shields (of *clipeus* type) that were dedicated "in honor of Tiberias" in 32 CE, as related by Philo of Alexandria (*Legatio ad Gaium* 299–305).[39] The introduction of the gilded shields into Jerusalem was seen as an act of desecration, infuriating the local population, with this event eventually reaching the ears of the emperor Tiberias, who insisted on having them removed.

The northern edge of the palace precinct was protected by a strong fortification system with three tall and impressive towers that were inserted at intervals in the Old (or First) wall. Herod the Great named these after friends and a former wife: Hippicus, Phasael, and Mariamne. The massive base of one of these towers (probably Hippicus) is visible today in the citadel near the Jaffa Gate.[40] Josephus wrote that "adjoining and on the inner side of these towers, which lay to the north of it, was the king's palace, baffling all description: indeed, in extravagance and equipment no building surpassed it" (*J.W.* 5.176–183).

The palace itself consisted of twin apartments or wings (the Caesareum and Agrippium) elevated upon a massive podium, parts of which have been uncovered in archeological excavations in the Armenian Garden.[41] The buildings are described by Josephus as being exceedingly large and high, and richly decorated with gold and stones and wall decorations. Duane W. Roller has discussed Josephus's description, suggesting that the "stones" he mentions refer to marble revetment and that the other wall decorations are paintings.[42] While wall paintings were quite typical for this period at sites in Jerusalem and elsewhere, marble was hardly used as a building material prior to the founding of the pagan city Aelia Capitolina in the early second century CE.[43] The "stones" therefore probably refer to highly polished local colored stones.[44] It is disappointing that so little has been recovered of the superstructure of the palace complex. It would appear that the magnificent

---

[39] Paul L. Maier, "The Episode of the Golden Roman Shields at Jerusalem," *HTR* 62/1 (1969): 109–21; Taylor, "Pontius Pilate and the Imperial Cult," 575–82.

[40] It is generally agreed that the one visible tower in the citadel known as the Tower of David must be Hippicus, though there is less agreement as to where the other two are situated; see Hillel Geva, "The 'Tower of David'—Phasael or Hippicus?" *IEJ* 31/1–2 (1981): 57–65; Dan Bahat, "David's Tower and Its Name in Second Temple Times," *Eretz-Israel* 15 (1981): 396–400 (Hebrew). I believe Phasael is the southernmost ancient tower uncovered in excavations in the citadel courtyard and that Mariamne should be identified with a prominent tower halfway along the present western Old City wall.

[41] Shimon Gibson, "The 1961–67 Excavations in the Armenian Garden, Jerusalem," *PEQ* 119 (1987): 81–96; Ehud Netzer, *The Architecture of Herod, the Great Builder* (Tübingen: Mohr Siebeck, 2006), 129–32.

[42] Duane W. Roller, *The Building Program of Herod the Great* (Berkeley: University of California Press, 1998), 176.

[43] Sylvia Rozenberg, "On Wall-Painting Workshops in the Land of Israel," *Michmanim* 22 (2010): 7*–20*.

[44] On the use of multicolored stones for pavements in Jerusalem, see Assaf Avraham, "Addressing the Issue of Temple Mount Pavements During the Herodian Period," in *New Studies on Jerusalem* (ed. E. Baruch et al.; Ramat Gan: University of Bar Ilan, 2007), 13:87–96 (Hebrew).

palace was dismantled down to its foundations in the Byzantine period, in the fifth century CE, to make way for Christian chapels and monastic dwellings. Sufficient features of the palace have however survived, enabling us to provide for the first time a fairly good reconstruction of where the palace was situated and what it looked like (Fig. 3).

The size of the actual palace building complex appears to have been 140 meters from north to south, judging by a set of broad, rock-cut steps uncovered in the present-day citadel moat, which ran along the north side of Herod's building and by the podium boundary wall delimiting it to the south.[45] Since, according to Josephus, the palace consisted of two wings, we may suggest that the palace was a square building with an equivalent distance of 140 meters from east to west. The service buildings, with kitchens, installations, and storerooms, were located north of the palace in the area of the present-day courtyard of the citadel. This fits in with the fairly basic domestic remains that have been uncovered there. This general area was enclosed to the northwest by the fortifications of the city and by the two monumental towers named Hippicus and Phasael. The principal road running today through the Armenian Quarter roughly marks the central line dividing the two wings of the palace. The southeast corner of Herod's palace falls roughly beneath the complex of the present-day Armenian Church of St. James. The southwest corner of the palace was marked by a large tower named Mariamne, remains of which have been found in archeological excavations.

Herod established a magnificent formal pleasure garden to the south of the palace that was regarded as one of the marvels of Jerusalem:

> All around were many circular cloisters, leading one into another, the columns in each being different, and their open courts all of greensward; there were groves of various trees intersected by long walks, which were bordered by deep canals, and ponds everywhere studded with bronze figures, through which the water was discharged, and around the streams were numerous cots for tame pigeons. All around were many circular cloisters, leading one into another, the columns in each being different, and their open courts all of greensward; there were groves of various trees intersected by long walks, which were bordered by deep canals, and ponds everywhere studded with bronze figures, through which the water was discharged, and around the streams were numerous cots for tame pigeons. (Josephus, J.W. 5:180–181)

Beyond the garden and to its south was the military barracks situated immediately within the west gate. In a number of places in his writings Josephus mentions the camp (*stratopedon*) in which a garrison of soldiers was lodged; this must be a reference to the barracks connected to the palace of Herod the Great, as a number of scholars have assumed.[46]

---

[45] Renée Sivan and Giora Solar, "Excavations in the Jerusalem Citadel," in *Ancient Jerusalem Revealed* (ed. H. Geva; Jerusalem: Israel Exploration Society, 1994), 168–76; Dan Bahat and Magen Broshi, "Excavations in the Armenian Garden," in *Jerusalem Revealed: Archaeology in the Holy City 1968–1974* (ed. Y. Yadin; Jerusalem: Israel Exploration Society, 1975), 55–56.

[46] On the camp and troops garrisoned there, see Dalman, *Sacred Sites and Ways*, 275, 336–37; Fergus Millar, *The Roman Near East 31 BC–AD 337* (Cambridge, MA: Harvard

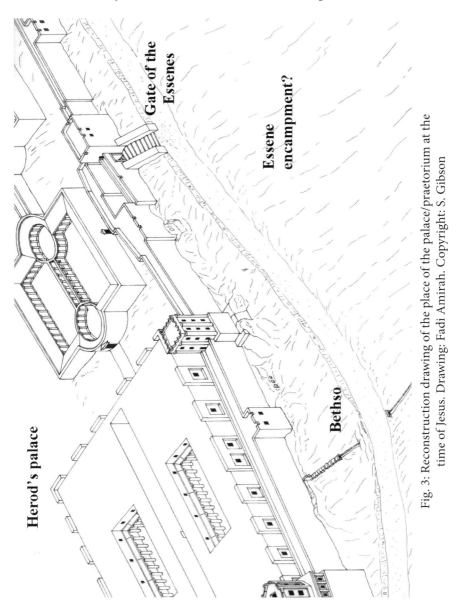

Fig. 3: Reconstruction drawing of the place of the palace/praetorium at the time of Jesus. Drawing: Fadi Amirah. Copyright: S. Gibson

**The Western Gate of the Palace of Herod/
Praetorium (the Gate of the Essenes)**

University Press, 1993): 45; Nikos Kokkinos, "The Royal Court of the Herods," in *The World of the Herods* (ed. Nikos Kokkinos; Stuttgart: Steiner, 2007), 279–303, esp. 285. This garrison would have had five hundred to one thousand men, according to Kraeling, "The Episode of the Roman Standards," 269.

In Josephus's description of the northwestern fortifications of Jerusalem, first built at the time of the Hasmoneans (c. 140 BCE) and restored and embellished by Herod the Great (probably c. 25 BCE), two landmarks are mentioned in association with a section of the defense wall running from the Hippicus tower southwards, which extended along the western side of Herod's palace/praetorium, namely, "Bethso" and the "Gate of the Essenes" (*J. W.* 5.145). The whereabouts of these landmarks have bedeviled scholars dealing with the reconstruction of the topography of Second Temple-period Jerusalem.[47]

Uncertainty has existed among scholars in regard to the location of the Gate of the Essenes, and many placed it near the southwest angle of the First wall, on the slope of the traditional Mount Zion, in an area where Frederick Bliss and Archibald Dickie uncovered a gate during their excavations of 1894–1897.[48] However, a gateway complex of definite Second Temple-period date was uncovered in Magen Broshi's excavations about midway along the western Old City wall to the south of the present citadel. It is this gate I suggest must be the Gate of the Essenes mentioned by Josephus, and its primary function was to provide direct access to Herod's palace and the later praetorium (Figs. 4–5).

---

[47]"Bethso" is believed to be the name associated with a substantial sewerage system of first century date uncovered immediately to the south of the citadel and extending beneath the medieval Sultan's Pool; see Magen Broshi and Shimon Gibson, "Excavations Along the Western and Southern Walls of the Old City of Jerusalem," in *Ancient Jerusalem Revealed* (ed. Hillel Geva; Jerusalem: Israel Exploration Society, 1994), 147–55; Gibson, "Suggested Identifications"; see now Amit Re'em, "First Temple Period Fortifications and Herod's Palace in the Kishle Compound," *Qadmoniot* 43 (2010): 96–101 (Hebrew).

[48]Michael Avi-Yonah, "Jerusalem in the Time of the Second Temple: Archaeology and Topography," in *Sepher Yerushalayim* (ed. Michael Avi-Yonah; Jerusalem and Tel Aviv; 2 vols.; Bialik Institute and Dvir, 1956), 305–19, 307 and Map 10 (Hebrew); Yigael Yadin, "The Gate of the Essenes and the Temple Scroll," in *Jerusalem Revealed: Archaeology in the Holy City 1968-1974* (ed. Yigael Yadin; Jerusalem: Israel Exploration Society, 1975), 90–91. J. A. Emerton has rightly expressed caution about the southwest gate location for the Gate of the Essenes and wrote, "We cannot be sure that Josephus gives us a complete list of gates, and it is possible that there was another gate that would also fit his description"; see J. A. Emerton, "A Consideration of Two Recent Theories about Bethso in Josephus's Description of Jerusalem and a Passage in the Temple Scroll," *Text and Context: Old Testament and Semitic Studies for F. C. Fensham* (ed. W. Claassen; JSOTSup 48; Sheffield: JSOT Press, 1988), 93–104, particularly 98. For a description of the excavation of the southwest gate on Mount Zion, see Frederick Jones Bliss and Archibald C. Dickie, *Excavations at Jerusalem 1894-1897* (London: John Murray, 1898), 14–16. The area of the gate was re-excavated by Bargil Pixner, Doron Chen, and Shlomo Margalit, and they dated the earliest gate to the Second Temple period based on the discovery of Second Temple-period potsherds in a small probe beneath the fills of the adjacent paving; see Bargil Pixner, Doron Chen, and Shlomo Margalit, "The 'Gate of the Essenes' Re-excavated," *Zeitschrift des Deutschen Palästina-Vereins* 105 (1989): 85–95, see 87; Doron Chen, Shlomo Margalit, and Bargil Pixner, "Mount Zion: Discovery of Iron Age Fortifications Below the Gate of the Essenes," in *Ancient Jerusalem Revealed* (ed. Hillel Geva; Jerusalem: Israel Exploration Society, 1994), 76–81, see 79. This dating, however, seems doubtful on methodological grounds, since the Second Temple potsherds may very well have been residuals in a consolidation fill poured beneath the Byzantine paving; see Gibson, "Suggested Identifications."

Fig. 4: The area of the palace/praetorium gate ("Gate of the Essenes") at the time of excavation, looking east. Photograph: Zeev Radovan. Copyright: S. Gibson / Mount Zion Archaeological Expedition

The gateway complex consists of an inner and outer curtain wall, with their respective gates; an inner open area between the walls (30 x 11 m) that was flanked by two large towers (20 x 9 m; 19.5 x 13.5 m); and a gateway approach (8 m wide) consisting of a series of paved steps laid on a sloping embankment, bordered on either side by walls (2.5 m thick) that led up to the gate in the outer wall.[49] Unfortunately, the stones belonging to the threshold of the outer (Herodian) gate were robbed down to the foundations of the wall in the Byzantine period. However, the width of the inner (Hasmonean) gate may still be ascertained (3 m); perhaps the gate in the outer wall had a similar width. The excavation of the fills and collapsed stone debris on top of the paved steps of the gateway approach suggests the gate complex

---

[49] Broshi and Gibson, "Excavations along the Western and Southern Walls," 153.

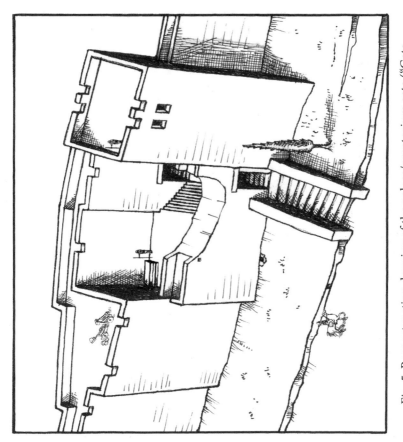

Fig. 5: Reconstruction drawing of the palace/praetorium gate ("Gate of the Essenes"). Drawing: S. Gibson. Copyright: S. Gibson

was destroyed in 70 CE, or in its immediate aftermath. The excavation of an area beneath the steps of the gateway approach and of pavements outside the outer wall suggest that it was built in the latter part of the first century BCE, probably at the time of Herod the Great. The characteristics of this gateway complex, with gates within two parallel curtain walls flanked by towers, bear general similarities to Late Hellenistic-type courtyard gates that are known in Greece and Anatolia.[50]

It is reasonable to assume that the gateway complex uncovered by Broshi was a private entrance into the palace/praetorium rather than a public thoroughfare. The construction of this gate may have been the direct response by Herod the Great to an occasion that arose at the time of the death of Antipater (c. 43 BCE), when the high priest Hyrcanus tried to refuse Herod entrance into Jerusalem on the grounds that some of his non-Jewish soldiers might accidentally contaminate

---

[50] F. E. Winter, *Greek Fortifications* (London: Routledge and Kegan Paul, 1971), 213, 244. For further information on gates of this period, see Oren Gutfeld, "The City Gate in Eretz-Israel in the Early Roman Period and Its Origins in the Hellenistic World" (MA thesis, Hebrew University of Jerusalem, 1999; Hebrew).

the purity of Jewish pilgrims who were gathered in the city for one of the festivals: "it was not proper to admit a crowd of foreigners when the people were in a state of ritual purity" (Josephus, *Ant.* 14.285; cf. *J.W.* 1.229). Although Herod did eventually manage to gain entrance into the city by stealth, he must have realized that having one's own private entrance into the city would have made things easier. Although it is a fair guess the gate was mainly used as a private entrance for Herod and later for the Roman governors, this does not exclude public activities taking place next to the gate and in the large open space (30 x 11 m) between the walls. Indeed, this spot would have been particularly suitable for proclamations and public trials, as we shall show below, and crowd control would have been easy owing to the fact that it was so well defended.

But why was it named after the Essenes? Perhaps this is because the Essenes were favored by the Herodian dynasty, as Philo (*Hypothetica* 11.18) and Josephus (*Ant.* 15.371–379) attest.[51] The story provided by Josephus is that an Essene prophet named Menachem predicted that Herod the Great would rule over the Jews, and "from that time he [Herod] continued to hold all Essenes in honor." It has been suggested that the Essenes might be the same as the Herodians, who are referred to as a religious group in the Gospels (Mark 3:6; 12:13; Matt 22:16).[52] The presence of Essenes in Jerusalem is not surprising, since we hear from Josephus (*J.W.* 2.124) that the Essenes "occupy no one city, but settle in every town." Because of the royal favor that was extended to them by Herod, members of the Essene community may have been allowed to establish themselves outside the palace gate (perhaps even in a closed encampment to ensure communal purity) and this resulted in the gate being named after them. The slope below the gate and above the upper Hinnom Valley would have been one possible location. The fact that the Essenes tended to live in separate communes is mentioned by Philo (*Prob.* 85; *Hypothetica* 11.1, 5) and Josephus (*Ant.* 18.21). Brian J. Capper has suggested that the Essene community house at Jerusalem numbered about one hundred or two hundred individuals.[53] Indeed, city gates in antiquity were inevitably named after features or places outside gates rather than those situated inside the city.[54] Yigael Yadin proposed that the gate was named after the Essenes because, unlike the rest of the inhabitants, they could "ease" themselves only in latrines situated outside the city for reasons of purity.[55]

---

[51] See Hartmut Stegemann, *The Library of Qumran: On the Essenes, Qumran, John the Baptist, and Jesus* (Grand Rapids: Eerdmans, 1998), 160–61; Joan E. Taylor, "Philo of Alexandria on the Essenes: A Case Study on the Use of Classical Sources in Discussions of the Qumran-Essene Hypothesis," *Studia Philonica Annual* 19 (2007): 1–28.

[52] Stegemann, *The Library of Qumran*, 267. For alternative views on the identification of the Herodians, see the most recent summary by John P. Meier, "The Historical Jesus and the Historical Herodians," *JBL* 119/4 (2000): 740–46.

[53] Brian J. Capper, "Essene Community Houses and Jesus' Early Community," in *Jesus and Archaeology* (ed. J. H. Charlesworth; Grand Rapids: Eerdmans, 2006), 472–502, see 478.

[54] A point also made by R. Steven Notley, "Historical Geography of the Gospels," in *The Sacred Bridge: Carta's Atlas of the Biblical World: An Overview of the Ancient Levant* (ed. Anson Rainey and R. Steven Notley; Jerusalem: Carta, 2006), 349–69, see 368.

[55] Yadin, "The Gate of the Essenes," 91; idem, *The Temple Scroll* (London: Weidenfeld & Nicolson, 1985), 182.

The frequent comings and goings of the Essenes, according to Yadin, ultimately led to the gate being named after them. I think this is highly unlikely for the simple reason that the gate I am proposing led directly into the property of the palace of Herod the Great and the later praetorium. Neither Herod nor the Roman governors would have allowed such activities to take place in their grounds.

I want to take this opportunity to reject the hypothesis put forward by Bargil Pixner that there was a separate Essene Quarter in the southern part of the Upper City on traditional Mount Zion, and in proximity to an exclusive aristocratic and priestly neighborhood.[56] The presence of a large (=4QFlor) number of *miqwao't* (ritual bathing pools) on Mount Zion is a sure indicator for Jewish houses,[57] but that does not in any way prove the existence of Essenes on Mount Zion as the late Pixner, followed by Rainer Reisner, has tried to show in numerous publications. R. Steven Notley is rightly skeptical about Pixner's ideas: "Quite simply, there exists today not a single piece of archaeological evidence to demonstrate that an Essene Quarter existed in Jerusalem in Jesus's day."[58]

Trials at the Palace/Praetorium

Now that I have demonstrated that the gate uncovered on the western side of Herod's palace is likely to be the Gate of the Essenes, what historical evidence may be adduced to support the idea that the courtyard situated within the gate was the

---

[56] Bargil Pixner, "An Essene Quarter on Mount Zion?" in *Studia Hierosolymitana I: Studi archeologici in onore a Bellarmino Bagatti* (Jerusalem: Franciscan Printing Press, 1976); idem, "The History of the 'Essene Gate' Area," *Zeitschrift des Deutschen Palästina-Vereins* 105 (1989): 96–104; idem, "Archäologische Beobachtungen zum Jerusalemer Essener-Viertel und zur Urgemeinde," in *Christen and Christliches in Qumran?* (Eichstätter Studien, Neue Folge 32; ed. B. Mayer; Regensburg: F. Pustet, 1992), 89–113; idem, "The Jerusalem Essenes, Barnabas, and the Letter to the Hebrews," in *Intertestamental Essays in Honour of Jósef Tadeusz Milik* (ed. Z. J. Kapera; Cracow: Enigma Press, 1992), 167–78; idem, "Jerusalem's Essene Gateway: Where the Community Lived in Jesus's Time," *BAR* 23/3 (1997): 23–31, 64–66; idem, "Mount Zion, Jesus, and Archaeology," in *Jesus and Archaeology* (ed. J. H. Charlesworth; Grand Rapids: Eerdmans, 2006), 309–22. Rainer Riesner, "Eseener und Urkirche in Jerusalem," in *Christen and Christliches in Qumran?* (Eichstätter Studien, Neue Folge 32; ed. B. Mayer; Regensburg: F. Pustet, 1992), 139–55; idem, "Das Jerusalemer Essenerviertel: Antwort auf einige Einwände," in *Intertestamental Essays in Honour of Jósef Tadeusz Milik* (ed. Z. J. Kapera; Cracow: Enigma Press, 1992), 179–86; idem, "Jesus, the Primitive Community, and the Essene Quarter of Jerusalem," in *Jesus and the Dead Sea Scrolls* (ed. J. H. Charlesworth; New York: Doubleday, 1992), 198–234. For criticism on the feasibility of an Essene quarter on the summit of the Upper City, see Emerton, "A Consideration of Two Recent Theories," 99; Lee I. Levine, *Jerusalem: Portrait of the City in the Second Temple Period (538 B.C.E.–70 C.E.)* (Philadelphia: Jewish Publication Society, 2002), 333; and Notley, "Historical Geography of the Gospels," 368; James F. Strange, "Archaeological Evidence of Jewish Believers," in *Jewish Believers in Jesus: The Early Centuries* (ed. Oskar Skarsaune and Reidar Hvalvik; Peabody, MA: Henrickson, 2007), 710–41, specifically 737–40.

[57] Gibson, "Jewish Purification Practices," 289 n. 36; see also previously Emerton, "A Consideration of Two Recent Theories," 97.

[58] Notley, "Historical Geography of the Gospels," 368.

place where Jesus was tried? As we shall see, there are a number of historical attestations for a tribunal being set up at the praetorium and, more particularly, on its western side.

First, when Pilate used temple funds for the purpose of building or restoring the upper-level aqueduct to bring water to Jerusalem, the local inhabitants, we are told by Josephus, "formed a ring round the tribunal of Pilate, then on a visit to Jerusalem, and besieged him with angry clamor" (*J.W.* 2.175–177; cf. *Ant.* 18.60–62). The date when this took place is unknown, but Brown suggests this was before Jesus' death.[59] Clearly this episode took place close to the praetorium but not inside it. Signaling from his tribunal, Pilate had many of the protestors beaten and killed by his soldiers, some of whom had previously infiltrated the crowd. Since Josephus describes this as an uprising in which many thousands took part, it cannot have taken place within the inner precincts of the praetorium, which was a closed compound surrounded by a wall. Hence a place on the outside to the west and in full view of the tribunal would fit the location outside the gate perfectly. The barracks for the soldiers had to be close by. This military camp (*stratopedon*) is mentioned by Josephus (*J.W.* 2.329) as adjoining the palace or praetorium, just inside the gate area and to the south of Herod's gardens. One should also mention the incident in which Herod Agrippa I seized Peter during Passover and threw him into prison in Jerusalem (Acts 12:3–9). This cannot have been at the Antonia fortress but must have been at the praetorium. The prison apparently had an "iron door which led into the city" (Acts 12:10), and since it gave access to a street it was probably located on the east side of the camp facing the city.

The second mention of a tribunal at the praetorium is in the story of the outbreak of the First Jewish Revolt (66 CE) against Rome. Gessius Florus, who was at that time the procurator, arrived at Jerusalem from Caesarea in an attempt to suppress the uprising. According to Josephus, Florus lodged at Herod's palace, and "on the following day had a tribunal placed in front of the building and took his seat; the chief priests, the nobles, and the most eminent citizens then presented themselves before the tribunal. Florus ordered them to hand over the men who had insulted him, declaring that they themselves would feel his vengeance if they failed to produce the culprits" (*J.W.* 2.301–309). When they refused to do so, Florus had his soldiers sack the Agora/Upper Market and the residential quarter that were in the close vicinity of the palace.

> There ensued a stampede through the narrow alleys, massacre of all who were caught, every variety of pillage; many of the peaceable citizens were arrested and brought before Florus, who had them first scourged and then crucified. The total number of that day's victims, including women and children, for even infancy received no quarter, amounted to about three thousand six hundred. The calamity was aggravated by the unprecedented character of the Roman cruelty. For Florus ventured that day to do what none had ever done before, namely to scourge *before his tribunal and nail to the cross* men of equestrian rank, men who, if Jews by birth, were at least invested with that Roman dignity. (Josephus, *J.W.* 2.301–309, italics added)

---

[59] Brown, *Death of the Messiah*, 700.

Since crucifixion was unlikely to have taken place within the city, the passage implies that the tribunal was set up adjacent to the palace/praetorium and next to, or alongside, the western city wall, with the crosses set up outside but still at a visible distance.[60] This fits perfectly the suggested location of the tribunal inside the courtyard of the Gate of the Essenes.

Conclusion

The discovery of a well-defended gateway—probably the Gate of the Essenes—that had an inner courtyard paved with flagstones and a rocky outcrop on one side corresponds perfectly with the situation of the place of the Roman tribunal as suggested by Josephus and in the Fourth Gospel. Hence, while it is a fair assumption that the gate was used mainly as a private entrance into the praetorium, this does not exclude public activities from taking place *inside* the gate and within the large court situated between the walls. Indeed, this spot would have been the ideal place for proclamations and public trials, and crowd control would have been easy owing to the fact that it was so well defended. It is where I think Jesus was brought to trial. The proceedings at the gate were probably very carefully monitored by the Roman soldiers from the praetorium barracks. The crowds that were allowed to observe the proceedings may have been angry, but they were powerless. Once Jesus had been condemned to death by Pilate, the milling crowds would have been ordered to move quickly beyond the gate outside, under the watchful eyes of the heavily armed Roman soldiers situated on the adjacent towers. Crowd control would have been extremely tight. Jesus was most likely taken back to the prison of the praetorium barracks and from there would have been paraded down the streets of the Upper City to the Gennath Gate, where he was led out of the city to Golgotha.[61]

---

[60] Lémonon, *Pilate et le Gouvernement de la Judée*, 124.
[61] See also Shimon Gibson, *The Final Days of Jesus: The Archaeological Evidence* (San Francisco: HarperOne, 2009).

Part Two

Interpreting the Scriptures in Jewish and Christian Communities

8

THE DEAD SEA SCROLLS AND THE INTERPRETATION OF SCRIPTURE

George J. Brooke

Introduction

The title of this chapter allows me to work in two ways simultaneously. First, it permits me to discuss all kinds of scriptural interpretation in the DSS.[1] I will address this aspect of the title by considering how the movement that preserved the scrolls in the eleven caves at and near Qumran conceived of itself as scripturally based by highlighting some key aspects of the history of the study of the interpretation of the scriptures in the DSS, by thinking about some of the characteristics of the scriptures that are being interpreted in both sectarian and non-sectarian compositions, by attempting to outline the various types and methods of scriptural interpretation that are attested in the scrolls, and by trying briefly to understand the significance of the settings in which interpretation took place.

---

[1] There are many surveys of this topic, but the following offer suitable guidance on the subject: Michael Fishbane, "Use, Authority, and Interpretation of Mikra at Qumran," in *Mikra: Text, Translation, Reading, and Interpretation of the Hebrew Bible in Ancient Judaism and Early Christianity* (ed. M. J. Mulder; CRINT 2/1; Assen: Van Gorcum; Philadelphia: Fortress, 1988), 339–77; Johann Maier, "Early Jewish Interpretation in the Qumran Literature," in *Hebrew Bible/Old Testament: The History of Its Interpretation,* vol. 1: *From the Beginnings to the Middle Ages (Until 1300)* (ed. M. Sæbø; Göttingen: Vandenhoeck & Ruprecht, 1996), 108–29; George J. Brooke, "Dead Sea Scrolls," in *Dictionary of Biblical Interpretation* (ed. J. H. Hayes; Nashville: Abingdon, 1999), 253–56; Moshe J. Bernstein, "Interpretation of Scriptures," in *Encyclopedia of the Dead Sea Scrolls* (ed. L. H. Schiffman and J. C. VanderKam; New York: Oxford University Press, 2000), 376–83; George J. Brooke, "Biblical Interpretation at Qumran," in *The Bible and the Dead Sea Scrolls,* vol. 1: *Scripture and the Scrolls* (ed. J. H. Charlesworth; The Second Princeton Symposium on Judaism and Christian Origins; Waco, TX: Baylor University Press, 2006), 287–319; Moshe J. Bernstein, "Biblical Interpretation in the Dead Sea Scrolls: Looking Back and Looking Ahead," in *The Dead Sea Scrolls and Contemporary Culture: Proceedings of the International Conference held at the Israel Museum, Jerusalem (July 6–8, 2008)* (ed. A. D. Roitman, L. H. Schiffman and S. Tzoref; STDJ 93; Leiden: Brill, 2011), 141–59.

But, second, the title of this chapter suggests to me that the handling of scripture in the DSS is suggestive for the interpretation of scripture more broadly, even in the present. Thus, I encourage you, if you are a member of a faith community that takes the reading and appropriation of scripture seriously, to reflect on the implications of this chapter for your own purposes. Throughout this chapter I will from time to time refer to phenomena that are parallel between the scrolls and the NT in their respective handlings of scripture. But, in addition, I will offer some more general reflective comments on the implications of what we are looking at, try to draw out several of these more general matters explicitly, and then pull them together tidily in my conclusion.

A Movement Based in Scripture

Categorizing the Scrolls from Qumran

The general release of all the previously unpublished DSS in 1991 has provoked a flurry of fresh interest in the scrolls. To begin with there was the matter of trying to put critical editions of the many fragmentary manuscripts in the public domain so that the hard task of the analysis of this range of material could be undertaken. That process of analysis is now in full sway, and collections of studies like those in this volume are steps along the way to the greater appreciation of the broad significance of the scrolls, both in themselves and as part of the wider world of early Judaism and its even more broadly conceived cultural context in the Greco-Roman world of the three centuries before the fall of the temple in 70 CE.

When scholars try to organize the library from the eleven Qumran caves into some sort of order, the first analytical description that is made usually involves a distinction between biblical and non-biblical manuscripts and compositions. This is not entirely a historical distinction between what is earlier and what is later, since some of the non-biblical compositions in the library have been dated by some to the mid-Second Temple period, the time when works like the books of Chronicles, the wisdom sayings of Qohelet, the book of Daniel, and the several forms of the books of Psalms were undergoing redaction. Rather, it seems to be a pragmatic recognition that in this library that was largely copied and collected in the first century BCE some priority has to be given to the collection of more or less authoritative literary traditions of earlier generations of Jews.[2]

Some scholars have suggested, with some validity, that the distinction between the biblical and non-biblical in the Qumran library is in some ways anachronistic, since there was not a Bible in the strict sense of a fixed list of books, even in the form of a codex, until well after the turn of the era.[3] Nevertheless the distinc-

---

[2] This distinction was in fact made from the outset with manuscripts from each cave being numbered first in the order of the biblical books and thereafter in relation to the proximity of the composition to the biblical material.

[3] See especially the insightful work of Eugene C. Ulrich, *The Dead Sea Scrolls and the Origins of the Bible* (Studies in the Dead Sea Scrolls and Related Literature; Grand Rapids: Eerdmans, 1999).

tion between biblical and non-biblical, or scriptural and non-scriptural, is strongly suggested by the overall contents of the library. How is this the case? It seems to me that this basic category distinction can be appreciated through the study of the non-biblical compositions by noting that nearly all of them in some way or other seem to depend upon earlier scriptural antecedents that are taken as authoritative in some way: "nearly all of the writings of the Qumran community, whether formally linked with scripture or not, are pervaded with scriptural interpretation."[4] The implication of this observation is striking. In a significant way the movement that put together the Qumran library saw itself as continuous with scriptural Israel. It was not strictly a postbiblical Jewish community, as the later rabbinic communities were. Rather, it thought of itself as Israel, as Israel indeed with a renewed covenant—not a new covenant to displace the old one, but a renewed covenant as Jeremiah had promised that was continuous with the old one that Noah, but especially Abraham, Moses, and David had been partners in.[5]

This point can be seen readily in two ways. First, if one opens up a collection of translations such as that widely used in colleges in the English-speaking world, Geza Vermes's *Complete Dead Sea Scrolls in English*, it is swiftly apparent that of his eight categories for the non-biblical compositions in the library, two are defined explicitly in terms of scriptural source materials as "biblical interpretation" and "biblically based apocryphal works" while the compositions classified as "rules," "hymns and poems," "calendars, liturgies and prayers," "historical and apocalyptic works," and "wisdom literature" all contain explicit or implicit references to scriptural antecedents.[6] Second, it might seem that among the compositions that appear to be the most independent of scriptural influence could be set the sectarian rules. After all, these are concerned with the community in the here and now and with how its members should behave in its meetings and toward one another. But recent studies have indicated forcefully just how much even these contemporary items of legislation depend on authoritative scriptural forebears in numerous ways.[7]

Scriptural Self-Designations of the Sectarian Movement

In addition it is worth briefly mentioning how the movement that collected the scrolls together refers to itself. Sadly for some, there is no clear use of the

---

[4]Bernstein, "Interpretation of Scriptures," 376. I have tried to demonstrate this point in George J. Brooke, "The Dead Sea Scrolls," in *The Biblical World* (ed. J. Barton; 2 vols.; London: Routledge, 2002), 1:250–69.

[5]On the importance of the phrase "renewed covenant" see Shemaryahu Talmon, "The Community of the Renewed Covenant: Between Judaism and Christianity," in *The Community of the Renewed Covenant: The Notre Dame Symposium on the Dead Sea Scrolls* (ed. E. Ulrich and J. C. VanderKam; Christianity and Judaism in Antiquity Series 10; Notre Dame: University of Notre Dame Press, 1994), 3–24.

[6]See Geza Vermes, *The Complete Dead Sea Scrolls in English* (rev. ed.; London: Penguin, 2004), vii–xii.

[7]See, e.g., Aharon Shemesh, "The Scriptural Background of the Penal Code in the *Rule of the Community* and *Damascus Document*," *DSD* 15 (2008): 191–224.

term "Essene," although, with a few loud dissenting voices, it seems to be generally agreed that the movement that was responsible for collecting the library together and part of which inhabited the site at Qumran for 150 years was Essene in some form.[8] But more particularly the movement's self-designations in the scrolls that come from the caves are scriptural epithets given new life in the sectarian compositions. For example, a good case can be made that the neologism of *yahad* as a noun referring to "those who are together," or "the union," or "community" can be related to a particular reading of the use of the word as an adverb in the context of the Sinai narrative.[9] Or again, the self-designation of members as *mitnadevim*, "freewill volunteers," depends on the roles such Israelites play in the book of Numbers: through the use of such a descriptor the community can be seen to be thinking of itself as those who offer themselves sacrificially as a freewill offering to God.[10] In other words this is a scriptural community. At least in part, Baptists and Presbyterians might be understood as making similar scriptural claims through their self-designations, whereas Anglicans, Lutherans, and the Orthodox are not.

Scripture as Given

Before leaving this section, I consider that at least one further point is significant. This positive attitude to prior scriptures as in large measure determining how identity and ideology should be constructed reflects an acceptance of that tradition as a given. It is a given in two senses. On the one hand it is a given of the past inherited by the movement that is tied to the scrolls. In it, or in part of it at least, that movement discovered its own continuities with what had gone before and could construct its own genealogy, its sense of authenticity and integrity. Sometimes that genealogy was made explicit through such scriptural priestly self-designations as "Sons of Aaron" or "Sons of Zadok"; sometimes other epithets were used, as we have already noted. On the other hand the tradition is a given in being the outward manifestation of the divine self-giving, the divine self-revelation to Israel in the past that was to be received as a gift. There may be fresh manifestations of the divine as the contents of the "heavenly tablets" are made known through angelic discourse in the book of *Jubilees* or as the "mysteries of existence" are revealed in the wisdom composition known as *Instruction* or the obscurities of prophetic oracles are made known through inspired exegesis as in the *Pesharim*, but the basic reference point in scripture is that it is a gift from God to which response is required. To my mind this is akin to what many Christians have described as grace, that which is suggestive of the divine initiative toward humanity, which seems to convey the divine anticipation of a human response. So, in my opinion, it is naive

---

[8]See, e.g., Vermes, *The Complete Dead Sea Scrolls in English*, 46–48.
[9]See J. C. VanderKam, "Sinai Revisited," in *Biblical Interpretation at Qumran* (ed. M. Henze; Studies in the Dead Sea Scrolls and Related Literature; Grand Rapids: Eerdmans, 2005), 44–60.
[10]See Devorah Dimant, "The Volunteers in the *Rule of the Community*—A Biblical Notion in Sectarian Garb," *RevQ* 23/90 (2007): 233–45.

to describe the members of this Jewish sectarian movement as straightforwardly legalistic, as if that adequately described their approach to life in general. Rather, their strict attitudes in interpreting Torah are best understood as an attempt at making an adequate response to the divine gift, which the Torah was (and for many continues to be).

Some Comments from the History of the Study of Scriptural Interpretation

It is not necessary in a short presentation like this to rehearse the whole of the history of the study of scriptural interpretation since the first DSS were discovered by that lost goat in 1947.[11] But a few points are worth bearing in mind as the rest of what I have to say unfolds.

Sectarian Interpretation as More than Pesher

In the first place, it is clear that until the general release of all the unpublished Cave 4 and Cave 11 fragmentary scrolls in 1991, it was commonly supposed that an adequate description of biblical interpretation in the DSS could be undertaken if the object of analysis was principally or exclusively the so-called *Pesharim*. The label *pesharim* (singular: *pesher*) refers principally to those exegetical compositions that present a biblical text in running order; the text is divided into small units of a few verses and interspersed with commentary. This is explicit exegesis. I shall return to make a few more detailed comments on this form of interpretation in a subsequent section, but the point here is to inform the reader that this prioritising of *pesher* resulted in Qumran biblical interpretation being characterized as almost exclusively about the fulfillment of prophecy in the lives and experiences of the Qumran community and its wider movement. F. F. Bruce, perhaps the greatest British evangelical biblical scholar of the twentieth century, began his study of *Biblical Exegesis in the Qumran Texts* with a chapter on the Qumran commentaries and referred to them intermittently throughout.[12]

In large measure the publication of the *Temple Scroll* with an extensive and detailed commentary by Yigael Yadin, first in Hebrew in 1977 and then in English in 1983,[13] changed the way in which biblical interpretation in the DSS was conceptualized. No longer was automatic priority given to discussion of the Qumran

---

[11] I have attempted to set out something of the history of the interpretation of interpretation in George J. Brooke, "From Bible to Midrash: Approaches to Biblical Interpretation in the Dead Sea Scrolls by Modern Interpreters," in *Northern Lights on the Dead Sea Scrolls: Proceedings of the Nordic Qumran Network 2003–2006* (ed. A. Klostergaard Petersen, T. Elgvin, C. Wassen, H. von Weissenberg, and M. Winninge with M. Ehrensvärd; STDJ 80; Leiden: Brill, 2009), 1–19.

[12] F. F. Bruce, *Biblical Exegesis in the Qumran Texts* (Grand Rapids: Eerdmans, 1959).

[13] Yigael Yadin, *The Temple Scroll* (Jerusalem: Israel Exploration Society, The Institute of Archaeology of the Hebrew University of Jerusalem, the Shrine of the Book, 1977 [Hebrew ed.], 1983 [English ed.]).

interpretations of scriptural texts that were the exegesis of unfulfilled prophecy. In place of the *Pesharim*, pride of place has more often been given to legal interpretation in its various forms, from being implicit in rewritten scriptural compositions, such as the *Temple Scroll* itself or in the so-called *Reworked Pentateuch* scrolls, to being explicit in the legal section of the *Damascus Document* and other compositions. In addition other forms of interpretation have also been discussed more extensively. All this has had a significant effect on the study of the use of scriptural tradition in the NT: not least there has been an increasing recognition that it was time to reconsider Jesus' attitude to the Torah and to re-evaluate Paul's views on the Jewish law.

Labeling the Methods of Interpretation in the Non-Scriptural Scrolls

Another issue that arises from making a few comments on the history of the study of scriptural interpretation in the DSS concerns the terminology that is used to describe what scholars observe. The sectarian scrolls do indeed use a few terms to indicate their method, but not enough for scholars to be able to describe adequately what is going on. For example, in the *Pesharim*, the term "pesher" is used with some kind of technical significance: most scholars subscribe to the view that the term is to be related to the use of its Aramaic counterpart in the book of Daniel and is to be understood principally in relation to the interpretation of dreams and visions.[14] New Testament scholars need to be aware that their rapid adoption of the term "pesher" to describe various kinds of scriptural exegesis in the NT is not altogether wise since an equivalent for the term is nowhere to be found there and there are as many differences as there are similarities between what is taking place in the exegesis of the scrolls and that of the NT.[15]

So where can supplementary terminology be found? Since the scrolls are all Jewish compositions, it might seem appropriate that Jewish interpretative terminology should be used, and indeed several scholars have tried to make use of exegetical terminology that is familiar from later rabbinic texts. In these cases it has not been uncommon to find scholars not just using the broad categories of halakhah (legal interpretation) and haggadah (narrative interpretation), but also using the more precise terminology of the expanding lists of middot (interpretative measures) as ascribed to Rabbi Hillel (late first century BCE), Rabbi Ishmael (second century CE), and Rabbi Eliezer (date uncertain). These rules contain several that expound the principles of "from the general to the particular" and "from the particular to the general" and refer to the application of interpretation by analogy.[16] Interestingly, the rich diversity of interpretative procedures in the

---

[14]See the helpful discussion in Maurya P. Horgan, *Pesharim: Qumran Interpretations of Biblical Books* (CBQMS 8; Washington, DC: Catholic Biblical Association of America, 1979), 230–37.

[15]An example of a NT scholar adopting the term "pesher" is Oskar Skarsaune, "Biblical Interpretation," in *The Early Christian World* (ed. P. F. Esler; New York: Routledge, 2000), 660–89, esp. 663–64.

[16]On rabbinic interpretation in general see Rimon Kasher, "The Interpretation of Scripture in Rabbinic Literature," in *Mikra: Text, Translation, Reading, and Interpretation of the*

DSS seems to indicate that there was not a gradual sophistication in rabbinic exegesis over the centuries, a developing subtlety requiring the formulation of ever more precise rules. Rather, the richness of method was there from earliest times, and what is visible in the expanding lists of interpretative measures is the rabbinic relaxation of earlier exegetical restrictions that probably went back to Pharisaic practices in the two centuries before the fall of the temple.[17]

Other scholars have wondered whether the contemporary Greco-Roman environment might not serve better as a source for descriptive terminology for the processes of interpretation in the scrolls, perhaps even because the Jewish methods may be a reflection of interpretative techniques that had been developed in the Hellenistic world since the time of Plato and Aristotle. In such a case, the most significant parallels to what is to be found in the DSS might be sought in the exegetical activities of the Jewish philosopher Philo, who was active in Egypt at the start of the first century CE.[18] Notable in his approach is the overall framework that acknowledges a plain or literal sense in scripture, but then commonly insists on adding a level of allegorical interpretation through which other moral or spiritual senses of scripture can also be expounded. However, by juxtaposing the interpretations of the DSS with those of Philo we raise acutely the as yet unresolved issue of how exposed the Qumran sectarians and their wider movement were to the influences of the programs and techniques of Hellenistic debate and rhetoric. And that raises other interesting questions, such as where and how many of the members of the sectarian movement had been educated and trained.

Whatever is decided about the terminology for describing the processes of interpretation that are evident in the non-biblical scrolls found in the Qumran caves, in recent years most scholars have become much more self-aware about what they are doing and attempt more often than not to use neutral terminology that will distort what is being discussed as little as possible. This is to be welcomed and applauded.

The Basis of Interpretation

Scriptural Pluralism

It is important to make a few observations about the character of the Jewish Scriptures that form the basis for so many of the ideas to be found in the DSS. In

---

Hebrew Bible in Ancient Judaism and Early Christianity (ed. M. J. Mulder; CRINT 2/1; Assen: Van Gorcum; Philadelphia: Fortress, 1988), 547–94.

[17] As I have argued in George J. Brooke, *Exegesis at Qumran: 4QFlorilegium in Its Jewish Context* (JSOTSup 29; Sheffield: JSOT Press, 1985), 8–17.

[18] See, e.g., Yehoshua Amir, "Authority and Interpretation of Scripture in the Writings of Philo," in *Mikra: Text, Translation, Reading, and Interpretation of the Hebrew Bible in Ancient Judaism and Early Christianity* (ed. M. J. Mulder; CRINT 2/1; Assen: Van Gorcum; Philadelphia: Fortress, 1988), 421–53; Peder Borgen, "Philo of Alexandria as Exegete," in *A History of Biblical Interpretation*, vol. 1: *The Ancient Period* (ed. A. J. Hauser and D. F. Watson; Grand Rapids: Eerdmans, 2003), 114–43.

first place, it has to be acknowledged now that in the late Second Temple period, as authoritative Scriptures were passed on, they were conveyed quite commonly in more than one form.[19] Though the pluralistic character of the scriptural text varies from book to book, it needs to be acknowledged that virtually no manuscript copy of a biblical book agrees letter for letter with the dominant form of the text that is found in the rabbinic Bibles of the Middle Ages (the tradition that was taken over by Protestant Christianity). Most of the variations are not doctrinally significant, but not uncommonly they open up exegetical possibilities. Let me cite just one small, well-known example that discloses that the ancient commentator was fully aware of such variant scriptural texts. In *Pesher Habakkuk* (1QpHab 11:8–14) we read:

> *You have been sated with dishonor instead of glory. Drink you also and stagger (hr'l). The cup of the right hand of the Lord will come round to you and* (will be) *shame upon your glory* (Hab 2:16). Its interpretation concerns the wicked priest whose dishonor exceeds his glory, for he did not circumcise (h'rl) the foreskin of his heart and he walked in the ways of drunkenness to quench the thirst . . .[20]

It is noteworthy that the reading "stagger" is reflected in the LXX, Aquila, the Syriac, and the Vulgate, whereas the reading of "being uncircumcised" is found in the MT. Which reading is the more original we will never know, since the metathesis (the interchange of letters), probably accidental, could be in either direction and could have taken place at any stage in the text's transmission in the Second Temple period.

In several ways it is important to reflect, albeit very briefly, on the overall significance of this textual pluralism. To my mind the authors of the NT indicate a very healthy attitude to the texts of Scripture, and we might do well in some respects to pay attention to their practices. Although their use of Scripture is often relatively precise, reflecting a form of the Greek text of the OT known to us from the manuscripts of late antiquity, sometimes they seem to adopt a form of the text other than that which was standard or quite possibly quote from memory, which turns out not to be exact. In some cases they seem to quote a form of the text that is particularly suitable for their purposes, and scholars have long wondered whether there was some adjustment of the citation as it was appropriated for its new interpretative context.[21] In all this one almost feels that Scripture is alive and fluid. Students of the NT should be among the first to recognize what is the case at Qumran in terms of the plurality of authoritative witnesses and not to be surprised by it.

---

[19] See the landmark essays in Frank Moore Cross and Shemaryahu Talmon, eds., *Qumran and The History of the Biblical Text* (Cambridge, MA: Harvard University Press, 1975); and the many important observations in Emanuel Tov, *Textual Criticism of the Hebrew Bible* (2nd ed.; Assen: Van Gorcum; Minneapolis: Fortress, 2001).

[20] Cited and discussed in Timothy H. Lim, *Holy Scripture in the Qumran Commentaries and Pauline Letters* (Oxford: Clarendon Press, 1997), 50.

[21] On Paul and Scripture see especially Christopher D. Stanley, *Paul and the Language of Scripture: Citation Technique in the Pauline Epistles and Contemporary Literature* (SNTSMS 74; Cambridge: Cambridge University Press, 1992).

Interpretation within Scripture

Second, it is important to note that there is much in the variety of the so-called biblical scrolls that is already scribal interpretation. Some of the variants in the scriptural manuscripts are interpretative variants. In the pre-rabbinic period, and even in several circles after the canonical fixing of Scripture, scribes did not conceive of themselves as slavish copyists. One might even say that the proper attitude toward the text, as that was conceived in some way as sacred or especially authoritative, was to seek ways to make it clearer as one transmitted it from one generation to another. The text was not thought of as eternally fixed and unalterable.

So it is the case that there are several examples where it seems as if the scribe of the particular manuscript copy of a biblical book has sought to improve it for his readers and hearers. One favorite example of mine involves just a single letter. There is an interpretative problem in the text of Gen 1, in Hebrew as in English, as it happens: does the word for "day" (*ywm*) refer to the full twenty-four-hour period or solely to the hours of daylight? The copyist of 4QGen[g] solved the problem by inserting a single letter (*mem*) in Gen 1:5 to read the adverbial form (*ywmm*), which we might translate as "daytime." With this single letter he is thus able to clarify the plain meaning of the text: the Hebrew word for "day" (*ywm*) refers consistently to the full twenty-four-hour period, "day one," "day two," "day three," whereas the adverbial form refers to "day" over against "night." In fact this same exegetical move is visible in the Targumim, the Jewish Aramaic paraphrastic translations of Scripture, and the Syriac, so it is quite possible that the scribe of 4QGen[g] was not the first to think of this clarificatory strategem.[22]

Another example might be seen in the *Damascus Document* (CD 3:21–4:1) where there is a quotation of Ezek 44:15: "As God promised them by Ezekiel the prophet, saying, 'The priests and the Levites and the sons of Zadok who have kept the courses of My sanctuary when the children of Israel strayed from Me, they shall bring Me fat and blood.'" This quotation then gives rise to an interpretation that identifies three groups of people, the priests ("the repentant of Israel"), the Levites ("those accompanying them"), and the sons of Zadok ("the chosen of Israel, the ones called by name, who are to appear in the Last Days").[23] The tripartite exposition depends neatly on the presence of two conjunctions in the Hebrew citation, but in the standard form of the Hebrew known to us there are no conjunctions, so all three labels need to be read as referring to the same group, "the levitical priests, the descendants of Zadok" (NRSV). Were the conjunctions introduced by the composer of the *Damascus Document* for his own clarificatory purposes or were they in a form of Ezekiel that he cited faithfully? We may never know.

---

[22] The text of 4QGen[g] is available in James R. Davila, "7. 4QGen[g]," in *Qumran Cave 4.VII: Genesis to Numbers* (DJD 12; Oxford: Clarendon Press, 1994), 57–60. Davila notes this systematic alteration of Gen 1:5 but wonders whether it originally arose from a scribal error, a dittography of the letter *mem* in an early manuscript; such an explanation does not seem to me to be necessary.

[23] The translations are taken from Michael Wise, Martin Abegg Jr., and Edward Cook, *The Dead Sea Scrolls: A New Translation* (rev. ed.; New York: HarperSanFrancisco, 2005), 54–55.

Scriptural Preferences

Third, it needs to be stated that, as for almost every faith community, not all parts of what was received as authoritative Scripture were treated as of equal significance. In fact a couple of matters need to be mentioned briefly. On the one hand it seems as if most, if not all, of what was later to become canonical for Jews was known to the members of the Qumran community and the parent movement from which they came. But it seems likely that they had ambivalent attitudes about some of it, such as the book of Esther, which celebrates a non-Torah festival and does not mention the name of God,[24] and the books of Chronicles, which were probably taken over for political reasons by the Hasmoneans with most of whom they seem to have had a strained relationship.[25] In addition it is likely that some works that are no longer in the Jewish canon, such as the book of *Jubilees*, were regarded as authoritative by these sectarian Jews (and possibly others).

On the other hand, it is also worthwhile trying to keep a diachronic perspective on things. Over the 250-year history of the movement of which the Qumran community was a part, it is quite likely that some books came in and out of favor. It might be the case, for example, that in the early stages of the movement some of the books of *Enoch* were particularly important for some members, whereas at a later stage they fell into disuse and so are not themselves widely used as the scriptural bases for interpretation in the explicit sectarian exegesis of the first centuries BCE and CE. Throughout their history, however, some books remained of constant interest, a kind of canon within the canon: these included Genesis, Deuteronomy, Isaiah, the Psalms, and several of the twelve minor prophets.[26]

Overall, modern readers should not be surprised that the collection of authoritative Scriptures for this movement in the strictly speaking prebiblical period fluctuates somewhat and that not all scriptures are perceived as of equal importance for the construction of the movement's identity and self-understanding.

Types of Interpretation

Alternative Ways of Categorizing Types of Interpretation

There are several possible ways of trying to come to terms with the enormously rich range of scriptural interpretation that is to be found in the scrolls from

---

[24]On knowledge of Esther in the Qumran community see Shemaryahu Talmon, "Was the Book of Esther Known at Qumran?" *DSD* 2 (1995): 249–67.

[25]On the attitude to Chronicles in the sectarian movement see George J. Brooke, "The Books of Chronicles and the Scrolls from Qumran," in *Reflection and Refraction: Studies in Biblical Historiography in Honour of A. Graeme Auld* (ed. R. Rezetko, T. H. Lim, and W. B. Aucker; VTSup 113; Leiden: Brill, 2007), 35–48.

[26]See George J. Brooke, "'The Canon within the Canon' at Qumran and in the New Testament," in *The Scrolls and the Scriptures: Qumran Fifty Years After* (ed. S. E. Porter and C. A. Evans; JSPSup 26; Roehampton Institute London Papers 3; Sheffield: Sheffield Academic Press, 1997), 242–66.

the Qumran caves. In addition to the kinds of inner-scriptural interpretation that were outlined briefly in the previous section of this chapter, there are many compositions in which the Jewish Scriptures play a larger or a smaller part. We might try to list the ways all this interpretation could be considered. Here are some.

Halakhah and Haggadah

A traditional way of considering early Jewish interpretations, often considered as the predecessors of subsequent rabbinic exegesis, is to suppose that it can be suitably categorized as either halakhic, concerned with how the authoritative texts lead one to adjust one's way of living in certain ways, broadly Jewish legal interpretation; or as haggadic, that is, as variously appealing to narrative as a source of explanation for the way things are, might be, or could be through juxtaposition with scriptural types.[27] Neither term is used in the strict sense in the DSS, but this has not prevented scholars from reading them back from the rabbinic period into earlier times. There is the possibility of some greater success with the term "midrash," though again its use at Qumran does not correspond with the later generic understanding in Judaism.[28]

Pure and Applied Exegesis

This use of Jewish categories to understand a Jewish phenomenon is sometimes expressed in a slightly different way, a way that speaks not so much of two basic categories according to content but rather thinks of the methods being used and their aims. This form of conceptualisation is expressed through the use of the labels "pure" and "applied" exegesis.[29] Pure exegesis is the name given to all kinds of interpretation that try to grapple with problems in the plain or literal meaning of the text (later defined as the *peshat*). In this approach priority is given to the text and the desire to understand what it might mean.[30] Applied exegesis generally begins from some phenomenon contemporary with the interpreter and then seeks to relate the text of scripture to such an issue, such as, in the case of the Qumran community, what scriptural tags might best be applied to describe and identify it.

---

[27] Despite earlier reservations about these labels, a recent example of their use is by P. R. Davies, "Biblical Interpretation in the Dead Sea Scrolls," in *A History of Biblical Interpretation*, vol. 1: *The Ancient Period* (ed. A. J. Hauser and D. F. Watson; Grand Rapids: Eerdmans, 2003), 144–66.

[28] As argued by Timothy H. Lim, "Midrash Pesher in the Pauline Letters," in *The Scrolls and the Scriptures: Qumran Fifty Years After* (ed. S. E. Porter and C. A. Evans; JSPSup 26; Roehampton Institute London Papers 3; Sheffield: Sheffield Academic Press, 1997), 280–92.

[29] This has been most explicitly used of Qumran sectarian exegesis by Geza Vermes, "Interpretation, History of: At Qumran and in the Targums," in *The Interpreter's Dictionary of the Bible: Supplementary Volume* (ed. K. Crim; Nashville: Abingdon, 1976), 438–43, esp. 440–41.

[30] On the importance of paying attention to the plain meaning of the text see George J. Brooke, "Reading the Plain Meaning of Scripture in the Dead Sea Scrolls," in *Jewish Ways of Reading the Bible* (ed. G. J. Brooke; JSSSup 11; Oxford: Oxford University Press, 2000), 67–90.

Implicit and Explicit Interpretation

Another way of creating a taxonomy of early Jewish scriptural interpretation is to think more of its various forms. Here the key matter to distinguish one subgroup of interpretative texts from another is the difference to be observed between implicit and explicit interpretation. Implicit interpretation is usually recognizable in those compositions that allude to scriptural antecedents in various ways, without using formulae or introductory statements that identify the source or sources being used. In this category it is easy to put many of the so-called rewritten Bible compositions found in the Qumran library, such as the *Genesis Apocryphon*, an Aramaic retelling of much of the book of Genesis—what survives concerns Lamech, Noah, Abraham, and their contemporaries. Also there is much implied interpretation of scripture in poetic, hymnic, and other liturgical compositions, though there are often extensive debates about whether a particular word or phrase was a deliberate use of scriptural phraseology or something more accidental, the result of the author's own vocabulary and usage that could have been influenced pervasively by scriptural works. Explicit interpretation is found in many different compositions, such as the *Pesharim*, the running commentaries on prophetic books, and in the admonitory section of the *Damascus Document* where short passages of scripture are explicitly cited and combined with others. One composition, which is probably dependent on a range of sources, contains both implicit interpretation in the form of rewritten scripture and explicit interpretation in the use of *pesher*; this *Commentary on Genesis A* might indicate how in the first century BCE there is a gradual shift toward greater use of explicit exegesis.[31]

Five Types by Content and Method

My own preference for some time has been to outline the various types of scriptural interpretation in the non-biblical DSS through their content and method.[32] In addition to the kind of inner-scriptural interpretation that we have noticed in 4QGen[g], I suggest that there are five broad categories to be considered.

Legal Interpretation

The first category is legal interpretation. This deserves to be put first in the list, because particularly in Christian readings of the scrolls its significance is some-

---

[31] George J. Brooke, "4Q252 as Early Jewish Commentary," *RevQ* 17 (1996): 385–401.

[32] See George J. Brooke, "Biblical Interpretation in the Qumran Scrolls and the New Testament," in *The Dead Sea Scrolls Fifty Years after Their Discovery: Proceedings of the Jerusalem Congress, July 20–25, 1997* (ed. L. H. Schiffman, E. Tov, and J. C. VanderKam; Jerusalem: Israel Exploration Society and the Shrine of the Book, Israel Museum, 2000), 60–73; idem, "Biblical Interpretation in the Wisdom Texts from Qumran," in *The Wisdom Texts from Qumran and the Development of Sapiential Thought* (ed. C. Hempel, A. Lange, and H. Lichtenberger; BETL 159; Leuven: Peeters and Leuven University Press, 2002), 201–20; idem, "Biblical Interpretation at Qumran," *The Bible and the Dead Sea Scrolls*, vol. 1: *Scripture and the Scrolls* (ed. J. H. Charlesworth; The Second Princeton Symposium on Judaism and Christian Origins; Waco, TX: Baylor University Press, 2006), 287–319.

times overlooked.[33] It is surely no accident that since the publication of several legal compositions from the Qumran caves, such as the *Temple Scroll, Miqṣat Maʿaśe Ha-Torah*, previously unknown halakhic materials in the *Damascus Document*, and other works, there has been a real awakening among scholars that much of the debate within Judaism in the last centuries before the fall of the temple was legal in nature. To be sure there were many factors that motivated such debates, but where and how one stood in relation to the Law seems to have mattered to many Jews at the time of Hillel and Jesus. The five books of the Law dominate the scene "at Qumran as objects of interpretation."[34] Among NT scholarship this awakening can be seen in the many studies on Jesus and the Law, especially considering whether he ever broke it or how he observed it, and many re-evaluations of Paul and the Law. Thus the legal interpretation of the scrolls has given permission and encouragement to NT scholars to put the most characteristic feature of Judaism back into the frame, whether it is the description of the Jewishness of Jesus or the nomistic attitude of Paul.

The chief characteristic of legal interpretation is the analogical extension or clarification of the Law through the juxtaposition of two texts that share some common feature, usually some common phraseology. A classic example with a significant parallel in the NT concerns marriage and divorce. In an admonitory section of the *Damascus Document* (CD 4:19–5:2) an example is given for how Israel has fallen into fornication, one of the traps of Belial. The text reads as follows:

> The builders of the wall who go after Zaw—Zaw is the preacher of whom he said: "Assuredly they will preach" (Mic 2:6)—are caught twice in fornication: by taking two wives in their lives, even though the principle of creation is "male and female he created them" (Gen 1:27), and the ones who went into the ark "went in two by two into the ark" (Gen 7:9). And about the prince it is written: "He should not multiply wives to himself" (Deut 17:17).[35]

There has been much debate about this passage, whether it rules against polygamy alone or against polygamy and divorce. The literal reading of the passage is that members of this movement were never allowed more than one wife, even if the wife died.[36] Whatever the case, it is important to see that the legal exposition

---

[33] A fine study is Moshe J. Bernstein and Shlomo A. Koyfman, "The Interpretation of Biblical Law in the Dead Sea Scrolls: Forms and Methods," in *Biblical Interpretation at Qumran* (ed. M. Henze; Studies in the Dead Sea Scrolls and Related Literature; Grand Rapids: Eerdmans, 2005), 61–87; see also the suggestions concerning how the Torah is used by Sidnie White Crawford, "The Use of the Pentateuch in the *Temple Scroll* and the *Damascus Document* in the Second Century BCE," in *The Pentateuch as Torah: New Models for Understanding Its Promulgation and Acceptance* (ed. G. N. Knoppers and B. M. Levison; Winona Lake, IN: Eisenbrauns, 2007), 301–17.

[34] Bernstein, "Interpretation of Scriptures," 377.

[35] Trans. Florentino García Martínez and Eibert J. C. Tigchelaar, *The Dead Sea Scrolls Study Edition* (Leiden: Brill; Grand Rapids: Eerdmans, 2000), 557.

[36] Jerome Murphy-O'Connor, "An Essene Missionary Document? CD II,14–VI,1," *RB* 77 (1970): 201–29, esp. 220; supported by P. R. Davies, *Behind the Essenes: History and Ideology in the Dead Sea Scrolls* (BJS 94; Atlanta: Scholars Press, 1987), 73–85.

rests on the juxtaposition of three scriptural texts, two from Genesis and one from Deuteronomy, which are combined to produce this strict and narrow ruling; additionally Gen 1:27 is identified as enshrining the "principle of creation" on the matter. In Mark 10:2–12 Jesus is presented as arguing against divorce and remarriage through the juxtaposition of Gen 1:27 (or Gen 5:2) and Gen 2:24; once again, Gen 1:27 is defined as foundational, "from the beginning of creation."

Narrative Interpretation

The second category is narrative interpretation. The existence of this form of interpretation among the DSS has been appreciated since the publication of the *Genesis Apocryphon* from Cave 1. However, because the composition is in Aramaic and does not contain any clear sectarian vocabulary, it has often been ignored by scholars who have focussed solely on the explicitly sectarian exegesis of the *Pesharim*. Yet, since the general release of the unpublished Cave 4 and Cave 11 manuscripts in 1991 the amount of narrative interpretation in the collection has increased significantly, so that it deserves a subcategory of its own.

The chief characteristic of narrative interpretation is explanatory expansion. Take the following example:

> And on the night of our entry into Egypt, I, Abram, dreamt a dream; [and behold], I saw in my dream a cedar tree and a palm tree . . . men came and they sought to cut down the cedar tree and to pull up its roots, leaving the palm tree (standing) alone. But the palm tree cried out saying, "Do not cut down this cedar tree, for cursed be he who shall fell [it]." And the cedar tree was spared because of the palm tree and [was] not felled.

> And during the night I woke from my dream, and I said to Sarai my wife, "I have dreamt a dream . . . [and I am] fearful [because of] this dream." She said to me, "Tell me your dream that I may know it." So I began to tell her this dream . . . [the interpretation] of the dream . . . that they will seek to kill me, but will spare you . . . [Say to them] of me, "He is my brother", and because of you I shall live, and because of you my life shall be saved . . .[37]

Here the wider context is the retelling of Gen 12:10–20. The inclusion of a dream at this juncture serves several explanatory purposes. "This haggadic insertion into the Genesis story seems intended to be an explanation of the lie that Sarai will have to tell to cover up the real identity of Abram her husband. The lie is to be told in conformity with a dream accorded to Abram, and though the origin of the dream is never ascribed to God, this is certainly the implication."[38] Thus there is an explanation for why Sarai lies and at the same time Abram is exonerated from being a man of deceit, since what happens seems to be at the divine behest. Perhaps Abram's deceit was perceived as a problem in the plain sense of the text of Genesis and some kind of clarification in his favor offered for it.

---

[37] Trans. Vermes, *The Complete Dead Sea Scrolls in English*, 487.
[38] Joseph A. Fitzmyer, *The Genesis Apocryphon of Qumran Cave 1 (1Q20): A Commentary* (BibOr 18/B; 3rd ed.; Rome: Pontifical Biblical Institute, 2004), 184.

Narrative interpretation can take several different forms. It can range from straightforward retelling to expansionist rewriting. Outside the scrolls there are many examples of this in the rehearsal of scripture by Josephus in his *Jewish Antiquities*,[39] and in the NT one way of viewing what Matthew and Luke respectively do to Mark is to consider them as explanatory narrative retellings of their authoritative source, particularly through the insertion of numerous extra sayings (probably from the source dubbed by scholars as Q). On occasions scriptural narratives can also form the typological basis for subsequent counterparts as in the way that elements of the narratives about Elijah and Elisha are used by Luke to narrate similar events in his portrayal of the ministry of Jesus.[40]

Hymnic and Poetic Interpretation

The third category is hymnic and poetic interpretation; this can also include the aphoristic use of scripture in wisdom compositions. Poets, sages, and those who write texts for use in the liturgy do not tend to cite their sources explicitly. Indeed, the obvious way to destroy the effect of a poem would be for the poet to interrupt his developing imagery with a confession that he was dependent on an earlier writer for his ideas. The use of scripture in poems and hymns influences form, content, and genre. Thus echoes of an earlier authoritative text can be used to structure a new poem, perhaps through repetition or chiasm. Or earlier source materials can be seen to provide vocabulary and themes for the new composition. Or the genre of a scriptural passage provides structural pointers and suitable language. Overall, however, the major characteristic of poetic interpretation is the creation of a fresh anthology of allusions, some of which may be picked up by the reader or listener, some of which may not.

Take the following short passage from one of the poems in the *Hodayot*:

And what then itself (is) flesh that it understands [these?
And a FORMATI]ON of dust how can it *direct* its steps?
You, you have FORMED the spirit
And its works you have *destined* [from before eternity].
And from you (is) the way of every living being. (1QHᵃ 7:34–35)[41]

This short extract is a reprise in a much larger wisdom poem. The elements of reprise are indicated by the words in italics: in the wisdom poem the theme of being destined for something occurs six times, in each subsection of the poem, and the

---

[39] See especially Louis H. Feldman, "Use, Authority, and Exegesis of Mikra in the Writings of Josephus," in *Mikra: Text, Translation, Reading, and Interpretation of the Hebrew Bible in Ancient Judaism and Early Christianity* (ed. M. J. Mulder; CRINT 2/1; Assen: Van Gorcum; Philadelphia: Fortress, 1988), 455–518; idem, *Studies in Josephus' Rewritten Bible* (JSJSup 58; Leiden: Brill, 1998).

[40] As shown in most detail by Thomas L. Brodie, *The Birthing of the New Testament: The Intertextual Development of the New Testament Writings* (New Testament Monographs 1; Sheffield: Sheffield Phoenix Press, 2004), 282–446.

[41] Trans. Julie A. Hughes, *Scriptural Allusions and Exegesis in the Hodayot* (STDJ 59; Leiden: Brill, 2006), 67; Hughes discusses the passage on pp. 71–77.

motif of having one's steps directed is also found in an earlier section. The words for "forming" and "formation" also occur elsewhere in the poem and are in small capital font here to indicate their fundamental thematic and theological significance for the poet. There are a string of possible scriptural allusions behind the choice of vocabulary in this section: for "formation" and its variations, consider Isa 45:9–12, and this term in combination with "spirit" is found in Zech 12:1 ("Thus says the Lord, who stretched out the heavens and founded the earth and formed the human spirit within"), and then "the way of every living being" may depend on a passage such as Job 12:9–10 ("In his hand is the life of every living thing"). The whole resonates with Jer 10:23, a verse that is significant in other parts of the poem and may provide some structural clues for the whole new poem: "I know, O Lord, that the way of human beings is not in their control, that mortals as they walk cannot direct their steps." The identification of the scriptural allusions is always open to question, but it is remarkable that the poet here does not simply borrow phrases at random—rather he seems to be aware of the contexts from which he borrows as he compiles a fresh composition that meditates on God as the one who forms the individual from eternity.

These kinds of allusory uses of scripture can be found in many places in early Jewish prayers and poems, not least as these are represented by such compositions as the canticles in Luke's infancy narrative[42] and the poetic pieces in Paul's epistles. Take, for example, the use of Scripture in Phil 2:6–11, with its allusions to Gen 1:27 and Gen 3:5 in relation to "form," its use of Isa 45:23 in formulating the ideas of "every knee shall bow" and "every tongue shall swear," as well as the possibility of other scriptural background echoes for motifs such as "equality with God," "slave," "obedience," and so on. All these are woven together in the hymn to create a fresh Christological statement for the Philippian believers to appropriate.[43]

Exhortatory Interpretation

In fourth place there is exhortatory interpretation. The chief characteristic of such interpretation is the way it uses scriptural precedents to encourage a particular form of behavior. Such precedents may be formulated as positive motivations, such as with the appeal to the figure of Abraham in the *Damascus Document* (CD 3:2–3), or they may be negative, such as with the recollection of the destructive power of the flood in the so-called *Admonition Based on the Flood* (4Q370):

> [And] he crowned the mountains with pro[duce and] poured out food upon them. And (with) good fruit he satisfied all. "Let all who do my will eat and be satisfied," said Y[H]WH. "And let them bless my [holy] name. But look! Now they have done what is evil in my eyes," said YHWH. And they rebelled against God in their deeds. And YHWH judged them according to [al]l their ways and according to the thoughts of the

---

[42] See Stephen Farris, *The Hymns of Luke's Infancy Narratives: Their Origin, Meaning, and Significance* (JSNTSup 9; Sheffield: JSOT Press, 1985).

[43] Most neatly and convincingly described by James D. G. Dunn, *Christology in the Making: An Inquiry into the Origins of the Doctrine of the Incarnation* (London: SCM, 1980), 114–19.

[evil] inclination of their heart. And he thundered against them with [his] strength. [And] all the foundations of the ea[rth] trembled, [and wa]ters broke forth from the depths. All the windows of the heavens were opened, and all the de[pths] overflowed [with] mighty waters. And the windows of the heavens p[our]ed forth rain. [So] he destroyed them in the deluge, [   ] he exterminated them (4Q370 1:1–5).[44]

The opening words of this section of text resonate with the similar phraseology of Deut 8:7–10: "For the Lord your God is bringing you into a good land . . . You shall eat your fill and bless the Lord your God for the good land that he has given you." This terminology is taken up in Neh 9:25–27, which may also be echoed in 4Q370: ". . . fruit trees in abundance; so they ate, and were filled and became fat, and delighted themselves in your great goodness." The references to Deuteronomy and Nehemiah show that 4Q370 is addressed to people who have occupied the land after the generation of the flood, and yet the recollection of the destruction brought on the wicked by the flood is used to good effect to warn the reader or listener against behaving like the last generation before the flood which followed the "thoughts of the evil inclination of their heart." A not entirely dissimilar exhortatory use of the flood account is to be found in Jesus' teaching according to Matt 24:36–44 and Luke 17:22–37: "Keep awake therefore, for you do not know on what day your Lord is coming."

Prophetic Interpretation

Lastly, there is prophetic interpretation. For the Qumran library this has been identified most obviously with the *Pesharim*.[45] Indeed, perhaps largely because *Pesher Habakkuk* from Cave 1 was among the very first manuscripts to be published, prophetic interpretation, *pesher*, has often been considered as the sole or dominant aspect of Qumran sectarian exegesis.[46] By putting it last in my list of types, I hope to dispel that impression somewhat.

---

[44] Trans. Carol A. Newsom, "Admonition on the Flood," in *Qumran Cave 4.XIV: Parabiblical Texts, Part 2* (ed. J. C. VanderKam; DJD 19; Oxford: Clarendon Press, 1995), 91.

[45] For a recent presentation of the *Pesharim* see Shani Berrin, "Qumran Pesharim," in *Biblical Interpretation at Qumran* (ed. M. Henze; Studies in the Dead Sea Scrolls and Related Literature; Grand Rapids: Eerdmans, 2005), 110–33. See also J. H. Charlesworth, *The Pesharim and Qumran History: Chaos or Consensus?* (Grand Rapids: Eerdmans, 2002); Timothy H. Lim, *Pesharim* (Companion to the Qumran Scrolls 3; London: Sheffield Academic Press, 2002).

[46] As, e.g., by Jonathan Campbell, "The Qumran Sectarian Writings," in *The Cambridge History of Judaism. Volume Three: The Early Roman Period* (ed. W. Horbury, W. D. Davies and J. Sturdy; Cambridge: Cambridge University Press, 1999), 810–11, who mentions under "biblical interpretation" almost no compositions other than the *Pesharim*; and note the title of the subsection in Craig Evans, *Ancient Texts for New Testament Studies: A Guide to the Background Literature* (Peabody, MA: Hendrickson, 2005), 146–48: "Pesharim: Qumran's Commentaries on Scripture." This attitude persists in the recent contribution by James H. Charlesworth, "Revelation and Perspicacity in Qumran Hermeneutics," in *The Dead Sea Scrolls and Contemporary Culture: Proceedings of the International Conference held at the Israel Museum, Jerusalem (July 6–8, 2008)* (ed. A. D. Roitman, L. H. Schiffman and S. Tzoref; STDJ 93; Leiden: Brill, 2011), 161–80.

The chief characteristic of prophetic interpretation is the way in which items in the prophetic text are identified in a "that is this"[47] fashion in the interpretation. As we have mentioned this is not unlike the methods applied for the interpretation of dreams and omens by Jews and others in antiquity. I have already provided an example of prophetic interpretation in the consideration of the use of variant scriptural texts discussed above so a further brief example will suffice here. The running commentary on Ps 37 has a section as follows:

> *But they who hope in YHWH will possess the land* (Ps 37:9). Its interpretation: they are the congregation of his chosen ones who carry out his will. *A little while, and the wicked will be no more. I will stare at his place and he will no longer be there* (Ps 37:10). Its interpretation concerns all the wickedness at the end of forty years, for they will be completed and upon the earth no [wic]ked person will be found (4QpPs[a] 1–10 ii, 4–8).[48]

The aspiration of the community to possess the land is represented by the straightforward way in which they, as the congregation of the chosen, are identified with those who hope in the Lord, but it is possible that their further identification as the ones who "carry out his will" is the result of a pun, since "land" (*'rṣ*) and "will" (*rṣwn*) share similar sounds. Scholars have for a long time designated this approach "atomization" or "specification":[49] a general item in the text is made to refer to something specific in the interpreter's concerns. The interpretation of Ps 37:10 continues the straightforward identifications, the "wicked" of the psalm being identified with collective wickedness, and the "little while" being seen to correspond with the final forty-year period, known from other sectarian compositions (1QM 2:6–15; CD 20:15). In addition the reference to "earth" or "land" in the interpretation may take forward the aspiration of the previous lemma: those who hope in the Lord will indeed be able to possess the land because all the wicked will have been removed. I have chosen these verses of Ps 37 because in the third beatitude in Matt 5:5, Matthew's Jesus refers to the same passage as the eschatological blessing for the meek.

Locations of Interpretation

The discussion of the interpretation of scripture in the DSS often takes place in conferences and in symposia, in seminaries and universities. Although it is not always the case, it often seems to be assumed that scriptural interpretation, both ancient and modern, was and is a kind of academic exercise, largely confined to the classroom and school. It may well be the case that ongoing habits of interpretation were learned through education in the schools of antiquity as they are also

---

[47] Bruce, *Biblical Exegesis in the Qumran Texts*, 67; though he prefers the formulation: "This is that."
[48] Trans. García Martínez and Tigchelaar, *The Dead Sea Scrolls Study Edition*, 343.
[49] For "specification" see Bernstein, "Interpretation of Scriptures," 381.

learned in such settings nowadays, but scriptural interpretation also took place in other settings. I consider it important to take note of this briefly in order to see that authoritative scriptures were at the basis of the lives of the Qumran community members and their Jewish contemporaries in a range of ways.

In addition to the schoolroom or study session (cf. 1QS 6:6–8), two particular settings are likely to have played a significant role in how Scripture was handled. On the one hand it is clear from a number of sectarian compositions that the community or part of it met for formal deliberations on all matters of business. There were rules for procedure at such meetings, many of which can themselves be derived from Scripture. But more significantly, it is likely that scriptural precedents influenced the decisions made at such meetings, and not just the community's own earlier decisions. It seems to me likely, for example, that the contents of the rulings in *Miqṣat Maʿaśe Ha-Torah* need to be seen as a collection of decisions about a wide range of topics relating to the priesthood and temple practice in Jerusalem, many of which can be related in various ways to scriptural statements on similar or the same topics.[50]

On the other hand, a key role is played by authoritative Scriptures in the worship of the community and of its individual members.[51] Not only would there normally be scriptural readings at worship gatherings, but such readings would be expounded. In addition, most, if not all, of the prayers and hymns used in such settings were full of the kinds of allusion to scriptural antecedents that I have hinted at briefly above in what has been said about the *Hodayot*, a text that may or may not have been used in corporate worship but which exemplifies much of the anthological use of Scripture found in liturgical texts in general.

Thus through study sessions, communal deliberations, and private and corporate prayer and worship, the members of the community would have encountered Scripture, engaged with it, used it for establishing their own self-understanding on a range of issues and, in doing all this, would have endorsed its authority.

Conclusion

We have ranged widely in this essay. Where have we arrived? I will conclude by drawing out two matters from what I have described.

First, I consider it important to note some key elements of the attitude to Scripture found in both the sectarian and non-sectarian compositions that have survived from the eleven caves at and near Qumran. The Jewish Scriptures as they are on their journey from authority to canon in the late Second Temple period, and possibly including some literary works that never completed the journey, are

---

[50] See George J. Brooke, "The Explicit Presentation of Scripture in 4QMMT," in *Legal Texts and Legal Issues: Proceedings of the Second Meeting of the International Organization for Qumran Studies, Cambridge 1995, Published in Honour of Joseph M. Baumgarten* (ed. M. Bernstein, F. García Martínez, and J. Kampen; STDJ 23; Leiden: Brill, 1997), 67–88.

[51] See Davies, "Biblical Interpretation in the Dead Sea Scrolls," 161–63.

the dominant carriers of the traditions with which the sectarian movement wishes to identify. They see themselves through the lenses of all kinds of interpretative compositions and in the various forms of the biblical books themselves as in continuity with biblical Israel—indeed they seem prepared to make exclusive claims to be the sole true heirs of that scriptural tradition. They are concerned with the plain meaning of scriptural texts, but they are also fully aware that Scripture is not just to be taken literally. They engage in a fascinating interactive exercise with the Scriptures as they convey the sense that the ancient texts were speaking to them directly. There is an admirable loyalty and devotion to the scriptural tradition. But modern students need to beware, especially those among Judaism and Christianity today who show similar affection and loyalty to the Scriptures. What reward meets this community with its exclusivist devoted reading? They are wiped out.

So it is, secondly and somewhat ironically perhaps, that it is important for all those devoted to Scripture to appreciate that ultimately their whole appropriation of Scripture cannot be derived from Scripture itself but depends on a range of factors external to Scripture. For the Qumran community, it is clear that at least two issues determined their selective reading of the Scriptures. On the one hand in their contemporary context they convinced themselves that everybody else's readings and interpretations were inappropriate, even evil. On the other hand, despite some warnings from some of their own members, they dressed up in scriptural language their daily experiences and the wider political context in Palestine and the emerging Roman Empire as the eschatological scenario in which and at the end of which God would decisively intervene on their behalf to vindicate them. We must wonder how anybody can think they know such things.

9

EXCAVATING IDEAS: THE QUMRAN
SCROLLS OF SAMUEL

Keith Bodner

If a reader of the *Wall Street Journal* on the first of June, 1954, chanced upon the classified advertisements of the newspaper, a number of deals were to be had in the "miscellaneous for sale" section: one could rent a picturesque and completely private summer property, or purchase a number of industrial-quality steel tanks, capable of holding upwards of ten thousand gallons. But sandwiched between these disparate deals was a notice that would ultimately prove to be the most lucrative for speculators. Headed with a bold font, the low-budget advertisement read as follows: "The Four Dead Sea Scrolls: Biblical manuscripts dating back to at least 200 BC are for sale. This would be an ideal gift to an educational institution or religious institution by an individual or group. Box F 206, The Wall Street Journal."[1] The Qumran manuscripts, it is fair to say, have not been out of the newspapers or related media ever since. Yet this advertisement in the *WSJ* was only one more intriguing twist in a tale that is worthy of a Broadway production, as the scrolls were first discovered some years before this notice. As Hershel Shanks relates the story, "In early 1947 (or late 1946), an Arab shepherd searching for a lost sheep threw a rock into a cave in the limestone cliffs on the northwestern shore of the Dead Sea. Instead of a bleating sheep, he heard the sound of breaking pottery. When he investigated, he found seven nearly intact ancient documents that became known as the Dead Sea Scrolls."[2]

---

[1] Reproduced in J. C. VanderKam, *The Dead Sea Scrolls Today* (2nd ed.; Grand Rapids: Eerdmans, 2010), 12. Related matters concerning the discovery of the scrolls are discussed by Timothy H. Lim, *The Dead Sea Scrolls: A Very Short Introduction* (Oxford: Oxford University Press, 2005). For an account of the many "battles of the scrolls" since their unearthing—battles that often seem as aggressive as the war between the sons of light and the sons of darkness in the scrolls themselves—see L. H. Schiffman, *Qumran and Jerusalem: Studies in the Dead Sea Scrolls and the History of Judaism* (Grand Rapids: Eerdmans, 2010), 15–44; H. Shanks, *Freeing the Dead Sea Scrolls and Other Adventures of an Archaeology Outsider* (London: Continuum, 2010).

[2] H. Shanks, "Dead Sea Scrolls: A Short History," *BAR* 33/3 (May/June 2007): 34–37, here 34. Note also the discussion of possible *earlier* discoveries of the scrolls in C. A. Evans,

It is hard to miss the historical and biblical appropriateness of this anecdote of discovery: in searching for a lost sheep, a faithful shepherd stumbled on an old and hidden library, a discovery that subsequently has been labeled as one of the most important archeological finds of the twentieth century. Altogether, as J. H. Charlesworth summarizes, the Qumran scrolls "comprise about eight hundred documents, actual leather or papyrus manuscripts that Jews held and read over two thousand years ago. All the Scrolls were hidden before 68 CE . . . and they were discovered in eleven caves on the northwestern shores of the Dead Sea."[3] Included in the cache of the fourth cave were some manuscripts of the biblical books of Samuel—not particularly well-preserved, but of great antiquity, certainly older than any previously known manuscripts—and the subject of my study here in this chapter. The three scrolls have come to be known as 4QSam[a], 4QSam[b], and 4QSam[c]. Of these, 4QSam[a] is the largest of the three scrolls, containing fragmentary representations from both 1 and 2 Samuel. In relative contrast, Kyle McCarter characterizes 4QSam[b] as "a poorly preserved MS of the mid-third century BCE containing fragments of a small part of 1 Samuel" and 4QSam[c] as "a MS of the early first century BCE preserving small fragments of I Samuel 25 and II Samuel 14–15."[4]

During the past few years a milestone for textual studies in the books of Samuel was reached as volume 17 in the series Discoveries in the Judean Desert was finally published in 2005. DJD 17 now represents an authoritative edition of the Samuel corpus from Qumran, previously known only through a smattering of photographs, scholarly articles, some doctoral dissertations, a pair of commentaries by Kyle McCarter, the critical apparatus to BHS, and the textual footnotes

---

Holman QuickSource Guide to the Dead Sea Scrolls (Nashville: Broadman & Holman, 2010), 24–43. For literary critics, a response to the scrolls can be found in R. Alter, "How Important Are the Dead Sea Scrolls?" *Commentary* 93/2 (1992): 34–41.

[3] J. H. Charlesworth, "The New Perspective on Second Temple Judaism and 'Christian Origins,'" in *The Bible and the Dead Sea Scrolls*, vol. 1: *Scripture and the Scrolls* (The Second Princeton Symposium on Judaism and Christian Origins; ed. J. H. Charlesworth; Waco, TX: Baylor University Press, 2006), xxiii. For one appraisal of the contribution of the Qumran material to modern scholarship, see E. Ulrich, "Our Sharper Focus on the Bible and Theology Thanks to the Dead Sea Scrolls," *CBQ* 66 (2004): 1–24.

[4] P. K. McCarter, *I Samuel* (AB 8; Garden City, NY: Doubleday, 1980), 6. See the early discussion of E. Tov, "The Textual Affiliations of 4QSam[a]," *JSOT* 14 (1979): 37–53, now assembled with other of his articles in E. Tov, *Hebrew Bible, Greek Bible, and Qumran: Collected Essays by Emanuel Tov* (TSAJ 121; Tübingen: Mohr Siebeck, 2008). See also D. W. Parry, "The Textual Character of the Unique Readings of 4QSam[a] (4Q51)," in *Flores Florentino: Dead Sea Scrolls and Other Early Jewish Studies in Honour of Florentino García Martínez* (ed. Anthony Hilhorst, Émile Puech, and Eibert J. C.Tigchelaar; JSJSup 122; Leiden: Brill, 2007), 163–82. In more general terms, see E. Tov, "The Many Forms of Hebrew Scripture: Reflections in Light of the Septuagint and 4QReworked Pentateuch," in *From Qumran to Aleppo: A Discussion with Emanuel Tov about the Textual History of Jewish Scriptures in Honor of His 65th Birthday* (ed. Armin Lange, Matthias Weigold, and József Zsengellér; FRLANT 230; Göttingen: Vandenhoeck & Ruprecht, 2009), 11–28. Further, a convenient review of several important works relevant to this study can be found in Kristin de Troyer, "Qumran Research and Textual Studies: A Different Approach," *RelSRev* 28 (2002): 115–22.

to the New American Bible translation. The official publication under the editorship of Frank Moore Cross, Eugene Ulrich, Donald Parry, and Richard Saley now opens the door for new avenues of research. Even in an age where our discipline enjoys fewer points of consensus than has been the case in the past, it nonetheless remains universally acknowledged that the Qumran scrolls of Samuel make a significant contribution to understanding the text-critical problems of this stretch of the Deuteronomistic History. To this point, however, comparatively less attention has been given to examining the contribution of the Qumran material as far as understanding the literary dynamics of the narrative.

In terms of method, my approach in this study takes its cue from a splendid article written by Alexander Rofé and published in *Dead Sea Discoveries*. Though his article deals with the Qumran text of Exodus, his approach can be adopted nicely for my purposes. Rofé is interested in a variant of Exod 2:3 attested in 4QExod[b], a detail that relates to an incident early in the life of Moses.[5] When the mother of Moses—because of Pharaoh's edict demanding that every Hebrew male baby be cast into the Nile—could hide her infant son no longer, she prepared an ark for him. The Hebrew MT at this point reads: "she set the child in it, and she set it among the reeds upon the lip of the Nile." Rofé opines, though, that the Qumran text contains an extra three words that can produce a different range of meaning. Consider Exod 2:3 now with the Qumran addition in italics: "But when she could no longer hide him, she took an ark for him, and coated it with tar and pitch. Then she put the child into it. *She said to her maidservant, 'Go!'* And she set it among the reeds by the bank of the Nile." I have discussed this variant and Rofé's analysis elsewhere, but one can immediately see that the Qumran addition changes the story in several interesting ways.[6] For instance, Rofé notes that the Greek LXX occasionally

---

[5] Alexander Rofé, "Moses' Mother and Her Slave-Girl according to 4QExod[b]," *DSD* 9 (2002): 38–43.

[6] Keith Bodner, *David Observed: A King in the Eyes of His Court* (Hebrew Bible Monographs 5; Sheffield: Sheffield Phoenix Press, 2008), 89–97, a revised version of an article that originally appeared as "The Royal Conscience According to 4QSam[a]," *DSD* 11 (2004): 158–66. My particular interest in the study is a variant of 2 Sam 11:3 attested in 4QSam[a] that, like the 4QExod[b] variant, has a number of intriguing literary possibilities. The MT reads: "And David sent and inquired about the woman, and he said, 'Is this not Bathsheba, the daughter of Eliam, the wife of Uriah the Hittite?'" but 4QSam[a] includes a further three words: "*armor-bearer of Joab?*" (נ]ושא כלי יואב). In the first instance, no speaker for this line is directly specified, and thus there is a teasing ambiguity as to whether these words are spoken by an unnamed messenger of David or by the king himself. Moreover, this additional information about Uriah's vocation—whereby he is now the armor-bearer to Joab in the Qumran text—must serve to accentuate his personal tragedy. As the high-level personal attendant of the general of Israel's armed forces, he would have to be considered the consummate loyal soldier, a paragon of constancy and faithful service, yet he is sacrificed by Joab because of the king's folly in Jerusalem. Bathsheba is the granddaughter of Ahitophel, who later joins the rebellion of Absalom that almost destroys David's kingship, In a small way, 2 Sam 11:3 foreshadows the coming destruction during the most turbulent phase of David's career, as he experiences betrayal from within his own household. I conclude the study by arguing that this 4QSam[a] variant provides evidence that 2 Sam 11—the turning point of the David story—was vigorously read and viewed as highly important to early readers of this

has secondary characters where none occur in the Hebrew text. So, Eli the priest has a servant in the LXX version of 1 Sam 1:14 who delivers a rebuke to Hannah, and likewise Ahijah the prophet has a servant who relays the prophet's words to the wife of Jeroboam, Israel's queen, and there is no counterpart servant in the Hebrew text (LXX 3 Reigns 12:24k; cf. MT 1 Kgs 14:4–6). Rofé explicates a number of reasons why such variants may be regarded as secondary—an argument that need not detain us here—but adds that such servants can be seen to augment the status of the respective main character; so, Eli the priest and Ahijah the prophet enjoy a heightened status owing to the presence of servants in their midst.[7] By extension, there could be a similar dynamic in the variant text of 4QExod[b], where the Qumran addition of a secondary character is entirely consistent with a phenomenon already known through the LXX. Moses' mother then could have an increased status in the Qumran text along the same lines as Eli and Ahijah in the Greek tradition. No doubt other reasons as to why the text is preserved could be adduced, but the additional words in 4QExod[b] hint at the forthcoming importance of Moses in the story, and the involvement of a servant girl in transporting him to the Nile River. A number of secondary female figures already contribute to the survival of Moses (Miriam, the midwives Shiphrah and Puah, as well as Pharaoh's daughter and her servant girl), and the 4QExod[b] variant includes one further character.

Utilizing an approach with some affinities to Rofé's analysis of 4QExod[b], in this chapter I am arguing that the 4QSam material presents alternative readings at several points that serve to enhance one's appreciation of the literary artistry of the 1 and 2 Samuel narratives. Overall, I would like to begin by making three main kinds of comments. First, I am keen to affirm that the Qumran material makes a quantifiable literary contribution for biblical exegetes in the often-neglected realms of plot, character, irony, motif, theme, temporal and spatial settings, point of view, intertextuality, structural design, and keywords.[8] Second, I would assert

---

narrative and illustrates the vitality of this verse and its dramatic purpose at such a decisive moment of David's reign. On several related issues, see F. Polak, "David's Kingship—A Precarious Equilibrium," in *Politics and Theopolitics in the Bible and Postbiblical Literature* (eds. Henning Graf Reventlow, Yair Hoffman, and Benjamin Uffenheimer; JSOTSup 171; Sheffield: Sheffield Academic Press, 1994), 134–35.

[7] See also Alexander Rofé, "The Methods of Late Biblical Scribes as Evidenced by the Septuagint Compared with the Other Textual Witnesses," in *Tehillah le-Moshe: Biblical and Judaic Studies in Honor of M. Greenberg* (ed. M. Cogan, B. L. Eichler, and J. H. Tigay; Winona Lake, IN: Eisenbrauns, 1997), 259–70.

[8] A working definition of narrative criticism and an extended example can be found in Keith Bodner, *Jeroboam's Royal Drama* (Oxford: Oxford University Press, forthcoming). Note also the categories and discussions in J. T. Walsh, *Style and Structure in Biblical Hebrew Narrative* (Collegeville, MN: Liturgical Press, 2001), and the summary of R. G. Bowman, "Narrative Criticism: Human Purpose in Conflict with Divine Presence," in *Judges and Method: New Approaches in Biblical Studies* (2nd ed.; ed. G. A. Yee; Minneapolis: Fortress, 2007), 19–45, here 19: "The basic presuppositions of narrative criticism are that (1) the final, present form of the text functions as a coherent narrative; (2) this narrative has a literary integrity apart from circumstances relating to the compositional process, the historical reality behind the story, or the interpretive agenda of the reader; and (3) an analysis of the literary features of this narrative will reveal an interpretive focus. The questions asked of the

that the Qumran texts of Samuel provide us an idea of the reception history of these compelling narratives: while the major details are often uniform, unique variations frequently come in the form of gap-filling or matters of characterization with a sense of vibrancy and creativity, and I would venture to submit, with an attuned sensitivity to storytelling flow and intent. Third, I would like to argue that the 4QSam material provides insight as far as the history of interpretation is concerned, since some of the variants indisputably testify to a dynamic understanding and application of the story; that is, an active engagement with the text, as though it is being read with a sense of imaginative vitality. So, to be sure, the Qumran texts of Samuel enhance our text-critical understanding, but to my mind, this material—as I hope is demonstrated in the two examples below—makes a useful literary and interpretive contribution as well.

My first example pertains to the Nazirite status of the prophet Samuel. The various traditions of 1 Sam 1:1–2:11 have proven to be a bonanza for textual critics. While the MT, LXX, and 4QSamᵃ material essentially agree on the major details of the narrative, there are some notable variations that create interesting implications for several of the major characters involved in the story. Indeed, the birth story of the prophet Samuel is a monumental event in the Deuteronomistic History, so it is not overly surprising that his mother, Hannah, is the subject of a rather complex characterization in the narrative. In fact, Hannah's song in 1 Sam 2:1–10 mirrors her own turn of fortune: she proclaims that the Lord will raise up the poor and humble from the dust and seat the lowly person among the princes; this is exactly what happens to her over the course of the narrative, as she moves from the status of a barren wife belittled by her rival, Peninnah, to a triumphant mother of young Samuel, whom she dedicates for divine service as she had promised before his birth. Both Hannah and Samuel, though—and perhaps this is because of their importance and complexity—are given unique shades of development in the various textual traditions. When Hannah is praying for a reversal of her barren estate, she prays fervently, and the quality of her vow endows any potential child with great expectations. Hannah's prayer takes place in the spatial setting of Shiloh within the precincts of the sanctuary that is under the stewardship of Eli the priest (1 Sam 1:11, MT): "Then she made a vow and said, 'O Lᴏʀᴅ of hosts, if you will indeed look on the affliction of your maidservant and remember me, and not forget your maidservant, but will give Your maidservant male seed, then I will give him to the Lᴏʀᴅ all the days of his life, and no razor shall come upon his head.'"

It is quite plausible that the general idea of a Nazirite vow is intimated here in Hannah's prayer, but it remains unstated. Her mention of the razor brings the text of Num 6 to mind, but the crucial term is not uttered in the MT. Nonetheless, other naziritic elements are apparent when one consults the LXX at 1 Sam 1:11: "if looking you will look on the humiliation of your slave and remember me and give to your slave an offspring of men, and I will give him as one devoted before you until the day of his death, *and wine or strong drink he shall not drink*, and no

---

text follow from these presuppositions and concern how the general elements of narrative are manifested in a particular narrative to yield a meaningful and meaning-filled story."

iron shall come upon his head."[9] There are several notable differences here, as the Greek text reads "until the day of his death" for "all the days of his life," as well as including a prohibition on fermented beverages ("he shall drink no wine nor strong drink"). Where does the prohibition on alcohol come from? The usual theories among scholars are that some sort of scribal accident resulted in the present divergence between the Greek and Hebrew texts, or that the LXX represents an expansion of the antecedent MT. But in the judgment of Stephen Pisano, there seems to be no identifiable textual accident or mechanical lapse that would account for the absence of wine and strong drink from the MT.[10] Furthermore, this temperance movement is also problematic in other places within the Greek text of 1 Sam 1, prompting my colleague Stanley Walters to very soberly point out that there is a drinking problem in this stretch of the LXX.[11] Still, despite the clear prohibition on alcohol, in the Greek text we do not have the outright mention of Samuel as a Nazirite—again, maybe it is assumed, but it is not mentioned, as it is with Samson in both the MT and LXX of Judg 13:5. In light of such matters, consider now the MT of 1 Sam 1:22, followed by the 4QSam[a] variant:

MT

And Elkanah the husband went up with all his household to offer to the Lord the annual sacrifice and his vow. But Hannah did not go up, for she said to her husband, "Only when the lad is weaned will I bring him, that he may appear in the presence of the Lord and live there forever."

4QSam[a]

. . . and I will [give] him as a Nazirite forever . . .

It is only the Qumran fragment where Samuel is explicitly labeled as a Nazirite; certainly in 1 Sam 1:22, although the way the text is presented in DJD 17—and as Eugene Ulrich and Kyle McCarter have also maintained—the line spacing seems to require the word "Nazirite" in 1 Sam 1:11 as well.[12] Since reconstructions based on line spacing and word requirements customarily have a speculative or at least provisional element, it is a rather bold and confident move when the NRSV

---

[9] I here consult the translation of B. A. Taylor, "The Kaige Text of Reigns," in *A New English Translation of the Septuagint, and the Other Greek Translations Traditionally Included under That Title* (ed. Albert Pietersma and Benjamin G. Wright; Oxford: Oxford University Press, 2007), 271–96, here 249.

[10] Stephen Pisano, *Additions or Omissions in the Books of Samuel: The Significant Pluses and Minuses in the Massoretic, LXX, and Qumran Texts* (OBO 57; Freiburg: Universitätsverlag; Göttingen: Vandenhoeck & Ruprecht, 1984), 22.

[11] S. D. Walters, "After Drinking (1 Sam 1:9)," in *Crossing Boundaries and Linking Horizons: Studies in Honor of Michael C. Astour on His 80th Birthday* (ed. Gordon D. Young, Mark W. Chavalas, and Richard E. Averback; Bethesda, MD: CDL Press, 1997), 527–56. Note also the larger study of the MT and LXX versions of 1 Sam 1 in Walters, "Hannah and Anna: The Greek and Hebrew Texts of 1 Samuel 1," *JBL* 107 (1988): 385–412.

[12] E. C. Ulrich, *The Qumran Text of Samuel and Josephus* (Missoula, MT: Scholars Press, 1978), 39–40; McCarter, *I Samuel*, 53–54.

separates itself from the crowd by including the term "Nazirite" in the translation of 1 Sam 1:11. The NRSV also includes "Nazirite" in 1 Sam 1:22, but at least the term *nazir* is attested in 4QSam[a] at that place. However, the rationale for NRSV decisions are not my point of inquiry here, nor, for that matter, is the larger issue of textual history (what Pisano refers to as the incremental naziritization of Samuel in these texts). What intrigues me as a commentator is the interpretive question of what happens to the story when Samuel is (or is not) labeled as a Nazirite. There are at least two kinds of questions that I think merit exploration in future research. First, does the specificity of Samuel's Nazirite status affect the intertextual relationship with Judg 13–16? What happens, therefore, to Samson's legacy when Samuel becomes a Nazirite? Is there a redeeming element, or is this a comment on Israel's national life at this crucial moment where the monarchy is introduced?[13]

Second, what happens to the character of Samuel when he unequivocally becomes a Nazirite? Is there a "nomistic" transformation along the lines argued by Rofé, or does the prophet simply become a more foreboding figure of uncommon austerity, and one with heightened qualification to call down judgments and condemnation of Israel's hapless inaugural monarch Saul?[14] In the short term—to be sure—Samuel's Nazirite status certainly enhances the sense of judgment hanging over the sanctuary of Shiloh, and the lad's prenatal commitment to ascetic rigor is surely in stark contrast to the sons of Eli and their profligacy. A helpful theoretical point emerges in a recent volume entitled *Biblical Interpretation at Qumran*, edited by Matthias Henze and part of the series Studies in the Dead Sea Scrolls and Related Literature. During his introductory remarks, Henze reminds us that not only have the scrolls made an invaluable contribution to our understanding of "the development of the biblical canon as it involves both the final stages in the formation of individual books and the emergence of the biblical canon as a whole," but also that the scrolls provide an unrivaled window into "Jewish biblical interpretation in antiquity."[15] Samuel as a Nazirite strikes me as precisely the kind of early interpretive activity that Henze describes in his introduction. When one considers the range of other interpretive issues on offer in 1 Sam 1—from Hannah's various activities to the conversations with Eli, and of course the variant texts of Hannah's song—one is in a better position to see how intensely this story was read in antiquity.[16]

---

[13] For one possibility, note S. Niditch, *"My Brother Esau Is a Hairy Man": Hair and Identity in Ancient Israel* (New York: Oxford University Press, 2008), 84.

[14] See Alexander Rofé, "4QMidrash Samuel?—Observations Concerning the Character of 4QSam[a]," *Textus* 19 (1998): 63–74, esp. 70. Cf. Rofé, "A Nomistic Correction in Biblical Manuscripts and Its Occurrence in 4QSam[a]," *RevQ* 14 (1989): 247–54.

[15] M. Henze, "Introduction," in *Biblical Interpretation at Qumran* (ed. M. Henze; Studies in the Dead Sea Scrolls and Related Literature; Grand Rapids: Eerdmans, 2005), 1–9, here 1–2.

[16] D. W. Parry, "Hannah in the Presence of the Lord," in *Archaeology of the Books of Samuel: The Entangling of the Textual and Literary History* (ed. Philippe Hugo and Adrian Schenker; VTSup 132; Leiden: Brill, 2010), 53–74; M. Tsevat, "Was Samuel a Nazirite?" in *"Sha'arei Talmon": Studies in the Bible, Qumran, and the Ancient Near East Presented to Shemaryahu Talmon* (ed. M. Fishbane and E. Tov; Winona Lake, IN: Eisenbrauns, 1992),

My next example is far less sanctified than the discussion of Samuel's Nazirite status but equally intriguing from a text-critical viewpoint. In the context of the civil war between David and the house of Saul in the early chapters of 2 Samuel, the assassination of Abner is one of the most politically contentious moments, as it creates a situation whereby David himself could be implicated in the murder, and coming as it does on the heels of Abner's efforts to negotiate a settlement. There is no doubt that Abner falls at the hands of Joab, but the various texts of the MT, LXX, and 4QSam[a] in 2 Sam 3:30 each highlight a unique shade of motive in this Deuteronomistic murder mystery. By way of buildup, two of the central characters in the narrative are rival military leaders of Israel and Judah, Abner and Joab. As a captain of David's troops, Joab evidently has a long association with David, but until the outbreak of direct war with Ishbosheth, he remained—in the description of Antony Campbell—a "shadowy figure" very much in the background.[17] As commander of the forces of Saul's house, Abner has been in the public spotlight longer than Joab, as it were, and has a history of enmity with David. Steven McKenzie is correct to point out that after the death of King Saul, "the most powerful man in Israel was Abner."[18]

Leading up to the sordid events of 2 Sam 3, a key piece of the backstory is that Abner has killed Joab's brother Asahel in battle (2 Sam 2:19–23), thus leaving the brothers Joab and Abishai without the third member of their fraternal triumvirate. One senses that this act of killing Asahel—even in the context of war—would somehow revisit Abner, who meanwhile proceeds to "strengthen himself" over the house of Saul. Accused by Ishbosheth of appropriating his father's concubine (an act that is tantamount to laying claim to the throne), Abner reacts by announcing his plans to defect and just as abruptly and surprisingly declares his intentions of making a deal with David.[19] Within moments, then, Abner joins the cause he was very recently trying to defeat, and this kind of vacillation has the effect of making him a far more unstable character. In terms of the deal between David and Abner, one wonders if there is a tacit understanding that Abner is to assume leadership over the army as compensation for his efforts to deliver the northern tribes to David. While unstated in the text, such a move would inconvenience Joab, who may well protest the promotion of such a one as Abner. Indeed, the deal between David and Abner is expediently ratified while Joab is out raiding, and upon returning to Hebron Joab upbraids David with a scathing invective. Stressing in no uncertain terms

---

199–204; J. Corley, "The Portrait of Samuel in Hebrew Ben Sira 46:13–20," in *Biblical Figures in Deuterocanonical and Cognate Literature: Deuterocanonical and Cognate Literature Yearbook 2008* (ed. Hermann Lichtenberger and Ulrike Mittmann-Richert; Berlin: de Gruyter, 2009), 31–56. For quantitative matters, see Frank Moore Cross and Richard J. Saley, "A Statistical Analysis of the Textual Character of 4QSamuel[a] (4Q51)," *DSD* 13 (2006): 46–54.

[17] A. F. Campbell, *2 Samuel* (FOTL 7; Grand Rapids: Eerdmans, 2005), 46.

[18] S. L. McKenzie, *King David: A Biography* (New York: Oxford University Press, 2000), 117.

[19] "Scornfully," writes Graeme Auld, "Abner neither accepts nor rejects the charge," and thus the reader is never sure exactly what transpired between Ishbosheth and Abner. See Graeme Auld, "1 and 2 Samuel," in *Eerdmans Commentary on the Bible* (ed. J. D. G. Dunn and J. W. Rogerson; Grand Rapids: Eerdmans, 2003), 231.

that Abner must be dissembling and has a devious purpose in making a deal with David, Joab storms off, sends messengers after Abner, and swiftly dispatches him personally (2 Sam 3:27). The narrator hastens to explain that Abner dies on account of Asahel's blood, but the reader must be feeling that Joab has multiple reasons for wanting Abner eliminated: personal revenge and his own job security. Bruce Birch has a convenient summary of some of the issues at stake:

> Joab must be seen as a figure with two interests that work against the acceptability of an alliance with Abner. The first is his hatred and distrust of Abner, stemming from Abner's killing of Joab's brother Asahel in the battle described in 2:12–32. Joab sees himself as the legitimate bearer of a claim for vengeance against Abner, although ordinarily bloodguilt would not be recognized for a death suffered in war—i.e., it was not considered murder. The second of Joab's interests in this matter has to do with influence on David. Joab eventually becomes commander of David's armies (8:16), but it is reasonable to think that Abner might have assumed this role if he had lived. In any case, Abner would have been a powerful and influential military adviser and leader within David's kingdom, and this would make him Joab's natural rival for David's favor.[20]

The possibility of twin motives for Joab's elimination of Abner needs to be kept in mind as we approach the pivotal verse (2 Sam 3:30). After David's vociferous avowal of innocence, there is a parenthetical remark by the narrator, a seeming intrusion that apparently repeats what the reader already knows. Yet this remark is pivotal for ascertaining the motives of the murderer, and it is here that some textual comparisons become illuminating, as the MT, LXX, and 4QSam^a each present unique shades of specificity regarding the motive for destroying Abner. Starting with the MT of 2 Sam 3:30, we read, "So Joab and his brother Abishai killed (הרג) Abner because he put their brother Asahel to death in Gibeon, in the war." The Hebrew verb deployed here implies the motive of blood vengeance and personal retribution for a brother's death. This is where Abishai's involvement becomes crucial; some commentators assert that Joab must have been acting alone, since Abishai is not mentioned in 2 Sam 3:26–27. But Abishai's inclusion here in 2 Sam 3:30 stresses the blood-feud dimension of Abner's death, which, incidentally, is exactly what Abner feared (2 Sam 2:23). The LXX of 2 Sam 3:30, though, reads as follows: "But Ioab and his brother Abessa *lay in wait* (διεπαρετηροῦντο) for Abenner." The idea of the ambush, as it is conveyed here, emphasizes the military side of the equation, as though the presence of Abner represents a vocational threat to the sons of Zeruiah, and it is to their professional advantage to have him removed.

4QSam^a has still a different reading: instead of the MT's *kill*, 4QSam^a informs the reader that Joab and Abishai "touched" (נג[עו]), Abner, following the proposed reconstruction of DJD 17. Since all the letters are not legible in the fragment, Donald Parry has alternatively suggested that a better option is פגע "reached out against," a verb with a similar enough semantic range.[21] The attraction with this

---

[20] B. C. Birch, "1 & 2 Samuel," in *The New Interpreter's Bible* (13 vols.; Nashville: Abingdon, 1998), 2:1225.

[21] D. W. Parry, "The Aftermath of Abner's Murder," *Textus* 20 (2000): 87: "A computer enhancement of two visible letters on the fragment indicates that they are *'ayin* and *waw*

verb option is that פגע can often be found in the Deuteronomistic History in pre-cisely this kind of context: that of "hostile touching." When we compare uses of "to reach out and touch someone" (whether נגע as reconstructed in DJD 17 or פגע as I am inclined to support), such a verb most often occurs in a context where a political opponent is neutralized; that is, the verb is frequently deployed when a king is protected from a political rival who invariably is permanently deleted by an assassin. There is a considerable fund of violent examples, including the order to Doeg the Edomite to "reach out against" the priests of Nob in 1 Sam 22; David's men "reaching out against" the Amalekite in 2 Sam 1; and Benaiah is a frequent subject of the verb in 1 Kgs 2 (under orders from Solomon).

With respect to Joab's actions against Abner in 2 Sam 3:30, the 4QSamª reading conceivably underscores the loyalty of Joab and Abishai to shield King David from the machinations of Abner, as explained in this otherwise redundant parenthetical aside. As J. C. VanderKam and others have argued, Joab is an underrated figure whose actions, grim as they often are, are politically advantageous to David and serve to strengthen his hold on the kingdom.[22] Abner—from Joab's point of view—potentially represents a dangerous threat to David, and thus he is "touched" just like other rivals in the Deuteronomistic History. It seems to me that the 4QSamª reading draws attention to these kinds of possibilities, with the most stinging irony saved for Joab himself. After all, in 1 Kgs 2 Benaiah is commanded by Solomon to march into the tent of meeting and "reach out against" (פגע) Joab, who is clinging to the horns of the altar, because Joab is guilty—so the newly crowned Solomon insists—of "reaching out against" (פגע) Abner those many years ago. Benaiah com-plies with the king's order, and before long, he is promoted as head of the army in place of Joab, who is buried in the wilderness. When the demise of Joab is coupled with his "touch" of Abner back in 2 Sam 3:30, it seems as though the Qumran frag-ment would invite the reader to compare these moments in Israel's monarchic his-tory. Far from confusing the matter, I think the variant reading attested in 4QSamª helps the reader to gain insight into the dynamics of the larger storyline. Abner's death was a politically contentious matter during the struggle for the kingdom, and evidently continued to be so throughout its textual history.

(reconstructed as ע]פג[]). . . . This rules out the reading of MT (הרגו) and the readings צפנו and אנו[. Note that the verb פגע is used elsewhere in the HB with the sense of "smite" (see, for example, Judg 8:21; 15:12; 1 Sam 22:17–18; 2 Sam 1:15), although its usage here with the prep-osition *lamed* is highly irregular." The other readings cited by Parry are found in McCarter, *I Samuel*, 110; and E. D. Herbert, *Reconstructing Biblical Dead Sea Scrolls: A New Method Applied to the Reconstruction of 4QSamª* (STDJ 22; Leiden: Brill, 1997), 95. Cf. E. D. Herbert and R. P. Gordon, "A Reading in 4QSamª and the Murder of Abner," *Textus* 19 (1998): 75–80.

[22] J. C. VanderKam, "Davidic Complicity in the Deaths of Abner and Eshbaal," *JBL* 94 (1980): 521–39. Cf. McKenzie, *King David*, 120: "To begin with, David had incentive to get rid of Abner. Abner would have been a constant source of worry for David if he had lived. He was obviously very influential—in the story he persuades both the army and the elders of Israel to go over to David. His dealings with Ishbaal demonstrated that he was indepen-dent and would be difficult to control." Given his interest in the political scheming at work, McKenzie concludes: "But Abner's removal had to be explained in such a way that David could claim innocence and ignorance of the deed. Enter Joab."

As I conclude this short study, there are of course numerous other variants that could have been explored, such as two of the most famous readings of 4QSam[a]—the additional material relating to Nahash, king of the Ammonites (see especially the NRSV translation of 1 Sam 10:27, where the Qumran material is included in the main body of the translation), and the height of Goliath (the MT measures the giant as "six cubits and a span" whereas the reading in 4QSam[a] [cf. LXX] presents a dramatic diminution as the famous Gathite is reduced to "four cubits and a span"). As with the examples of Samuel's Nazirite status and Abner's murder canvassed above, the issues of Nahash's actions and Goliath's height unfold numerous kinds of possibilities for literary interpretation. Such opportunities are bound to increase with the publication of DJD 17. I earlier mentioned the series Studies in the Dead Sea Scrolls and Related Literature, and here I cite the words of the general editors Peter Flint, Martin Abegg, and Florentino García Martínez: "the field of Qumran studies has undergone a renaissance. Scholars have begun to question the established conclusions of the last generation; some widely held beliefs have withstood scrutiny, but others have required revision or even dismissal. . . . At the same time, the scholarly task of establishing reliable critical editions of the texts is nearing completion. The opportunity is ripe, therefore, for directing renewed attention to the task of analysis and interpretation." The Qumran scrolls of Samuel—chronologically not far from the early church community—alert us to the reality that these readers and scribes knew how to hear a story, and on the eve of the birth of the NT Gospel narratives, were familiar with matters of plot, character, point of view, irony, wordplay, direct speech, ambiguity, spatial and temporal settings, and the role of the narrator. Contemporary literary critics view the books of Samuel as a repository of narrative artistry, and it is apparent that ancient readers and scribes held a similar conviction. E. J. Kenney has remarked, "A text is not a concrete artifact, like a pot or a statue, but an abstract concept or idea."[23] A wealth of ideas have been unearthed in the Qumran caves that provide us with insight into reading practices and early hermeneutical habits, and literary analysis of these texts in the days ahead will elevate our appreciation.[24]

---

[23] E. J. Kenney, "Textual Criticism," in *Encyclopaedia Britannica* (15th ed.; Chicago: University of Chicago Press, 1984), 18:189–95, here 191; cited in R. S. Hendel, "The Oxford Hebrew Bible: Prologue to a New Critical Edition," a later version of which was published in *VT* 58 (2008): 324–51.

[24] This article was originally presented in the 2008 spring edition of the Hayward Lectures at Acadia Divinity College, Wolfville, NS. I am extremely grateful to Craig Evans for his invitation and gracious hospitality during the lectures.

10

THE OLDEST ATTESTED HEBREW SCRIPTURES AND THE KHIRBET QEIYAFA INSCRIPTION

Stephen J. Andrews

The Khirbet Qeiyafa Inscription

In July 2008, Oded Yaar, a seventeen-year-old volunteer, was excavating in a square near one of the gates at Khirbet Qeiyafa.[1] Located in the western Shephelah at the top of a hill above the Elah Valley, this ancient site was definitely a strategic location on the main thoroughfare between Philistia on the coastal plain and Jerusalem and Hebron in the hill country.[2] In the debris where he was working, Oded discovered a large trapezoid piece of pottery, 15 x 16.5 cm (5.9 x 6.5 in). He thought it was important, so he put it in the pottery bucket to be brought back to camp.

Eventually it was discovered that Oded's find was an ostracon, a piece of pottery with writing on it. Ostraca are rare but important epigraphs. Some are incised with a sharp tool, but this one was written with ink. There were at least five rows of writing on the shard with black lines separating the rows. The writing was placed on the concave inside of the ostracon. The ancient script was closer to the Proto-Sinaitic or Proto-Canaanite script found at Serabit el-Khadim in Egypt then the later Paleo-Hebrew script.[3] The locus in which the ostracon was discovered was clearly Iron IIA and dated to the early tenth century BCE, the time

---

[1] The content of this chapter was originally presented at The Scrolls and the Scriptures Conference at Midwestern Baptist Theological Seminary, Kansas City, MO, April 3, 2010. The material has been revised and edited.

[2] Yosef Garfinkel and Saar Ganor, "Khirbet Qeiyafa: Sha'arayim," *JHS* 8/22 (2008): 2. For excavation reports, see Yosef Garfinkel and Saar Ganor, "Kirbet Qeiyafa, 2007–2008," *IEJ* 58 (2008): 243–48; Yosef Garfinkel et al., "Khirbet Qeiyafa, 2009," *IEJ* 59 (2009): 214–20; and Yosef Garfinkel and Saar Ganor, *Khirbet Qeiyafa Vol. 1: Excavation Report 2007–2008* (Jerusalem: Israel Exploration Society, 2009).

[3] For a discussion on the history of the West Semitic scripts, including Proto-Canaanite, see Joseph Naveh, *Early History of the Alphabet* (2nd rev. ed.; Jerusalem: Magnes Press, 1987), 23–42.

of King David. Needless to say, the find created quite a stir among the archeological and scholarly world.[4]

Two months later, Haggai Misgav, the expedition's epigraphist, presented the discovery of this particular ostracon privately to forty professional archeologists in Jerusalem. At this meeting, Misgav offered photographs and a preliminary reading of a few words of the inscription. One of the archeologists present leaked the news on his blog.[5]

The news created a sensation, and about eighty websites picked up on the find. The public announcement came at Hebrew University later. Misgav told the world that they had found an ostracon that appeared to be the oldest example of Hebrew writing ever found. Still only a few words were deciphered. Photographs were soon released, and the ostracon attracted media attention from all over the world. If this was the oldest "Hebrew" text ever found, it would likely have a major impact on our knowledge of the history of literacy and the development of the alphabet.

Some claimed that it would alter our notions of the biblical David.[6] Even Yosef Garfinkel, co-excavator of the site, stated, "The chronology and geography of Khirbet Qeiyafa create a unique meeting point between the mythology, history, historiography and archaeology of King David."[7] There is no doubt that the Khirbet Qeiyafa inscription could shed valuable light in our understanding of the history of the period of David's kingdom.

Then the ostracon was flown to the United States and subjected to a number of tests, including various imaging spectrometer sessions. In late 2009 Misgav again presented an analysis of the inscription in Jerusalem. This time a detailed article with a photograph and drawing accompanied the lectures. Other scholars were asked to respond, and the proceedings were published. The final report on the 2007–2008 excavations at Khirbet Qeiyafa was published in late December 2009.[8] This report included three chapters on the inscription. At this time, Misgav offered a proposed reading of the text.

Galil's Translation

By January 2010, Gershon Galil, chair of the Department of Jewish History at Haifa University, also offered a proposed reconstruction of the inscription in a

---

[4] The chronology of the discovery of the ostracon and subsequent study is documented on two Hebrew University of Jerusalem web pages: "Qeiyafa Ostracon Chronicle," Khirbet Qeiyafa Archaeological Project, 2008, Hebrew University of Jerusalem, accessed March 30, 2010, http://qeiyafa.huji.ac.il/ostracon.asp, and "Qeiyafa Ostracon Chronicle," Khirbet Qeiyafa Archaeological Project 2009–2010, Hebrew University of Jerusalem, accessed March 10, 2010, http://qeiyafa.huji.ac.il/ostracon2.asp.

[5] "Qeiyafa Ostracon Chronicle," Khirbet Qeiyafa Archaeological Project, 2008.

[6] Ethan Bronner, "Find of Ancient City Could Alter Notions of Biblical David," *New York Times* (October 30, 2008), http://www.nytimes.com/2008/10/30/world/middleeast/30david.html?_r=1&ref=ethanbronner (accessed January 24, 2011).

[7] Cited in Reuters, "Archaeologists Report Finding Oldest Hebrew Text" (October 30, 2008), http://www.reuters.com/article/idUSTRE49T52620081030.

[8] Garfinkel and Ganor, *Khirbet Qeiyafa Vol. 1: Excavation Report 2007–2008.*

press release.[9] Galil's translation and comments caused a great deal of interest and controversy. His proposed interpretation is as follows:

1' you shall not do [it], but worship the [Lord].

2' Judge the sla[ve] and the wid[ow] / Judge the orph[an]

3' [and] the stranger. [Pl]ead for the infant / plead for the po[or and]

4' the widow. Rehabilitate [the poor] at the hands of the king.

5' Protect the po[or and] the slave / [supp]ort the stranger.

Galil made several controversial statements about the inscription. In a press release he claimed the find "indicates that the kingdom of Israel already existed in the 10th century BCE, and that at least some of the biblical texts were written hundreds of years before the dates presented in current research."[10] Specifically, the ostracon is

> a social statement, relating to slaves, widows and orphans. It uses verbs that were characteristic of Hebrew, such as asah ("did") and avad ("worked"), which were rarely used in other regional languages. Particular words that appear in the text, such as almanah ("widow") are specific to Hebrew and are written differently in other local languages. The content itself was also unfamiliar to all the cultures in the region besides the Hebrew society: The present inscription provides social elements similar to those found in the biblical prophecies and very different from prophecies written by other cultures postulating glorification of the gods and taking care of their physical needs.[11]

In addition, Galil declared, "It can now be maintained that it was highly reasonable that during the 10th century BCE, during the reign of King David, there were scribes in Israel who were able to write literary texts and complex historiographies such as the books of Judges and Samuel."[12]

The biggest claim in the press release from Haifa University relates to Scripture:

> The contents of the text express social sensitivity to the fragile position of weaker members of society. The inscription testifies to the presence of strangers within the Israeli society as far back as this ancient period, and calls to provide support for these strangers. It appeals to care for the widows and orphans and that the king—who at that time had the responsibility of curbing social inequality—be involved. This inscription is similar in its content to biblical scriptures (Isaiah 1:17, Psalms 72:3, Exodus 23:3, and others), but it is clear that it is not copied from any biblical text.[13]

---

[9] University of Haifa, "Most Ancient Hebrew Biblical Inscription Deciphered" (January 7, 2010), accessed March 24, 2010, http://www.eurekalert.org/pub_releases/2010-01/uoh-mah010710.php.

[10] Ibid.

[11] Ibid.

[12] Ibid.

[13] Ibid.

Galil's claims are substantial.[14] According to him, the inscription, written in Hebrew, offers proof that the kingdom of Israel existed in the tenth century BCE. It proves that scribes existed in Israel at the time, and that they were able to write literary texts and complex historiographies. It also ostensibly demonstrates that the biblical texts were written centuries before current research supposes them to be. In addition, the inscription contains a highly complex "social statement" displaying a more advanced sensitivity to social inequality than existed in the surrounding cultures. Finally, the ostracon is not copied from any biblical text but contains words and phrases very similar in content.

Biblical Echoes?

Can the Khirbet Qeiyafa ostracon substantiate all of Galil's claims? Is it the earliest evidence of a Hebrew text? Does it contain echoes or allusions to biblical texts or prophecies? Before these questions can be discussed properly, we need to identify some basic assumptions about the value of the ostracon.

The Khirbet Qeiyafa ostracon is an epigraphic find, an inscribed pottery shard. Ostraca are extremely rare in archeological excavations and, thus, are very valuable. Archeologists are reluctant to privilege texts to the exclusion of other material remains discovered on site. But this inscription is important because it was discovered *in situ*, that is, in a specific location or *locus* in a controlled dig. Consequently, we can date it, not only paleographically but also by its find spot, the ceramic typology, and the stratigraphy associated with it.

An epigraphic find will also speak to the issue of literacy, that is, who wrote it. Further, at what time was it written? The ostracon should provide linguistic evidence as well. What does it tell us about the language used at the time? How did it convey meaning?

One of the most important questions concerns its literary type. To what genre does the inscription belong? What type of literature does it contain? Is it like other ostracon discovered at other sites, or is it unique? This is a very significant question.

If the inscription is a letter, it can teach us about the social and political history of the time, maybe mentioning prominent people such as kings or nobles. If it is a lawsuit or judgment, we can learn about the legal climate. If it is a list of wages or products, it may inform us about the economic, social, and cultural circumstances.

A list of names generally provides insight into the prosopography of the period. Prosopography is the study of genealogy, vocation, and demography based on the names common to a period. A name can reveal familial relationships: father, son, or child. At times, the vocations of individuals are listed. Since theophoric

---

[14]Galil's reconstruction appears to support other agendas as well. The first is the very sensitive political issue in Israel about who has the right to the land. The other concerns the minimalist-maximalist debate, whether or not there was a David or a Solomon, or whether they were just tribal chiefs, and whether or not the Bible could have been written at that time since it contains complex theological material.

names include the designation of a deity, some insight into popular religion can also be ascertained.

An ostracon may also reveal possible historical information. Galil's reconstruction claims the inscription speaks of the social sensitivity of David's monarchy, linking it with the biblical historiographies and prophecies. But how does it connect to the Bible? Does it provide direct or indirect evidence of any biblical connections?

Like the Gezer Calendar, the Khirbet Qeiyafa ostracon contributes to our knowledge of literacy in the early Iron Age. It also speaks about the mechanics of writing, the use of pen and ink. This point is essential for understanding how a biblical book was written.[15] If biblical books were written during this period, how were they created? What medium were they written on and with what? It is hard to believe that an ostracon would be used to write down a complex literary text.

How early do we have attested Scripture that we can talk about? Is the Khirbet Qeiyafa ostracon one of those types of texts, as implied by Galil? Other than the DSS and later manuscripts, there are two other early texts that directly quote biblical material.[16] These are the Nash Papyrus and the silver amulets from Ketef Hinnom. Both of them contain quotations from Scripture. We need to discuss both before we come back to the Khirbet Qeiyafa inscription.

The History of the Transmission of the Hebrew Scriptures

Five periods in the transmission of the Hebrew Scriptures may be roughly identified. And although this may reflect an oversimplification, it will prove helpful in understanding the nature of the texts under discussion here. The five periods are:

Early Period: Composition to 250 BCE

Intermediate Period: 250 BCE to 150 CE

Masoretic Period: 150 to 1000 CE

Medieval Period: 1000 to 1500 CE

Modern Period: 1500 CE to Present

---

[15] On this issue, see J. Philip Hyatt, "The Writing of an Old Testament Book," *BA* 6 (December 1943): 71–80.

[16] Ziony Zevit correctly notes that the Deir 'Alla plaster inscriptions and the Kuntillet Ajrud wall inscriptions possess echoes of certain biblical texts. However, these two texts cannot be said to quote a canonical text and are not examined here. See Ziony Zevit, "Scratched Silver and Painted Walls: Can We Date Biblical Texts Archaeologically?" *HS* 48 (2007): 32–37.

Unfortunately, the modern period with the invention of the printing press and printed Bibles often subtly and anachronistically frames the way we think about the canon of Scripture. Approximately two thousand or so manuscripts are attested from the medieval period. The pre-Masoretic and Masoretic period established a standardized text and vocalization. This includes Talmud debate and the period of the Ben Asher family.

The discovery of the DSS radically challenged scholarly views on the transmission of the Hebrew text. The intermediate period provides evidence of several important text types. Obviously, the texts were composed at some time prior to 250 BCE. In general, the existence of the biblical DSS presuppose a period of prior composition.[17] How early is not important here. The Nash Papyrus was written (or copied out) in the intermediate period, but the Ketef Hinnom silver amulets date back to the early period. If the Khirbet Qeiyafa does in fact connect in some way to the biblical text, then it, like the Ketef Hinnom amulets, belongs in the early period.

One other issue requires attention before we continue. What does it mean to say that a text contains a biblical connection? Galil has argued that his reconstruction of the text of the Qeiyafa ostracon is similar in content to biblical Scriptures. Obviously, Galil does not suppose that the ostracon quotes or cites a canonical biblical text. What then does he mean?

There are at least four concepts that may help to answer this question more precisely. First, a text might directly quote another text. This is accomplished with a formulaic identification, such as "it is written in the book of . . ." The NT often does this in quoting the OT. Second, a text may indirectly quote another text. This may be without any formula or with an abbreviated formula; such as, "it says. . ."

Third, a text may contain a direct allusion to another text through the use of a phrase or partial sentence. The allusion may be the exact words or a close paraphrase. Finally, a text may contain an echo of another text. This is the most difficult to establish. The echo may be argued to be a phrase, a word, or even a very loose paraphrase.

The Qeiyafa inscription does not contain direct or indirect quotes of the Bible. There are no clear direct allusions either. In Galil's reconstruction there are words, phrases, and combinations of phrases that remind us clearly of something in the biblical text. I think Galil is arguing that the Khirbet Qeiyafa inscription contains echoes of biblical material, maybe just a word or two that brings to mind theological concepts and ideas that we also find in the biblical texts.

Nash Papyrus

The oldest biblical Hebrew text discovered before the DSS is the Nash Papyrus. W. L. Nash purchased it from a dealer in 1902, and Stanley Cook published the fragments of the text in 1903.[18] The four adjoining fragments may have come from Fayuum, a city about 80 miles southwest of Cairo.

---

[17] Depending, of course, on when Daniel and Esther are dated.

[18] On the Nash Papyrus, see Stanley A. Cook, "A Pre-Massoretic Biblical Papyrus," *Proceedings of the Society of Biblical Archaeology* 25 (1903): 34–56; F. C. Burkitt, "The Hebrew Papyrus

Papyrus is made from reeds that grow in the Nile delta. The reed was sliced open, flattened out, and then crisscrossed together with other pieces to make what is more or less the first type of paper. The four pieces of the adjoining fragments that make up the papyrus are very small. Measured together, the fragments are less than 7.62 x 12.7 cm (3 x 5 in). The papyrus contained twenty-five lines of square Hebrew script without vowel points, accents, or diacritical marks.

The script on the papyrus was originally dated to the second century CE, but later, with the discovery of the DSS and the advancement of Hebrew paleography, the text was redated to between 250 BCE to 150 CE. In fact, when John Trevor was given the opportunity to examine one of the first scrolls to be discovered in the caves along the Dead Sea (1QIsaᵃ), he consulted a publication on the Nash Papyrus and recognized that the script of this new manuscript was almost exactly the same. The similarity of script led him to conclude that the DSS manuscript was ancient and very valuable.[19]

The twenty-five lines of the Nash Papyrus contains a composite text of the Ten Commandments (mostly from Deut 5 but also reflecting Exod 20 at several places), and the *Shema' Israel* pericope (Deut 6:4–5). The Tetragrammaton occurs seven times in the text.

The papyrus contains a different order of commandments from that found in the HB for six (murder), seven (adultery), and eight (theft). The LXX has seven (adultery) first, followed by eight (theft), and then six (murder). The Nash Papyrus agrees with Luke 18, Rom 13, and Philo in the order being first seven (adultery), then six (murder), and then eight (theft). There is even a different order in Jer 7:9. This difference in order may be a clue to the purpose of the Nash Papyrus:[20]

Hebrew Bible (Exod–Deut)	6. Murder	7. Adultery	8. Theft
Septuagint	7. Adultery	8. Theft	6. Murder
Nash Papyrus; Luke 18:20; Rom 13:9; Philo	7. Adultery	6. Murder	8. Theft
Jer 7:9; cf. the order of violation in Joshua, Judges, Samuel	8. Theft	6. Murder	7. Adultery

of the Ten Commandments," *JQR* 15 (1903): 392–408; W. F. Albright, "A Biblical Fragment from the Maccabaean Age: The Nash Papyrus," *JBL* 56 (1937): 145–76; idem, "On the Date of the Scrolls from 'Ain Feshkha and the Nash Papyrus," *BASOR* 115 (1949): 10–19; S. A. Birnbaum, "The Dates of the Cave Scrolls," *BASOR* 115 (1949): 20–22; M. Greenberg, "Nash Papyrus," *Encyclopedia Judaica*, 14:783–84; Innocent Himbaza, "Le Décalogue de Papyrus Nash, Philon, 4QPhyl G, 8QPhyl 3 et 4QMez A," *RevQ* 20 (2002): 411–28; and Marvin A. Sweeney, "The Nash Papyrus: Preview of Coming Attractions," *BAR* 36/4 (July/August 2010): 43–48, 77.

[19] Sweeney, "The Nash Papyrus," 43–45.

[20] Chart adapted from "Order of Commandments Six, Seven, and Eight," *BRev* 5/6 (December 1989), http://www.basarchive.org/bswbBrowse.asp?PubID=BSBR&Volume=5&Issue=6&ArticleID=17 (accessed March 25, 2010).

What is the Nash Papyrus? What is its genre? For the most part it contains the canonical Deuteronomy text of the Decalogue and the *Shema' Israel*. There are a small number of variations. But it is not a fragment of a Bible manuscript; it is not part of a Torah scroll. It seems to have possessed a different purpose.

The general consensus is that the Nash Papyrus is an early liturgical text used in a prayer service in a Jewish community.[21] The Mishnah (*Tamid* 5:1) notes that the Decalogue was read before the *Shema'* in the Jewish prayer service of the Greco-Roman period. By 600 CE, the Babylonian Talmud (*Berakot* 12a) noted that the practice of reading the Ten Commandments in worship services was discontinued.

The problem with this theory is that the Nash Papyrus is very small. Twenty-five lines are written on the size of a small index card. If one intended to read or recite a biblical text as a prayer, then it is reasonable to write it larger so that it would be clearly legible for day and evening services. The script on the papyrus is miniscule. It is written as if someone was deliberately trying to squeeze a set amount of text onto a very small document.

There have been a number of small texts like the Nash Papyrus discovered among the DSS. They are called *Tefillin* texts.[22] *Tefillin* or phylacteries are small leather boxes wrapped around the head and left arm of an observant Jew during daily prayers. The practice arises from a literal interpretation of the *Shema'* where Israel is enjoined to "bind [the *Shema'*] as a sign on your hand, and . . . as frontlets between your eyes" (Deut 6:8). Very small texts of the *Shema'* would be copied out, rolled or folded up, and placed in the *Tefillin*. The *Tefillin* were then wrapped around the head and left arm, and the worshiper would recite the daily prayers. Most importantly, the phylacteries discovered at Qumran also included the Decalogue.[23] This custom is reflected in the Nash Papyrus.

Documents like the Nash Papyrus and the Qumran *Tefillin* are a type of apotropaic text. An apotropaic text is intended to protect someone from evil by means of a magical formula, incantation, amulet, or talisman. I am not suggesting that Israel used the *Tefillin* and its text simply as a good-luck charm. The text was employed to ask God for the blessing of protection, to safeguard one from evil or the evil one. Even Jesus prayed that God would keep the disciples from the evil one (John 17:15; cf. 2 Thess 3:3).

Tefillin are a way of surrounding oneself with the name of the Lord (name theology), so that the Lord would bless and protect that person. Deuteronomy 6 tells Israel to put the *Shema'* before their eyes, before what they see, perceive, and think (Ps 101:3). That is the purpose of the phylactery, the frontlet. They were to bind them on their hands, their arms, so whatever they did was pleasing to God (cf. Matt 18:8). This was an act of worship, symbolizing the confession of faith in God in the act of binding the *Tefillin*.

A *Tefillin* text was not meant to be seen. They were mass-produced and, therefore, scribes were often casual in copying. They could be written out from memory (*b. Megillah* 18b). If a person writes a *Tefillin* text from memory, he is not copying it

---

[21] Sweeney, "The Nash Papyrus," 45.
[22] Ruth S. Fagen, "Phylacteries," *ABD* 5:369.
[23] Ibid., 370.

from an exemplar. The Tosefta contains a tradition that phylacteries, mezuzot, and even scrolls could be written for the poor by a Gentile (*t. ʾAbodah Zarah* 3:6–8)!

Consequently, a text like the Nash Papyrus has questionable value for textual criticism. Because these texts were often written from memory, they differ from the MT.[24] Therefore, the idea that the textual affinities of Nash Papyrus with the LXX and Philo bears witness to a Hebrew text in Egypt significantly different from the MT is untenable.[25] Since a scribe could have written the text from memory, he could have been expansive, paraphrasing or adding other textual readings into the Decalogue. So we cannot argue from the existence of the Nash Papyrus that there was a separate text type or *vorlage* in Egypt even though it has similarities with Philo or the LXX.

But the Nash Papyrus is very important in recognizing that this is a text that points to Scripture. It gives direct knowledge of Scripture because it quotes it. It is not a canonical biblical scroll, but it quotes selections from a Scripture that pre-dated its own composition. The Nash Papyrus does not quote the MT verbatim. The orthography of the Nash Papyrus is fuller. It copied the preexisting biblical text for a purpose. It is a text that is meant to be folded up and put away where no one would see it. The scribe designed the text to be used in worship, in order to symbolize confession, faith, and trust in God.

Silver Amulets from Ketef Hinnom

In 1975 Gabriel Barkay began digging in a tomb outside of Jerusalem on the shoulder of the Hinnom, the Ketef Hinnom.[26] After several years of work, the archeologists found an untouched repository in chamber 25 of cave 24.[27] One of the volunteers showed Barkay a little purplish colored object that looked like a cigarette butt.[28] The object turned out to be a small cylinder of rolled-up silver that may have been worn around the neck like an amulet. The roll, Ketef Hinnom I (KH I) was approximately 2.5 cm wide by 10 cm long (1 x 4 in) and 99 percent pure silver. It was difficult to unroll the silver scroll properly. But when it was finally unrolled, it contained a very delicately incised inscription of eighteen lines in Paleo-Hebrew script. And what is more, Barkay recognized the Tetragrammaton, the name of Yahweh, on the scroll.

---

[24] Emanuel Tov, *Textual Criticism of the Hebrew Bible* (2nd rev. ed.; Minneapolis: Fortress, 2001), 118–19.

[25] James R. Adair Jr., "Nash Papyrus," in *EDB*, 948.

[26] An account of the archeological contex and the problem of translating both scrolls, along with a list of references, may be found in Gabriel Barkay et al., "The Amulets from Ketef Hinnom: A New Edition and Evaluation," *BASOR* 334 (May 2004): 41–71. See also Gabriel Barkay, "The Priestly Benediction on Silver Plaques from Ketef Hinnom in Jerusalem," *Journal of the Institute of Archaeology of Tel Aviv University* 19 (1992): 139–92; Erik Waaler, "A Revised Date for Pentateuchal Texts? Evidence from Ketef Hinnom," *TynBul* 53 (2002): 29–50.

[27] A popular account of the discovery of the silver amulets is given in Gabriel Barkay, "The Riches of Ketef Hinnom: Jerusalem Tomb Yields Biblical Text Four Centuries Older Than the Dead Sea Scrolls," *BAR* 35 (July/August 2009; September/October 2009): 22–28, 30–33, 35, 122–26.

[28] Ibid., 35.

The excavation team sifted the dirt from the repository and found a second scroll, Ketef Hinnom II (KH II). KH II was even smaller than the first one, less than 4 cm in length (1.1 x 3.92 cm). Again, in unrolling the second amulet, the team found Hebrew letters inscribed in a kind of casual small script. On this scroll there were three references to the Tetragrammaton. The only place where the Tetragrammaton occurs in that proximity in the Bible is in the priestly blessing of Num 6:24–26: "May the LORD bless you, and keep you; May the LORD cause his face to shine upon you, and be gracious to you; May the LORD lift up his countenance upon you, and grant you peace."

The announcement that these silver scrolls contained an inscription quoting the priestly benediction caused a stir. They were the earliest known artifacts to cite passages from the HB. But because the amulets were found *in situ*, they could be dated precisely to the end of the seventh century or the beginning of the sixth, just prior to the destruction of the temple in 586–587 BCE. Paleographically, both texts may also be dated to the late seventh century BCE.

The silver amulets were unquestionably written during the early period of the composition and transmission of the HB. Both texts were written in a very small Paleo-Hebrew script. The scrolls were written in an "informal" or casual script, to the point of being "negligent."[29] The scribes who wrote them were not too concerned about who read it. In other words, the script was small and light and a bit sloppy. Apparently, one scribe wrote KH I and another scribe incised KH II.

In the 1990s Barkay approached Bruce Zuckerman and the University of Southern California's West Semitic Research Project and asked if they could use modern high-resolution technology to photograph the scrolls.[30] These new photographs revealed something amazing concerning the scrolls. The amulets contained traces of new letters and clarifications of partially visible letters, both of which were undetectable by the naked eye. As a result, the new discoveries have enabled scholars to ascertain more clearly the purpose for the texts. It will be helpful to examine KH II first and then look at KH I.

KH II was found in the sifting of the dirt from chamber 25 and is very small, only 11 by 39.2 mm (less than 1/2 x 1 1/2 in). The scribe seemed to scratch the tiny letters on the silver as if the text was not meant to be seen or read. Some mistakes were evident as well. Perhaps this was because after the inscription was written on the silver, it was rolled up and worn like an amulet, a kind of charm or bracelet.[31]

The translation offered by Barkay et al. is as follows:

[For PN, (the son/daughter of) xxxx]h/hu. May h[e]/sh[e] be blessed by Yahweh, the warrior [or: helper] and the rebuker of [E]vil: May Yahweh bless you, keep you. May Yahweh make his face shine upon you and grant you p[ea]ce.[32]

---

[29] Barkay et al., "The Amulets from Ketef Hinnom," 46.

[30] Gabriel Barkay et al., "The Challenges of Ketef Hinnom: Using Advanced Technologies to Reclaim the Earliest Biblical Texts and Their Context," *NEA* 66 (2003): 164.

[31] Ibid., 163.

[32] Barkay et al., "The Amulets from Ketef Hinnom," 68. The inaccurate line numbers are removed.

The missing line(s) before the first visible line of the text contained a personal name and possibly a patronym. The lines identifying the owner may have been similar to texts carved on stone vessels from Kuntillet ʿAjrud.[33] The last name listed may have been theophoric, ending in the well-known divine eponym "-yahu." Because of a lack of vowel letters (*matre lectiones*), the text is silent concerning the gender of the owner.

The new readings make it clear the silver amulet contained a personal apotropaic blessing for the protection of the wearer, but not necessarily in a magical way as a good-luck charm.[34] The aim was to surround the wearer with the name of the Lord for his or her protection. Once again this is name theology.

The unique thing here is that the amulet contains an abridged rendition of the priestly blessing in Num 6:24–26. The amulet quotes four of the six phrases (1, 2, 3, 6) in the blessing, and except for one missing conjunction, the quotation is literally word for word. The text also appears to contain echoes of biblical theology. Prior to the Aaronic blessing, the amulet identifies Yahweh as "the warrior" or "the helper" depending on which root of עזר is read (l. 3; cf. 1 Chr 12:1; Gen 49:25; Ps 54:4; 146:5 and *passim* in the Psalms).[35] The text labels Yahweh "the rebuker of evil"[36] as well (ll. 4–5). The root גער is found in the HB where God rebukes the sea or the deep (Isa 17:13; Nah 1:4; Ps 106:9; cf. the noun in Ps 18:16). In a later biblical text God rebukes Satan (Zech 3:2). The root is also found in Hebrew incantation texts where the context suggests that גער may have the nuance "exorcise."[37] Yahweh will rebuke and remove the evil forces. It is clear that Yahweh serves as the guardian of the owner of the amulet (cf. Ps 121).

KH I was found in about 65 cm of accumulation among 125 silver objects, 49 arrowheads, 150 semiprecious stones, and numerous gold, ivory, glass, and bone artifacts. It was discovered *in situ* in square D in the middle of chamber 25. The script was also very small and casually written, as if the scribe was not worried about who would read it. Some of the letters were written quickly and sloppily with the result that the text is difficult to read in several places.

KH I also contains a personal apotropaic blessing. The beginning and the end are broken off. The missing lines at the beginning most likely contained the same type of opening formula as KH II. Here the owner of the silver scroll would be identified and blessed (cf. KH II: 1–2). The remaining eighteen lines may be translated as follows:

> . . .]YHW . . . the grea[t . . . who keeps] the covenant and [G]raciousness toward those who love [him] and those who keep [his commandments . . .]. the Eternal? [. . .]. [the?] blessing more than any [sna]re and more than Evil. For redemption is in him. For Yahweh is our restorer and rock. May Yahweh bles[s] you and [may he] keep you. [May] Yahweh make [his face] shine . . ."[38]

---

[33] Ibid., 64.
[34] Ibid., 46.
[35] Ibid., 65.
[36] The reading of "evil" is dependent on the proposed reconstruction of the beginning of line 5.
[37] Barkay et al., "The Amulets from Ketef Hinnom," 65.
[38] Adapted from Barkay et al., "The Amulets from Ketef Hinnom," 61.

Like KH II, KH I quotes the priestly blessing of Num 6:24–26 at the end of its text. However, in KH I the bottom of the amulet is broken off, and there is no way to tell whether the text of the blessing was abridged as in KH II or cited *in toto*. The fact that KH I cites the priestly benediction is remarkable. But in this case there is even more significant text on the scroll.

The careful study conducted by Zuckerman and USC's West Semitic Research Project revealed some new discoveries about the beginning of the KH I. This amulet also alluded to a parallel text in Deut 7:9 as part of a confessional statement. Yahweh is the "great [God who keeps] the covenant and steadfast love for those who love him and keep [his commandments] . . ." The lacunae in KH I can be filled in on the basis of three texts: Deut 7:9; Dan 9:4; and Neh 1:5:

"... the faithful God who keeps covenant and steadfast love with those who love him and keep his commandments . . ." (Deut 7:9 ESV)

"... the great and awesome God, who keeps covenant and steadfast love with those who love him and keep his commandments . . ." (Dan 9:4 ESV)

"... the great and awesome God who keeps covenant and steadfast love with those who love him and keep his commandments . . ." (Neh 1:5 ESV)

Not only does KH I quote the Aaronic blessing; it also contains a clear reference to the covenant theology advocated in the three cited texts above. Yahweh is the one who keeps covenant and shows חֶסֶד to those who love him and keep his commandments. This concept is well known in OT theology. Presumably, the owner of the amulet believed that Israel had a covenantal relationship with God that was based upon obedience to the covenant.

Much of the middle lines on the scroll are difficult to read. But the overall sense seems to be clear. The inscription was intended to remind the owner that Yahweh's blessing would protect him or her from evil. In this regard both KH II and KH I possess the same purpose. KH II may or may not have employed the definite article with the preposition בּ in lines 4–5 for its use of the word "evil" (ברע), but it is clear that KH I did in line 10 (הרע). It is just not evil in KH I; it is "the evil." This reminds one of the model prayer (Matt 6:13) and the high-priestly prayer of Jesus (John 17:15), both of which contain an article with reference to "the" evil.

But there may be more echoes. According to KH I "redemption" (גְּאֻלָּה) is in Yahweh (l. 11f.). Compare Isa 41:14, where the Holy One of Israel helps and redeems. Psalm 19:15 declares that Yahweh is both rock and redeemer. KH I also states that Yahweh is "our restorer [and] rock" (ll. 12–13). Three verses of Ps 80 (4, 8, 20) repeat a stanza imploring God to "restore us" with language reminiscent of the priestly blessing: "Restore us, O God; Let your face shine, that we may be delivered." In addition, "rock" (צוּר) is a common epithet applied to Yahweh (1 Sam 2:2; 2 Sam 22:32; etc.). Although these examples may not be direct quotes or allusions, it is hard to reject the idea that they functioned at least as echoes of Yahwistic theology common to the time of the owner of the amulet.

KH I aims at providing its owner with a personal apotropaic blessing. Nevertheless, if the reading of "our restorer" in line 13 is correct, then the amulet also contains a corporate covenantal statement. The first person plural pronominal suffix asserts that Yahweh is the protector of all his people. The owner invokes Yahweh to be not only his protector but also the guardian of his family and community. Thus the text possesses a corporate theological understanding as well.

The accumulated evidence provided by the quotes, allusions, and echoes in KH I points to the conclusion that the text was not meant to be a magical incantation. It was instead a confessional statement of the owner's trust in the Lord. In short order KH I speaks of the God who keeps covenant with those who love him and keep his commandments (Deut 7:9), who protects from evil, who is the locus of redemption, who restores, and who is solid as a rock. Finally, it ends with a recitation of the priestly benediction. There could be more, because we are not sure how to read lines 7–9!

Therefore, KH I and KH II are more than simple magical apotropaic amulets or jewelry. They are personal theological confessions of faith and trust in the owner's god. They provide evidence of the popular faith of the period. The scribes wrote them quickly; they were to be rolled up and hidden much like the Tefillin texts.[39] No one was supposed to read the text. The owner held the confession dear—enough to pay a price for the silver scroll.

It is possible that both amulets were made up ahead of time, as a boilerplate item. The scribe wrote the name in on the top, and in the case of one of them, the name is on the back. It could also have been written quickly from memory and then rolled up and given to the wearer. The purchaser may have been able to choose what type of text to have. KH I and KH II could represent a longer and shorter text respectively. They were possibly worn by the living in order to confess a covenant relationship. In the end they were buried with the dead in testimony to their owner's faith.

Back to Khirbet Qeiyafa

By means of quotation, allusion, and echoes, the Nash Papyrus and the Ketef Hinnom silver amulets attest to the existence of some type of canonical Scripture prior to the time of their respective creation. If Gershon Galil's Hebrew reconstruction of the Khirbet Qeiyafa ostracon is correct, and if, as he claims, the text is similar in content to biblical Scriptures, then it would be entirely reasonable to expect to find in the inscription comparative biblical concepts, if not even possible biblical allusions and echoes. Galil does claim that similarities exist between the content of the inscription and Isa 1:17, Ps 72:3, Exod 23:3, and other texts. If all this were true, then the Khirbet Qeiyafa would be the oldest inscription attesting to biblical literature and theology as yet discovered. Such a discovery would force a rewrite of current scholarly opinion.

However, other individuals have weighed in on the matter. The reading of Haggai Misgav, the actual expedition epigrapher, is different. The reconstructions

---

[39] Barkay et al., "The Amulets from Ketef Hinnom," 46.

of other scholars are even more so. Galil's sensational arguments have been questioned, and he has been severely criticized.[40]

Shouldn't we be able just to look at the artifact and tell what is on it? The problem is that the plain photographs are difficult to read clearly. The infrared photo is not that much better. This is understandable because the faded ink is approximately three thousand years old. More investigations using the newest technology need to be done.

The problem is that Galil's reconstruction may be more a picture of what Galil thought was there. Other excellent scholars have not confirmed the same reading. Galil claims to read characters that other scholars say are not there. Because of this Galil's work is open to the charge of circular reasoning. If Galil's reading is not there, then neither are the comparisons or echoes with the biblical text. Who is correct?

Misgav's Translation

Part of the problem is reading the Proto-Canaanite script. Not enough samples have been found to provide a clear picture of its paleography. Misgav offered a less enthusiastic reconstruction. He argued that several words are clear: *mlk* (king), *špṭ* (judge or rule), *ʿbd* (servant or serve), and *srn* (Philistine king). In addition Misgav argues that the inscription is in Hebrew because it uses the root *ʿsh* "to do" at the beginning of the inscription. This root (עשה) is distinctive to Hebrew and not found in Phoenician or some other dialect of West Semitic.

Aren Maeir's rough translation of Misgav's reconstruction is as follows:[41]

Do not do [ ] and servant a[. . .]
Judge . . . . . [ ] El(?) . . .
El(?) and Ba'all
Pe[rso]n will revenge, YSD king (of) G[ath(?)]
Seren(?) a[. . .] from Gederot (?)

This is quite different from Galil's translation. Understandably, Misgav has a different view of the purpose of the inscription:

The inscription begins with several words of command which may be judicial or ethical in content. . . . The end of the inscription contains words which may relate to the area of politics or government. It is difficult to extract more meaning from this text at the present stage. We can determine, however, that the text has continuity of meaning, and is not merely a list of unconnected words. It is phrased as a message from one

---

[40] See "Open Letter to Prof. Gershon Galil, Haifa University," Khirbet Qeiyafa Archaeological Project, 2009–2010, Hebrew University of Jerusalem, accessed January 24, 2011, http://qeiyafa.huji.ac.il/galil.asp.

[41] See Aren Maier, "For Those Who Don't Know Any Biblical Hebrew," The Tell Es-Safi/Gath Excavations Official (and Unofficial) weblog, October 16, 2009, accessed January 24, 2011, http://gath.wordpress.com/2009/10/16/for-those-who-don't-know-any-biblical-hebrew/#more-1195.

person to another. We cannot know if this is a private or public document, although it does appear to be part of some correspondence.[42]

Misgav believes that the writer of the letter was a professional. It was not a scribal exercise. In light of its find spot and assuming that Qeiyafa was a royal fortress, Misgav considers this ostracon to be a testimony to the presence of literate administrators in the early days of the united monarchy.[43]

The importance of this inscription has already caused a number of scholars to weigh in on the nature of the text. Suggestions include a list of names, a draft of a monumental inscription, a lexical list of various titles in society, and others. No doubt that there will be many more refinements in the future.

Conclusion

What do we really know then about this inscription? We know that it is an ostracon, a pottery shard containing writing. Ostraca were used to record mostly letters and lists of various sorts. Military commanders wrote letters to military outposts reporting things or giving instructions. Other ostraca include those from Arad, Lachish, and Samaria. This was a convenient way to write a message and send it.

The script of the Qeiyafa inscription is an old Canaanite form of the alphabet also called Proto-Canaanite or Proto-Sinaitic. It is an early alphabetical script, a poor man's kind of writing, possibly invented by illiterate Canaanite workers at Serabit el-Khadim.[44] The direction of the writing of the script is unusual. Later Biblical Hebrew inscriptions are written sinistrograde (right to left). The Qeiyafa ostracon, however, is written dextrograde (left to right), just as modern English is written. If the inscription is Hebrew, a normative direction of writing was not established yet. A few ancient inscriptions have also been written boustrephedon. Boustrephedon writing starts on one line in one direction (e.g., right to left) and then switches in the next line to the other direction (left to right).

This text will help contribute to a more detailed paleographic typology for Proto-Canaanite. The Qeiyafa ostracon needs to be studied in tandem with other comparative finds. For example, the Izbet Sartah ostracon is incised on a piece of pottery and is dated between 1200 and 1000 BCE. It also contains unusual letter stance and unidentified characters. The Tel Zayit "abecedary" is dated to the tenth century BCE. Its text is written sinistrograde and is incised on the pottery shard. The script is appears to be a precursor to Paleo-Hebrew. It also points to the existence of scribes and literate culture.

---

[42] Cited in Hershel Shanks, "Prize Find: Oldest Hebrew Inscription Discovered in Israelite Fort on Philistine Border," *BAR* 36/2 (March/April 2010): 54.

[43] Ibid.

[44] Orly Goldwasser, "How the Alphabet Was Born from Hieroglyphs," *BAR* 36/2 (March/April 2010): 43.

What about the language of the text? Nobody agrees. It is a Northwest Semitic language. It could be Old Hebrew, Phoenician, or "Canaanite." The text can be dated based on the find spot to the late eleventh or early tenth century. But it could also have been written somewhere else and carried to Khirbet Qeiyafa. Without a clear translation, the provenance of the ostracon is impossible to ascertain. Without a good translation, it is also difficult to identify the inscription's genre.

What then is the significance of Qeiyafa inscription? Is it the earliest Hebrew inscription? Maybe, maybe not. Does the text contain an allusion to the biblical text? According to Galil it does, but if he has heavily reconstructed it, he has read more of the Bible into it than it originally had.

The inscription makes a contribution to our understanding of the development of writing. It points to cultural literacy. If this script was that of the poor, unlike the cuneiform script or the hieroglyphs, then literacy among the lower classes existed at the time. The idea of a written tradition of the exodus and the monarchy would not be so unlikely.

What about the historicity of David's kingdom? Khirbet Qeiyafa may have been one of David's outposts. Consequently, David was not a mere tribal chieftain but the monarch of a growing and developing kingdom called Israel. Given the archeological context in which the inscription was found, it is difficult to avoid the conclusion that some kingdom or political entity existed on the eastern border of the Philistine states in the early Iron Age. The accounts in 1 and 2 Samuel preserve the tradition that this kingdom belonged to David.

The Khirbet Qeiyafa inscription remains an extremely rare and important find. It will prove its worth in helping to understand the language and literacy of the early Iron Age. It will have an impact on the issue of the historicity of David and the united monarchy. Nevertheless, the sensational claims about the Khirbet Qeiyafa ostracon and Scripture are unfounded. The text does not echo biblical prophecy; nor does it quote or allude to any biblical text. Any similarities are merely linguistic.

The Nash Papyrus and the Ketef Hinnom silver amulets are different. They attest to the existence of canonical Scripture. Both artifacts quote or allude to these Scriptures. They presuppose Scripture and employ it for a distinct purpose. As theological apotropaic texts they speak about Yahweh and their worship of him as the creator God. Yahweh is the protector and rock; he is the one who will watch over them and will keep them from all harm.

11

Biblia Hebraica Quinta

James A. Sanders

Five fascicles of the fifth edition in the Biblia Hebraica series of the text of the HB have appeared, heralding a new approach in publication of the standard single-volume handbook (*Handausgabe*) presentation of the text and critical apparatuses.[1] A review of the history of this important project will be useful.[2]

The first four editions of the series appeared in the course of the twentieth century. The first (BHK[1] = Biblia Hebraica Kittel) was published in 1906 by the Württembergische Bibelanstalt (the Deutsche Bibelgesellschaft since 1981) and distributed through the Hinrichs Verlag in Leipzig, and the second as well in 1913. Both editions used the 1524–1525 Bomberg text of Jacob ben Hayyim, essentially the Bible Jews have used for four and a half centuries, as in the Koren edition, which is still largely favored by rabbis and other observant Jews. The BH editions have made the text of the HB available for critical use among Christian and Jewish scholars because they included a critical apparatus that offered a succinct history of the text of problem passages. Those histories were often limited in scope and accuracy, since the best of text critics had to copy from earlier scholarly apparatuses and publications. Images of manuscripts were often hard for the individual scholar to access; the principal reason for the founding of the Ancient Biblical Manuscript Center (ABMC) in Claremont, California, was to provide open access to photographic and then digital images of as many ancient witnesses to the biblical text as possible.

The third edition (BHK[3] = Kittel/Kahle) of 1929–1937, published in Stuttgart also by the Württembergische Bibelanstalt, introduced major changes to the series: use of the newly recovered text of codex EBP. I B 19a, Codex Leningradensis (L), housed in the Saltikov-Shchedrin Library in Leningrad (now the National Public Library of St. Petersburg) as base text, including for the first time the *masorah parva* of the Leningrad text, and an entirely new apparatus. Codex L (1005 CE) is the oldest complete HB in the world. Paul Kahle had pursued major studies

---

[1] Adrian Schenker et al., eds., *Biblia Hebraica Quinta: Fascicle 18: General Introduction and Megilloth* (Stuttgart: Deutsche Bibelgesellschaft, 2004).

[2] The present chapter is an edited version of my review of *Biblia Hebraica Quinta: Fascicle 18*, which first appeared in *RBL* 8 (2006): 1–10.

of the masoretic phenomenon and convinced Rudolf Kittel, the BH founder and editor, to delay publication of the third edition of BHK so that films taken of the codex in Leningrad could be used as the text of BHK[3], and not the Bomberg again, as in the first two. Kahle was in Leningrad in 1926 and managed to have the codex sent to Leipzig in 1927 for two years, where it was filmed. Fortunately, a copy was made of the films in the Bonn Oriental Seminar because the ones taken in Leipzig were destroyed in World War II; one assumes that BHK and BHS were based on the Bonn photos.[3]

This was a major advance for scholarship of the HB. Kahle's in-depth studies of the masoretes (Eastern and Western) had earlier taken him in the early 1920s to Aleppo, where he unfortunately failed to persuade the leaders of the synagogue there to let him photograph the *Keter 'Aram Tsova* (Codex Aleppensis = A), the codex apparently approved of by Maimonides and supposedly the most reliable. This turned out eventually to be a major setback for scholarship. Codex A was later partially destroyed by fire during the Arab-Jewish War of 1947–1948 and lost some of its inner leaves (apparently by theft or sale to raise money for the Aleppo congregation). Codex A was taken to Jerusalem after the war, published in facsimile in 1953 and in 1976, and is being used as the base text of the Hebrew University Bible (HUB), of which three volumes (Isaiah, Jeremiah, Ezekiel) have now appeared, but it is still uncertain how HUB is going to present the text of the missing portions of A.[4]

BHK[3] served scholars and students for almost forty years, but it wielded a rather heavy hand in its judgments as to which readings were corrupt ("crrp") and which to choose ("lege"), sometimes offering textual conjectures based on the stage of scholarship of the time. I have had inexperienced students try to read their BHK following all the lege and prps readings in the apparatus! Textual criticism, on the contrary, should start with as careful a reading and understanding of the involved MT passage as possible; it then does the same with each witness—before deciding on a reading that is most responsible. Each witness, beginning with the MT, deserves full respect and understanding in its own right. The text critic now knows that each tradent, scribe, or translator had a prior concept of the passage in question and that she or he must take a whole pericope into account before being able to understand the specific reading or variant in question.

The fourth edition of Biblia Hebraica Stuttgartensia (BHS = BH[4]) was published in Stuttgart in 1977. It offered a new, less subjective apparatus and, for the first time, a collation of the *masorah magna* compiled by Gérard Weil from the

---

[3] P. Kahle, *The Cairo Geniza* (2nd ed.; New York: Praeger, 1960), 131–38. I am grateful to Harold Scanlin of the Bible Societies for sharing his personal knowledge about the films. He wrote Kahle's son some years back, who responded that he did not know what happened to the Bonn films. Kahle probably took them with him to Oxford and then to Turin, where they may be housed in the Kahle Institute there. One assumes they were used to make the Makor facsimile edition of 1971.

[4] See my review of *Hebrew University Bible: The Book of Ezekiel*, by Moshe Goshen-Gottstein, Shemaryahu Talmon, and Galen Marquis, eds., *RBL* (2005). http://www.bookreviews.org/BookDetail.asp?TitleId=4662.

masorah of L and of other available manuscripts. It is this fourth edition that is in common use today by scholars the world over, but it was published too early to take advantage of the full impact of study of the Judean desert scrolls upon the art of textual criticism of the HB. The apparatus in BHS presents a better history of the transmission of the text than do the first three editions, including variants from the biblical scrolls found in the Judean desert. The apparatus has fewer biased judgments, and the text itself, edited by Hans Peter Rüger of Tübingen (then Adrian Schenker after Rüger's untimely death in 1990), better reflects readings in the microfilms of L.

This fifth edition (BHQ) as a *Handausgabe* is a major step forward for textual criticism of the HB. The text used is still that of L, since it is the oldest complete manuscript of the HB available, but it is based on new photographs taken in Leningrad in 1990 (at the first hints of *glasnost*) by the Ancient Biblical Manuscript Center at the Claremont School of Theology in California, executed by its photographic team from West Semitic Research at the University of Southern California.[5] A set of transparencies of L was made available as soon as feasible, well before their publication in the facsimile edition, to the editorial committee appointed to produce BHQ. The new films clarified a number of uncertain readings in the text of the Kahle films, including amazingly clear images of the masorah magna of L in the top and bottom margins. The text of L is reproduced in BHQ as it appears on the films, even patent scribal errors. These are treated ad loc in the apparatus and in the editor's commentary to the apparatus. Readings in damaged portions of the codex are provided in the base text but clearly signaled in the apparatus. The BHQ editorial committee has been scrupulous in representing the text of L as it appears in the manuscript, preferring to deal with such anomalies in the apparatus, rather than pretending to be latter-day scribes by "correcting" the text itself. BHQ pursues the same practice in this regard that is used by the HUB in presenting Aleppensis as base text. Also like the HUB, the text of BHQ is presented in a single column rather than attempting, like Nahum Ben Zvi's *Keter Yerushalayim* (2000) to emulate the codex, which normally has three columns of prose and two of poetic texts.[6]

Another highly commendable trait of BHQ is that of presenting the text honoring the *te'amim* or masoretic accent marks. Earlier BH editions presented poetic texts using modern poetic analysis, largely ignoring the accent marks in the MT. Much of that effort obscured and denigrated what the masoretic tradition understood the text to mean. In fact, BHQ is the first edition in the BH series that is totally free of the bias that only the consonants of the MT are authentic. That bias came from Martin Luther's "hermeneutic of textual criticism," which he called *Res et Argumentum*, by which the vowels, masorot, accents, and intervals could be ignored if other readings yielded a text that "pointed to the Gospel of Jesus Christ."

---

[5] David Noel Freedman et al., eds., *The Leningrad Codex: A Facsimile Edition* (Grand Rapids: Eerdmans, 1998).

[6] See my review of *Jerusalem Crown: The Bible of the Hebrew University of Jerusalem*, by Nahum ben Zvi, ed., *RBL* (2004). http://www.bookreviews.org/bookdetail.asp?TitleId= 4090&CodePage=4090.

Then, when the Enlightenment induced critical readings of the text, the bias against the full MT continued even though the hermeneutic shifted 180 degrees to point to "original readings." Actually, the bias had its roots in the Jewish- Christian dialogue from early days of debates about the reading and understanding of texts crucial to Christian arguments about the witness of the First Testament to Christ and the church. In those early dialogues the arguments centered in the differences between the proto-MT texts of the rabbis and the Greek translations used by Christians.[7] Origen's transliteration of the Hebrew text in Greek in the Hexapla showed respect for the vocalization he had learned from his rabbinic dialogue partners in Alexandria and Caesarea. But it was Luther who believed that only the textual consonants were authentic, so that vowels, accent marks, the textual intervals, and the masorot could be ignored when need be. They have been ignored or depreciated also in critical scholarship in its efforts to reconstruct "original texts."[8]

One of the major results of a half century of study of the Judean desert scrolls has been clearer understanding of the history of transmission of the text and hence a gradual growth in appreciation of the MT's being made up of five integral elements: consonants, vowels, accents, intervals, and masorot. Along with the recent, fuller recovery of the actual masoretic phenomenon in critical study of the text, largely boosted by close study of the scrolls, has been a gradual shedding of bias against the MT's being a Jewish propaganda device in the perennial Jewish-Christian and then later critical debates about the meanings of biblical texts. The BH series stands as an ongoing witness to that recovery: first the use of L beginning with BHK[3], in which at least the *masorah parva* was printed in the lateral margins but in which the *te'amim* and the intervals were largely ignored in the layout of poetry in favor of modern means of parsing the text; then, the addition of the masorah magna in BHS but in which masoretic accents and intervals were largely ignored in the textual *mise-en-page* of poetry; and now, the full integration of all five elements of the MT in HUB and BHQ. The reader should understand that rabbis and Jewish students of the biblical text still by and large prefer to use the old Koren edition of the Bomberg Bible even though Aron Dotan has published a rabbinic-traditional edition of L and Nahum Zvi a rabbinic-traditional edition of A, in neither of which is the full masorah offered and in which traditional intervals are used and not alone those in the MT of either L or A. Whether Qara'ite or Rabbanite, the masoretic text in crucial ways does not follow traditional-rabbinic (Talmudic) practice in the *mise-en-page* or layout of the text, or indeed in other essential traits of the classical Tiberian MT manuscripts. The MT is not strictly speaking a rabbinic form of the HB, nor is it a Jewish anti-Christian polemic, as was sometimes charged in the debates.

BHQ thus valorizes the full masoretic phenomenon and takes advantage of its gifts, which critical scholarship has finally come to realize. In this respect, while

---

[7] See James A. Sanders, "Origen and the First Christian Testament," in *Studies in the Hebrew Bible, Qumran, and the Septuagint Presented to Eugene Ulrich* (ed. P. W. Flint, J. C. VanderKam, and E. Tov; VTSup 101; Leiden: Brill, 2006), 134–42.

[8] See James A. Sanders, "Hermeneutics of Text Criticism," *Textus* 18 (1995): 1–26.

BHQ is a true heir of the BH series, it improves greatly on its appreciation of the MT, shedding earlier biases about it.

The second principal characteristic of BHQ is a basic change in its hermeneutic of textual criticism over against its predecessors. Like the earlier editions (and unlike the HUB), it deals with only a selection of textual cases, emphasizing those that are of substance for translation and exegesis. But unlike the earlier editions, the BHQ apparatus serves the truly critical purpose of an apparatus: the evidence necessary for the reader or user to locate true variants in the history of transmission of a passage as over against pseudo-variants so that the reader can make judgments with a minimum of subjective intervention from the editors. The task of text criticism is that of locating true variants in the history of transmission of the text.[9] BHQ provides separate sections titled "notes on the *masorah parva*," "notes on the *masorah magna*," and "a commentary on the critical apparatus" for each book to make clear to the user how that task was pursued for each problem addressed. These are major advances over any prior edition. With these improvements BHQ follows in the basic format of the BH series since its inception— except for the felicitous, totally new additions of critical commentaries on the mp, the mm, and on the apparatuses (see infra).

But it has another basic trait that is quite different from the earlier editions in that the editorial committee of BHQ is the heir of the Hebrew Old Testament Text Project (HOTTP). The HOTTP was constituted in 1969 by Eugene Nida of the United Bible Societies (UBS). The Württembergische or Deutsche Bibelgesellschaft, a part of the UBS since 1981, has all along had the responsibility of publishing the BH series. The HOTTP was composed of six scholars (Dominique Barthélemy of Fribourg, Hans Peter Rüger of Tübingen, Norbert Lohfink of Frankfurt, A. R. Hulst of Utrecht, W. D. McHardy of Oxford, and myself). It met for a month each summer for twelve years in Europe, mainly at the Erholungsheim in Freudenstadt, through 1980. Each member had a specific assignment of preparation for each annual session addressing textual problems assigned the project by the Translations Department of the UBS. Those problems came from the difficulties the national translation committees of the UBS encountered in their work around the world—precisely the ones for which the local committees would turn to the modern translations in their former colonial tongues to find solutions. And they often found disagreement and confusion in doing so. They needed expert text-critical help, and the HOTTP was asked to offer it. The BH series has always selected the readings difficult for translation and exegesis to address in the apparatuses; the work of the HOTTP was no different.

The situation was not unlike that in antiquity, when translators would turn to the LXX for solutions to difficult textual problems; in fact many of the more than five thousand problems we were asked to address showed that the LXX had in a number of cases provided the solutions in antiquity for later translations, and we often had to adjudicate between the MT and the LXX to choose the critically most

---

[9] See James A. Sanders, "The Task of Text Criticism," in *Problems in Biblical Theology* (ed. H. Sun et al.; Grand Rapids: Eerdmans, 1997), 315–27.

responsible text. This we found difficult to do in many cases because the LXX either had a different *Vorlage* from which it made its translations, or the Greek translator had a different concept of what the text was about, even though the *Vorlage* would have been basically the MT. In the case of some books we felt we had to deal with two equally valid but quite different *Vorlagen* (e.g., Samuels, Jeremiah, portions of Exodus, Proverbs, Ecclesiastes). This is so much the case that some of us began to call for a pluriform Bible in which both texts would be ranged side by side.[10]

Though our assigned task was to offer current translation committees around the globe critical help in their important work (parallel to the UBS Greek New Testament Committee formed by Nida in 1955 that has produced five editions of the Greek NT), we made it clear that while we were committed to doing that we also wanted to take advantage of the opportunity to work on textual problems in all the books of the First Testament, to work out a hermeneutic of textual criticism that would be built on the quite new textual situation created by the discovery of the Judean desert scrolls. We all agreed on the new history of transmission of the text that the scrolls had induced: the premasoretic period, the protomasoretic period, and the masoretic period. We agreed with the HUBP that there had been a "great divide" at the end of the first century CE, when stabilization of the text was clear in the later Hebrew texts in the biblical scrolls as well as in the Greek translations of the second century (Aquila, Theodotion, and Symmachus).[11]

At issue was how to view the textual fluidity of the premasoretic period. We clearly could no longer view it principally as a matter of different *Vorlagen* only, or of scribal errors principally. It was important to see that the hermeneutic of the text changed with the birth of rabbinic Judaism at the end of the first century CE.[12] Prior to the "great divide" it was not uncommon even for scribes, certainly for translators, to manipulate the text in minor ways to render an archaic or difficult word or phrase clear to the communities the ancient tradents were serving; but after the divide at the end of the first century CE scribes and translators began to revere each word of the text as somehow sacred so that meaning could be sacrificed to transmitting the text with verbal accuracy. The change provided the stability needed for application of the tannaitic and rabbinic *midot,* modes of interrelating words and phrases from throughout the HB for midrashic exegesis, halakic and haggadic.

The change in hermeneutic at the great divide was the reason also for development of the *masorah finalis* in which the number of words in a book is noted along

---

[10]See James A. Sanders, "Stability and Fluidity in Text and Canon," in *Tradition of the Text* (ed. G. Norton and S. Pisano; Göttingen: Vandenhoeck & Ruprecht, 1991), 203–17. Note that the Oxford University Bible, being edited by Ronald Hendel, will place the LXX and MT Jeremiahs in parallel columns, though its purpose is an eclectic edition purportedly reflecting a current understanding of an early stage in transmission of the text.

[11]The Hebrew University Bible Project (HUBP) was launched in 1956 by the late Moshe Goshen-Gottstein (1925–1991), who was succeeded by Chaim Rabin (1915–1996) and later Shemaryahu Talmon (1920–2010). The base text is the Aleppo Codex. Thus far editions of Isaiah (1995), Jeremiah (1997), and Ezekiel (2004) have been published.

[12]See James A. Sanders, "Text and Canon: Concepts and Method," *JBL* 98 (1979): 5–29.

with other information to aid the scribe to be scrupulous in copying each word in place as received—no matter the apparent meaning. And it was the beginning of the development of the *masorot parva* and *magna* as scribal sentinels in the margins of the text to guard scrupulous verbal transmission, but not necessarily a particular meaning as the *teʾamim* and intervals aided in doing. In fact, there is an occasional mp designed to protect an anomaly in the text, which a scribe might otherwise want to correct out of habit or memory of the doublet passage. Often there is an mp for a word in a doublet passage designed to keep a scribe from harmonizing the two passages even though they were essentially but two different forms of the same text (as in the case of Ps 18 and 2 Sam 23, which the BHS apparatuses ad loc tend to harmonize in efforts to reflect some early form of the poem). We had also to address the fact that the earlier history of formation of the text sometimes overlapped with the ensuing history of transmission of the text, and this underscored the need to decide on the stage in the transmission at which to aim the state of the most critically responsible text.

During the first session of the HOTTP in 1969 we accepted individual responsibilities for the work of the whole. Hans Peter Rüger prepared the sheets for each problem we were assigned, providing all the witnesses to it. Norbert Lohfink and his assistant prepared summaries of the best of critical scholarship in modern times on each problem we would face in a given session. My assistant and I, most notably Richard Weis, now a member of the BHQ editorial committee, from the ABMC collection provided the team with any and all variants in the Judean desert scrolls. (For this we gratefully had the full cooperation of the Caves 4 and 11 teams of scholars for biblical texts not yet published, especially Frank Moore Cross of Harvard.) And Dominique Barthélemy brought to each session in-depth study of the ancient and medieval exegetes and grammarians, which proved crucial in many of our discussions. We drew up a list of fifteen factors important to discern in scribal activity, among which were those that helped most in isolating facilitating pseudo-variants.

The factors *lectio difficilior* and *brevior* were used, but not slavishly if other factors seemed more important. The more difficult reading was often the cause of the diverse variants, showing that it had been difficult also for early tradents. This left us often with a term or phrase that it was tempting to label "crrp," as many critics had been doing up to our time. But more often than not we found from Barthélemy's searches that the expert medieval grammarians who wrote in Judeo-Arabic, notably Yefet ben Eli and Abulwalid, had a grammatical or syntactic solution to difficult readings. We learned to trust the Judeo-Arabic grammarians largely because their analysis of Hebrew grammar was based on their intimate acquaintance with Arabic grammar, whereas Western Hebrew grammars take their point of departure from classical grammatical and syntactic analysis, just as the presentation of poetry in the earlier BH editions was based on classical or Western poetic analysis, which it tried to adapt to the Semitic.

We found that doing a structure analysis of the full pericope in which a textual problem occurs helped to discern the concept lying behind a passage and not a trivial observation based on only the troublesome word or on just the sentence in which it is found.[13] We further obligated ourselves to take sides when an apparently true variant was identified so that each reading would receive the best possible argument. Sometimes it was difficult to decide between the readings so that we gave the resultant decision a lower "grade" to show our respect for the other reading. Our work was published in five volumes of a preliminary report so that UBS committees could continue their work without relying on modern translations.[14] That satisfied the primary purpose of our assignment. In addition, four volumes of a final report have appeared in *Critique textuelle de l'Ancien Testament*.[15] These, especially the introductions to each volume, provide the scholarly world with a full review and reassessment of the whole field of textual criticism of the HB in all its aspects. We have found that few scholars have read these and fewer still understood them, so that an English translation is being prepared of the introductions of the first three volumes. English is the lingua franca of today, as witnessed by the fact that BHQ is essentially in English, not Latin or German, as was the case in the early editions.

In August 1990 in Fribourg, at a final meeting of members of the HOTTP, an editorial committee was appointed to create a fifth edition of BH that would critically set forth the full MT of L based on the hermeneutic principles established by the HOTTP as described above. The editorial committee is chaired by Adrian Schenker, Barthélemy's successor at Fribourg, and composed of Yohanan Goldman, Gerald Norton, Arie van der Kooij, Steve Pisano, Jan de Waard, and Richard Weis. De Waard was head (now retired) of the Translations Department of the UBS; van der Kooij of Leiden had been A. R. Hulst's assistant on the HOTTP, and Richard Weis of the Twin Cities in Minnesota mine. The others had been students of Barthélemy in Fribourg. Aron Dotan of Tel Aviv University is consultant on matters concerning the masorah.

Once the successor committee had been appointed, the HOTTP gave full authority to the new editorial committee and withdrew, realizing that the new committee would freely need to address problems along the way that we had perhaps not faced. The BHQ editorial committee set about its task of working with the Deutsche Bibelgesellschaft, the publisher of the BH series and the principal sponsor of HOTTP, and to appoint editors for the biblical books other than those the committee members would edit.

The book editors of BHQ are Avraham Tal of Tel Aviv University (Genesis), Peter Schwagmeier of Zürich (Exodus), Innocent Himbaza of Fribourg (Leviticus), Martin Rösel of Rostock (Numbers), Carmel McCarthy of University College, Dublin (Deuteronomy), Leonard Greenspoon of Creighton University and

---

[13] See Sanders, "The Task of Text Criticism."

[14] D. Barthélemy, A. Schenker, and J. A. Thompson, eds., *Preliminary and Interim Report on the Hebrew Old Testament Text Project* (London: United Bible Society, 1975–80).

[15] D. Barthélemy and A. R. Hulst, eds., *Critique textuelle de l'Ancien Testament* (Göttingen: Vandenhoeck & Ruprecht, 1982, 1986, 1992, 2005). Broken down, the respective volumes are as follows: 1. Josué, Juges, Ruth, Samuel, Rois, Chroniques, Esdras, Néhémie, Esther (1982); 2. Isaïe, Jérémie, Lamentations (1986); 3. Ézéchiel, Daniel et les 12 Prophètes (1992); 4. Psaumes (2005).

Seppo Sipilä of Helsinki (Joshua), Natalio Fernández Marcos of Madrid (Judges), Stephen Pisano of the Pontifical Biblical Institute in Rome (1–2 Samuel), Adrian Schenker (1–2 Kings), Arie van der Kooij (Isaiah), Richard Weis (Jeremiah), Johan Lust of Leuven (Ezekiel), Anthony Gelston of Durham (the Twelve), Gerard Norton of Dublin (Psalms), Robert Althann of the PBI (Job), Jan de Waard (Proverbs and Ruth), Yohanan Goldman of Fribourg (Qohelet), Piet Dirksen of Leiden (Canticles), Rolf Schäfer of the DBG in Stuttgart (Lamentations), Magne Saebo of Oslo (Esther), Augustinus Gianto of the PBI (Daniel), David Marcus of the Jewish Theological Seminary in New York (Ezra–Nehemiah), and Zipora Talshir of Ben Gurion University (1–2 Chronicles). Aside from Gérard Weil's work on the masorah for BHS, this is the first time that the editors have been other than European Protestant. It is the first truly international, interfaith, and ecumenical edition of the Hebrew Bible.

Each of the five biblical books in the volume under review has (1) an introduction, (2) notes on the *masorah parva*, (3) notes on the *masorah magna*, (4) commentaries on the critical apparatuses to each of the five books, and (5) bibliographic data provided for works cited. All the introductions are grouped together and provide all the available data on the ancient sources for study of the principal witnesses to the text of each book: Hebrew, Greek, Latin, Syriac, and Aramaic. They also include valuable parallel lists of where in the text of each Hebrew witness the intervals occur and usually conclude with appropriate acknowledgments of the help of others by the book editor. The notes to the *masorah parva* are generally explanatory comments by the editor on the entry, while the notes to the masorah magna are basically expanded "translations" of the entry ad loc, thus giving the scribal cross-references by the more familiar chapter and verse numbers.

There is a general introduction to BHQ in English, German, and Spanish followed by two sample pages illustrating how to use both text and apparatus. In addition, there are the usual lists of sigla, symbols, and abbreviations; definitions of the terms used to characterize readings with an alphabetical list of them and their definitions; a glossary of common terms in the *masorah parva*; and tables of the masoretic accents used for both prose and poetry.

The commentaries to the critical apparatuses of each book are very valuable in that they offer the critical and subjective judgments of each editor about the succinct and largely neutral notations provided for each apparatus, placed as usual under the text. Here is where the editor expresses his opinion about what he sees going on in the several witnesses to the history of the text, sometimes comparing the entries with the apparatuses of earlier editions of BH; and here is where the editor is free to state reasons for preferences in readings and even rarely a conjecture as to the early reading that perhaps gave rise to the later conflicting witnesses. Many such subjective judgments were included in the apparatuses themselves of the earlier editions of BH, whereas in BHQ they occur seldom in the apparatus but are offered quite properly in the editor's personal comments. In this manner the apparatuses provide the basic data needed for the reader to make his or her own judgments about distinguishing true and false variants to the text, while the commentary offers the current expertise of the editor, arguably the most competent at the moment of composing it for making such judgments but not necessarily so in future use of BHQ. In this mode the commentaries can be updated in the future without having to create a whole new BH edition to do so.

Along with the publication of the Hebrew University Bible, these five fascicles of BHQ (three more are at the press, the rest in preparation) herald the redemption of the way textual criticism has been done in modern times. The task of textual criticism is to locate true variants in the available ancient and medieval witnesses to the text; the aim of textual criticism is to determine at what stage in the ancient history of transmission of the text the critically most responsible text should be located; and the goal of textual criticism is to suggest how that text might read for translation and critical study. BHQ succeeds in addressing the task and in providing the means to determine the aim and the goal in each case addressed.

With both HUB and BHQ in process, the field of textual criticism of the HB is in the process of being redeemed, rectified, and made fully available to fledgling students as well as the most advanced scholars of the text of the HB.

12

What Do the Earliest Christian Manuscripts Tell Us about Their Readers?

Larry Hurtado

Introduction

My purpose in the following discussion is to focus on the physical and visual features of the earliest Christian manuscripts to consider what we can learn from them about those who prepared and read them. The manuscripts I will speak to are among the earliest artifacts of Christianity. Indeed, the oldest of these manuscripts are probably the earliest Christian artifacts extant, some of them dated to the late second century CE, a few perhaps a bit earlier. So, for any historical interests in the transmission of the writings concerned, and for other historical questions as well, these manuscripts are unexcelled in importance. They are, however, often overlooked by scholars beyond the circles of papyrologists and textual critics. I hope to show that they cast light on several important matters of broader import that will be relevant to anyone interested in early Christianity.

But you may be thinking that there is a prior question lurking here that needs to be addressed: How, in fact, do we identify ancient manuscripts as Christian items in the first place? So, let us turn to this question immediately. In answering it we will also derive some observations directly relevant to the main question stated in my title.

How Do We Recognize Early Christian Manuscripts?

There are essentially two main types of evidence that can be used to identify a manuscript as Christian, by which I mean a manuscript that was used (and probably produced) by Christians. The first and most obvious indication that some manuscripts are Christian ones is their contents. In this early time, we can safely conclude that a copy of a text that is itself expressly Christian in origin was used by Christians. So, for example, copies of the writings that came to form the NT, other known Christian texts such as *Shepherd of Hermas,* and identifiably Christian theological tractates and homilies would all readily be classified as of Christian provenance. Of course, Christians also copied and used other texts as well that were not composed by Christians, prominent among which were the OT writings. Deciding whether a given copy of one of these texts is of Christian provenance requires other indicators that I will turn to shortly.

Indeed, one of the observations we can make on the basis of earliest Christian manuscripts, as well as references in early Christian writings themselves, is that already in the earliest centuries and probably earliest decades Christians were heavily involved in writing, copying, reading, exchanging, and disseminating a great number of texts.[1] In recent decades there has been a good deal of justifiable interest in ancient "orality," the spoken word, and oral "performance" as features of early Christianity in its ancient Roman-era setting. But, without denying for a moment that oral speech was important in that period, I must emphasize the prominent place of texts as a distinguishing feature of earliest Christianity. Indeed, in the Roman religious environment, early Christianity seems to have been unexcelled, and perhaps unique, in the comparative scale of the production, use, and distribution of texts, devoting impressive personnel and financial resources to the activities involved.

It is interesting to take a moment to note the range of texts attested in the extant Christian manuscripts of the first three centuries CE.[2] We have remnants of copies of many texts, such as most of those that comprise the Greek OT, which includes the writings regarded as Apocrypha by Judaism and Protestants.[3] Indeed, for a number of OT texts we have remnants of multiple copies. There are copies of all NT writings except for 1–2 Timothy and 3 John. In addition, there are remnants of well over twenty other literary texts, plus a number of others such as prayers, magical texts, and exorcistic texts.

When we note that virtually all of our extant manuscript evidence of these earliest centuries comes from Egypt (indeed well into Egypt, in places such as Oxyrhynchus), the range of writings attested is impressive.[4] To be sure, we can-

---

[1] For discussion, see esp. Harry Y. Gamble, *Books and Readers in the Early Church: A History of Early Christian Texts* (New Haven: Yale University Press, 1995). To get an idea of the number of Christian texts produced in the early centuries (many of them now lost or extant only in fragments or as quotations in other texts) see Claudio Moreschini and Enrico Norelli, *Early Christian Greek and Latin Literature: A Literary History* (trans. Matthew J. O'Connell; 2 vols.; Peabody, MA: Hendrickson, 2005).

[2] In what follows I draw upon my fuller discussion in *The Earliest Christian Artifacts: Manuscripts and Christian Origins* (Grand Rapids: Eerdmans, 2006), 16–41. See also Appendix 1 (209–27) for a table of manuscripts with identifying data.

[3] The following OT texts are not attested: 1 Chronicles, 1–2 Kings, Song of Solomon, Nehemiah, 1–2 Samuel, Lamentations, 1 Maccabees, Judith.

[4] Peter Parsons, *City of the Sharp-Nosed Fish: Greek Lives in Roman Egypt* (London: Weidenfeld & Nicolson, 2007), provides a fascinating description of Oxyrhynchus based on the large trove of manuscripts found there, among which the Christian manuscripts are a small portion.

not know how many of the writings attested in the manuscript remains were read by any one Christian or group of Christians. But, as most of our evidence comes from Oxyrhynchus, we can say that Christians there seem collectively to have had an interest in, and to have made use of, an impressive list of writings, and this can suggest things about what kind of Christians they probably were.[5] For example, it appears that these were believers who regarded the OT as Scriptures, and so were not Marcionites, and probably not so-called Gnostics.

The manuscripts also reflect a noteworthy range of geographical derivation of texts. In this material from a provincial town well over a hundred miles up the Nile from Alexandria, we have copies of writings of Irenaeus (from Lyons), Melito (Sardis), and multiple copies of *Shepherd of Hermas* (Rome). Moreover, these copies are all dated palaeographically close to the time of their composition. So, these manuscript remains attest a vibrant and energetic networking of Christians all around the Mediterranean basin that involved the production, distribution, and exchange of texts. That is, these fragmentary manuscript remains reflect a desire by their early Christian readers to develop a certain translocal outlook on their faith. They may have lived in a provincial town, but they seem not to have been provincial in the scope of their reading tastes and religious interests.

But we can make a further inference as well. Prominent among the writings from afar are those connected with early Christian figures and locations that reflected what we may call proto-orthodox Christianity, the various circles of Christians that came to comprise the mainstream. We have copies of works by Irenaeus of Lyons, the doughty exponent of the fourfold Gospel and opponent of various Christian sects; Melito of Sardis, the eloquent advocate of a recognizably traditional Christian faith; and Hermas of Rome, the author of the somewhat puzzling text that was, nevertheless, intended and received widely for its advocacy of Christian holiness. These are all key representatives of the emergent catholic/orthodox Christian faith in the first few centuries. We would be entitled to suppose, therefore, that the Christians who read these texts in Oxyrhynchus were believers who tended in this faith direction.

To be sure, we also have copies of other texts, some of which seem to reflect a more sectarian, or perhaps elitist, or esoteric outlook. These include *The Gospel of Thomas*, *The Gospel of Mary*, and several other so-called apocryphal Christian writings. So, collectively, the Egyptian Christians whose manuscript remains we have from this period may have included either a diversity of faith stances or

---

[5]For discussion of copies of NT texts from Oxyrhynchus, see Eldon Jay Epp, "The New Testament Papyri at Oxyrhynchus in Their Social and Intellectual Context," in *Sayings of Jesus: Canonical and Non-Canonical, Essays in Honour of Tjitze Baarda* (ed. William L. Peterson, Johan S. Vos, and Henk J. de Jonge; NovTSup 89; Leiden: Brill, 1997), 47–68; idem,"The Oxyrhynchus New Testament Papyri: 'Not Without Honor Except in Their Hometown'?" *JBL* 123 (2004): 5–55. Indeed, Oxyrhynchus more broadly seems to exhibit a strong literary interest. Peter Parsons, "Copyists of Oxyrhynchus," in *Oxyrhynchus: A City and Its Texts* (ed. A. K. Bowman et al.; London: Egypt Exploration Society, 2007), 262–70, noted "a much higher proportion of literary to documentary texts than any comparable Egyptian site" (262).

simply some Christians with eclectic interests and tastes. I must note, however, that from these manuscript remains it is hard to posit separate groups such as "Thomas" Christians or "Mary" Christians. There may well have been such groups, but my point is that the mere existence of these texts does not in itself require the inference that they reflect discrete groups or versions of Christianity.[6] In any case, the copies of these apocryphal Christian writings further demonstrate the place of composing, copying, and reading texts in earliest Christianity, and the rich diversity of the texts involved.

To judge from the extant number of copies, however, some texts seem to have been more popular, or at least more frequently copied, than others. Psalms leads the way with 18 extant copies from these earliest centuries, followed by the Gospel of John (16 copies), the Gospel of Matthew (12 copies), then *Shepherd of Hermas* (11 copies), Genesis (8 copies), Luke and Acts (7 copies each), Isaiah (6 copies), Revelation (5 copies), Romans and Hebrews (4 copies each), and then an extended list of other texts with fewer copies numbering from three down to one each. Broadly speaking, the greater number of copies of some texts, for example, Psalms, John, Matthew, and Isaiah, is reflected also in the greater number of citations and allusions to them in early Christian writings, confirming the view that these texts were read more frequently than those with fewer extant copies.

You may well ask about copies of other texts that were not written by Christians and were not used exclusively by them. The OT writings are the most obvious examples. How would one decide whether a copy of one of these texts was of Jewish or Christian origin, for they were Scriptures to both faith traditions?[7] In these cases especially, we must take account of another type of evidence, in particular certain physical and visual features that are commonly accepted among scholars familiar with these ancient manuscripts as indicative that they derive from Christian circles.

The Codex

One of the distinguishing features of early Christianity was a strong preference for the codex book form for literary texts, over the roll (scroll) which was the overwhelmingly preferred book form in the larger culture of the time.[8] The

---

[6] For some cogent cautionary discussion about inferring groups from texts, see Frederik Wisse, "The Use of Early Christian Literature as Evidence for Inner Diversity and Conflict," in *Nag Hammadi, Gnosticism, and Early Christianity* (ed. Charles W. Hedrick and Robert Hodgson; Peabody, MA: Hendrickson, 1986), 177–90.

[7] Scholars rightly debate the degree to which "Judaism" and "Christianity" were fully distinguishable as early as the second century CE. Nevertheless, I think that it is correct to speak of two faith communities in this period, in at least some locations, although there were likely individuals and perhaps circles of Christian believers who also considered themselves Jews (and may have been considered so by the larger Jewish community). See, e.g., Judith Lieu, *Neither Jew nor Greek? Constructing Early Christianity* (Edinburgh: T&T Clark, 2002); Thomas A. Robinson, *Ignatius of Antioch and the Parting of the Ways* (Peabody, MA: Hendrickson, 2009).

[8] For a fuller discussion, see my chapter in *The Earliest Christian Artifacts*, 43–93. On the bookroll, see William A. Johnson, *Bookrolls and Scribes in Oxyrhynchus* (Toronto: Uni-

codex was essentially a leaf-book, the ancestor of the book form with which we are familiar, constructed of sheets of writing material folded to form leaves, the folded sheets bound at the folded edge. By contrast, the roll (scroll) was constructed by joining sheets of writing material to form a continuous length of this material. In a codex, the text was written on both sides of the leaves, whereas with a roll the text was written in narrow columns on what would be the inner side of the rolled-up writing material.

As we will note shortly, the differences between Christian and non-Christian preferences in this matter are stark and undeniable. Moreover, it is noteworthy that early Christians seem to have preferred the codex book form especially for those literary texts that they regarded most highly and used as Scripture. Indeed, for these texts, the codex seems to have been used almost exclusively and from the earliest years from which we have any evidence. By contrast, all our evidence of identifiably Jewish manuscripts (e.g., Qumran and other Judean sites) indicates an equally strong preference for the roll, especially for their copies of Scriptures. So well known is the Christian preference for the codex that if papyrologists come across a portion of an identifiable OT text, even a single large fragment, and if this fragment can be identified as a leaf or part of a leaf from a codex (which can be determined if the same text continues from one side of the fragment onto the other), they typically judge the fragment to be a portion of a Christian manuscript.

To avoid misunderstanding, let me emphasize that the codex was not a Christian invention. We have references to the use of the small parchment codex for portable copies of pagan literary texts in the late first-century CE Roman writer Martial (*Epigrams* 1.2; 14.184, 188, 190, 192), and we have examples of pagan use of the codex among extant manuscripts.[9] The codex (parchment and papyrus) was used more commonly, however, for non-literary material, such as astrological tables, and simpler forms of the codex served for purposes such as note taking, shopping lists, and "things to do." It was, essentially, viewed as a utilitarian form of book, and generally not particularly as appropriate for literary texts, at least in the early centuries with which we are concerned here.

We get a good idea of the strong general preference for the roll in this period by comparing the percentage of extant manuscripts that are rolls and codices. A recent check on the Leuven Database of Ancient Books (LDAB) is revealing. Of items dated to the second century CE, the LDAB lists 1848 rolls compared with 113 codices. For the third century CE, the LDAB lists 420 codices and 1184 rolls. Put another way, codices make up about 6% of the total of second-century items catalogued and about 26% of the total of third-century items. By the fourth century CE, however, codices make up the majority of manuscripts. It is an obvious question why we see this shift across these centuries, but we cannot take time here to engage it. Instead, I want to show how starkly different the data are for identifiably Christian manuscripts.

---

versity of Toronto Press, 2004).
   [9] A list of parchment codices containing pagan literary texts is given by Eric G. Turner, *The Typology of the Early Codex* (Philadelphia: University of Pennsylvania Press, 1977), 39.

Of 41 Christian manuscripts dated to the second century in the LDAB catalogue, 24% are rolls and 76% codices; and of about 190 third-century CE Christian manuscripts 23% are rolls and 77% codices.[10] Although Christian items make up a very small percentage of the total of manuscripts from these centuries, it is still clear that the Christian preference for the codex went against dominant preferences in the book culture of the time. For example, although Christian items make up about 2% of the total of second-century manuscripts, about 27% of the total of second-century codices are identifiably Christian books. Christian items make up about 12% of the total of third-century manuscripts but 38% of third-century codices.

But the differences are starker still if we confine ourselves to copies of texts that functioned in these centuries as Scriptures. I made a more detailed analysis of copies of Christian literary texts a few years ago, and the data will not have shifted enough since then to change the results significantly. Essentially, Christians massively preferred the codex for Scriptures but were a bit more ready to use the roll for other texts, though even here the codex was favored. In a list of 58 Christian copies of non-biblical texts dated to the second or third centuries, about 34% are rolls. These are copies of theological tractates (such as Irenaeus, *Against Heresies*) and a number of other texts, including copies of several apocryphal writings. But when we consider copies of OT writings or those writings that came to comprise the NT, the preference for the codex is nearly total. Among about 75 copies of OT texts dated to the second and third centuries CE, probably no more than 7% of those that may be Christian manuscripts are rolls. So far as NT writings are concerned, we do not have a single extant copy written on an unused roll.[11]

The clear impression is that early Christians thought the codex particularly appropriate for their most prized writings, those that functioned in their churches as Scriptures. Indeed, I suggest that we can infer that any copy of a Christian text written on a roll was probably not intended to function as Scripture, at least in the sense of being read as part of corporate worship, but was likely used in personal reading and/or study. In short, the book forms in which texts were copied likely give us artifactual evidence of early Christian attitudes about these texts, or at least about these particular copies. The preference for the codex is certainly a feature relevant to the formation of the Christian canon of Scriptures.

Scholars have offered various ideas about why Christians so strongly preferred the codex, and as yet there is probably not a clearly dominant position on the matter. I will return to this question a bit later, after we have dealt with another interesting feature that helps us to identify Christian manuscripts.

---

[10]Consultation of LDAB on February 22, 2010. I omit from my count items classified as "fragment" (which means that the editor was unable or unwilling to identify whether it came from a codex or roll) or "sheet" (which means a portion of writing material that derived from neither a roll nor a codex).

[11]There are a very few copies of NT texts on reused rolls, e.g., $\mathfrak{P}^{22}$, but these do not indicate any preference between book forms. These opisthographs were typically personal copies for study purposes.

The Nomina Sacra

Another earmark that identifies a manuscript even more confidently as of Christian provenance is the curious scribal practice known among scholars as the *nomina sacra* ("sacred words/names").[12] The term *nomina sacra* designates a collection of words central in early Christian religious discourse that were typically written in a distinctive manner. They were abbreviated (usually first and last letters, but often with one or more middle letters as well), and with a distinctive horizontal stroke placed over the abbreviation. The words earliest and most consistently treated in this manner are the Greek words *Theos, Kyrios, Christos, and Iēsous* (respectively, "God," "Lord," "Christ," and "Jesus"); other words came to be included in the practice as time went on across the first several centuries (some fifteen or more words are so treated with varying frequency, e.g., Greek words for "man," "son," "father," "Jerusalem," "Spirit," "mother," "David"). These abbreviated forms are so distinctive that, even if all we have is a fragment and we cannot identify the text it contains, the appearance of any of the *nomina sacra* is sufficient to lead papyrologists to suspect that the fragment must be from a Christian manuscript.

Several factors make the *nomina sacra* remarkable. First, although abbreviations of various frequently used words are common in copies of documentary texts such as contracts, deeds, and land registers, abbreviations are rarer in copies of literary texts. But in Christian literary texts, especially copies of OT and NT writings, these particular abbreviations are frequent, indeed probably more frequent and consistent than in Christian documentary texts.

Second, abbreviations typically functioned to save space on a small or limited writing surface. The most common abbreviations were on coins and inscriptions, where the many titles of a ruler would need to be accommodated.[13] But the *nomina sacra* have nothing to do with saving space. The manuscripts in which they are found typically have wide margins, generous-sized writing, ample spacing between lines, and in every way suggest that the copyist was unconcerned about the available space on the writing material.

Third, even the specific, typical forms of the *nomina sacra* set them apart. The usual way that one made an abbreviation in ancient Greek or Latin was to write the first letter or first few letters of a word. This is called abbreviation by suspension. With one particularly interesting exception, which I cannot take time to discuss here, the *nomina sacra* are typically what are called contractions, the first and final letters (and one or more medial letters in some longer words).[14]

---

[12] I give a much fuller discussion and engagement with other scholars in *The Earliest Christian Artifacts*, 95–134.

[13] E.g., imperial titles were frequently abbreviated on coins and inscriptions: PP (Pater Patriae), Cos (Consul), F (Filio), Divi (Divine), Aug (Augustus).

[14] In some early instances, Jesus' name (Ιησους) is abbreviated by suspension, as Iη. I have proposed that the numerical value of Iη (18) may have been a factor prompting this abbreviation (reflecting ancient Jewish interest in gematria), and that Iη may have been the first of the *nomina sacra*. Larry W. Hurtado, "The Origin of the *Nomina Sacra*: A Proposal," *JBL* 117 (1998): 655–73.

Finally, perhaps the most puzzling feature of the *nomina sacra* is the horizontal stroke placed over the abbreviated forms. This is not a typical feature of other abbreviations, in Christian or non-Christian evidence. Sometimes a similar stroke is placed over the end of an abbreviated word, a suspended form, especially if it occurs at the end of a line, to signal to readers that some letters of the word have been omitted. But the stroke that forms part of the *nomina sacra* is placed right over the abbreviated form, and irrespective of where the *nomina sacra* forms occur in lines of text.

So, to summarize, these are the principal factors that are used to identify earliest Christian manuscripts. When we can recognize the contents of a manuscript as Christian texts, then we can be rather confident that the manuscript comes from Christian hands. In addition, there are two physical earmarks that reflect early Christian copying practices and that can be taken as indicating a highly likely Christian provenance of a manuscript: the codex book form, especially in texts used as Scripture, and the *nomina sacra*.

Early Christian Manuscripts in Historical Perspective

The next obvious questions that present themselves are why Christians preferred the codex and deployed the *nomina sacra*, and what these features represent in historical perspective. In addition, I want to present some other features of Christian manuscripts that will further help us to learn something about those who prepared and used them.

Let us begin by taking up again the early Christian preference for the codex book form.[15] Some scholars have proposed that the codex was preferred because Christians saw in this book form some practical advantage over the roll. For instance, some have suggested that the codex may have been more convenient for itinerant preachers, or because readers could supposedly more easily find a particular passage by leafing through the pages of a codex. Another proposal is that Christians preferred the codex because they were largely people from lower social strata in which the codex (which was more typically used for non-literary purposes) was a more familiar book form than the roll. So, in this view, the predominance of the codex in early Christian circles was a reflection of their socioeconomic makeup.

Other scholars, however, contend that in the historical context the strong preference for the codex must have been intended to distinguish Christian book practice. Regardless of whether one was or was not a frequent user of literary texts, in that setting one would know that the roll was deemed the appropriate book form for literary texts and that the codex was regarded as more appropriate for "subliterary" purposes (e.g., manuals, tables of data, etc.). I tend to find this view more persuasive. I think that it is particularly relevant to remember that early

---

[15]I quickly mention proposals discussed more fully in Hurtado, *The Earliest Christian Artifacts*, 43–89.

Christians seem to have preferred the codex especially for their scriptural texts, and Christians were a bit more ready to use the roll for their other literary texts. I submit that this suggests that the preference for the codex likely represents a deliberate choice against the dominant cultural preference for the roll. That is, Christians may have appropriated the codex as their preferred book form as an expression of their emerging sense of being distinctive. More specifically, they may have preferred the codex to distinguish physically their copies of scriptural texts from Jewish copies and from pagan religious texts.

We should also note that the commitment to use of the codex for serious literary purposes required copyists to acquire and develop skills beyond those typically involved in copying on rolls.[16] For a roll, all copyists needed was an adequate length of writing material and the abilities to copy in sequential columns. But use of a codex for any sizeable text required several further abilities, such as estimating how many sheets would be needed, deciding how to construct the codex (whether in a single gathering or multiples, and if the latter, how many sheets per gathering), and writing on both surfaces of papyrus or skin. It is evident that Christians in the second and third centuries were at the leading edge of developing the codex for literary purposes. So they had to invest some serious thought and effort into the use of this book form. In short, they did not adopt the codex because it was already serviceable for their needs; instead, they adapted and developed the codex book form to make it serviceable for their needs, specifically the need to accommodate large texts and then collections of texts in one manuscript.

As for the *nomina sacra*, here too we are dealing with a notable feature of early Christian books that requires some explanation. Although there has been the occasional proposal that the *nomina sacra* may have served some practical purpose, such as helping readers orient themselves on a page, most scholars have concluded that these curious abbreviations originated as expressions of early Christian piety.[17] That is, these words seem to have been written in this distinctive manner to set them off visually from the surrounding text out of reverence for the referents of the words so treated. This fits with the observation that the four words for "God," "Lord," "Jesus," and "Christ" are the words earliest and most consistently treated as *nomina sacra*.

Those familiar with ancient Jewish manuscripts will note some rough similarity to the Jewish scribal tendency to mark off the divine name (*YHWH*) in copies of scriptural texts. In Hebrew OT manuscripts, this was often done by writing *YHWH* in archaic Hebrew characters or by writing a series of dots where the name belonged, and sometimes by substituting *Elohim* ("God") for the divine name. In Greek OT manuscripts, the name was often written in Hebrew characters. Jewish scribal practices concerning the divine name varied and do not correspond exactly with the Christian *nomina sacra* practice. But there is a certain similarity in the

---

[16] Colin H. Roberts and T. C. Skeat, *The Birth of the Codex* (London: Oxford University Press, 1983).

[17] For further discussion of the issues, see Hurtado, *The Earliest Christian Artifacts*, 120–33.

likely motivation and the attitude that lie behind both Jewish scribal treatment of the divine name and early Christian handling of the *nomina sacra*; in both cases we are dealing with scribal practices intended to express a religious attitude of reverence for what the words designate.

There is, however, a further interesting difference between the *nomina sacra* and Jewish scribal treatment of the divine name. The latter probably is connected to the Jewish avoidance of pronouncing the divine name, a scruple already well developed by the first century CE. So, setting off the divine name visually was almost certainly intended to alert readers to use a reverential substitute word, such as *Adonay* in Hebrew or *Kyrios* in Greek. But the *nomina sacra* did not function in this way. That is, early Christians simply pronounced normally (e.g., in public or liturgical reading) the words written as *nomina sacra*, their abbreviated forms making no difference. This means that the *nomina sacra* forms were purely visual phenomena. If, as most scholars believe, they were expressions of early Christian piety, they could be noted only by seeing them on the written page.

So, both in their physical form, the codex, and in the deployment of the *nomina sacra*, the copies of texts, especially scriptural texts, typically used by early Christians were distinctive. That is, early Christians seem to have been concerned to mark off their texts physically and visually. I have proposed that the preference for the codex book form and the *nomina sacra* comprise our earliest evidence of an emerging Christian material and visual culture. The dates of our earliest manuscripts require us to place the emergence of these manifestations of this material and visual culture no later than sometime in the second century CE, and perhaps even a bit earlier.

Other Manuscript Evidence of Early Christian Readers

In "Toward a Sociology of Reading in Antiquity," the American papyrologist William Johnson explored textual references to the reading of pagan literary texts in the Roman period, and then considered the physical and visual features of ancient high-quality manuscripts of pagan literary texts.[18] The textual references tend to place the reading of literary texts in small groups of sophisticated cultural elites. Typically, these texts (e.g., historical or philosophical writings, poetry, or fiction) were read in small dinner settings of social elites, and the occasion could include ensuing discussion among the dinner party about the text read. Johnson then noted the rather severe and demanding format of the high-quality manuscripts of these texts, especially prose texts, which typically have little or no punctuation and are written in a strict *scriptio continua* (that is, writing with no spacing between words or sentences), producing tall, narrow columns of writing

---

[18] William A. Johnson, "Toward a Sociology of Reading in Classical Antiquity," *American Journal of Philology* 121 (2000): 593–627. He has now produced a fuller discussion, *Readers and Reading Culture in the High Roman Empire: A Study of Elite Communities* (Oxford: Oxford University Press, 2010).

with strict left and right justification.[19] Indeed, individual words are line wrapped to achieve a rather strict right justification. He accounted for this layout by proposing that these manuscripts were intentionally formatted to make them demanding, to reflect the elite cultural circles in which they were to be read. That is, these manuscripts were intentionally difficult to read by anyone who was not very well trained to handle their format and highly experienced in reading them. In short, their visual layout is a direct reflection of the elite and exclusive social circles in which they were to be used.

I want to highlight now some typical format features of early Christian manuscripts by comparison.[20] I propose that these features likewise comprise artifactual evidence of the (very different) circles for which these manuscripts were copied. The broad thrust of the following discussion will be to propose that the format of earliest manuscripts of Christian literary texts was intended to facilitate reading them and to enable the somewhat wider spectrum of readers and reading abilities that was found in early Christian groups. That is, these manuscripts give us physical evidence of the more inclusive and diverse social composition of earliest Christian circles, in comparison with the elite circles noted by Johnson.

The most readily noted difference is the somewhat less elegant, less calligraphic nature of the copyists' hands typical of earliest Christian manuscripts. There is some variation among early manuscripts, to be sure, with one or two approaching the calligraphic end of ancient Greek hands of the time (e.g., 𝔓[4/64/67]). But the overwhelming number of Christian manuscript hands fall into what we could characterize as careful, conscientious, and competent, but workmanlike and not equal to the elegance of high-quality pagan and Jewish manuscripts of the time. For example, there is less consistency in letter sizes, and some of the letters reflect an informality (e.g., rounded letters) that leads some palaeographers to describe some copyists' hands as "semi-cursive" or "semi-documentary."

In his PhD thesis completed in the University of New England (Australia), Alan Mugridge surveyed well over five hundred early Christian manuscripts of the first four centuries or so to determine the quality and character of the copyists' hands.[21] Classifying ancient copyists into three broad categories, calligrapher-quality, professional but less skilful than calligraphers, and unskilled, Mugridge demonstrates persuasively that the great majority are what he calls professional quality. By this term he means hands of competent, trained copyists, but not those who prepared high-quality literary manuscripts of the sort that Johnson highlighted. Although I find Mugridge's term "professional" less helpful than other descriptors such as "competent" and "experienced," Mugridge's detailed analysis of the specific scribal features of early Christian manuscripts gives a more

---

[19] By comparison, poetic texts were often written with staggered lines, to indicate the poetic structure. But the more appropriate comparison to early Christian texts is with pagan prose texts and their layout in manuscripts.

[20] See my fuller discussion in Hurtado, *The Earliest Christian Artifacts*, 155–89.

[21] Alan Mugridge, "Stages of Development in Scribal Professionalism in Early Christian Circles" (PhD thesis, University of New England, 2010).

thoroughgoing confirmation of what most students of early Christian manuscripts have judged for some time.[22]

The general character of the copyists' hands in these Christian manuscripts suggests an intention to provide a clear, readable text, that is, a concern for facilitating reading rather than a concern for elegance. The hands evidence a conscientious effort and, usually, competence in copying. So, for example, the individual letters are written without ligatures, clearly spaced apart, and typically of ample size, except for miniature manuscripts and some other copies that seem to have been intended for personal reading. Also, the spacing between lines is generous, which likewise seems intended to make reading easier. This produces copies with fewer lines per column than in more elegant pagan literary texts of equivalent column height, as noted by Sir Eric Turner many years ago.[23]

Early Christian manuscripts often have some punctuation, such as a dot written mid-height on a line, indicating a sense unit roughly like our sentence. They also often feature the use of a diaeresis (two horizontal dots, like a German *umlaut*) placed over the initial vowel of words that follow immediately after words ending in a vowel (to alert the reader that the final vowel of the one word and the initial vowel of the other are to be read as part of separate words). Pagan poetic texts were sometimes copied with some punctuation and with lines of text written to reflect the poetic cadences, but punctuation is less common in ancient pagan prose manuscripts. We have examples of pagan literary manuscripts in which the reader (not the copyist) has marked up the text for reading, putting in punctuation and other markers. But early Christian manuscripts often have punctuation and other readers' aids that are clearly from the hand of the copyists. That is, to use an automobile metaphor, these sorts of readers' aids were not added as customizations by owners but were factory equipment!

We also see instances where enlarged spaces were used to mark off sentence-size units and larger sense units that are roughly equivalent to paragraphs or sections of text. In his 1912 edition of the Washington Gospels Codex, Henry Sanders noted that sections of text were marked off by use of such enlarged spaces, and he judged that the sections in this early fifth-century CE Greek manuscript corresponded significantly with the sections of the same texts in early Latin, Coptic, and Syriac manuscripts of the Gospels. He proposed that the wide distribution of what seems to be a relatively standardized scheme of sections of the Gospels suggests a pattern that goes back to the second century.[24] Decades later, in his 1956 edition of the Bodmer Gospels codex, $\mathfrak{P}^{66}$ (P.Bodmer II), Victor Martin noted the

---

[22] Mugridge seeks to argue that many Christian manuscripts may have been prepared by professional copyists who were not necessarily Christians themselves. This is possible, of course. But I think that he fails to consider adequately the evidence that many Christian manuscripts were copied by Christians "privately" and "in house." See, e.g., Kim Haines-Eitzen, *Guardians of Letters: Literacy, Power, and the Transmitters of Early Christian Literature* (Oxford: Oxford University Press, 2000).

[23] Turner, *Typology of the Early Codex*, esp. 85–87.

[24] H. A. Sanders, *New Testament Manuscripts in the Freer Collection, Part 1, the Washington Manuscript of the Four Gospels* (New York: Macmillan, 1912), 14.

use of spaces to mark off sections in this manuscript, which is dated c. 200 CE, and judged that these sections tended to correspond to the sections that Sanders had identified in the Washington Codex (though more thoroughly developed in Codex W). A few years later, in their edition of P. Bodmer XIV ($\mathfrak{P}^{75}$), which likewise dates from c. 200 CE, Martin and Kasser again noted a similar scheme of marking off sections of text in the Gospels, concluding that Sanders's proposal was basically correct, and that the practice of laying out the texts of the Gospels in sections did indeed go back as remarkably early as Sanders had suggested.[25]

This practice of marking off sections of a text is another effort to facilitate the reading of the text, another readers' aid. But, as every author today knows, the choice of where to make one paragraph end and another begin also involves an effort to shape the text and guide the readers' engagement with it. The sections that we see marked off in early Christian manuscripts were probably identified in the course of the transmission and copying of the texts in question. So, we should probably see the identification of larger sense units such as paragraphs or sections as reflecting exegesis of the text and as efforts to facilitate (and perhaps to guide) the understanding of the text by subsequent readers.

It is worth noting that this use of spaces to mark off sense units, though uncommon in pagan prose-text copies of the time, is something found in Jewish manuscripts.[26] This was noticed many decades ago by C. H. Roberts in his editing of P.Rylands 458, a portion of the Greek text of Deuteronomy.[27] Indeed, in Hebrew manuscripts (e.g., from Qumran) we even have word separation. So, it is plausible to think that early Christian scribal practice was influenced by Jewish scribal practice in the use of spaces.

In sum, we have a body of evidence that the earliest Christian manuscripts of prose literary texts (especially Scriptures) reflect efforts by their copyists to produce clear, readable copies, with various devices intended to facilitate readers' use of them. If Johnson's analysis is correct that the format of high-quality pagan literary manuscripts was intended to make them demanding and even off-putting for anyone but highly skilled readers, and that their appearance was deliberately indicative of the elite, cultured circles for which these manuscripts were prepared, then the earliest Christian manuscripts indicate a quite different aim and the very different and more inclusive social makeup of the circles for which they were intended.

Early Christian groups seem typically to have comprised people of a certain variety of social levels, males and females, from slaves and day laborers to free(d) people who owned property, and even, occasionally, minor civic officials.

---

[25] Victor Martin and J. W. B. Barns, *Papyrus Bodmer II, Supplément: Évangile de Jean, chap. 14–21, nouvelle édition aumentée et corrigée* (Cologny-Geneva: Bibliotheca Bodmeriana, 1962), 18–20; Victor Martin and Rodolphe Kasser, *Papyrus Bodmer XIV, Evangile de Luc, chap. 3–24* (Cologny-Geneva: Bibliotheca Bodmeriana, 1961), 14–17.

[26] Emanuel Tov, *Scribal Practices and Approaches Reflected in the Texts Found in the Judean Desert* (STDJ 54; Leiden: Brill, 2004), is now the fullest discussion of the features of earliest Jewish manuscripts.

[27] C. H. Roberts, *Two Biblical Papyri in the John Rylands Library Manchester* (Manchester: Manchester University Press, 1936).

As the apostle Paul noted, there were "not many of noble birth" (1 Cor 1:26) in early Christian churches. Moreover, given recent estimates of literacy in the early Roman period (c. 10 to 15% of the general population), many, perhaps most, believers of this time were unable to read.[28] Many others likely had limited reading competence. Very few came from the sort of elite circles that Johnson linked with high-quality pagan manuscripts. In short, there was a spectrum of reading competence in early Christian circles, with very few believers having the level of reading ability characteristic of the cultured elite.

I propose that the earliest Christian manuscripts were prepared for a certain variety of reading competence, particularly to enable believers with less-than-sophisticated reading abilities to read them out in worship gatherings for their fellow Christians. This means that, in comparison with high-quality pagan manuscripts, these early Christian copies give us physical evidence of the more inclusive and socially diverse nature of early churches.

We could also note that we have manuscripts that are artifacts of private or personal reading. These include the examples of small copies of texts, such as P. Oxyrhynchus 655, a roll of about 16 cm height containing a copy of *The Gospel of Thomas*, the text written in a small but skillful hand, and P. Antinopolis 1.12, a third-century miniature codex that contained 2 John and perhaps a few other NT texts as well. Reused rolls, opisthographs, likewise probably represent personal copies of texts intended for private reading (e.g., $\mathfrak{P}^{18}$, a copy of Revelation, and P. Oxyrhynchus 654, another copy of *Gospel of Thomas*). So, early Christian manuscripts tell us that some were used or read corporately and other copies, privately.

Conclusion

I have tried to show briefly that we can learn a good deal from the physical and visual features of the earliest Christian manuscripts. We have manuscripts indicating private or personal reading of texts, and others likely intended for reading in churches. In the latter especially, we have evidence that they were formatted to facilitate public reading of the texts that they contained. These manuscripts give us, thus, physical, artifactual evidence of the use of Scriptures among Christians of the time.

Early manuscripts also show that Christians of this early period were already developing a sense of particularity, a distinctive corporate identity as Christians, and were developing and deploying expressions of this identity in their production of copies of their texts, particularly their most cherished ones, those that they read in churches as Scripture. That is, in spite of the evident diversity in beliefs and practices among Christians in these early centuries, their manuscripts also indicate some interesting signs of emerging conventions and identifying features that seem to have been embraced translocally and across various circles of believers.

---

[28] See, e.g., William V. Harris, *Ancient Literacy* (London: Harvard University Press, 1989), which has, however, received some criticism; see Mary Beard et al., *Literacy in the Roman World* (Journal of Roman Archaeology Supplement Series 3; Ann Arbor: University of Michigan, 1991).

13

Bold Claims, Wishful Thinking, and Lessons about Dating Manuscripts from Papyrus Egerton 2

Paul Foster

Introduction

In the summer of 1934 a collection of fascinating papyri was purchased by the British Museum from an unnamed dealer.[1] Beyond this, the *editio princeps* and subsequent discussions of these texts provide little information concerning the location of the discovery of these fragments or the circumstances that led to their being acquired by the British Museum. Assessing the collection as a whole, the editors note,

> Unfortunately the provenance of the fragments is unknown. They formed part of a miscellaneous collection bought from a dealer. Most of the papyri acquired with them contain no evidence of provenance; of those which do (so far as a preliminary examination goes) one only comes from the Arsinoite nome, five certainly and one probably from Oxyrhynchus; and an Oxyrhynchite origin is likely for the rather high proportion of literary texts. Hence Oxyrhynchus is the most natural place of origin for the Gospel fragments also; but not much weight can really be attached to these arguments.[2]

Consequently for *P.Egerton* 2 (which is the catalogue reference for the Gospel fragments mentioned above), it is likely, as is the case with the bulk of surviving papyrus fragments from antiquity, that these fragments originated in Egypt. In his recent treatment, T. J. Nicklas states that "*P.Egerton* 2 came from an Egyptian dealer in antiquities who sold it to the British Library."[3] The precise source of Nicklas's statement that the antiquities dealer was Egyptian is unknown, and it

---

[1] H. I. Bell and T. C. Skeat, eds., *Fragments of an Unknown Gospel and Other Early Christian Papyri* (London: The Trustees of the British Museum, 1935), v.

[2] Bell and Skeat, *Fragments of an Unknown Gospel*, 7.

[3] T. J. Nicklas, "'Unknown Gospel' on Papyrus Egerton 2 (+ Papyrus Cologne 225)," in *Gospel Fragments* (ed. T. J. Kraus, M. Kruger, and T. J. Nicklas; OECGT; Oxford: Oxford University Press, 2009), 11.

may be the case that this is a sensible and probably correct supposition, rather than derived from documented evidence.

Significance and Description

The sensational aspect of the publication was not its provenance; huge hoards of Greek and Coptic Christian papyrus manuscripts had been discovered in Egypt prior to 1934. Neither was the fact that it contained a non-canonical gospel-like text; various apocryphal sayings of Jesus had been discovered at Oxyrhynchus in Upper Egypt three to four decades earlier. What caused a stir was the antiquity of this text. The four fragments that comprise this manuscript were confidently dated to the period before the middle of the second century. Thus, at the time of publication *P.Egerton* 2 was the earliest known Christian text. The date assigned to this text was at least half a century earlier than that given to the far more extensive Chester Beatty manuscript of the Pauline epistles, $\mathfrak{P}^{46}$, which according to its editor were penned probably "in the first half of the third century."[4] However, this exciting discovery was not a source of jubilation for some pious believers. For although an obviously Christian text had been published that was dated half a century earlier than any other surviving Christian gospel-like manuscript, this was a non-canonical text. Those who theorized that the apocryphal gospels were later perversions of the earlier settled fourfold canonical Gospels were thus confronted with seemingly irrefutable evidence that non-canonical texts may in fact be contemporaneous with the earliest stages of the transmission of the NT Gospels. Therefore, such non-canonical gospels could not be dismissed as late forgeries; instead they were at least contemporary rivals, and who could tell—perhaps they were even earlier predecessors to the four texts that later became canonical Gospels. The neat understanding of "heresy" as a later deviation from the pristine bedrock of apostolic "orthodoxy" was thrown into confusion. Perhaps the origins of Christianity and the emergence of gospel traditions were far messier than had previously imagined. Thus, for some, *P.Egerton* 2 threatened to rip a seismic fault line through the previous belief in the solid early bedrock of apostolic Christianity.

It is necessary to pause at this juncture, and before responding to such concerns, to describe the actual physical features of the fragments that constitute *P.Egerton* 2. On the verso of fragment 4 only a single letter is preserved, a lunate sigma; no text was observed on the recto. No images or dimensions of the fragment are given in the standard editions; it will not be discussed further. The remaining fragments have the following dimensions:

Fragment 1   11.5 cm x 9.2 cm

Fragment 2   11.8 cm x 9.7 cm

Fragment 3   6.0 cm x 2.3 cm

---

[4] F. G. Kenyon, *The Chester Beatty Biblical Papyri*, part 3 (London: E. Walker, 1936), xiv–xv.

The amount of text preserved on fragment 3 at the most generous enumeration consists of thirty letters over six lines on the recto, and twenty-six letters over six lines on the verso. As Nicklas states, "[t]hese fragments are too small to allow any kind of translation or commentary."[5] However, they do contribute data for the overall palaeographical analysis of the manuscript, which in turn provides an indication of the dating.

Other preliminary issues involve the relative order of both the fragments, as well as that of the sequence of the recto and verso sides of the two major fragments, and determining the number of pericopae preserved on these two fragments. Since there are no page numbers preserved, and because the narrative appears to continue uninterrupted on to the reverse page, yet without tops or bottoms of pages to provide continuity, it must therefore be admitted that the ordering is arbitrary. Consequently, the decision adopted here has been to follow the arrangement proposed by the original editors, which has been adopted by the majority of scholars who worked subsequently on these fragments, although there have been dissenting voices. That order is frag. 1 verso (?), frag. 1 recto (?), frag. 2 verso (?), frag. 2 recto (?). Given this order, then maybe five separate pericopae can be identified:

1. Debate with experts in law/testimony of Scripture   frag. 1 (?), lines 1–20

2. Attempt to arrest Jesus   frag. 1 (?), lines 1–10

3. Jesus heals a leper   frag. 1 (?), lines 11–20

4. Strange questions and Jesus beside the Jordan   frag. 2 (?), lines 1–16

5. Questioning over payment of taxes   frag. 2 (?), lines 1–18

Because of the highly fragmentary nature of the text such descriptions and divisions remain highly tentative. Nonetheless, what is apparent is that the fragments contain at least five separate pericopae, that some of these have parallels with material in the canonical Gospels, and that the parallels span both traditions found in the Synoptic and Johannine Gospels.

Different inferences have been drawn from the mixture of Synoptic and Johannine-type traditions. Some have inferred that this implies the text was composed with some kind of knowledge of both Synoptic and Johannine Gospels. However, others have drawn a very different conclusion. For instance, John Dominic Crossan has stated that "considering the random and fragmentary nature of the text and the fact that each leaf gives a curious mix of both Johannine and Synoptic material, the gospel gives important evidence of the stage in the transmission prior to the separation of these twin traditions."[6] In many ways such theories are at

---

[5] Nicklas, "Papyrus Egerton 2," 95.
[6] John Dominic Crossan, *Four Other Gospels: Shadows on the Contours of Canon* (Minneapolis: Winston Press, 1985), 75.

best tangential to the concerns of this discussion. Decisions concerning the dating of a text carried in a given manuscript are related to the dating of the manuscript (in that the earliest manuscript of the given text provides a *terminus ad quem* for the text). While this fixes the latest possible date for the composition of a text, unless one is dealing with an autograph, then the date of the composition of the text will be somewhat earlier. Here the concern will be to look at the way in which the manuscript of *P.Egerton* 2 was dated, since this provides the latest possible date for the composition of the text that the sole manuscript witness to this text provides.

Opinions Concerning the Dating of *P.Egerton* 2

As has been mentioned, *P.Egerton* 2 caused quite a stir when it was published since it was at the time of its publication the earliest Christian text to have been discovered. For objective observers this was a matter of great historical interest; for some pious believers the fact that this text deviated from the supposed bedrock of pristine orthodoxy was a challenge to theories concerning the emergence of Christianity and the ideological belief in the safeguard of the apostolic faith.

The actual dating was based on a palaeographical analysis. Since the text is undated and contains no historical reference to the time of its composition, scholars must examine the style of handwriting against other dated or datable exemplars. Fortunately in antiquity a large number of texts are dated, yet using a dating system differing from the current continuous numerical progression of dates. The most common system in antiquity was to date an event to the regnal year of the current emperor. Such a reference can be found in P.Oxy. 1643, a letter authorizing an agent to pursue a runaway slave. The author of the letter, Aurelius Sarapammon, dates his document in the following manner:

> Year 14 and year 13 of our lords Diocletianus and Maximianus Augusti and year 6 of our lords Constantius and Maximianus the most illustrious Caesars, Pascho 16, of the consulship of Festus and Gallus.[7]

Without discussing the history of the tetrarchy, this document can securely be dated to the year 298/299. Such references abound especially, but not exclusively, in documentary papyri. This results in a set of dated documents against which to compare undated manuscripts. In essence palaeography then looks for shared handwriting features and aligns undated manuscripts against dated documents with similar handwriting. Since handwriting style for an alphabet such as Greek can be shown to have undergone an evolutionary process of shifts in the way in which letters were formed, mapping such temporal developments allows for the broad dating of manuscripts that do not come with self-contained date references. Handbooks of reference texts containing plates of datable Greek exemplars, such

---

[7]S. R. Llewelyn, *New Documents Illustrating Early Christianity* (vol. 8; Grand Rapids: Eerdmans, 1997), 32–33.

as Sir Eric Turner's *Greek Manuscripts of the Ancient World*,[8] have proved invaluable in assigning more precise dates to undated manuscripts. However, it immediately needs to be acknowledged that there are limits to the precision that can be attained by this method.

To illustrate the problem an analogy is helpful. If a letter is received from one's grandmother (dated or undated) it is likely the handwriting would represent the style current during the time of her schooling rather than contemporary writing style. If the letter were undated, palaeographers practicing their craft in several centuries' time might date the document to a period fifty years earlier than was the actual case. Alternatively, if the document were dated, it might be included among the set of documents indicative of a writing style that *could* be used in contemporary manuscripts. However, it might represent a somewhat anachronistic style or even reflect regional variations. These limitations must be borne in mind when applying palaeographic techniques to ancient documents. This is not an exact science that can provide precise dates; rather, it is indicative of a broad period. Thus one should operate with a certain suspicion when an undated document from antiquity is given a precise dating such as AD 125.

When it comes to the dating of *P.Egerton* 2 it is useful to revisit the arguments put forward in the initial studies to see how they arrived at the suggested date. The *editio princeps* devoted most of the first seven pages to the issue of dating. Without replicating all of the comparative dating assembled, the most pertinent points in the cumulative argument will be drawn out of this discussion. Three comparative dated documents were considered:

1. P.Berol. ined. 6854, "a document written in the reign of Trajan (died A.D. 117), in a hand sufficiently like the literary script [of *P.Egerton* 2] to be usefully comparable";

2. P.Lond. 130, "a horoscope calculated from 1 April A.D. 81 and therefore not likely to be later than the early years of the second century";

3. P.Fay. 110, "a letter written in a semi-literary hand, which is perhaps most like of the three to the present hand . . . dated in A.D. 94."[9]

The editors, Bell and Skeat, also anticipated possible objections to their conclusion that "it seems extremely improbable . . . that [*P.Egerton* 2] can be dated later than the middle of the second century."[10] They noted that the codex format of this document was characteristic of Christian communities and consequently did not rule out a date in the first half of the second century. The presence of the Christian system of abbreviations known as the *nomina sacra* that were widely used was argued to be consonant with the proposed date. Both the unusual nature of some of the contracted forms, and the fact that the name Jesus is abbreviated consistently by suspension rather than by using what emerged as the dominant practice

---

[8] Eric G. Turner, *Greek Manuscripts of the Ancient World* (2nd ed., rev. and enlarged by P. J. Parsons; London: Institute for Classical Studies, 1987).

[9] Bell and Skeat, *Fragments of an Unknown Gospel*, 1–2.

[10] Ibid., 2.

of contraction, is seen as further supporting a date in the first half of the second century. The advantage of contracted forms is that they preserve case endings and consequently provide greater ease of use for lectors. Thus it was inferred that this apparently embryonic form of the *nomen sacrum* for the name Jesus was another indicator of the date in the early second century. To their credit, Bell and Skeat consulted with other papyrologists such as Schubert and Kenyon, who provided corroboration for the proposed dating of before the middle of the second century. The opinion of the former is described at some length:

> It may be added in conclusion that Professor Schubert, to whom a photograph was sent and whose authority on such a matter none will question, pronounced the date here assigned "as good as certain", that is in the degree to which palaeographical datings can ever be certain; and he remarked that some features of the hand might suggest an even earlier date.[11]

In addition to the *editio princeps*, Bell and Skeat also published a more popular pamphlet describing *P.Egerton* 2. In that work they made the following comment about the date of the manuscript:

> The result of a careful examination and comparison of the fragments with other papyri is the conclusion that the manuscript was written not very far from the middle of the second century, with perhaps some preference for a date slightly before over one after A.D. 150. If the upward and downward limits of date be fixed at respectively 130 and 165 we shall probably not be far wrong as to the period within which the manuscript is likely to have been written.[12]

Many subsequent treatments of the fragments concurred with this initial assessment. Writing a decade after the initial publication, G. Mayeda echoed the sentiments of Bell and Skeat, "so daß sie nicht als Gründe gegen die Ansetzung des Papyrus vor 150 gelten können."[13] Several decades later this view was still being affirmed. Thus, R. Cameron observed, "[o]n paleographical grounds the papyrus has been assigned a date in the first half of the second century C.E."[14] Similarly, Crossan, in what was one of his earliest publications on the subject, held to the widely proposed dating by citing the statement from Bell and Skeat's more popular publication of 1935 on the topic, thereby reiterating the range for the writing of the fragments between 130 and 165.[15] Perhaps the most recent affirmation of a dating to the first half of the second century is to be found in a recent volume by Philip W. Comfort. He states, "[t]his gospel was probably composed around 120–130, yet

---

[11] Ibid., 7.

[12] H. I. Bell and T. C. Skeat, *The New Gospel Fragments* (London: The Trustees of the British Museum, 1935), 10.

[13] ". . .thus there are not valid reasons against locating the papyrus before 150." G. Mayeda, *Das Leben-Jesu-Fragment Papyrus Egerton 2 und seine Stellung in der urchristlichen Literaturgeschichte* (Bern: Paul Haupt, 1946), 14.

[14] R. Cameron, *The Other Gospels: Non-Canonical Gospel Texts* (Philadelphia: Westminster Press, 1982), 72–75.

[15] Crossan, *Four Other Gospels*, 69.

the copy which was discovered could be not later than 150. It bears remarkable resemblance to 𝔓⁵²."[16] It is to the subject of 𝔓⁵² that this discussion now turns.

𝔓⁵² Saves the Day, or Does It?

Soon after the sensational report in *The Times* of January 23, 1935 (accompanied with photographs of the fragment) and the publication of *editio princeps*, those who had been disquieted by the fact that the earliest surviving text was a non-canonical gospel text found solace. Later the same year another early Christian fragment was published. This was a fragment of a leaf from a codex, preserving part of the text of the Fourth Gospel (John 18:31–33, 37–38). Apparently it had been discovered among a cache of unsorted papyri that had obtained by B. P. Grenfell as early as 1920, although the papyri were not sorted until 1934 and subsequently published late in 1935 by C. H. Roberts.[17] The hand was described as Hadrianic in style, and the fragment later catalogued as 𝔓⁵² was consequently dated by Roberts to the first half of the second century. The midpoint of that range, 125, is often cited in reference works as the date of this papyrus fragment.[18] Such a precise date is, of course, nonsense. Palaeographical analysis does not allow such precision for undated texts—but there was theological importance in assigning such a date that was earlier than the lower date in Bell and Skeat's proposed range of 130 to 165 for *P.Egerton* 2.

In actual fact Roberts was far more cautious than many who cited his analysis, in dating 𝔓⁵² to the "first half of the second century."[19] Employing the usual methods of palaeographical analysis, Roberts identified a set of comparator texts to identify the likely date range of this fragment of John. In terms of handwriting style the two texts discussed by Roberts that exhibited the closest affinities with 𝔓⁵² were both undated. The first was part of a roll containing *Iliad* IX, which Roberts stated was "assigned to the end of the first or beginning of the second century in the original publication, but which Schubart now prefers to date to the closing decades of the first century."[20] The second text that was seen to demonstrate extremely similar features is particularly pertinent to the current discussion; it was *P.Egerton* 2. Unlike the manuscript of the *Iliad,* the similarity between *P.Egerton* 2 and 𝔓⁵² also extended to the physical form of both texts, which are fragments from a codex. Describing the affinities in handwriting between 𝔓⁵² and this comparator text, Roberts stated,

---

[16] Philip W. Comfort, *Encountering the Manuscripts: An Introduction to the New Testament Palaeography and Textual Criticism* (Nashville: Broadman & Holman, 2005), 32.

[17] C. H. Roberts, *An Unpublished Fragment of the Fourth Gospel in the John Rylands Library* (Manchester: Manchester University Press, 1935).

[18] In the standard textbook on the text of the NT, the Alands state the date as "*ca.* 125.". See K. Aland and B. Aland, *The Text of the New Testament* (rev. and enlarged ed.; trans. E. F. Rhodes; Grand Rapids: Eerdmans, 1987), 99.

[19] Roberts, *An Unpublished Fragment of the Fourth Gospel*, 11.

[20] Ibid., 14.

$\mathfrak{P}^{52}$ Recto $\mathfrak{P}^{52}$ Verso
Reproduced by courtesy of the University Librarian and Director, The
John Rylands University Library, The University of Manchester.

The second text—and this resemblance, by no means the only one between the two manuscripts, is suggestive—is P. Egerton 2, assigned by the editors to the middle of the second century, a judgment which, as they remark, errs, if at all, on the side of caution. Although P. Egerton 2 is written in a lighter and less laboured hand, the family resemblance between the two is unmistakable; the forms of the upsilon, the mu and the delta in the two texts are akin and most of the charactistics of our hand are to be found, though in a less accentuated form, in P. Egerton 2.[21]

Therefore, one of the main reference points for establishing the date of $\mathfrak{P}^{52}$ was based upon the decision concerning the date of *P.Egerton* 2. Consequently it is implausible to argue that the date of $\mathfrak{P}^{52}$ is earlier than *P.Egerton* 2. They are seen by palaeographers as contemporaneous. While *P.Egerton* 2 may have been written in a slightly more careful hand, nothing can be inferred from this concerning the date order between it and $\mathfrak{P}^{52}$. Both texts date to broadly the same time span; it is impossible to determine the relative age of the two texts.

However, the importance, for some people, in having an early NT fragment is perhaps more of an ideological commitment than something that is established on the basis of close analysis. In a series of publications Philip Comfort has affirmed the date of $\mathfrak{P}^{52}$ as being in the range "ca. 110–125,"[22] or even "early second century (ca. 100–125)."[23] One may enquire as to the basis for such a downward

---

[21] Ibid.

[22] Comfort, *Encountering the Manuscripts*, 69.

[23] Philip W. Comfort and D. P. Barrett, eds., *The Complete Text of the Earliest New Testament Manuscripts* (Grand Rapids: Baker, 1999), 355.

drift in dating that locates the text not in the first half but in the first quarter of the second century. The expectation might be that it is based on new comparator texts that have been shown through palaeographic analysis to have closer affinities with $\mathfrak{P}^{52}$ than those originally used by Roberts. Instead it appears to be based upon a throwaway suggestion in a German newspaper by Adolf Deissmann that while a Hadrianic hand was more likely, a Trajanic date was not impossible.[24] In the title of his article, Deissmann explicitly referred to a fragment "from the days of Hadrian," and this should be understood as his preferred option.

A New Insight into Dating *P.Egerton* 2

Papyrology is both a strange and sometimes serendipitously fascinating discipline. From the initial publication of *P.Egerton* 2 until the mid-1980s the uniform and unchallenged assessment of the date of the manuscript remained constant; namely, sometime in the first half of the second century. In 1987 the German scholar Michael Gronewald published a discussion of Papyrus Köln 255.[25] Like two pieces of a jigsaw puzzle, Gronewald noted, P.Köln 255 was the continuation of what Bell and Skeat had labeled as fragment 1 of *P.Egerton* 2. In relation to the frag. 1 verso (?) of *P.Egerton* 2, P.Köln 255 offers partial completions of two lines and an additional five lines of partial text; in relation to frag. 1 recto (?) P.Köln 255 offers partial completions of three lines and an additional five lines of partial text. Due to certain edges being abraded the fit is not as perfect as a newly milled jigsaw puzzle, but there are sufficient places where broken letters can be joined[26] and where identical letter formation can be recognized, in order to guarantee that these two fragments are adjoining sections of the same papyrus leaf.

Obviously, finding a continuation of the Egerton text was exciting in itself. Being from the same hand the date of the two fragments would obviously be identical especially as the left-hand lines at top of the recto of P.Köln 255 would have been written moments before the right-hand completions on the recto of *P.Egerton* 2. However, on line 4 of the recto of P.Köln 255 a punctuation mark can be read; an oblique apostrophe above the right-hand termination of the letter gamma.

Prior to the publication of P.Köln 255, Turner had noted that this punctuation feature is a characteristic that is exemplified in third-century manuscripts.[27] Gronewald's interpretation of Turner's observation in relation to the presence of the apostrophe in P.Köln 255 was as follows:

---

[24] Adolf Deissmann, "Ein Evangelienblatt aus den Tagen Hadrians," *Deutsche allgemeine Zeitung* (December 3, 1935): 564.

[25] Michael Gronewald, "Papyrus Köln 255: Unbekanntes Evangelium oder Evangelienharmonie (Fragment aus dem "Evangelium Egerton")," in *Papyrologica Coloniensia: Kolner Papyri—Vol. VII, Band 6* (ARWAW; ed. M. Gronewald, B. Kramer, K. Maresch, M. Parca, und C. Romer; Opladen: Westdeutscher Verlag, 1987), 136–45.

[26] In particular see line 18 of the recto of *P.Egerton* 2, where the right-hand vertical leg of the initial p, which is incomplete, has its completion on line 1 of the recto of P.Köln 255.

[27] Eric G. Turner, *Greek Papyri: An Introduction* (Oxford: Clarendon Press, 1980), 13, 3.

Nachzutragen ist, daß sich in dem Kölner Fragment nun auch Apostroph zwischen Konsonanten (ανενεγ'κον) wie in P.Bodmer II findet, was nach E.G. Turner, *Greek Manuscripts* 13, 3 eher ins dritte Jahrhundert weist. Doch auch bei einer eventuellen Datierung um 200 würde P.Egerton 2 immer noch zu den frühesten christlichen Papyri zählen.[28]

This portion of P.Köln VI 255 is reproduced with the
kind permission of Dr. Robert Daniel.

Whereas Gronewald's reading of Turner leads him to conclude that P.Köln 255 (and consequently also *P.Egerton* 2) could not be dated earlier than 200, Nicklas is perhaps more correct in reading Turner's statement as not precluding a late second-century date, although the punctuation apostrophe is far more prevalent in third-century texts. Thus Nicklas observes that the presence of the apostrophe "suggests that the papyrus should not be dated too early; it points more to the third than to the second century."[29]

The implications that arise from the publication of P.Köln 255 are more wide-reaching than simply the redating of *P.Egerton* 2 by approximately half a century, to around 200. It also provides a sobering lesson concerning the degree of precision that can be gained even from unanimous opinions concerning palaeographical analysis of manuscripts. Despite the strong statements from Bell and Skeat that "it seems extremely improbable . . . that [*P.Egerton* 2] can be dated later than the middle of the second century," the manuscript in fact appears to be maybe fifty years later than that terminal date.[30] The expert opinion of Schubart that Bell and

---

[28] "It is only now in the Cologne fragment with the apostrophe that one finds between consonants (ανενεγ'κον), as in P.Bodmer II, which according to E. G. Turner (Greek Manuscripts, 13,3) points rather to the third century. But even with a possible date of 200, P.Egerton 2 would still rank among the earliest Christian papyri." Gronewald, "Papyrus Köln 255," 136–45.

[29] Nicklas, "Papyrus Egerton 2," 20.

[30] Bell and Skeat, *Fragments of an Unknown Gospel*, 2.

Skeat were conservative in their estimate suggested moving the date further in the wrong direction. An obvious implication, perhaps welcomed by those who were discomforted (maybe for pious reasons) by the suggestion that *P.Egerton* 2 may have been the earliest extant Christian text is that this is almost certainly not the case. Even certain champions of the theory that non-canonical gospels emerged at the same time as their canonical counterparts have given up the claim that the manuscript of the Egerton Gospel stems from the early years of the second century. While some have continued to maintain that the actual text carried by P.Köln 255 and *P.Egerton* 2 was composed in the second half of the first century,[31] the evidential base for this theory has been severely weakened, and it is far more plausible that this text is both dependent upon and a pastiche of canonical Gospel texts.

However, while this apparently secure later dating of *P.Egerton* 2 may provide comfort in some circles, there is a further implication that has not been fully explored that may arouse the opposite feeling. It has already been shown that the *editio princeps* of $\mathfrak{P}^{52}$ was dependent upon *P.Egerton* 2 for fixing the date of the fragment of John 18. In fact *P.Egerton* 2 was seen as one of the two closest comparator texts, and given not only the palaeographical similarities but also the commonalities in the use of the codex form one must acknowledge that the issues of dating these two texts are closely linked. If *P.Egerton* 2 is no longer a likely contender for the label of earliest Christian text, it would seem equally impossible to place that label on $\mathfrak{P}^{52}$ given its palaeographical affinities with the former.

In assessing this issue it first needs to be noted that Roberts himself was more circumspect, maintaining the date range of the "first half of the second century." The ideological pressure to revise the date downwards stands in direct opposition to the rigors of palaeographical analysis. While preferring an early date for $\mathfrak{P}^{52}$, Roberts observes that "some similarities are to be found in P.Flor. 1, a cursive document of A.D. 153."[32] While the implication of the redating of *P.Egerton* 2 for $\mathfrak{P}^{52}$ has either been missed or neglected by many scholars, a few seem to have become more cautious. In opposition to an earlier statement made by the Alands dating $\mathfrak{P}^{52}$ to "*ca.* 125,"[33] by contrast in the appendix in the NA[27] the date is listed more broadly as second century.[34] More explicitly based on the new evidence from P.Köln 255, Andreas Schmidt favors a date around 170 with a range of plus or minus twenty-five years.[35] This assessment is made in light of perceived similarities with Chester Beatty X and the redated *P.Egerton* 2. Most recently Brent Nongbri's discussion of

---

[31] See John Dominic Crossan, "The Egerton Gospel," in *The Complete Gospels* (ed. R. J. Miller; rev. and expanded ed.; Santa Rosa, CA: Polebridge, 1994), 413.

[32] These similarities include the upsilon, omega, and alpha, although it is noted that there are also divergences with a number of other letters. Roberts, *An Unpublished Fragment of the Fourth Gospel*, 16.

[33] Aland and Aland, *Text of the New Testament*, 99.

[34] B. Aland, K. Aland, et al., eds., *Novum Testamentum Graece* (27. revidierte Auflage, 8. korrigierter und um die Papyri 99–116; Stuttgart: Deutsche Bibelgesellschaft, 2001), appendix 1.

[35] Andreas Schmidt, "Zwei Anmerkungen zu P. Ryl. III 457," *Archiv für Papyrusforschung* 35 (1989): 11–12.

the dating of 𝔓⁵² makes the point being emphasised here; palaeographic analysis provides only a broad range for dating manuscripts.[36] Moreover, NT scholars who advocate precise dates, such as 125 or earlier in the case of 𝔓⁵², are engaged in an exercise in wishful thinking usually to back up theological claims that should be argued on other grounds. Was John's Gospel written before the end of the first century? Yes, probably. Does 𝔓⁵² prove this to be the case? No, probably not.

A Wider Phenomenon in New Testament Scholarship

Revisionist dating of manuscripts, nearly always in the direction of earlier dates, is not limited to discussions of *P.Egerton* 2 and 𝔓⁵². The early Greek fragments of the *Gospel of Thomas* have been subject to new claims about their date. Taking the example of P.Oxy. 1 as representative, B. P. Grenfell and A. S. Hunt made the following initial estimate of date:

> We are of the opinion that the hand of the Logia fragment is far from belonging to the latest type of uncials used before 300 A.D., and therefore the papyrus was probably not written much later than the year 200.[37]

However, according to A. E. Bernhard's recent edition, the date given, cited with the authority of Grenfell and Hunt, is "late second or early third century."[38] With the texts associated with the *Gospel of Peter* the same tendency has been apparent. P.Cair. 10759 discovered at Akhmîm in the winter season dig of 1886/87 contained four texts, including two fragments of *1 Enoch* written in different hands. The first text contained in the codex, identified as the *Gospel of Peter*, was initially very broadly dated between the eighth to twelfth centuries in the *editio princeps*.[39] Almost immediately, and based on closer examination, this range was narrowed and the lower limit was placed a century earlier. Therefore, the most commonly proposed dating for the text advanced by papyrologists since the discovery of the codex has been sometime between the seventh to ninth centuries.[40] However, more recently G. Cavallo and H. Maehler suggest a date "near the end of the VI century."[41] This same tendency has been seen with the dating of P.Oxy. 2949, which comprises two small papyrus fragments. Some scholars have suggested that this

---

[36] Brent Nongbri, "Use and Abuse of 𝔓⁵²: Papyrological Pitfalls in the Dating of the Fourth Gospel," *HTR* 98 (2005): 23–52.
[37] B. P. Grenfell and A. S. Hunt, *Sayings of Our Lord* (London: Henry Frowde, 1897), 6.
[38] A. E. Bernhard, *Other Early Christian Gospels: A Critical Edition of the Surviving Greek Manuscripts* (LNTS (JSNTS) 315; London: T&T Clark International, 2006), 18.
[39] U. Bouriant, "Fragments du texte grec du livre d'Énoch et de quelques écrits attribués à saint Pierre," in *Mémoires publiés par les membres de la Mission archéologique française au Caire* (t. IX, fasc. 1; Paris: Ernest Leroux 1892), 93.
[40] See J. van Haelst's *Catalogue des papyrus littéraires juifs et chrétiens* (Paris: Publication de la Sorbonne, 1976), 597, no. 598.
[41] G. Cavallo and H. Maehler, *Greek Bookhands of the Early Byzantine Period A.D. 300–800* (BICS.S 47; London: University of London, Institute of Classical Studies, 1987), 75.

text is an early witness to the *Gospel of Peter*.[42] Palaeographically, according to R. A. Coles, the editor of these fragments, the handwriting should be assigned to the "early third or possibly the late second century."[43] Interestingly, most scholars who have made use of the assessment of dating provided by Coles give the dating mentioned in the subheading "late second or early third century."[44] Consequently they miss the fact that Coles put the third-century dating first in the body of his discussion and only haltingly introduced the possibility of a late second-century dating. Helmut Koester exemplifies this trend.

> No other manuscript or fragment was known until Dieter Lührmann discovered that two small papyrus fragments from Oxyrhynchus, written ca. 200 CE, which had been published in 1972, actually belonged to the Gospel of Peter. This confirms a *terminus ad quem* for the composition of the *Gospel of Peter* of 200 CE.[45]

From this summary statement it would appear that Koester has not read Coles's publication report on P.Oxy. 2949 closely and instead bases his assessment on Lührmann's follow-up article. Yet even here, Koester turns the more flexible date of "ca. 200 CE" into an absolute *terminus ad quem*. There appears to be a theological agenda at work here, which is based upon pushing the date of non-canonical gospel texts earlier in order to make them rival the canonical Gospels in terms of priority.

However, the tendency to redate texts to an earlier period without any supporting palaeographical analysis, or with acknowledgment of the lack of precision that such methods provide, is not limited to non-canonical gospels. Within the most recent printed edition of the first appendix to the NA[27] the following papyri are assigned second-century dates: $\mathfrak{P}^{52}$, $\mathfrak{P}^{90}$, $\mathfrak{P}^{104}$, with the date of $\mathfrak{P}^{98}$ being followed by a question mark, i.e., "II (?)."[46] Consultation of the recently updated *Kurzgefasste Liste* (February 2010)[47] shows that in the catalogued list of NT papyri that run to $\mathfrak{P}^{127}$, no further items have been identified as second century. However, instead of three or four second-century papyrus fragments, the champion of revisionist datings for the NT papyri, Comfort, has suggested that ten papyrus fragments, including the four listed above, date from the second century. The six additional items he includes are as follows (with the date given in the NA[27] provided in square brackets):

> 1. $\mathfrak{P}^{4+}$ $\mathfrak{P}^{64+}$ $\mathfrak{P}^{67}$, three fragments initially published separately which probably came from the same codex, $\mathfrak{P}^4$ containing Lk 1.58–59; 1.62–2.1, 6–7; 3.8–4.2, 29–32, 34, 35; 5.3–8; 5.30–6.16; $\mathfrak{P}^{64+}$ $\mathfrak{P}^{67}$ containing Matt 3.9, 15; 5.20–22, 25–28; 26.7–8, 19, 14–15, 22–23, 31–33 [$\mathfrak{P}^4$ III; $\mathfrak{P}^{64+}$ $\mathfrak{P}^{67}$ c. 200 CE].

---

[42] This identification has been challenged by Paul Foster, "Are There Any Early Fragments of the So-called *Gospel of Peter*?" *NTS* 52 (2006): 1–28.

[43] R. A. Coles, "2949. Fragments of an Apocryphal Gospel(?)," in G. M. Browne (ed.), *The Oxyrhynchus Papyri,* vol. 41 (Cambridge: Cambridge University Press, 1972), 15.

[44] Ibid.

[45] Helmut Koester, *Ancient Christian Gospels: Their History and Development* (London: SCM; Philadelphia: Trinity Press International, 1990), 216–17.

[46] Aland, Aland, et al., *Novum Testamentum* Graece (27).

[47] http://www.uni-muenster.de/NTTextforschung/KgLSGII2010_02_04.pdf (accessed March 26, 2010).

2. $\mathfrak{P}^{32}$, a small fragment containing Titus 1.11–15; 2.3–8 [c. 200 CE].

3. $\mathfrak{P}^{46}$, a major codex containing large sections of Paul's epistles—Romans, 1 and 2 Corinthians, Galatians, Ephesians, Philippians, 1 Thessalonians, Hebrews [c. 200 CE].

4. $\mathfrak{P}^{66}$, a largely complete manuscript containing John 1.1–6.11; 6.35–14.26, 29–30; 15.2–26; 16.2–4, 6–7; 16.10–20.20, 22–23; 20.25–21.9 [c. 200 CE].

5. $\mathfrak{P}^{77}$, a small fragment containing Matt 23.30–39 [II/III].

6. $\mathfrak{P}^{103}$, a small fragment containing Matt 13.55–56; 14.3–5 [II/III].[48]

Perhaps what is interesting (without considering the details of palaeography) is that for any manuscript that the NA[27] appendix gives the slightest possibility of originating in the second century, Comfort sees these all as definitely being written in the second century. One might perhaps think, just in terms of natural probability, that although some might be slightly earlier than the cusp of the year 200, others might have been later—especially given the imprecision that has been demonstrated in using palaeographic techniques.

It is instructive to consider the arguments advanced by Comfort in support of these proposed datings, which place the ten fragments in the second century. First, $\mathfrak{P}^{52}$, which Comfort maintains is likely to be the earliest extant NT text and which he dates to very early in the second century (i.e., 100,[49] 110,[50] or 115,[51] but never later than 125[52]). Perhaps Comfort even entertains an earlier date for $\mathfrak{P}^{52}$, although he only alludes to this possibility: "A few New Testament manuscripts (namely, $\mathfrak{P}^{52}$ and $\mathfrak{P}^{104}$) resemble hands of the late first century or early second century."[53] What is of interest is the way in which Comfort handles the relationship between *P.Egerton* 2 and $\mathfrak{P}^{52}$ in light of the discovery of P.Köln 255. As has been noted, when describing *P.Egerton* 2, Comfort states that "[i]t bears remarkable resemblance to $\mathfrak{P}^{52}$."[54] He notes that some palaeographers have followed the obvious implication of Turner's observation that the separating apostrophe employed between consonant emerged at the beginning of the third century[55] to redate *P.Egerton* 2 to c. 200.[56] Thus Comfort cavils at this redating of *P.Egerton* 2 in the following manner:

> I would argue that the previously assigned date of such manuscripts was given by many scholars according to their observations of several palaeographic features. Thus the presence of this particular feature (the hook or apostrophe between double consonants) determines an early date for its emergence, not the other way around. Thus, the Egerton

---

[48] Comfort, *Encountering the Manuscripts*, 31–32.

[49] Comfort and Barrett, *Complete Text of the Earliest New Testament Manuscripts*, 355.

[50] Comfort, *Encountering the Manuscripts*, 69.

[51] Ibid., 31.

[52] Comfort and Barrett, *Complete Text of the Earliest New Testament Manuscripts*, 355; Comfort, *Encountering the Manuscripts*, 31, 69.

[53] Comfort, *Encountering the Manuscripts*, 11.

[54] Ibid., 32.

[55] Turner, *Greek Manuscripts of the Ancient World*, 1–23.

[56] See A. Schmidt, "Zwei Anmerkungen zu P.Ryl. III 457," *Archiv fur Papyrusforschung* (1989): 11–12.

Gospel, dated by many to ca. 150, should still stand, and so should the date for 𝔓⁵² (as early second century). Another way to come at this is to look at 𝔓⁶⁶, dated by several scholars to ca. 150 (see discussion below). Turner, however, would date 𝔓⁶⁶ later (early third) largely because of the hook between double consonants. What I would say is that the predominant dating of 𝔓⁶⁶ (i.e., the dating assigned by most scholars) predetermines the date for this particular feature.[57]

Thus, in a breathtaking *tour de force*, Comfort not only inverts the more likely implication of the presence of the apostrophe in P.Köln 255 (admittedly the earliest examples of this feature may date to late in the second century) but also privileges the broad approximation of palaeographic dating over what is potentially a more precise indication of the emergence of a new punctuation feature. Furthermore, he drags 𝔓⁶⁶ (one might almost say kicking and screaming) into the second century despite both the presence of the hook apostrophe and the independent analysis of palaeographic features. As an aside, the decision to date 𝔓⁶⁶ to c. 200 by the majority of palaeographers is based on far more than the presence or absence of the separating apostrophe.

It is instructive to consider a second example from Comfort's list of second-century NT papyri. The case of 𝔓⁴⁶ offers the benefit of a far more extensive text, and consequently there are multiple examples of scribal features such as letter formation and quality of penmanship. Moreover, it is possible to assess methods involved with codex preparation and care given to correcting the manuscript. It is perhaps worth noting that the classic study of this remarkable manuscript, 𝔓⁴⁶, is by G. Zuntz, who refrains from explicitly dating the manuscript; however, many indirect indications of his assessment of dating are given. Zuntz saw the *Corpus Paulinum* being formed around the year 100 and notes that "roughly 250 years separate the archetype from the codex Vaticanus," and that "with the emergence of the Chester Beatty papyrus this gap has been reduced by more than one half."[58] On his "graphic presentation" of the stream of the Pauline tradition, Zuntz placed 𝔓⁴⁶ slightly before the year 200 datum. Hence one may infer a suggested date of c. 180 to 200. More recently James R. Royse has affirmed that "dated *ca.* 200, 𝔓⁴⁶ is a remarkable ancient text."[59]

While a date around 200 remains the majority position both on the basis of palaeographical analysis and other arguments, this manuscript has perhaps been subjected to the most staggering downward revision in dating. A 1988 article, by Young-Kyu Kim, made comparisons between 𝔓⁴⁶ and several first-century manuscripts. He concluded that this evidence "strongly suggests that 𝔓⁴⁶ was written some time before the reign of Domitian."[60] The suggestion that 𝔓⁴⁶ is to be dated to the period prior to 81 CE has not gained much support. While Comfort finds

---

[57] Comfort, *Encountering the Manuscripts*, 108–9.

[58] G. Zuntz, *The Text of the Epistles: A Disquisition upon the* Corpus Paulinum, *The Schweich Lectures* (Oxford: Oxford University Press, 1953), 17.

[59] James R. Royse, *Scribal Habits in Early Greek New Testament Papyri* (NTTS 36; Leiden: Brill, 2008), 201.

[60] Young-Kyu Kim, "Palaeographical Dating of P46 to the Later First Century," *Biblica* 69 (1988): 248.

II CORINTHIANS XI, 33 – XII, 9

$\mathfrak{P}^{46}$ 2 Corinthians 11:33–12:9. Reproduced with the kind
permission of the Chester Beatty Library.

much to affirm in Kim's thesis, he has become more circumspect in his comments. Initially Comfort dated $\mathfrak{P}^{46}$ to 85 to 150;[61] however, he has returned to a mid-second-century date (which is still optimistic) in his more recent publications.[62] Other reviews of Kim's thesis have found even less to affirm. B. W. Griffin refutes

---

[61] P. W. Comfort, *The Quest for the Original Text of the New Testament* (Grand Rapids: Baker, 1992), 30–31, 77.

[62] Comfort, *Encountering the Manuscripts*, 131–37.

the palaeographical arguments put forward by Kim;[63] Bruce Metzger and Skeat believe the developed system of *nomina sacra* found in $\mathfrak{P}^{46}$ undercut this radical proposal;[64] and Royse sees the presence of eight readings that conflate Western and Alexandrian text traditions as pointing to a later date.[65] Thus, the historical probability of the Pauline corpus being gathered some time in the seventies of the first century, in codex form of large proportion, and with the developed system of *nomina sacra* may stretch plausibility a little too far.

Royse's argument against Kim's dating also has implications for Comfort's mid-second-century dating. Similarly Griffin's detailed palaeographic analysis resulted in the proposal of "a date of A.D. 175–225."[66] Moreover, Griffin notes that utilizing the data assembled in Turner's *Typology of the Early Codex*,[67] it is to be seen that $\mathfrak{P}^{46}$ falls into his group 8, of which only three examples exist that are c. 200 or earlier. Therefore, $\mathfrak{P}^{46}$ is a fascinating early manuscript that may at the earliest date to the latter decades of the second century, or perhaps have been written during the early decades of the third century.

Conclusion

This discussion has attempted to show the limitations of palaeographic dating. At best it provides a broad range of possible dates for manuscripts that contain no internal chronological indicators. Often dates are placed in a fifty-year bandwidth, that is, plus or minus twenty-five years. However, the limited levels of confidence even in this range should be noted. The case of *P.Egerton* 2 demonstrates how spectacularly incorrect even the most eminent palaeographers can be in their estimates. Moreover, because for some scholars much seems to hang to early datings, even strong evidence (such as that provided by P.Köln 255) is often resisted because of the implications that this might have for cherished beliefs—such as the antiquity of $\mathfrak{P}^{52}$. However, the reality is that bad history never makes for good faith. Having the wealth of NT manuscripts from c. 200 onward is remarkable; the desire to push these dates earlier with little evidential basis fails to recognize the strength of the textual evidence that exists. Moreover, it appears to be based on an implicit false premise that early manuscripts somehow prove Christianity. Futhermore, such radical redatings are also in danger of playing into the hands of those who wish to represent the work of Christian scholars as naïve and faith-driven rather than being evidenced-led; and maybe in some cases one would have to admit that such assessments have not been without

---

[63] B. W. Griffin, "The Palaeographical Dating of P[46]" (unpublished paper, SBL, 1996). See http://www.biblical-data.org/P-46%20Oct%201997.pdf (accessed March 28, 2010).

[64] Bruce M. Metzger, *The Text of the New Testament* (3rd ed.; Oxford: Oxford University Press, 1992), 265–66.

[65] Royse, *Scribal Habits*, 201.

[66] Griffin, "Palaeographical Dating of P[46]."

[67] Eric G. Turner, *The Typology of the Early Codex* (Philadelphia: University of Pennsylvania Press, 1977).

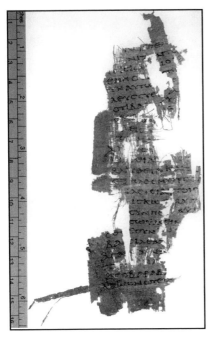 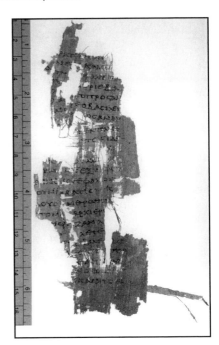

$\mathfrak{P}^{90}$ // P.Oxy. 3523 recto $\mathfrak{P}^{90}$ // P.Oxy. 3523 verso

Photograph courtesy of the Egypt Exploration Society and
The Imaging Papyri Project, University of Oxford.

foundation. If $\mathfrak{P}^{52}$ were to date from the late second century instead of the precise year 125, does this disprove the case for the Fourth Gospel being composed in the first century? The earliest extant copy of Arrian's *Anabasis of Alexander* is a damaged copy of around 1200 CE; however, this does not invalidate the case for dating the composition to the second century CE.[68]

However, inquisitive minds being what they are, it is neither likely nor desirable that questions such as "What is the earliest surviving manuscript of the New Testament?" will cease to be asked. This discussion has not set out to debar that mantle from being assigned to $\mathfrak{P}^{52}$, although that case is perhaps far less certain given the necessary revision to the dating of *P.Egerton* 2. Do other manuscripts have a better claim to being the earliest extant NT text? Well it may be the case that $\mathfrak{P}^{90}$ (also classified as P.Oxy. 3523) dating from the second half of the second century is perhaps the earlier than $\mathfrak{P}^{52}$.

If that were the case, it would be surprising to find that the manuscript that was thought to be the earliest, $\mathfrak{P}^{52}$, has contents (John 18:31–33, 37–38) that overlap at least partially with the text that might challenge its temporal preeminence

---

[68] See P. A. Brunt, trans., *Arrian, Anabasis of Alexander*, books 1–4 (LCL 236; Cambridge, MA: Harvard University Press, 1976), xiv–xv.

($\mathfrak{P}^{90}$, John 18:36–19:1, 2–7).[69] While such coincidences are fascinating, they are perhaps little more than coincidences. Perhaps what is even more remarkable is the fact that maybe only one or two decades later than the date of these partial fragments, one finds the survival of a near complete codex containing the Pauline Epistles.

Thus, NT scholars are confronted with a rich range of early manuscripts, some of which may reach back to the last decades of the second century. That is no bold claim but an assessment that is accepted by all who work in the field of palaeography and papyrology. While one may wish for an early-second-century or late-first-century manuscript, there has been a certain tendency in the absence of such discoveries to redate surving texts to transform them into what one wants. This is surely an exercise in wishful thinking that runs counter to best practice in scholarship. The lessons from *P.Egerton* 2 and the related dating of $\mathfrak{P}^{52}$ illustrate the dangers of overly optimistic datings and of striving for too great a temporal precision. The lack of granularity in palaeographical dating should be frankly acknowledged, and extreme caution should be exercised in assigning early dates to highly fragmentary scraps of papyrus. Instead, NT scholars should be happy to celebrate the diversity of third-century (and perhaps even some late-second-century) manuscript witnesses to the text that is the center of their scholarly attention.

---

[69] For an extended discussion see R. Rodgers, "The Text of the New Testament and Its Witnesses before 200 A.D.: Observations on $\mathfrak{P}^{90}$ (P.Oxy. 3523)," in *The Text of the New Testament in Early Christianity: Le texte du Nouveau Testament au début du christianisme* (ed. Christin-B. Amphoux and J. Keith Elliott; Lausanne: Éditions du Zèbre, 2003), 83–91.

BIBLIOGRAPHY

Aasgaard, Reidar. *The Childhood of Jesus: Decoding the Apocryphal Infancy Gospel of Thomas.* Eugene, OR: Cascade Books, 2009.

———. "Paul as a Child: Children and Childhood in the Letters of the Apostle." *JBL* 126 (2007): 129–59.

Abegg, Jr., Martin G., James E. Bowley, and Edward M. Cook. "Qumran Sectarian Manuscripts." *Accordance Bible Software* 8.05. Altamonte Springs, FL: Oaktree Software Specialists, 2008.

Abegg, Jr., Martin G., Peter W. Flint, and Eugene Ulrich, trans. *The Dead Sea Scrolls Bible: The Oldest Known Bible Translated for the First Time into English.* San Francisco: HarperSanFrancisco, 1999.

Adair, Jr., James R. "Nash Papyrus." In *EDB*, 948.

Aland, Barbara and Kurt Aland, et al., eds. *Novum Testamentum Graece.* 27th ed. Stuttgart: Deutsche Bibelgesellschaft, 2001.

Aland, Kurt, and Barbara Aland. *The Text of the New Testament.* Translated by Erroll F. Rhodes. Rev. and enlarged ed. Grand Rapids: Eerdmans, 1987.

Albright, W. F. "A Biblical Fragment from the Maccabaean Age: The Nash Papyrus." *JBL* 56, no. 3 (1937): 145–76.

———. "On the Date of the Scrolls from 'Ain Feshkha and the Nash Papyrus." *BASOR* 115 (1949): 10–19.

Alcock, Susan E. "The Eastern Mediterranean." In *The Cambridge Economic History of the Greco-Roman World,* edited by Walter Scheidel, Ian Morris, and Richard P. Saller, 671–97. Cambridge: Cambridge University Press, 2007.

Aletti, Jean-Noël. *Saint Paul, Épitre aux Colossiens: Introduction, traduction et commentaire.* Paris: J. Galbalda, 1993.

Alexander, Philip S. *Mystical Texts: Songs of the Sabbath Sacrifice and Related Manuscripts.* London: T&T Clark, 2006.

———. "The Redaction History of Serek ha Yahad: A Proposal." *RevQ* 17 (Milik Festschrift, 1996), 437–53.

Alföldy, G. "Pontius Pilatus und das Tiberieum von Caesarea Maritima." *Scripta Classica Israelitica* 18 (1999): 85–108.

Allert, Craig D. *A High View of Scripture? The Authority of the Bible and the Formation of the New Testament Canon.* Grand Rapids: Baker Academic, 2007.

Alter, Robert. "How Important Are the Dead Sea Scrolls?" *Commentary* 93, no. 2 (1992): 34–41.

Amir, Yehoshua. "Authority and Interpretation of Scripture in the Writings of Philo." In *Mikra: Text, Translation, Reading, and Interpretation of the Hebrew Bible in Ancient Judaism and Early Christianity,* edited by Martin Jan Mulder, 421–53. CRINT 2, no. 1. Assen: Van Gorcum; Philadelphia: Fortress, 1988.

Andreau, Jean. "Twenty Years after Moses I. Finley's *Ancient Economy.*" In *The Ancient Economy,* edited by Walter Scheidel and Sitta von Reden, 33–49. New York: Routledge, 2002.

Arnal, William E. *Jesus and the Village Scribes: Galilean Conflicts and the Setting of Q.* Minneapolis: Augsburg Fortress, 2001.

Aschim, Anders. "Melchizedek and Jesus: 11QMelchizedek and the Epistle to the Hebrews. In *The Jewish Roots of Christological Monotheism: Papers from the St. Andrews Conference on the Historical Origins of the Worship of Jesus.* Edited by Carey C. Newman, James R. Davila, and Gladys S. Lewis. Supplements to the Journal for the Study of Judaism 63, 129–47. Leiden: Brill, 1999.

Ascough, Richard A. *Lydia: Paul's Cosmopolitan Hostess.* Paul's Social Network: Brothers and Sisters in Faith. Collegeville, MN: Liturgical Press, 2009.

Attridge, Harold W. *The Epistle to the Hebrews: A Commentary on the Epistle to the Hebrews.* Philadelphia: Fortress, 1989.

Auld, Graeme. "1 and 2 Samuel." In *Eerdmans Commentary on the Bible,* edited by James D. G. Dunn and John W. Rogerson, 213–245. Grand Rapids: Eerdmans, 2003.

Aune, David E. *Revelation 1–5.* Edited by Bruce M. Metzger. WBC 52A. Nashville: Nelson, 1997.

———. *Revelation 6–16.* Edited by Bruce M. Metzger. WBC 52B. Nashville: Nelson, 1997.

Aviam, Mordechai. "Regionalism of Tombs and Burial Customs in the Galilee during the Hellenistic, Roman, and Byzantine Periods." In *Jews, Pagans, and Christians in the Galilee: Twenty-Five Years of Archaeological Excavations and Surveys: Hellenistic to Byzantine Periods,* 257–313. Institute for Galilean Archaeology. Rochester, NY: University of Rochester Press, 2004.

Avi-Yonah, Michael. "Jerusalem in the Time of the Second Temple: Archaeology and Topography." In *Sepher Yerushalayim,* edited by Michael Avi-Yonah, 305–19 and Map 10. Jerusalem and Tel Aviv: Bialik Institute and Dvir, 1956 (Hebrew).

Avraham, Assaf. "Addressing the Issue of Temple Mount Pavements during the Herodian Period." In *New Studies on Jerusalem,* edited by E. Baruch et al, 13:87–96. Ramat Gan: University of Bar Ilan, 2007 (Hebrew).

Bagnall, Roger S. "Evidence and Models for the Economy of Roman Egypt." In *The Ancient Economy: Evidence and Models,* edited by J. G. Manning and Ian Morris, 187–204. Palo Alto, CA: Stanford University Press, 2005.

Bahat, Dan. "David's Tower and Its Name in Second Temple Times." *Eretz-Israel* 15 (1981): 396–400 (Hebrew).

Bahat, Dan, and Magen Broshi. "Excavations in the Armenian Garden." In *Jerusalem Revealed: Archaeology in the Holy City 1968–1974,* edited by Yigael Yadin, 55–56. Jerusalem: Israel Exploration Society, 1975.

Bakke, O. M. *When Children Became People: The Birth of Childhood in Early Christianity.* Translated by Brian McNeil. Minneapolis: Augsburg Fortress, 2005.

Balch, David L. *Let Wives Be Submissive: The Domestic Code in 1 Peter.* SBLMS 26. Chico, CA: Scholars Press, 1981.

———. "Neopythagorean Moralists and the New Testament Household Codes." *ANRW* II.26.1 (1992): 380–411.

Balch, David L., and Carolyn Osiek, eds. *Early Christian Families in Context: An Interdisciplinary Dialogue.* Grand Rapids: Eerdmans, 2003.

Balla, Peter. *The Child-Parent Relationship in the New Testament and Its Environment.* WUNT 155. Tübingen: Mohr Siebeck, 2003.

Bang, Peter Fibiger. "Romans and Mughals: Economic Integration in a Tributary Empire." In *The Transformation of Economic Life under the Roman Empire,* edited by Lukas de Blois and John Rich, 1–27. Impact of Empire (Roman Empire) 2. Amsterdam: J. C. Gieben, 2002.

Barkay, Gabriel. "The Priestly Benediction on Silver Plaques from Ketef Hinnom in Jerusalem." *Journal of the Institute of Archaeology of Tel Aviv University* 19 (1992): 139–92.

———. "The Riches of Ketef Hinnom: Jerusalem Tomb Yields Biblical Text Four Centuries Older Than the Dead Sea Scrolls." *BAR* 35 (July/August 2009; September/October 2009): 22–28, 30–33, 35, 122–26.

Barkay, Gabriel, et al. "The Amulets from Ketef Hinnom: A New Edition and Evaluation." *BASOR* 334 (May 2004): 41–71.

———. "The Challenges of Ketef Hinnom: Using Advanced Technologies to Reclaim the Earliest Biblical Texts and Their Context." *NEA* 66 (2003):162–71.

Barthélemy, Dominique, ed. *Critique textuelle de l'Ancien Testament 1: Josué, Juges, Ruth, Samuel, Rois, Chroniques, Esdras, Néhémie, Esther,* edited by H. Peter Roger and James A. Sanders. OBO 50, no. 1. Fribourg, Suisse: Editions Universitaires; Göttingen: Vandenhoeck & Ruprecht, 1982.

———. *Critique textuelle de l'Ancien Testament 2: Isaïe, Jérémie, Lamentations,* edited by H. Peter Roger and James A. Sanders. OBO 50, no. 2. Fribourg, Suisse: Editions Universitaires; Göttingen: Vandenhoeck & Ruprecht, 1986.

———. *Critique textuelle de l'Ancien Testament 3: Ézéchiel, Daniel et les 12 Prophètes,* edited by H. Peter Roger and James A. Sanders. OBO 50, no. 3. Fribourg, Suisse: Editions Universitaires; Göttingen: Vandenhoeck & Ruprecht, 1992.

———. *Critique textuelle de l'Ancien Testament 4: Psaumes,* edited by H. Peter Rogers and James A. Sanders. OBO 50, no. 4. Fribourg, Suisse: Editions Universitaires; Göttingen: Vandenhoeck & Ruprecht, 2005.

Barthélemy, Dominique, et al., eds. *Preliminary and Interim Report on the Hebrew Old Testament Text Project.* 5 vols. London: United Bible Societies, 1979–1980.

Bauckham, Richard. *The Climax of Prophecy: Studies on the book of Revelation.* Edinburgh: T&T Clark, 1993.

Baumgarten, Joseph M., ed. *Qumran Cave 4. XIII: The Damascus Document (4Q266–273)*. DJD 18. Oxford: Clarendon Press, 1996.

Beard, Mary, et al. *Literacy in the Roman World*. Journal of Roman Archaeology Supplement Series 3. Ann Arbor: University of Michigan, 1991.

Bell, Harold Idris, and T. C. Skeat. *The New Gospel Fragments*. London: The Trustees of the British Museum Press, 1935.

Bell, Harold. Idris, and T. C. Skeat, eds. *Fragments of an Unknown Gospel and Other Early Christian Papyri 1935*. London: The Trustees of the British Museum, 1935.

Benoit, Pierre. "Le prétoire de Pilate à l'époque Byzantine." *RB* 91, no. 2 (1984): 161–77.

———. "Prétoire, Lithostroton et Gabbatha." *RB* 59 (1952): 531–50.

Berg, Laura L. "The Illegalities of Jesus' Religious and Civil Trials." *BSac* 161, no. 643 (July–September 2004): 330–42.

Berg, Shane A. "An Elite Group within the Yahad: Revisiting 1QS 8–9." In *Qumran Studies: New Approaches, New Questions*, edited by Michael Thomas Davis and Brent A. Strawn, 161–77. Grand Rapids: Eerdmans, 2007.

Berges, Ulrich. *Jesaja 40–48*. HThKAT. Freiburg: Herder, 2008.

Bernhard, Andrew. *Other Early Christian Gospels: A Critical Edition of the Surviving Greek Manuscripts*. LNTS (JSNTS) 315. London: T&T Clark International, 2006.

Bernstein, Moshe J. "Biblical Interpretation in the Dead Sea Scrolls: Looking Back and Looking Ahead." In *The Dead Sea Scrolls and Contemporary Culture: Proceedings of the International Conference held at the Israel Museum, Jerusalem (July 6–8, 2008)*, edited by Adolfo D. Roitman, Lawrence H. Schiffman, and Shani Tzoref, 141–59. STDJ 93. Leiden: Brill, 2011.

———. "Interpretation of Scriptures." In *Encyclopedia of the Dead Sea Scrolls*, edited by Lawrence H. Schiffman and James C. VanderKam, 1:376–83. New York: Oxford University Press, 2000.

———. "Pseudepigraphy in the Qumran Scrolls: Categories and Functions." In *Pseudepigraphic Perspectives: The Apocrypha and Pseudepigrapha in Light of the Dead Sea Scrolls. Proceedings of the [Second] International Symposium of the Orion Center for the Study of the Dead Sea Scrolls and Associated Literature, 12–14 January 1997*, edited by Esther G. Chazon and Michael E. Stone, 1–26. STDJ 31. Leiden: Brill, 1999.

Bernstein, Moshe J., and Shlomo A. Koyfman. "The Interpretation of Biblical Law in the Dead Sea Scrolls: Forms and Methods." In *Biblical Interpretation at Qumran*, edited by Matthias Henze, 61–87. Studies in the Dead Sea Scrolls and Related Literature. Grand Rapids: Eerdmans, 2005.

Berrin, Shani. "Qumran Pesharim." In *Biblical Interpretation at Qumran*, edited by Matthias Henze, 110–33. Studies in the Dead Sea Scrolls and Related Literature. Grand Rapids: Eerdmans, 2005.

Best, Ernest. *A Critical and Exegetical Commentary on Ephesians*. ICC. Edinburgh: T&T Clark, 1998.

Birch, Bruce C. "1 & 2 Samuel." In *The New Interpreter's Bible*, 2: 949–1383. Nashville: Abingdon, 1998.

Birnbaum, S. A. "The Dates of the Cave Scrolls." *BASOR* 115 (1949): 20–22.

Bliss, Frederick Jones. *Excavations in Jerusalem 1894–1897.* London: Palestine Exploration Fund, 1898.

Blue, Bradley. "Acts and the House Church." In *The Book of Acts in Its First Century Setting: Volume 2 Graeco Roman Setting,* edited by David W. J. Gill and Conrad Gempf, 119–221. Grand Rapids: Eerdmans, 1994

Bock, Darrell L. *Jesus According to Scripture: Restoring the Portrait from the Gospels.* Grand Rapids: Baker Academic, 2007.

Bodner, Keith. *David Observed: A King in the Eyes of His Court.* Hebrew Bible Monographs 5. Sheffield: Sheffield Phoenix Press, 2008.

———. *Jeroboam's Royal Drama.* Oxford: Oxford University Press, forthcoming.

———. "The Royal Conscience According to 4QSam[a]." *DSD* 11 (2004): 158–66.

Bond, Helen K. *Caiaphas: Friend of Rome and Judge of Jesus?* Louisville: Westminster John Knox, 2004.

———. *Pontius Pilate in History and Interpretation.* SNTSMS 100. Cambridge: Cambridge University Press, 1998.

Borg, Marcus, and John Dominic Crossan. *The Last Week: A Day-by-Day Account of Jesus's Final Week in Jerusalem.* New York: HarperCollins, 2006.

Borgen, Peder. "Philo of Alexandria as Exegete." In *A History of Biblical Interpretation,* vol. 1: *The Ancient Period,* edited by Alan J. Hauser and Duane F. Watson, 114–43. Grand Rapids: Eerdmans, 2003.

Bouriant, U. "Fragments du texte grec du livre d'Énoch et de quelques écrits attribués à saint Pierre." In *Mémoires publiés par les membres de la Mission archéologique française au Caire* (t. IX, fasc. 1), 93–147. Paris: Ernest Leroux, 1892.

Bowman, Richard G. "Narrative Criticism: Human Purpose in Conflict with Divine Presence." In *Judges and Method: New Approaches in Biblical Studies,* edited by Gale A. Yee, 19–45. 2nd ed. Minneapolis: Fortress, 2007.

Boylston, Anthea. "Evidence for Weapon-Related Trauma in British Archaeological Samples." In *Human Osteology: In Archaeology and Forensic Science,* ed. Margaret Cox and Simon Mays, 357–80. London: Greenwich Medical Media, 2000.

Brandon, S. G. F. *The Trial of Jesus of Nazareth.* New York: Stein and Day, 1968.

Braund, David C. *Rome and the Friendly King: The Character of Client Kingship.* London: Croom Helm; New York: St. Martin's Press, 1984.

Brodie, Thomas L. *The Birthing of the New Testament: The Intertextual Development of the New Testament Writings.* New Testament Monographs 1. Sheffield: Sheffield Phoenix Press, 2004.

Bronner, Ethan. "Find of Ancient City Could Alter Notions of Biblical David." *New York Times,* October 29, 2008. Accessed January 24, 2011. http://www.nytimes.com/2008/10/30/world/middleeast/30david.html?_r=1&ref=ethanbronner

Brooke, George J. "Between Authority and Canon: The Significance of Reworking the Bible for Understanding the Canonical Process." In *Reworking the Bible: Apocryphal and Related Texts at Qumran. Proceedings of a Joint Symposium by the Orion Center for the Study of the Dead Sea Scroll and Associated Literature and the Hebrew University Institute for Advanced Studies Research on Qumran,15–17 January, 2002,* edited by Esther G. Chazon, Devorah Dimant, and Ruth A. Clements, 85–104. STDJ58. Leiden: Brill, 2005. ————. "Biblical Interpretation at Qumran." In *The Bible and the Dead Sea Scrolls,* vol. 1: *Scripture and the Scrolls,* edited by James H. Charlesworth, 287–319. The Second Princeton Symposium on Judaism and Christian Origins, 1997. Waco, TX: Baylor University Press, 2006.

————. "Biblical Interpretation in the Qumran Scrolls and the New Testament." In *The Dead Sea Scrolls Fifty Years after Their Discovery: Proceedings of the Jerusalem Congress, July 20–25, 1997,* edited by Lawrence A. Schiffman, Emanuel Tov, and James C. VanderKam, 60–73. Jerusalem: Israel Exploration Society and the Shrine of the Book, Israel Museum, 2000.

————. "Biblical Interpretation in the Wisdom Texts from Qumran." In *The Wisdom Texts from Qumran and the Development of Sapiential Thought,* edited by C. Hempel, A. Lange, and H. Lichtenberger, 201–20. BETL 159. Leuven: Peeters and Leuven University Press, 2002.

————. "The Books of Chronicles and the Scrolls from Qumran." In *Reflection and Refraction: Studies in Biblical Historiography in Honour of A. Graeme Auld,* edited by Robert Rezetko, Timothy H. Lim, and W. Brian Aucker, 35–48. VTSup 113. Leiden: Brill, 2006.

————. " 'The Canon within the Canon' at Qumran and in the New Testament." In *The Scrolls and the Scriptures: Qumran Fifty Years After,* edited by Stanley E. Porter and Craig A. Evans, 242–66. JSPSup 26. Roehampton Institute London Papers 3. Sheffield: Sheffield Academic Press, 1997.

————. "Dead Sea Scrolls." In *Dictionary of Biblical Interpretation,* edited by John H. Hayes, 253–56. Nashville: Abingdon, 1999.

————. "The Dead Sea Scrolls." In *The Biblical World,* edited by John Barton, 1:248–66. London: Routledge, 2002.

————. *Exegesis at Qumran: 4QFlorilegium in Its Jewish Context.* JSOTSup 29. Sheffield: JSOT Press, 1985.

————. "The Explicit Presentation of Scripture in 4QMMT." In *Legal Texts and Legal Issues: Proceedings of the Second Meeting of the International Organization for Qumran Studies, Cambridge 1995, Published in Honour of Joseph M. Baumgarten,* edited by M. Bernstein, F. García Martínez, and J. Kampen, 67–88. STDJ 23. Leiden: Brill, 1997.

————. "4Q252 as Early Jewish Commentary." *RevQ* 17 (1996): 385–401.

————. "From Bible to Midrash: Approaches to Biblical Interpretation in the Dead Sea Scrolls by Modern Interpreters." In *Northern Lights on the Dead Sea Scrolls: Proceedings of the Nordic Qumran Network 2003–2006,* edited by Anders Klostergaard Petersen, Torleif Elgvin, Cecelia Wassen, Hanne von Weissenberg, and Mikael Winninge with Martin Ehrensvärd, 1–19. STDJ 80. Leiden: Brill, 2009.

————. "Isaiah 40:3 and the Wilderness Community." In *New Qumran Texts and Studies: Proceedings of the First Meeting of the International Organization for*

Qumran Studies New Qumran Texts and Studies Paris 1992, edited by George J. Brooke with Florentino García Martínez, 117–32. STDJ 15. Leiden: Brill, 1994.

———. "Reading the Plain Meaning of Scripture in the Dead Sea Scrolls." In *Jewish Ways of Reading the Bible,* edited by George J. Brooke, 67–90. JSSSup 11. Oxford: Oxford University Press, 2000.

Broshi, Magen, and Shimon Gibson. "Excavations along the Western and Southern Walls of the Old City of Jerusalem." In *Ancient Jerusalem Revealed,* edited by Hillel Geva, 147–55. Jerusalem: Israel Exploration Society, 2000.

Brown, Raymond E. *The Death of the Messiah: From Gethsemane to the Grave: A Commentary on the Passion Narratives in the Four Gospels.* 2 vols. ABRL. New York: Doubleday, 1994.

Bruce, F. F. *Biblical Exegesis in the Qumran Texts.* Grand Rapids: Eerdmans, 1959.

Brunt, P. A. trans. *Arrian, Anabasis of Alexander,* books 1–4. LCL 236. Cambridge, MA: Harvard University Press, 1976.

Bunge, Marcia J., ed. *The Child in the Bible.* Grand Rapids: Eerdmans, 2008.

Burkill, T. A. "The Condemnation of Jesus: A Critique of Sherwin-White's Thesis." *NovT* 12, no. 4 (1970): 321–42.

———. "The Trial of Jesus." *Vigiliae Christianae* 12, no. 1 (1958): 1–18.

Burkitt, F. C. "The Hebrew Papyrus of the Ten Commandments." *JQR* 15 (1903): 392–408.

Burrows, Millar. *The Dead Sea Scrolls.* New York: Viking, 1961.

Callaway, Philip R. *The History of the Qumran Community: An Investigation.* JSPSup 3. Sheffield: JSOT Press, 1988.

Cameron, Ron, ed. *The Other Gospels: Non-Canonical Gospel Texts.* Philadelphia: Westminster Press, 1982.

Campbell, Anthony F. *2 Samuel.* FOTL 8. Grand Rapids: Eerdmans, 2005.

Campbell, Jonathan. "The Qumran Sectarian Writings." In *The Cambridge History of Judaism. Volume Three: The Early Roman Period,* edited by William Horbury, W. D. Davies, and John Sturdy, 798–821. Cambridge: Cambridge University Press, 1999.

Campbell, William Sanger. "Engagement, Disengagement and Obstruction: Jesus' Defense Strategies in Mark's Trial and Execution Scenes (14:53–64; 15:1–39)." *JSNT* 26, no. 3 (2004): 283–300.

Capper, Brian J. "Essene Community Houses and Jesus' Early Community." In *Jesus and Archaeology,* edited by James H. Charlesworth, 472–502. Grand Rapids: Eerdmans, 2006.

Carmichael, Joel. *The Death of Jesus.* New York: Macmillan, 1962.

Cascio, Elio Lo. "The Early Roman Empire: The State and the Economy." In *The Cambridge Economic History of the Greco-Roman World,* edited by Walter Scheidel, Ian Morris, and Richard P. Saller, 619–47. Cambridge: Cambridge University Press, 2007.

Cavallo, G., and H. Maehler. *Greek Bookhands of the Early Byzantine Period A.D. 300–800.* BICS.S 47. London: University of London, Institute of Classical Studies, 1987.

Chancey, Mark A. "Archaeology, Ethnicity, and First-Century CE Galilee: The Limits of Evidence." In *A Wandering Galilean: Essays in Honour of Sean Freyne,* edited by Zuleika Rodgers with Margaret Daly-Denton and Anne Fitzpatrick McKinley, 205–18. JSJSup 132. Leiden: Brill, 2009.

———. *Greco-Roman Culture and the Galilee of Jesus.* SNTSMS 134. Cambridge: Cambridge University Press, 2005.

———. *The Myth of a Gentile Galilee.* SNTSMS 118. Cambridge: Cambridge University Press, 2002.

Charlesworth, James H. "The New Perspective on Second Temple Judaism and 'Christian Origins.'" In *The Bible and the Dead Sea Scrolls,* vol. 1: *Scripture and the Scrolls,* ed. James H. Charlesworth, xxiii–xxxi. The Second Princeton Symposium on Judaism and Christian Origins, 1997. Waco, TX: Baylor University Press, 2006.

———. *The Pesharim and Qumran History: Chaos or Consensus?* Grand Rapids: Eerdmans, 2002.

———. "Revelation and Perspicacity in Qumran Hermeneutics." In *The Dead Sea Scrolls and Contemporary Culture: Proceedings of the International Conference held at the Israel Museum, Jerusalem (July 6–8, 2008),* edited by Adolfo D. Roitman, Lawrence H. Schiffman, and Shani Tzoref, 161–80. STDJ 93. Leiden: Brill, 2011.

Chavarría, Alexandra, and Tamara Lewit. "Archaeological Research on the Late Antique Countryside: A Bibliographic Essay." In *Recent Research on the Late Antique Countryside,* edited by William Bowden, Luke Lavan, and Carlos Machado, 3–51. Late Antique Archaeology, vol. 2. Leiden: Brill, 2004.

Chen, Doron, Shlomo Margalit, and Bargil Pixner. "Mount Zion: Discovery of Iron Age Fortifications Below the Gate of the Essenes." In *Ancient Jerusalem Revealed,* edited by Hillel Geva, 76–81. Reprint. Jerusalem: Israel Exploration Society, 2000.

Cohen, Haim. *The Trial and Death of Jesus.* Old Saybrook, CT: Konecky & Konecky, 2000.

Coles, R. A. "2949. Fragments of an Apocryphal Gospel (?)." In *The Oxyrhynchus Papyri,* 41, edited by Gerald M. Browne, 15–16. Graeco-Romans Memoirs 57. Cairo: Egypt Exploration Society, 1972.

Collins, John J. *Beyond the Qumran Community: The Sectarian Movement of the Dead Sea Scrolls.* Grand Rapids, MI: Eerdmans, 2010.

———. "Sectarian Communities in the Dead Sea Scrolls." In *The Oxford Handbook of the Dead Sea Scrolls,* edited by Timothy H. Lim and John J. Collins, 151–72. Oxford: Oxford University Press, 2010.

———. "The Yahad and 'The Qumran Community.'" In *Biblical Traditions in Transmission: Essays in Honour of Michael A. Knibb,* edited by Charlotte Hempel and Judith Lieu, 81–96. JSJSup 111. Leiden: Brill, 2006.

Comfort, Philip W. *Encountering the Manuscripts: An Introduction to the New Testament Palaeography and Textual Criticism.* Nashville: Broadman & Holman, 2005.

————. *The Quest for the Original Text of the New Testament.* Eugene, OR: Wipf and Stock, 2003.

Comfort, Philip W., and David P. Barrett, eds. *The Complete Text of the Earliest New Testament Manuscripts.* Grand Rapids: Baker, 1999.

Consultation of LDAB, February 22, 2010.

Coogan, Michael D., ed. *The New Oxford Annotated Apocrypha.* 3rd ed. Oxford: Oxford University Press, 2001.

Cook, Stanley A. "A Pre-Massoretic Biblical Papyrus." *Proceedings of the Society of Biblical Archaeology* 25 (1903): 34–56.

Corley, Jeremy. "The Portrait of Samuel in Hebrew Ben Sira 46:13–20." In *Biblical Figures in Deuterocanonical and Cognate Literature: Deuterocanonical and Cognate Literature Yearbook 2008,* edited by Hermann Lichtenberger and Ulrike Mittmann-Richert, 31–56. Berlin: Walter de Gruyter, 2009.

Cotton, Hannah M., and Werner Eck. "Governors and Their Personnel on Latin Inscriptions from Caesarea Maritima." *The Israel Academy of Sciences and Humanities Proceedings* 7, no. 7 (2001): 215–40.

Crawford, Sidnie White. "4QTales of the Persian Court (4Q550a–e) and Its Relation to Biblical Royal Courtier Tales, Especially Esther, Daniel, and Joseph." In *The Bible as Book: The Hebrew Bible and the Judaean Desert Discoveries,* edited by Edward D. Herbert and Emanuel Tov, 121–37. London: The British Library and Oak Knoll Press in association with The Scriptorium: Center for Christian Antiquities, 2002.

Crawford, Sidnie White. "The Use of the Pentateuch in the *Temple Scroll* and the *Damascus Document* in the Second Century BCE." In *The Pentateuch as Torah: New Models for Understanding Its Promulgation and Acceptance,* edited by Gary N. Knoppers and Bernard M. Levison, 301–17. Winona Lake, IN: Eisenbrauns, 2007.

Cross, Frank Moore. *The Ancient Library of Qumran.* 3rd ed. New York: Doubleday, 1958. Reprint, Sheffield: Sheffield Academic Press, 1995.

Cross, Frank Moore, and Richard J. Saley. "A Statistical Analysis of the Textual Character of 4QSamuel^a (4Q51)." *DSD* 13 (2006): 46–54.

Cross, Frank Moore, and Shemaryahu Talmon, eds. *Qumran and the History of the Biblical Text.* Cambridge, MA: Harvard University Press, 1975.

Crossan, John Dominic. *The Birth of Christianity: Discovering What Happened in the Years Immediately After the Execution of Jesus.* New York: HarperCollins, 1998.

————. "The Egerton Gospel." In *The Complete Gospels.* Ed. Robert J. Miller. Rev. and enlarged ed. Santa Rosa, CA: Polebridge, 1994.

————. *Four Other Gospels: Shadows on the Contours of Canon.* Eugene, OR: Wipf and Stock, 2008.

————. *God and Empire: Jesus against Rome, Then and Now.* New York: HarperCollins, 2007.

————. *The Historical Jesus: The Life of a Mediterranean Jewish Peasant.* New York: HarperCollins, 1991.

————. *Who Killed Jesus? Exposing the Roots of Anti-Semitism in the Gospel Story of the Death of Jesus.* New York: HarperCollins, 1995.

Crossan, John Dominic, and Jonathan L. Reed. *Excavating Jesus: Beneath the Stones, behind the Texts.* New York: HarperSanFrancisco, 2001.

Dalman, Gustaf. *Sacred Sites and Ways: Studies in the Topography of the Gospels.* London: SPCK, 1935.

Daniels, Jon B. "Egerton Gospel." In *The Complete Gospels,* edited by Robert J. Miller, 412–17. Rev. and expanded edition. Santa Rosa, CA: Polebridge Press, 1994.

Dar, Shimon. *Landscape and Pattern: An Archaeological Survey of Samaria 800 BCE–636 CE.* BAR International Series 308. Oxford: BAR, 1986.

Davies, Philip R. *Behind the Essenes: History and Ideology in the Dead Sea Scrolls.* BJS 94. Atlanta: Scholars Press, 1987.

————. "Biblical Interpretation in the Dead Sea Scrolls." In *A History of Biblical Interpretation,* vol. 1: *The Ancient Period,* edited by Alan J. Hauser and Duane F. Watson, 144–66. Grand Rapids: Eerdmans, 2003.

————. *The Damascus Covenant: An Interpretation of the "Damascus Document."* JSOTSup 25. Sheffield: JSOT, 1982.

————. "Redaction and Sectarianism in the Qumran Scrolls." In *Sects and Scrolls: Essays on Qumran and Related Topics,* edited by Philip R. Davies, 151–61. South Florida Studies in the History of Judaism. Reflection and Theory in the Study of Religion, vol. 134. Atlanta: Scholars Press, 1996.

Davila, James R. "7. 4QGen^g." In *Qumran Cave 4.VII: Genesis to Numbers,* edited by E. Ulrich et al., 57–60. DJD 12. Oxford: Clarendon Press, 1994.

De Blois, Lukas, Harry W. Pleket, and John Rich. "Introduction." In *The Transformation of the Economic Life under the Roman Empire,* edited by Lukas de Blois and John Rich, ix–xx. Impact of Empire (Roman Empire) 2. Amsterdam: J. C. Gieben, 2002.

De Blois, Lukas, and John Rich, eds. *The Transformation of the Economic Life under the Roman Empire.* Impact of Empire (Roman Empire) 2. Amsterdam: J. C. Gieben, 2002.

De Troyer, Kristin. "Qumran Research and Textual Studies: A Different Approach." *RelSRev* 28, no. 2 (2002): 115–22.

De Vaux, Roland. *Archaeology and the Dead Sea Scrolls.* The Schweich Lectures of the British Academy. Vol. 1959. Oxford: Oxford University Press, 1973.

Deissmann, Adolf. "Ein Evangelienblatt aus den Tagen Hadrians," *Deutsche allgemeine Zeitung* (December 3, 1935): 564.

Dimant, Devorah. "The Volunteers in the *Rule of the Community*—A Biblical Notion in Sectarian Garb." *RevQ* 23, no. 90 (2007): 233–45.

Doudna, Gregory L. *4Q Pesher Nahum: A Critical Edition.* JSPSup 35. CIS 8. London: Sheffield Academic Press, 2001.

Downing, F. Gerald. "In Quest of First-Century CE Galilee." *CBQ* 66 (2004): 78–97.

Duling, Dennis C. "Empire: Theories, Methods, Models." In *The Gospel of Matthew in its Roman Imperial Context,* edited by John Riches and David C. Sim, 49–74. LNTS. London: T&T Clark International, 2005.

Dunn, James D. G. *Christology in the Making: An Inquiry into the Origins of the Doctrine of the Incarnation.* 2nd ed. Grand Rapids: Eerdmans, 1989.

Eckardt, R. "Das Praetorium des Pilatus." *Zeitschrift des Deutschen Palästina-Vereins* 34 (1911): 39–48.

Edwards, Douglas R. "First Century Urban-Rural Relations in Lower Galilee: Exploring the Archaeological and Literary Evidence." In *SBLSP,* edited by David J. Lull, 169–82. Atlanta: Scholars Press, 1988.

———. "Identity and Social Location in Roman Galilean Villages." In *Religion, Ethnicity, and Identity in Ancient Galilee,* edited by Jürgen Zangenberg, Harold W. Attridge, and Dale B. Martin, 357–74. WUNT 210. Tübingen: Mohr Siebeck, 2007.

———. "The Socio-Economic and Cultural Ethos of the Lower Galilee in the First Century: Implications for the Nascent Jesus Movement." In *The Galilee in Late Antiquity,* edited by Lee I. Levine, 53–73. New York: Jewish Theological Seminary of America, 1994.

Ehrman, Bart D. "Jesus' Trial before Pilate: John 18:28–19:16." *BTB* 13, no. 4 (1983): 124–31.

Elgvin, Torleif. "Jewish Christian Editing of the Old Testament Apocrypha." In *Jewish Believers in Jesus: The Early Centuries,* edited by Oskar Skarsaune and Reidar Hvalvik, 278–304. Peabody, MA: Hendrickson, 2007.

———. "Priests on Earth as in Heaven: Jewish Light on the Book of Revelation." In *Echoes from the Caves: Qumran and the New Testament,* edited by Florentino García Martínez, 257–78. STDJ 85. Leiden: Brill, 2009.

———. "Qumran and the Roots of the Rosh Hashanah Liturgy." In *Liturgical Perspectives: Prayer and Poetry in Light of the Dead Sea Scrolls,* edited by Esther G. Chazon, 49–67. Proceedings of the Fifth International Symposium of the Orion Center, 19–23 January, 2000. STDJ 48. Leiden: Brill, 2003.

———. "Temple Mysticism and the Temple of Men." In *The Dead Sea Scrolls: Text and Context,* edited by Charlotte Hempel, 227–42. STDJ 90. Leiden: Brill, 2010.

———. "The Yahad Is More Than Qumran." In *Enoch and Qumran Origins: New Light on a Forgotten Connection,* edited by Gabriele Boccaccini, 273–79. Grand Rapids: Eerdmans, 2005.

Elitzur, Yoel. *Ancient Place Names in the Holy Land: Preservation and History.* Winona Lake, IN: Eisenbrauns, 2004.

Emerton, J. A. "A Consideration of Two Recent Theories about Bethso in Josephus's Description of Jerusalem and a Passage in the Temple Scroll." *Text and Context: Old Testament and Semitic Studies for F. C. Fensham*, edited by W. Claassen, 93–104. JSOTSup 48. Sheffield: JSOT Press, 1988.

Epp, Eldon Jay. "The New Testament Papyri at Oxyrhynchus in Their Social and Intellectual Context." In *Sayings of Jesus: Canonical and Non-Canonical, Essays in Honour of Tjitze Baarda,* edited by William L. Peterson, Johan S. Vos, and Henk J. de Jonge, 47–68. NovTSup 89. Leiden: Brill, 1997.

———. "The Oxyrhynchus New Testament Papyri: 'Not Without Honor except in Their Hometown'?" *JBL* 123, no. 1 (2004): 5–55.

Eshel, Hanan. *The Dead Sea Scrolls and the Hasmonean State*. Grand Rapids: Eerdmans, 2008.

———. "4QMMT and the History of the Hasmonean Period." In *Reading 4QMMT:
New Perspectives on Qumran Law and History*, edited by John Kampen and
Moshe J. Bernstein, 53–65. SBLSymS 2. Atlanta: Scholars Press, 1996.

———. "Qumran Archaeology," *JAOS* 125 (2005): 389–94.

Evans, Craig A. *Ancient Texts for New Testament Studies: A Guide to the Background Literature*. Peabody, MA: Hendrickson, 2005.

———. "Excavating Caiaphas, Pilate, and Simon of Cyrene: Assessing the Literary and Archaeological Evidence." In *Jesus and Archaeology*, edited by J. H.
Charlesworth, 323–40. Grand Rapids: Eerdmans, 2006.

———. *Holman QuickSource Guide to the Dead Sea Scrolls*. Nashville: Broadman
& Holman, 2010.

———. *Jesus and the Ossuaries: What Jewish Burial Practices Reveal about the
Beginning of Christianity*. Waco, TX: Baylor University Press, 2003.

Evans, Craig A., and N. T. Wright. *Jesus, the Final Days: What Really Happened*.
Edited by Troy A. Miller. Louisville: Westminster John Knox, 2009.

Facella, Margherita. "The Economy and Coinage of Commagene (First Century
BC–First Century AD)." In *Patterns in the Economy of Roman Asia Minor*,
edited by Stephen Mitchell and Constantina Katsari, 225–50. Swansea: The
Classical Press of Wales, 2005.

Fagen, Ruth S. "Phylacteries," *ABD* 5:368–70.

Falk, Daniel K. *The Parabiblical Texts: Strategies for Extending the Scriptures among
the Dead Sea Scrolls*. Companion to the Qumran Scrolls no. 8; Library of Second Temple Studies no. 63. New York: T&T Clark, 2007.

Farris, Stephen. *The Hymns of Luke's Infancy Narratives: Their Origin, Meaning,
and Significance*. JSNTSup 9. Sheffield: JSOT Press, 1985.

Feldman, Louis H. *Studies in Josephus' Rewritten Bible*. JSJSup 58. Leiden: Brill, 1998.

———. "Use, Authority, and Exegesis of Mikra in the Writings of Josephus." In
*Mikra: Text, Translation, Reading, and Interpretation of the Hebrew Bible in
Ancient Judaism and Early Christianity*, edited by Martin J. Mulder, 455–518.
CRINT 2, no. 1 Assen: Van Gorcum; Philadelphia: Fortress, 1988.

Fiensy, David A. "Ancient Economy and the New Testament." In *Understanding the
Social World of the New Testament*, edited by Dietmar Neufeld and Richard E.
DeMaris, 194–206. London: Routledge, 2010.

———. "Assessing the Economy of Galilee in the Late Second Temple Period: Five
Considerations." In *The Galilean Economic Life in the Time of Jesus*. Edited by
Ralph Hawkins and David A. Fiensy. (in preparation).

———. *Jesus the Galilean: Soundings in a First Century Life*. Piscataway, NJ: Gorgias Press, 2007.

———. Review of *Palestine in the Time of Jesus: Social Structures and Social Conflicts*, by K. C. Hanson and Douglas E. Oakman. *CBQ* 70 (2008): 842–44.

———. *The Social History of Palestine in the Herodian Period: The Land Is Mine*.
Studies in the Bible and Early Christianity, no. 20. Lewiston, NY: Edwin Mellen Press, 1991.

Finley, M. I. "The Ancient City: From Fustel de Coulanges to Max Weber and Beyond." *Comparative Studies in Society and History* 19 (1977): 305–27.

———. *The Ancient Economy.* Sather Classical Lectures, vol. 43. Berkeley: University of California Press, 1973.

Fiorato, Veronica, Anthrea Boylston, and Christopher Knüsel, eds. *Blood Red Roses: The Archaeology of a Mass Grave from the Battle of Towton AD 1461.* Rev. ed. Oxford: Oxbow, 2007.

Fishbane, Michael. "Use, Authority, and Interpretation of Mikra at Qumran." In *Mikra: Text, Translation, Reading, and Interpretation of the Hebrew Bible in Ancient Judaism and Early Christianity,* edited by Martin Jan Mulder, 339–77. CRINT 2, no. 1. Assen: Van Gorcum; Philadelphia: Fortress, 1988.

Fitzmyer, Joseph. *The Genesis Apocryphon of Qumran Cave 1 (1Q20): A Commentary.* BibOr 18B. 3rd ed. Rome: Pontifical Biblical Institute, 2004.

Flint, Peter W. "Noncanonical Writings in the Dead Sea Scrolls; Apocrypha, Other Previously Known Writings, Pseudepigrapha." In *The Bible at Qumran: Text, Shape, and Interpretation,* edited by Peter W. Flint, 80–123. Studies in the Dead Sea Scrolls and Related Literature. Grand Rapids: Eerdmans, 2001.

Flusser, David. "Caiaphas in the New Testament." *'Atiqot* 21 (1992): 81–87.

———. *Jesus.* New York: Herder & Herder, 3rd ed. Jerusalem: Magnes Press, 2001.

———. *Judaism and the Origins of Christianity.* Jerusalem: Magnes Press, 1998.

Foster, Paul. "Are There Any Early Fragments of the So-called *Gospel of Peter*?" *NTS* 52 (2006): 1–28.

Frankel, Rafael, Nimrod Getzov, Mordechai Aviam, and Avi Degani. *Settlement Dynamics and Regional Diversity in Ancient Upper Galilee: Archaeological Survey of Upper Galilee.* IAA Reports 14. Jerusalem: Antiquities Authority, 2001.

Freedman, David Noel, et al., eds. *The Leningrad Codex: A Facsimile Edition.* Grand Rapids: Eerdmans, 1998.

Freyne, Sean. *Galilee and Gospel.* Leiden: Brill, 2002.

———. *Jesus, A Jewish Galilean: A New Reading of the Jesus-Story.* London: T&T Clark, 2004.

Frova, Antonio. "L'Inscrizione di Ponzio Pilato a Cesarea." *Rendiconti, Classe di Lettere, Instituto Lombardo* 95 (1961): 419–34.

Galor, Katharina, et al., eds. *Qumran: The Site of the Dead Sea Scrolls: Archaeological Interpretations and Debates, Proceedings of a Conference Held at Brown University, November 17–19, 2002.* STDJ 57. Leiden: Brill, 2006.

Gamble, Harry Y. *Books and Readers in the Early Church: A History of Early Christian Texts.* New Haven: Yale University Press, 1995.

Garfinkel, Yosef, and Saar Ganor. "Khirbet Qeiyafa: Sha'arayim." *JHS* 8/22 (2008): 2–10.

———. "Kirbet Qeiyafa, 2007–2008." *IEJ* 58 (2008): 243–48.

———. *Khirbet Qeiyafa Vol. 1: Excavation Report 2007–2008.* Jerusalem: Israel Exploration Society, 2009.

Garfinkel, Yosef, et al. "Khirbet Qeiyafa, 2009." *IEJ* 59 (2009): 214–20.

Gärtner, M. *Die Familienenerziehung in der alten Kirche.* Cologne: Bohlau, 1985.

George, Michele. "Domestic Architecture and Household Relations: Pompeii and Roman Ephesos." *JSNT* 21 (2004): 7–25.

———. "*Servus* and *Domus*: The Slave in the Roman Household." In *Domestic Space in the Roman World: Pompeii and Beyond,* edited by Andrew Wallace-Hadrill and Ray Laurence, 15–24. Portsmouth, RI: Journal of Roman Archaeology Supplementary Series 22, 1997.

Geva, Hillel. "The 'Tower of David'—Phasael or Hippicus?" *IEJ* 31/1–2 (1981): 57–65.

Gibson, Shimon. "The Archaeology of Jesus in Jerusalem." In *Loy H. Witherspoon Lecture Booklet in Religious Studies.* Charlotte: University of North Carolina at Charlotte, 2009.

———. "The Excavations at the Bethesda Pool in Jerusalem: Preliminary Report on a Project of Stratigraphic and Structural Analysis." *Proche-Orient Chrétien* (forthcoming).

———. *The Final Days of Jesus: The Archaeological Evidence.* San Francisco: HarperCollins, 2009.

———. "Jewish Purification Practices and the Bethesda Pools in Jerusalem." *Proche-Orient Chrétien* 55 (2005): 270–93.

———. "New Excavations on Mount Zion in Jerusalem and an Inscribed Stone Cup/Mug from the Second Temple Period." In *New Studies in the Archaeology of Jerusalem and Its Region,* edited by David Amit et al., 4:32–43. Jerusalem: IAA, 2010.

———. "The 1961–67 Excavations in the Armenian Garden, Jerusalem." *PEQ* 119 (1987): 81–96.

———. "Stone Vessels of the Early Roman Period from Jerusalem and Palestine: A Reassessment." In *One Land—Many Cultures: Archaeological Studies in Honour of S. Loffreda,* edited by G. Claudio Bottini, Leah Di Segni, and L. Daniel Chrupcala, 287–308. Jerusalem: Franciscan Printing Press, 2003.

———. "Suggested Identifications for 'Bethso' and the 'Gate of the Essenes' in the Light of Magen Broshi's Excavations on Mount Zion." In *New Studies in the Archaeology of Jerusalem and Its Region,* edited by Joseph Patrich et al., 1:29–33. Jerusalem: IAA, 2007.

Gilbert, Gary. Review of *Excavating Jesus: Beneath the Stones, behind the Text,* by John Dominic Crossan and Jonathan L. Reed. *RBL.* Posted June 7, 2003 at http://www.bookreviews.org/

Glancy, Jennifer A. *Slavery in Early Christianity.* Oxford: Oxford University Press, 2002.

Gleason, Kathryn L. "The Promontory Palace at Caesarea Maritima: Preliminary Evidence for Herod's *Praetorium.*" *Journal of Roman Archaeology* 11 (1998): 41–52

Golden, M. *Children and Childhood in Classical Athens.* Baltimore: John Hopkins University Press, 1990.

Goldwasser, Orly. "How the Alphabet Was Born from Hieroglyphs." *BAR* 36/2 (March/April 2010): 43.

Goodman, Martin. "Josephus' Treatise *Against Apion.*" In *Apologetics in the Roman Empire: Pagans, Jews, and Christians,* edited by Mark Edwards, Martin Goodman, and Simon Price, in association with Christopher Rowland, 45–58. Oxford: Oxford University Press, 1999.

Grant, Michael. *Jesus.* London: Rigel, 1977.

Greenberg, M. "Nash Papyrus." *Encyclopedia Judaica*, 14:783–84.

Greenfield, Jonas C., Michael E. Stone, and Esther Eshel. *The Aramaic Levi Document: Edition, Translation, and Commentary.* SVTP. Leiden: Brill, 2004.

Greenhut, Zvi. "The 'Caiaphas' Tomb in North Talpiyot, Jerusalem." *'Atiqot* 21 (1992): 63–72.

Grenfell, B. P., and A. S. Hunt. *Sayings of Our Lord.* London: Henry Frowde, 1897.

Griffin, Bruce W. "The Palaeographical Dating of P[46]." Paper presented at the New Testament Textual Criticism Section, 1996 SBL Annual Meeting. http://www.biblical-data.org/P-46%20Oct%201997.pdf.

Gronewald, Michael. "Papyrus Köln 255: Unbekanntes Evangelium oder Evangelienharmonie (Fragment aus dem "Evangelium Egerton")." In *Papyrologica Coloniensia: Kolner Papyri—Vol. VII, Band 6* (ARWAW), edited by M. Gronewald, B. Kramer, K. Maresch, M. Parca, und C. Romer, 136–45. Opladen: Westdeutscher Verlag, 1987.

Gundry-Volf, Judith M. "The Least and the Greatest: Children in the New Testament." In *The Child in Christian Thought,* edited by Marcia J. Bunge, 29–60. Grand Rapids: Eerdmans, 2001.

Gutfeld, Oren. "The City Gate in Eretz-Israel in the Early Roman Period and its Origins in the Hellenistic World." Unpublished MA thesis, Hebrew University of Jerusalem, 1999 (Hebrew).

Haas, N. "Anthropological Observations on the Skeletal Remains from Giv'at ha-Mivtar." *IEJ* 20 (1970): 38–59.

Haelst, J. van. *Catalogue des papyrus littéraires juifs et chrétiens.* Paris: Publication de la Sorbonne, 1976.

Haines-Eitzen, Kim. *Guardians of Letters: Literacy, Power, and the Transmitters of Early Christian Literature.* Oxford: Oxford University Press, 2000.

Hales, Shelley. *The Roman House and Social Identity.* Cambridge: Cambridge University Press, 2009.

Hanson, K. C. "The Galilean Fishing Economy and the Jesus Tradition." *BTB* 27, no. 3 (1997): 99–111.

Hanson, K. C., and Douglas E. Oakman. *Palestine in the Time of Jesus: Social Structures and Social Conflicts.* 2nd ed. Minneapolis: Fortress, 2008.

Harding, G. Lankaster. "Khirbet Qumrân and Wady Murabba'at: Fresh Light on the Dead Sea Scrolls and New Manuscript Discoveries in Jordan." *PEQ* 84 (1952): 109.

Harland, Phillip A. "The Economy of First-Century Palestine: State of the Scholarly Discussion." In *Handbook of Early Christianity: Social Science Approaches,* edited by Anthony J. Blasi, Jean Duhaime, and Paul-André Turcotte, 511–28. Walnut Creek, CA: Altamira, 2002.

Harmon, M., T. I. Molleson, and J. L. Price. "Burials, Bodies and Beheadings in Romano-British and Anglo-Saxon Cemeteries." *Bulletin of the British Museum of Natural History: Geology* 35 (1981): 145–88.

Harris, William V. *Ancient Literacy.* London: Harvard University Press, 1989.

———. "Between Archaic and Modern: Some Current Problems in the History of the Roman Economy." In *The Inscribed Economy: Production and Distribution*

in the Roman Empire in the Light of Instrumentum Domesticum, edited by
W. V. Harris, 11–29. Ann Arbor: Journal of Roman Archaeology, 1993.

Hendel, R. S. "The Oxford Hebrew Bible: Prologue to a New Critical Edition." *VT*
58 (2008): 324–51.

Henten, Jan Willem Van, and Athalya Brenner, eds. *Family and Family Relations
as Represented in Early Judaisms and Early Christianities: Texts and Fictions.*
Studies inTheology and Religion, 2. Leiden: Deo, 2000.

Henze, Matthias. "Introduction." In *Biblical Interpretation at Qumran,* edited by
Matthias Henze, 1–9. Studies in the Dead Sea Scrolls and Related Literature.
Grand Rapids: Eerdmans, 2005.

Herbert, Edward D. *Reconstructing Biblical Dead Sea Scrolls: A New Method Applied to the Reconstruction of 4QSamᵃ.* STDJ 22. Leiden: Brill, 1997.

Herbert, E. D., and R. P. Gordon. "A Reading in 4QSamᵃ and the Murder of Abner."
Textus 19 (1998): 75–80.

Herzog II, William R. *Jesus, Justice, and the Reign of God: A Ministry of Liberation.*
Louisville: Westminster John Knox, 2000.

———. *Parables as Subversive Speech: Jesus as Pedagogue of the Oppressed.* Louisville: Westminster John Knox, 1994.

Hewitt, J. W. "The Use of Nails in the Crucifixion." *HTR* 25 (1932): 29–45.

Himbaza, Innocent. "Le Décalogue de Papyrus Nash, Philon, 4QPhyl G, 8QPhyl 3
et 4QMez A." *RevQ* 20 (2002): 411–28.

Hirschfeld, Yizhar. "Farms and Villages in Byzantine Palestine." *Dumbarton Oaks
Papers* 51 (1997): 33–71.

———. "Jewish Rural Settlement in Judaea in the Early Roman Period." In *The
Early Roman Empire in the East,* edited by Susan E. Alcock, 72–88. Oxford:
Oxbow, 1997.

———. *Qumran in Context: Reassessing the Archaeological Evidence.* Peabody,
MA: Hendrickson, 2004.

———. "Ramat Ha-Nadiv." In *The New Encyclopedia of Archaeological Excavations,* edited by Ephraim Stern et al., 5:2004–6. Jerusalem: Israel Exploration
Society, Washington, DC: Biblical Archaeology Society, 2008.

Hopkins, Keith. "Rome, Taxes, Rent, and Trade." *Kodai* 6, no. 7 (1995–1996):
41–75.

———. "Taxes and Trade in the Roman Empire." *JRS* 70 (1980): 101–125.

Horbury, W. "The 'Caiaphas' Ossuaries and Joseph Caiaphas." *PEQ* 126 (1994):
32–48.

Horgan, Maurya P. *Pesharim: Qumran Interpretations of Biblical Books.* CBQMS 8.
Washington, DC: Catholic Biblical Association of America, 1979.

Horn, Cornelia B., and John W. Martens. *"Let the little children come to me": Childhood and Children in Early Christianity.* Washington, DC: The Catholic University Press of America, 2009.

Horrell, David G. "Domestic Space and Christian Meetings at Corinth: Imagining
New Contexts and the Buildings East of the Theatre." *NTS* 50 (2004): 349–69.

Horsley, Richard A. *Archaeology, History, and Society in Galilee: The Social Context
of Jesus and the Rabbis.* Valley Forge, PA: Trinity Press International, 1996.

———. *Covenant Economics: A Biblical Vision of Justice for All.* Louisville: West-minster John Knox, 2009.

———. *Galilee: History, Politics, People.* Valley Forge, PA: Trinity Press International, 1995.

———. *Jesus and Empire: The Kingdom of God and the New World Disorder.* Minne-apolis: Fortress, 2003.

Horvath, Tibor. "Why Was Jesus Brought to Pilate?" *NovT* 11/3 (1969): 174–84.

Hughes, Julie A., trans. *Scriptural Allusions and Exegesis in the Hodayot.* STDJ 59. Leiden: Brill, 2006.

Humbert, Jean-Baptiste. "Reconsideration of the Archaeological Interpretation." In *Khirbet Qumrân et 'Aïn Feshkha: II Études d'anthropologie, de physique et de chimie, [Studies of Anthropology, Physics, and Chemistry]*, edited by Jean-Baptiste Humbert and Jan Gunneweg, 419–25. NTOA.SA 3. Fribourg: Aca-demic Press, 2003.

Hurtado, Larry W. *The Earliest Christian Artifacts: Manuscripts and Christian Origins.* Grand Rapids: Eerdmans, 2006.

———. "The Origin of the *Nomina Sacra*: A Proposal." *JBL* 117, no. 4 (1998): 655–73.

Hyatt, J. Philip. "The Writing of an Old Testament Book." *BA* 6 (December 1943): 71–80.

Jensen, Morten Hørning. *Herod Antipas in Galilee.* WUNT 2, no. 215. Tübingen: Mohr Siebeck, 2006.

Jewett, R. "Tenement Churches and Communal Meals in the Early Church: The Implications of a Form-Critical Analysis of 2 Thessalonians 3:10." *BR* 38 (1993): 23–43.

Johnson, William A. *Bookrolls and Scribes in Oxyrhynchus.* Toronto: University of Toronto Press, 2004.

———. *Readers and Reading Culture in the High Roman Empire: A Study of Elite Communities.* Oxford: Oxford University Press, 2010.

———. "Toward a Sociology of Reading in Classical Antiquity." *American Journal of Philology* 121 (2000): 593–627.

Jongman, Willem M. "The Roman Economy: From Cities to Empire." In *The Trans-formation of the Economic Life Under the Roman Empire*, edited by Lukas De Blois and John Rich, 28–47. Impact of the Empire (Roman Empire) vol. 2. Amsterdam: J. C. Gieben, 2002.

Kahle, Paul E. *The Cairo Geniza.* 2nd ed. New York: Praeger, 1960.

Kasher, Rimon. "The Interpretation of Scripture in Rabbinic Literature." In *Mikra: Text, Translation, Reading, and Interpretation of the Hebrew Bible in Ancient Judaism and Early Christianity*, edited by M. J. Mulder, 547–94. CRINT 2, no. 1. Assen: Van Gorcum; Philadelphia: Fortress, 1988.

Katsari, Constantina. "The Monetization of Rome's Frontier Provinces." In *The Monetary Systems of the Greeks and Romans*, edited by W. V. Harris, 242–67. Oxford: Oxford University Press, 2008.

Kautsky, John H. *The Politics of Aristocratic Empires.* Chapel Hill: University of North Carolina Press, 1982.

Keel, O. "Zeichen der Verbundenheit: Zur Vorgeschichte und Bedeutung der Forderungen von Deuteronomium 6, 8f. und Par." In *Mélanges Dominique Barthelemy: études bibliques offertes à l'occacion de son 60e anniversaire,* edited by P. Casetti et al., 159–240. Göttingen: Vandenhoeck & Ruprecht, 1981.

Kenney, E. J. "Textual Criticism." In *Encyclopaedia Britannica,* 18:189–95. 15th ed. Chicago: University of Chicago Press, 1984.

Kenyon, F. G. *The Chester Beatty Biblical Papyri,* part 3. London: E. Walker, 1936.

Kim, Young-Kyu. "Palaeographical Dating of P46 to the Later First Century." *Biblica* 69 (1988): 248.

Klausner, Joseph. *Jesus of Nazareth: His Life, Times, and Teaching.* Translated by Herbert Danby. New York: Macmillan, 1945.

Kloppenborg, John S. *The Tenants in the Vineyard: Ideology, Economics, and Agrarian Conflict in Jewish Palestine.* WUNT 195. Tübingen: Mohr Siebeck, 2006.

Knibb, Michael A. *The Qumran Community.* Cambridge Commentaries on Writings of the Jewish and Christian World 200 BC to AD 200 2. Cambridge: Cambridge University Press, 1987.

Koester, Helmut. *Ancient Christian Gospels: Their History and Development.* Harrisburg, PA: Trinity Press International, 1990.

Kokkinos, Nikos. "The Royal Court of the Herods." In *The World of the Herods,* edited by Nikos Kokkinos, 279–303. Stuttgart: Steiner, 2007.

Kraeling, Carl H. "The Episode of the Roman Standards at Jerusalem." *HTR* 35, no. 4 (1942): 263–89.

Laes, Christian. *Kinderen bij de Romeinen: Zes Eeuwen Dagelijks Leven* [Children among the Romans: Six Centuries of Daily Life]. Leuven: Uitgeverij Davidsfonds NV, 2006.

Leaney, A. R. C. *The Rule of Qumran and Its Meaning: Introduction, Translation, and Commentary.* Philadelphia: Westminster Press, 1966.

Légasse, Simon. *The Trial of Jesus.* London: SCM, 1997.

Leibner, Uzi. *Settlement and History in Hellenistic, Roman, and Byzantine Galilee: An Archaeological Survey of the Eastern Galilee.* Texte und Studien zum antiken Judentum 127. Tubingen: Mohr Siebeck, 2009.

Lémonon, Jean-Pierre. *Pilate et le gouvernement de la Judée: Textes et monuments.* Paris: Gabalda, 1981.

Lenski, Gerhard E. *Power and Privilege: A Theory of Social Stratification.* Chapel Hill: University of North Carolina Press, 1966.

Lenski, Gerhard, and Jean Lenski. *Human Societies: An Introduction to Macrosociology.* 4th ed. New York: McGraw-Hill, 1982.

Levenson, Jon. "The Jerusalem Temple in Devotional and Visionary Experience." In *Jewish Spirituality: From the Bible through the Middle Ages,* edited by Arthur Green, 1:32–61. London: SCM, 1989.

Levine, Lee I. *Jerusalem: Portrait of the City in the Second Temple Period (538 B.C.E.–70 C.E.).* Philadelphia: Jewish Publication Society, 2002.

Lieu, Judith. *Neither Jew nor Greek? Constructing Early Christianity.* London: T&T Clark, 2002.

Lim, Timothy H. *The Dead Sea Scrolls: A Very Short Introduction.* Oxford: Oxford University Press, 2005.

———. *Holy Scripture in the Qumran Commentaries and Pauline Letters.* Oxford: Clarendon Press, 1997.

———. "Midrash Pesher in the Pauline Letters." In *The Scrolls and the Scriptures: Qumran Fifty Years After,* edited by S. E. Porter and C. A. Evans, 280–92. JSP-Sup 26. Roehampton Institute London Papers 3. Sheffield: Sheffield Academic Press, 1997.

———. *Pesharim.* Companion to the Qumran Scrolls 3. London: Sheffield Academic Press, 2002.

Lincoln, Andrew T. *Ephesians.* Edited by Bruce M. Metzger. WBC 42. Dallas: World Publishing, 1990.

Llewelyn, S. R. *New Documents Illustrating Early Christianity,* vol. 8. Grand Rapids: Eerdmans, 1997.

Lund-Andersen, Jens, and Torleif Elgvin. *Hør, Israel! Ved disse ord skal du leve! Tekster og tider i 5 Mosebok.* Oslo: Norsk Luthersk Forlag, 2000.

MacDonald, Margaret Y. "A Place of Belonging: Perspectives on Children from Colossians and Ephesians." In *The Child in the Bible,* edited by Marcia J. Bunge, 278–304. Grand Rapids: Eerdmans, 2008.

———. "Slavery, Sexuality, and House Churches: A Reassessment of Col 3.18–4.1 in Light of New Research on the Roman Family." *NTS* 53 (2007): 94–113.

Magen, Yishak, and Yuval Peleg. "Back to Qumran: Ten Years of Excavation and Research, 1993–2004." In *The Site of the Dead Sea Scrolls: Archaeological Interpretations and Debates,* edited by Katharina Galor et al., 55–113. STDJ 57. Leiden: Brill, 2006.

Magness, Jodi. *The Archaeology of Qumran and the Dead Sea Scrolls.* Grand Rapids: Eerdmans, 2002.

Maier, Aren. "For Those Who Don't Know Any Biblical Hebrew." The Tell Es-Safi/Gath Excavations Official (and Unofficial) Weblog, October 16, 2009. Accessed January 24, 2011, at http://gath.wordpress.com/2009/10/16/for-those-who-don't-know-any-biblical-hebrew/#more-1195

Maier, Johann. "Early Jewish Interpretation in the Qumran Literature." In *Hebrew Bible/Old Testament: The History of Its Interpretation,* vol. 1: *From the Beginnings to the Middle Ages (Until 1300),* edited by Magne Sæbø, 108–129. Göttingen: Vandenhoeck & Ruprecht, 1996.

Maier, Paul L. "The Episode of the Golden Roman Shields at Jerusalem." *HTR* 62/1 (1969): 109–121.

———. "Pilate in the Dock: For the Defense." *BRev* 20/3 (2004): 27–30, 32.

Manning, J. G. "The Relationship of Evidence to Models in the Ptolemaic Economy (332 BC–30 BC)." In *The Ancient Economy: Evidence and Models,* edited by J. G. Manning and Ian Morris, 163–85. Palo Alto, CA: Stanford University Press, 2005.

Manning, J. G., and Ian Morris, eds. *The Ancient Economy: Evidence and Models.* Stanford, CA: Stanford University Press, 2005.

Mantel, Hugo. "Sanhedrin." *Encyclopedia Judaica,* 18:22–23. 2nd ed. New York: Macmillan, 2007.

Martin, Dale B. "Slave Families and Slaves in Families." In *Early Christian Families in Context: An Interdisciplinary Dialogue,* edited by David L. Balch and Carolyn Osiek, 207–230. Grand Rapids: Eerdmans, 2003.

———. *Slavery as Salvation: The Metaphor of Slavery in Pauline Christianity.* New Haven: Yale University Press, 1990.

_____. "Review Essay: Justin J. Meggitt, *Paul, Poverty, and Survival.*" *JSNT* 84 (2001): 51–64.

Martin, Victor, and J. W. B. Barns. *Papyrus Bodmer II, Supplément: Évangile de Jean, chap. 14–21, nouvelle édition aumentée et corrigée.* Cologny-Geneva: Bibliotheca Bodmeriana, 1962.

Martin, Victor, and Rodolphe Kasser. *Papyrus Bodmer XIV, Evangile de Luc, chap. 3–24.* Cologny-Geneva: Bibliotheca Bodmeriana, 1961.

Martinez, Florentino García, and Eibert J. C. Tigchelaar, trans. *The Dead Sea Scrolls Study Edition.* 2 vol. Leiden: Brill; Grand Rapids: Eerdmans, 2000.

Mattila, Sharon Lea. "Jesus and the 'Middle Peasants': Challenging a Model of His Socioeconomic Context." PhD. diss., University of Chicago, 2006.

Mattingly, David J., and John Salmon, eds. *Economies Beyond Agriculture in the Classical World.* Leicester-Nottingham Studies in Ancient Society, vol. 9. London: Routledge, 2001.

Mayeda, G. *Das Leben-Jesu-Fragment Papyrus Egerton 2 und seine Stellung in der urchristlichen Literaturgeschichte.* Bern: Paul Haupt, 1946.

McCane, B. R. "'Let the Dead Bury Their Own Dead': Secondary Burial and Matt 8:21–22." *HTR* 83 (1990): 31–43.

McCarter, Jr., P. Kyle. *I Samuel.* AB 8. Garden City, NY: Doubleday, 1980.

McKenzie, Steven L. *King David: A Biography.* New York: Oxford University Press, 2000.

McKinley, J. L. "A Decapitation from the Romano-British Cemetery at Baldock, Hertfordshire." *International Journal of Osteoarchaeology* 3 (1993): 41–44.

Meggitt, Justin J. *Paul, Poverty, and Survival.* Edited by John Barclay, Joel Marcus, and John Riches. Studies of the New Testament and Its World. Edinburgh: T&T Clark, 1998.

———. "The Social Status of Erastus [Rom 16:23]." *NovT* (1996): 218–23.

Meier, John P. "The Historical Jesus and the Historical Herodians." *JBL* 119, no. 4 (2000): 740–46.

Messner, Brian E. "Pontius Pilate and the Trial of Jesus: The Crowd." *Stone-Campbell Journal* 3 (2000): 195–207.

Metso, Sarianna. "In Search of the Sitz im Leben of the Community Rule." In *The Provo International Conference on the Dead Sea Scrolls: Technological Innovations, New Texts, and Reformulated Issues,* edited by Donald W. Parry and Eugene Ulrich, 306–315. STDJ 30. Leiden: Brill, 1999.

———. *The Textual Development of the Qumran Community Rule.* STDJ 21. Leiden: Brill, 1997.

————. "Whom Does the Term Yahad Identify?" In *Biblical Traditions in Transmission: Essays in Honour of Michael A. Knibb,* edited by Charlotte Hempel and Judith Lieu, 213–35. JSJSup 111. Leiden: Brill, 2006.

Metzger, Bruce M. *The Text of the New Testament: Its Transmission, Corruption, and Restoration.* 3rd ed. Oxford: Oxford University Press, 1992.

Meyers, Eric M. "Jesus and His Galilean Context." In *Archaeology and the Galilee: Texts and Contexts in the Graeco-Roman and Byzantine Periods,* edited by Douglas R. Edwards and C. Thomas McCollough, 57–66. South Florida Studies in the History of Judaism 143. Atlanta: Scholars Press, 1997.

————. *Jewish Ossuaries: Reburial and Rebirth.* BibOr 24. Rome: Pontifical Biblical Institute Press, 1971.

Milik, Jozef T. *The Books of Enoch: Aramaic Fragments of Qumran Cave 4.* Oxford: Clarendon Press, 1976.

————. *Ten Years of Discovery in the Wilderness of Judea.* Translated by J. Strugnell. Studies in Biblical Theology 26. London: SCM, 1963.

Millar, Fergus. "Reflections on the Trial of Jesus." In *A Tribute to Geza Vermes: Essays on Jewish and Christian Literature and History,* edited by Philip R. Davies and Richard T. White, 355–81. Sheffield: JSOT Press, 1990.

————. *The Roman Near East 31 BC–AD 337.* Cambridge, MA: Harvard University Press, 1993.

Moreland, Milton. "The Jesus Movement in the Villages of Roman Galilee: Archaeology, Q, and Modern Anthropological Theory." In *Oral Performance, Popular Tradition, and Hidden Transcript in Q,* edited by Richard A. Horsley, 159–180. Semeia Studies 60. Atlanta: Society of Biblical Literature, 2006.

Moreschini, Claudio, and Enrico Norelli. *Early Christian Greek and Latin Literature: A Literary History.* Translated by Matthew J. O'Connell. 2 vols. Peabody, MA: Hendrickson, 2005.

Morris, Ian. "Foreword." In *The Ancient Economy,* edited by M. I. Finley, ix–xxxvi. Updated ed. Berkeley: University of California Press, 1999.

Moxnes, Halvor. "The Construction of Galilee as a Place for the Historical Jesus— Part II." *BTB* 31, no. 2 (2001): 64–77.

Moxnes, Halvor, ed. *Constructing Early Christian Families: Family as Social Reality and Metaphor.* London: Routledge, 1997.

Mugridge, Alan. "Stages of Development in Scribal Professionalism in Early Christian Circles." PhD thesis, University of New England, 2010.

Müller, Peter. *In der Mitte der Gemeinde: Kinder im Neuen Testament.* Neukirchen-Vluyn: Neukirchener, 1992.

Murphy-O'Connor, Jerome. "An Essene Missionary Document? CD II,14–VI,1." *RB* 77 (1970): 201–229.

————. "La genèse littéraire de la règle de la communauté." *RB* 66 (1969): 528–49.

————. *St. Paul's Corinth: Texts and Archaeology.* 3rd rev. and expanded ed. Collegeville, MN: Liturgical Press, 2002.

Nagar, Y., and H. Torgeë. "Biological Characteristics of Jewish Burial in the Hellenistic and Early Roman Periods." *IEJ* 53 (2003): 164–71.

Najman, Hindy. *Seconding Sinai: The Development of Mosaic Discourse in Second Temple Judaism*. JSJSup 77. Leiden: Brill, 2003.

Nathan, Geoffrey S. *The Family in Late Antiquity: The Rise of Christianity and the Endurance of Tradition*. London: Routledge, 2000.

Naveh, Joseph. *Early History of the Alphabet*. 2nd rev. ed. Jerusalem: Magnes Press, 1982.

Neils, J., and J. H. Oakley. "Introduction." In *Coming of Age in Classical Greece: Images of Childhood from the Classical Past*, 1–6. New Haven: Yale University Press, 2003.

Netzer, Ehud. *The Architecture of Herod, the Great Builder*. TSAJ 117. Tübingen: Mohr Siebeck, 2006.

Nevett, Lisa C. *Houses and Society in the Ancient Greek World*. New Studies in Archaeology. Cambridge: Cambridge University Press, 1999.

Newsom, Carol A., trans. "Admonition on the Flood." In *Qumran Cave 4.XIV: Parabiblical Texts, Part 2*, DJD 19. Oxford: Clarendon Press, 1995.

Nickelsburg, George W. E. *1 Enoch 1. Hermeneia: A Critical and Historical Commentary on the Bible*. Minneapolis: Fortress, 2001.

Nickelsburg, George W. E., and James C. VanderKam. *1 Enoch: A New Translation*. Minneapolis: Fortress, 2004.

Nicklas, Tobias. "The 'Unknown Gospel' on *Papyrus Egerton 2 + Papyrus Cologne 225*." In *Gospel Fragments*, edited by Thomas J. Kraus, Michael J. Kruger, and Tobias Nicklas, 11–122. OECGT. Oxford: Oxford University Press, 2009.

Niditch, Susan. *"My Brother Esau Is a Hairy Man": Hair and Identity in Ancient Israel*. New York: Oxford University Press, 2008.

Nongbri, Brent. "Use and Abuse of P[52]: Papyrological Pitfalls in the Dating of the Fourth Gospel." *HTR* 98 (2005): 23–52.

Notley, R. Steven. "Historical Geography of the Gospels." In *The Sacred Bridge: Carta's Atlas of the Biblical World: An Overview of the Ancient Levant*, edited by Anson E. Rainey and R. Steven Notley, 349–69. Jerusalem: Carta, 2006.

Oakman, Douglas E. "The Ancient Economy." Chapter 5 in *Jesus and the Peasants*, 53–69. Eugene, OR: Cascade Books, 2008.

———. *Jesus and the Economic Questions of His Day*. Lewiston, NY: Edwin Mellen Press, 1986.

———. *Jesus and the Peasants*. Eugene, OR: Cascade Books, 2008.

———. "Models and Archaeology in the Social Interpretation of Jesus." In *Social Scientific Models for Interpreting the Bible: Essays by the Context Group in Honor of Bruce J. Malina*, edited by John J. Pilch, 102–131. BIS 53. Leiden: Brill, 2001.

"Open Letter to Prof. Gershon Galil, Haifa University." Khirbet Qeiyafa Archaeological Project, 2009-2010. Hebrew University of Jerusalem. Accessed January 24, 2011. http://qeiyafa.huji.ac.il/galil.asp.

"Order of Commandments Six, Seven, and Eight." *BAR* 5, no. 6 (December 1989). Accessed March 25, 2010. http://www.basarchive.org/bswbBrowse.asp?PublD=BSBR&Volume=5&Issue=6&ArticleID=17.Origen. *Contra Celsum*. Trans. Henry Chadwick. Cambridge: Cambridge: University Press, 1953.

Osiek, Carolyn, and David L. Balch. *Families in the New Testament World: Households and House Churches.* Louisville: Westminster John Knox, 1997.

Osiek, Carolyn, and Margaret Y. MacDonald, with Janet Tulloch. *A Woman's Place: House Churches in Earliest Christianity.* Minneapolis: Fortress, 2006.

Overman, J. Andrew. "Jesus of Galilee and the Historical Peasant." In *Archaeology and the Galilee: Texts and Contexts in the Graeco-Roman and Byzantine Periods,* edited by Douglas R. Edwards and C. Thomas McCollough, 67–73. South Florida Studies in the History of Judaism 143. Atlanta: Scholars Press, 1997.

Overstreet, R. Larry. "Roman Law and the Trial of Christ." *BSac* 135 (October–December 1978): 323–32.

"Papyri." http://www.uni-muenster.de/NTTextforschung/KgLSGII2010_02_04. pdf (accessed March 26, 2010).

Parry, Donald W. "The Aftermath of Abner's Murder." *Textus* 20 (2000): 83–96.

———. "Hannah in the Presence of the Lord." In *Archaeology of the Books of Samuel: The Entangling of the Textual and Literary History,* edited by Philippe Hugo and Adrian Schenker, 53–74. VTSup 132. Leiden: Brill, 2010.

———. "The Textual Character of the Unique Readings of 4QSam^a (4Q51)." In *Flores Florentino: Dead Sea Scrolls and Other Early Jewish Studies in Honour of Florentino García Martínez,* edited by Anthony Hilhorst, Émile Puech, and Eibert J. C.Tigchelaar, 163–82. JSJSup 122. Leiden: Brill, 2007.

Parsons, Peter. *City of the Sharp-Nosed Fish: The Lives of the Greeks in Roman Egypt.* London: Weidenfeld & Nicolson, 2007.

———. "Copyists of Oxyrhynchus." In *Oxyrhynchus: A City and Its Texts,* edited by A. K. Bowman et al., 262–70. Greco-Roman Memoirs 93. London: Egypt Exploration Society, 2007.

Pastor, Jack. *Land and Economy in Ancient Palestine.* London: Routledge, 1997.

Patrich, Joseph. "A Chapel of St. Paul at Caesarea Maritima." *Liber Annuus* 50 (2000): 363–82.

Patterson, J. "Pilate in the Dock: For the Prosecution." *BRev* 20/3 (2004): 30–32.

Paulien, J. "The role of the Hebrew Cultus, Sanctuary, and Temple in the Plot and Structure of the Book of Revelation." *AUSS* 33 (1995), 245–64.

Peters, Dorothy M. *Noah Traditions in the Dead Sea Scrolls: Conversations and Conversations in Antiquity.* SBLEJL 26. Atlanta: Society of Biblical Literature, 2008.

Pisano, Stephen. *Additions or Omissions in the Books of Samuel: The Significant Pluses and Minuses in the Massoretic, LXX, and Qumran Texts.* OBO 57. Freiburg: Universitätsverlag; Göttingen: Vandenhoeck & Ruprecht, 1984.

Pixner, Bargil. "Archäologische Beobachtungen zum Jerusalemer Essener-Viertel und zur Urgemeinde." In *Christen and Christliches in Qumran?* edited by B. Mayer, 89–113. Eichstätter Studien, Neue Folge 32. Regensburg: F. Pustet, 1992.

———. "An Essene Quarter on Mount Zion?" In *Studia Hierosolymitana I: Studi archeologici in onore a Bellarmino Bagatti.* Jerusalem: Franciscan Printing Press, 1976.

———. "The History of the 'Essene Gate' Area." *Zeitschrift des Deutschen Palästina-Vereins* 105 (1989): 96–104.

———. "The Jerusalem Essenes, Barnabas, and the Letter to the Hebrews." In *Intertestamental Essays in Honour of Jósef Tadeusz Milik,* edited by Z. J. Kapera, 167–78. Cracow: Enigma Press, 1992.

———. "Das Jerusalemer Essenerviertel: Antwort auf einige Einwände." In *Intertestamental Essays in Honour of Jósef Tadeusz Milik,* edited by Z. J. Kapera, 179–86. Cracow: Enigma Press, 1992.

———. "Jerusalem's Essene Gateway: Where the Community Lived in Jesus's Time." *BAR* 23, no. 3 (1997): 23–31, 64–66.

———. "Mount Zion, Jesus, and Archaeology." In *Jesus and Archaeology*, edited by James H. Charlesworth, 309–322. Grand Rapids: Eerdmans, 2006.

———. "Noch einmal das Prätorium. Versuch einer neuen Lösung." *Zeitschrift des Deutschen Palästina-Vereins* 95 (1979): 56–86.

Pixner, Bargil, Doron Chen, and Shlomo Margalit. "The 'Gate of the Essenes' Re-excavated." *Zeitschrift des Deutschen Palästina-Vereins* 105 (1989): 85–95.

Polak, F. "David's Kingship—A Precarious Equilibrium." In *Politics and Theopolitics in the Bible and Postbiblical Literature,* edited by Henning Graf Reventlow, Yair Hoffman, and Benjamin Uffenheimer, 119–47. JSOTSup 171. Sheffield: Sheffield Academic Press, 1994.

"Qeiyafa Ostracon Chronicle." Khirbet Qeiyafa Archaeological Project, 2008. Hebrew University of Jerusalem. Accessed March 30, 2010. http://qeiyafa.huji.ac.il/ostracon.asp.

"Qeiyafa Ostracon Chronicle." Khirbet Qeiyafa Archaeological Project, 2009-2010. Hebrew University of Jerusalem. Accessed March 30, 2010. http://qeiyafa.huji.ac.il/ostracon2.asp.

Qimron, Elisha. "The Halakha." In *Qumran Cave 4: V. Miqsat Ma'ase Ha-Torah,* edited by Elisha Qimron and John Strugnell, 123–77. DJD 10. Oxford: Clarendon Press, 1994.

Qimron, Elisha, and John Strugnell, eds. *Qumran Cave 4: V. Miqsat Ma'ase Ha-Torah.* DJD 10. Oxford: Clarendon Press, 1994.

Rabinovitch, Ari. "Archaeologists Report Finding Oldest Hebrew Text" Accessed October 30, 2008). http://www.reuters.com/article/idUSTRE49T52620081030.

Rahmani, L. Y. *A Catalogue of Jewish Ossuaries in the Collections of the State of Israel.* Jerusalem: Israel Antiquities Authority, 1994.

Rapinchuk, Mark. "The Galilee and Jesus in Recent Research." *Currents in Biblical Research* 2 (2004): 197–222.

Rawson, Beryl. *Children and Childhood in Roman Italy.* Oxford: Oxford University Press, 2003.

Reed, Jonathan L. *Archaeology and the Galilean Jesus: A Re-examination of the Evidence.* Harrisburg, PA: Trinity Press International, 2000.

———. "Instability in Jesus' Galilee: A Demographic Perspective." *JBL* 129, no. 2 (2010): 343–65.

———. "Reappraising the Galilean Economy: The Limits of Models, Archaeology, and Analogy." Paper presented at the 2008 meeting of the Westar Institute.

Reʾem, Amit. "First Temple Period Fortifications and Herod's Palace in the Kishle Compound." *Qadmoniot* 43 (2010): 96–101 (Hebrew).

Regev, Eyal. "Family Burial, Family Structure, and the Urbanization of Herodian Jerusalem." *PEQ* 136 (2004): 109–31.

———. "Josephus on Gibeah: Versions of a Toponym." *The Jewish Quarterly Review* 89, nos. 3–4 (1999): 351–59.

———. *Sectarianism in Qumran: A Cross-Cultural Perspective.* Religion and Society 45. Berlin: de Gruyter, 2007.

Reinhartz, Adele. "Parents and Children: A Philonic Perspective." In *The Jewish Family in Antiquity,* edited by Shaye J. D. Cohen, 61–88. BJS 289. Atlanta: Scholars Press, 1993.

———. "Philo on Infanticide." *Studia Philonica Annual* 4 (1992): 42–58.

Rensberger, David. "The Politics of John: The Trial of Jesus in the Fourth Gospel." *JBL* 103, no. 3 (1984): 395–411.

Richardson, Peter. "Architectural Transitions from Synagogues and House Churches to Purpose-Built Churches." In *Common Life in the Early Church: Essays Honoring Graydon F. Snyder,* edited by J. V. Hill, 373–89. Harvard Theological Studies. Harrisburg, PA: Trinity Press International, 1998.

Richardson, Peter, and Douglas Edwards. "Jesus and Palestinian Social Protest: Archaeological and Literary Perspectives." In *Handbook of Early Christianity: Social Science Approaches,* edited by Anthony J. Blasi, Jean Duhaime, and Paul-André Turcotte, 247–66. Walnut Creek, CA: Altamira, 2002.

Riesner, Rainer. "Eseener und Urkirche in Jerusalem." In *Christen and Christliches in Qumran?* edited by B. Mayer, 139–55. Eichstätter Studien, Neue Folge 32. Regensburg: F. Pustet, 1992.

———. "Jesus, the Primitive Community, and the Essene Quarter of Jerusalem." In *Jesus and the Dead Sea Scrolls: The Controversy Resolved,* edited by James H. Charlesworth, 198–234. ABRL. New York: Doubleday, 1992.

———. "What Does Archaeology Teach Us about House Churches?" *Tidsskrift for Teologi og Kirche* 78 (2007): 159–85.

Roberts, Colin H. *Two Biblical Papyri in the John Rylands Library Manchester.* Manchester: Manchester University Press, 1936.

———. *An Unpublished Fragment of the Fourth Gospel in the John Rylands Library.* Manchester: Manchester University Press, 1935.

Roberts, C. H., and T. C. Skeat. *The Birth of the Codex.* London: Oxford University Press, 1989.

Robinson, Thomas A. *Ignatius of Antioch and the Parting of the Ways.* Peabody, MA: Hendrickson, 2009.

Rodgers, R. "The Text of the New Testament and Its Witnesses before 200 A.D.: Observations on P^{90} (P.Oxy. 3523)." In *The Text of the New Testament in Early Christianity: Le texte du Nouveau Testament au début du christianisme,* edited by Christin-B. Amphoux and J. Keith Elliott, 83–91. Lausanne: Éditions du Zèbre, 2003.

Rofé, Alexander. "4QMidrash Samuel?—Observations Concerning the Character of 4QSam^a." *Textus* 19 (1998): 63–74.

————. "The Methods of Late Biblical Scribes as Evidenced by the Septuagint Compared with the Other Textual Witnesses," in *Tehillah le-Moshe: Biblical and Judaic Studies in Honor of M. Greenberg*, edited by Mordechai Cogan, Barry L. Eichler, and Jeffrey H. Tigay, 259–70. Winona Lake, IN: Eisenbrauns, 1997.

————. "Moses' Mother and Her Slave-Girl according to 4QExod[b]." *DSD* 9 (2002): 38–43.

————. "A Nomistic Correction in Biblical Manuscripts and Its Occurrence in 4QSam[a]." *RevQ* 14 (1989): 247–54.

Roller, Duane W. *The Building Program of Herod the Great.* Berkeley: University of California Press, 1998.

Roth, Jonathan. "The Army and the Economy in Judaea and Palestine." In *The Roman Army and the Economy,* edited by Paul Erdkamp, 375–97. Amsterdam: J. C. Gieben, 2002.

Royse, James R. *Scribal Habits in Early Greek New Testament Papyri.* NTTS 36. Leiden: Brill, 2008.

Rozenberg, Sylvia. "On Wall-Painting Workshops in the Land of Israel." *Michmanim* 22 (2010): 7*–20*.

Safrai, Ze'ev. *The Economy of Roman Palestine.* London: Routledge, 1994.

Saller, Richard. "Framing the Debate over Growth in the Ancient Economy," In *The Ancient Economy: Evidence and Models*, edited by J. G. Manning and Ian Morris, 223–38. Stanford, CA: Stanford University Press, 2005.

————. "*Pater Familias, Mater Familias*, and the Gendered Semantics of the Roman Household." *CP* 94:182–97.

Sanders, E. P. *The Historical Figure of Jesus.* London: Allen Lane, 1993.

Sanders, Henry Arthur. *New Testament Manuscripts in the Freer Collection, Part 1, the Washington Manuscript of the Four Gospels.* New York: Macmillan, 1912.

Sanders, James A. "Hermeneutics of Text Criticism." *Textus* 18 (1995): 1–26.

————. "Origen and the First Christian Testament." In *Studies in the Hebrew Bible, Qumran, and the Septuagint Presented to Eugene Ulrich,* edited by Peter W. Flint, Emanuel Tov, and James C. VanderKam, 134–42. VTSup 101. Leiden: Brill, 2006.

————. Review of *Biblia Hebraica Quinta: Fascicle 18,* by Adrian Schenker et al., eds. *RBL* 8 (2006): 1–10.

————. Review of *Hebrew University Bible: The Book of Ezekiel,* by Moshe Goshen-Gottstein, Shemaryahu Talmon, and Galen Marquis, eds. *RBL* (2005). http://www.bookreviews.org/BookDetail.asp?TitleId=4662.

————. "Stability and Fluidity in Text and Canon." In *Tradition of the Text: Studies Offered to Dominique Barthélemy in Celebration of his 70th Birthday,* edited by Gerald J. Norton and Stephen Pisano, 203–217. OBO 109. Göttingen: Vandenhoeck & Ruprecht, 1991.

————. "The Task of Text Criticism." In *Problems in Biblical Theology: Essays in Honor of Rolf Knierim,* edited by Henry T. C. Sun, et al., 315–27. Grand Rapids: Eerdmans, 1997.

————. "Text and Canon: Concepts and Method." *JBL* 98, no. 1 (1979): 5–29.

Sands, Percy Cooper *The Client Princes of the Roman Empire*. Cambridge: Cambridge University Press, 1908.

Sauer, Norman J. "The Timing of Injuries and Manner of Death: Distinguishing among Antemortem, Perimortem, and Postmortem Trauma." In *Forensic Osteology: Advances in the Identification of Human Remains*, edited by Kathleen J. Reichs, 321–32. 2nd ed. Springfield, IL: Charles C. Thomas, 1998.

Scheidel, Walter. "Demography." In *The Cambridge Economic History of the Greco-Roman World*, edited by Walter Scheidel, Ian Morris, and Richard P. Saller, 38–86. Cambridge: Cambridge University Press, 2007.

Scheidel, Walter, Ian Morris, and Richard P. Saller, eds. *The Cambridge Economic History of the Greco-Roman World*. Cambridge: Cambridge University Press, 2008.

Scheidel, Walter, and Sitta von Reden, eds. *The Ancient Economy*. New York: Routledge, 2002.

Schenker, Adrian, et al., eds. *Biblia Hebraica Quinta: Fascicle 18: General Introduction and Megilloth*. Stuttgart: Deutsche Bibelgesellschaft, 2004.

Schiffman, Lawrence H. *The Eschatological Community of the Dead Sea Scrolls: A Study of the Rule of the Congregation*. SBLMS 38. Atlanta: Scholars Press, 1989.

———. *Qumran and Jerusalem: Studies in the Dead Sea Scrolls and the History of Judaism*. Grand Rapids: Eerdmans, 2010.

———. *Reclaiming the Dead Sea Scrolls: The History of Judaism, the Background of Christianity, the Lost Library of Qumran*. Philadelphia: Jewish Publication Society, 1994.

Schmidt, Andreas. "Zwei Anmerkungen zu P.Ryl. III 457." *Archiv fur Papyrusforschung* 35 (1989): 11–12.

Schofield, Alison. *From Qumran to the Yahad: A New Paradigm of Textual Development for the Community Rule*. STDJ 77. Leiden: Brill, 2009.

———. "Rereading S: A New Model of Textual Development in Light of the Cave 4 *Serekh* Copies." *DSD* 15 (2008): 96–120.

Schofield, Alison, and James C. VanderKam. "Were the Hasmoneans Zadokites?" *JBL* 124, no. 1 (2005): 73–87.

Schwartz, Daniel R. "Pontius Pilate." In *ABD*, 5:395–401. New York: Doubleday, 1992.

Schwartz, Earl. "The Trials of Jesus and Paul." *Journal of Law and Religion* 9/2 (1992): 501–513.

Seim, Turid Karlsen. "A Superior Minority: The Problem of Men's Headship in Ephesians 5." In *Mighty Minorities? Minorities in Early Christianity—Positions and Strategies. Essays in Honor of Jacob Jervell on his 70th Birthday*, edited by David Hellholm, Halvor Moxnes, and Turid Karlsen Seim, 167–81. Oslo: Scandinavian University Press, 1995.

Shanks, Hershel. "Dead Sea Scrolls: A Short History." *BAR* 33, no. 3 (May/June 2007): 34–37.

———. *Freeing the Dead Sea Scrolls and Other Adventures of an Archaeology Outsider*. London: Continuum, 2010.

———. "Prize Find: Oldest Hebrew Inscription Discovered in Israelite Fort on Philistine Border." *BAR* 36, no. 2 (March/April 2010): 54.

Shemesh, Aharon. "The Scriptural Background of the Penal Code in the *Rule of the Community* and *Damascus Document*." *DSD* 15 (2008): 191–224.

Sherwin-White, A. N. *Roman Society and Roman Law in the New Testament: The Sarum Lectures, 1960–61.* Oxford: Clarendon Press, 1965.

Silver, Morris. Review of *The Ancient Economy*, by Walter Scheidel and Sitta von Reden. EH.net. Posted January 2, 2003 at http://eh.net/book_reviews/ancient-economy

Sivan, Renée, and Giora Solar. "Excavations in the Jerusalem Citadel, 1980–1988." In *Ancient Jerusalem Revealed*, edited by Hillel Geva, 168–76. Jerusalem: Israel Exploration Society, 1994.

Skarsaune, Oskar. "Biblical Interpretation." In *The Early Christian World*, edited by Philip F. Esler, 1:660–89. New York: Routledge, 2000.

Smit, Peter-Ben. "The Final Verdict: A Note on the Structure of Jesus' Trial in the Gospel of John." *RB* 115, no.3 (2008): 383–95.

Smith, P. "The Human Skeletal Remains from the Abba Cave." *IEJ* 27 (1977): 121–24.

Stanley, Christopher D. *Paul and the Language of Scripture: Citation Technique in the Pauline Epistles and Contemporary Literature.* SNTSMS 74. Cambridge: Cambridge University Press, 1992.

Stegemann, Hartmut. *The Library of Qumran: On the Essenes, Qumran, John the Baptist, and Jesus.* Grand Rapids: Eerdmans, 1998.

Stern, Menahem, ed. *Greek and Latin Authors: On Jews and Judaism.* 3 vols. Jerusalem: Israel Institute of Science and Humanities, 1980.

Strange, James F. "Archaeological Evidence of Jewish Believers." In *Jewish Believers in Jesus: The Early Centuries*, edited by Oskar Skarsaune and Reidar Hvalvik, 710–41. Peabody, MA: Henrickson, 2007.

Strange, W. A. *Children in the Early Church: Children in the Ancient World, the Ne Ancient Jerusalem Revealed, w Testament, and the Early Church.* Carlisle: Paternoser, 1966; repr., Eugene OR: Wipf & Stock, 2004.

Strugnell, John. "Second Thoughts on a Forthcoming Edition." In *The Community of the Renewed Covenant: The Notre Dame Symposium on the Dead Sea Scrolls, Volume 1993*, edited by Eugene Ulrich and James VanderKam, 57–62. Christianity and Judaism in Antiquity 10. Notre Dame, IN: University of Notre Dame Press, 1994.

Stuckenbruck, Loren T. *The Book of Giants from Qumran: Texts, Translation, and Commentary.* TSAJ 63. Tübingen: Mohr Siebeck, 1997.

Sussmann, Y. "Appendix 1. The History of the Halakha and the Dead Sea Scrolls." In *Qumran Cave 4: V. Miqsat Ma'ase Ha-Torah*, edited by Elisha Qimron and John Strugnell, 179–200. DJD 10. Oxford: Clarendon Press, 1994.

Sutcliffe, E. F. "The First Fifteen Members of the Qumran Community." *JSS* 4 (1959): 134–38.

Sweeney, Marvin A. "The Nash Papyrus: Preview of Coming Attractions." *BAR* 36, no. 4 (July/August 2010): 43–48, 77.

Syon, Danny. "Tyre and Gamla: A Study in the Monetary Influence of Southern Phoenician on Galilee and the Golan in the Hellenistic and Roman Periods." PhD diss., Hebrew University (Jerusalem), 2004.

Talbert, Charles H. *Ephesians and Colossians*. Paideia Commentaries on the New Testament. Grand Rapids: Baker Academic, 2007.

Talmon, Shemaryahu. "The Community of the Renewed Covenant: Between Judaism and Christianity." In *The Community of the Renewed Covenant: The Notre Dame Symposium on the Dead Sea Scrolls*, edited by Eugene Ulrich and James C. VanderKam, 3–24. Christianity and Judaism in Antiquity, vol. 10. Notre Dame, Ind.: University of Notre Dame Press, 1994

———. "Was the Book of Esther Known at Qumran?" *DSD* 2 (1995): 249–67.

Taylor, Bernard A, trans. "Reigns." In *A New English Translation of the Septuagint and the other Greek Translations Traditionally Included under that Title,* edited by Albert Pietersma and Benjamin G. Wright, 244–96. Oxford: Oxford University Press, 2007.

Taylor, Joan E. "Philo of Alexandria on the Essenes: A Case Study on the Use of Classical Sources in Discussions of the Qumran-Essene Hypothesis." *Studia Philonica Annual* 19 (2007): 1–28.

———. "Pontius Pilate and the Imperial Cult in Roman Judaea." *NTS* 52 (2006): 555–82.

Tov, Emanuel. *Hebrew Bible, Greek Bible, and Qumran*. TSAJ 121. Tübingen: Mohr Siebeck, 2008.

———. "The Many Forms of Hebrew Scripture: Reflections in Light of the Septuagint and 4QReworked Pentateuch." In *From Qumran to Aleppo: A Discussion with Emanuel Tov about the Textual History of Jewish Scriptures in Honor of His 65th Birthday,* edited by Armin Lange, Matthias Weigold, and József Zsengellér, 11–28. FRLANT 230. Göttingen: Vandenhoeck & Ruprecht, 2009.

———. *Scribal Practices and Approaches Reflected in the Texts Found in the Judean Desert*. STDJ 54. Atlanta: Society of Biblical Literature, 2009.

———. "The Textual Affiliations of 4QSamᵃ." *JSOT* 14 (1979): 37–53.

———. *Textual Criticism of the Hebrew Bible*. 2nd rev. ed. Minneapolis: Fortress, 2001.

Tsevat, Matthiahu. "Was Samuel a Nazirite?" In *"Sha'arei Talmon": Studies in the Bible, Qumran, and the Ancient Near East Presented to Shemaryahu Talmon,* edited by Michael Fishbane and Emmanuel Tov, 199–204. Winona Lake, IN: Eisenbrauns, 1992.

Turner, E. G. *Greek Manuscripts of the Ancient World*. Edited by P. J. Parsons. 2nd ed. Rev. and enlarged. London: Institute for Classical Studies, 1987.

———. *Greek Papyri: An Introduction*. Oxford: Clarendon Press, 1980.

———. *The Typology of the Early Codex*. Haney Foundation Series, vol. 18. Philadelphia: University of Pennsylvania Press, 1977.

Tyson, Joseph B. "The Lukan Version of the Trial of Jesus." *NovT* 3, no. 4 (1959): 249–58.

Udoh, Fabian E. *To Caesar What Is Caesar's: Tribute, Taxes, and Imperial Administration in Early Roman Palestine (63 BCE–70 CE)*. BJS 343. Providence: Brown Judaic Studies, 2005.

Ulfgard, Hakan. *Feast and Future: Revelation 7:9–17 and the Feast of Tabernacles.* CBNTS 22. Stockholm: Almquist & Wiksell, 1989.

Ulrich, Eugene. *The Dead Sea Scrolls and the Origins of the Bible.* Studies in the Dead Sea Scrolls and Related Literature. Grand Rapids: Eerdmans, 1999.

———. "Our Sharper Focus on the Bible and Theology Thanks to the Dead Sea Scrolls." *CBQ* 66 (2004): 1–24.

———. *The Qumran Text of Samuel and Josephus.* Harvard Semitic Monograph 19. Missoula, MT: Scholars Press, 1978.

University of Haifa. "Most Ancient Hebrew Biblical Inscription Deciphered." January 7, 2010. Accessed March 24, 2010. http://www.eurekalert.org/pub_releases/2010-01/uoh-mah010710.php.

VanderKam, James C. "Davidic Complicity in the Deaths of Abner and Eshbaal: A Historical and Redactional Study." *JBL* 94, no. 4 (1980): 521–39.

———. *The Dead Sea Scrolls Today.* 2nd ed. Grand Rapids: Eerdmans, 2010.

———. *From Joshua to Caiaphas: High Priests after the Exile.* Minneapolis: Fortress, 2004.

———. "Identity and History of the Community." In *The Dead Sea Scrolls after Fifty Years: A Comprehensive Assessment,* edited by Peter W. Flint, James C. VanderKam, and Andrea E. Alvarez, 2: 507–523. Leiden: Brill, 1999.

———. "The Origins and Purposes of the *Book of Jubilees.*" In *Studies in the Book of Jubilees,* edited by Matthias Albani, Jorg Frey, and Armin Lange, 3–24. TSAJ 65. Tübingen: Mohr Siebeck, 1997.

———. "Sinai Revisited." In *Biblical Interpretation at Qumran,* edited by Matthias Henze, 44–60. Studies in the Dead Sea Scrolls and Related Literature. Grand Rapids: Eerdmans, 2005.

VanderKam, James C., and Peter W. Flint. *The Meaning of the Dead Sea Scrolls: Their Significance for Understanding the Bible, Judaism, Jesus, and Christianity.* San Francisco: HarperSanFrancisco, 2002.

Vermes, Geza, trans. *The Complete Dead Sea Scrolls in English.* Rev. ed. London: Penguin Books, 2004.

———. "Eschatological Worldview in the Dead Sea Scrolls and in the New Testament." In *Emanuel: Studies in Hebrew Bible, Septuagint, and Dead Sea Scrolls in Honor of Emanuel Tov,* edited by Shalom M. Paul, Robert A. Kraft, Lawrence H. Schiffman, and Weston W. Fields, 479-496. VTSup 94. Leiden: Brill, 2003.

———. "Interpretation, History of: At Qumran and in the Targums." In *The Interpreter's Dictionary of the Bible: Supplementary Volume,* edited by Keith Crim, 438–43. Nashville: Abingdon, 1976.

———. *Les manuscrits du désert de Juda.* 2nd ed. Paris: Desclée, 1954.

———. *The Passion.* London: Penguin Books, 2005.

Vermes, Geza, and Martin D. Goodman, eds. *The Essenes According to the Classical Sources.* JSOT 1. Sheffield: JSOT Press, 1989.

Waaler, Erik. "A Revised Date for Pentateuchal Texts? Evidence from Ketef Hinnom." *TynBul* 53 (2002): 29–50.

Walaskay, Paul W. "The Trial and Death of Jesus in the Gospel of Luke." *JBL* 94, no. 1 (1975): 81–93.

Wallace-Hadrill, Andrew. "*Domus* and *Insulae* in Rome: Families and Housefuls." In *Early Christian Families in Context,* edited by David L. Balch and Carolyn Osiek, 3–18. Grand Rapids: Eerdmans, 2003.

———. *Houses and Society in Pompeii and Herculaneum.* Princeton: Princeton University Press, 1994.

Walsh, Jerome T. *Style and Structure in Biblical Hebrew Narrative.* Collegeville, MN: Liturgical Press, 2001.

Walters, Stanley D. "After Drinking (1 Sam 1:9)." In *Crossing Boundaries and Linking Horizons: Studies in Honor of Michael C. Astour on His 80th Birthday,* edited by Gordon D. Young, Mark W. Chavalas, Richard E. Averback, and Kevin L. Danti, 527–56. Bethesda, MD: CDL Press, 1997.

———. "Hannah and Anna: The Greek and Hebrew Texts of 1 Samuel 1." *JBL* 107, no. 3 (1988): 385–412.

Wassen, Cecilia. *Women in the Damascus Document.* SBLABib 21. Atlanta: Society of Biblical Literature; Leiden: Brill, 2005.

Watt, Robin J. "Evidence for Decapitation." In *The Roman Cemetery at Lankhills,* edited by Giles Clarke, 342–44. Winchester Studies 3: Pre-Roman and Roman. Oxford: Clarendon Press, 1979.

Weissenberg, Hanne von. *4QMMT: Reevaluating the Text, the Function, and the Meaning of the Epilogue.* STDJ 82. Leiden: Brill, 2009.

Wells, G. A. *The Jesus of the Early Christians: A Study in Christian Origins.* London: Pemberton, 1971.

White Crawford, Sidnie. "The Use of the Pentateuch in the *Temple Scroll* and the *Damascus Document* in the Second Century BCE." In *The Pentateuch as Torah: New Models for Understanding Its Promulgation and Acceptance,* edited by Gary N. Knoppers and Bernard M. Levison, 301–317. Winona Lake, IN: Eisenbrauns, 2007.

Wilson, C. W. *Golgotha and the Holy Sepulchre.* Edited by C. M. Watson. London: Committee of the Palestine Exploration Fund, 1906.

Wilson, William Riley. *The Execution of Jesus: A Judicial, Literary, and Historical Investigation.* The Scribner Library 104. New York: Scribners, 1970.

Winter, F. E. *Greek Fortifications.* Toronto: University of Toronto Press, 1971.

Winter, Paul. *On the Trial of Jesus.* Edited by T. A. Burkill and Geza Vermes. 2nd ed. Studia Judaica. Forschungen zur Wissenschaft des Judentums. Berlin: de Gruyter, 1974.

———. "The Trial of Jesus." *Commentary* 38 (September 1964): 35–41.

Wise, Michael O. *The First Messiah: Investigating the Savior Before Jesus.* San Francisco: HarperSanFrancisco, 1999.

———. "The Origins and History of the Teacher's Movement." In *The Oxford Handbook of the Dead Sea Scrolls,* edited by Timothy H. Lim and John J. Collins, 92–122. Oxford: Oxford University Press, 2010.

Wise, Michael Owen, Martin Abegg Jr., and Edward Cook. *The Dead Sea Scrolls: A New Translation.* New York: HarperSanFrancisco, 2005.

Wisse, Frederik. "The Use of Early Christian Literature as Evidence for Inner Diversity and Conflict." In *Nag Hammadi, Gnosticism, and Early Christianity,* edited by Charles W. Hedrick and Robert Hodgson, 177–90. Peabody, MA: Hendrickson, 1986.

Yadin, Yigael. "Epigraphy and Crucifixion." *IEJ* 23 (1973): 18–22 + plate.

———. "The Gate of the Essenes and the Temple Scroll." In *Jerusalem Revealed: Archaeology in the Holy City 1968–1974,* edited by Yigael Yadin, 90–91. Jerusalem: Israel Exploration Society, 1975.

———. *The Temple Scroll.* Jerusalem: Israel Exploration Society, The Institute of Archaeology of the Hebrew University of Jerusalem, the Shrine of the Book, 1977 [Hebrew ed.], 1983 [English ed.].

———, ed. *The Temple Scroll.* London: Weidenfeld & Nicolson, 1985.

———, ed. *The Temple Scroll.* 3 vols. Jerusalem: Israel Exploration Society, 1977–1983.

Zevit, Ziony. "Scratched Silver and Painted Walls: Can We Date Biblical Texts Archaeologically?" *HS* 48 (2007): 32–37.

Zias, Joe. "Anthropological Evidence of Interpersonal Violence in First-Century A.D. Jerusalem." *Current Anthropology* 24 (1983): 233–34.

Zias, Joe, and E. Sekeles. "The Crucified Man from Giv'at ha-Mivtar: A Reappraisal." *IEJ* 35 (1985): 22–27.

Zias, Joe, and James H. Charlesworth. "Crucifixion: Archaeology, Jesus, and the Dead Sea Scrolls." In *Jesus and the Dead Sea Scrolls,* edited by James H. Charlesworth, 273–89. ABRL. New York: Doubleday, 1992.

Zuntz, G. *The Text of the Epistles: A Disquisition upon the Corpus Paulinum.* The Schweich Lectures of the British Academy, 1946. Eugene, OR: Wipf & Stock, 2007.

Index of Modern Authors

INDEX OF ANCIENT SOURCES